Music in American Religious Experience

Music in American Religious Experience

Edited by

PHILIP V. BOHLMAN

EDITH L. BLUMHOFER

MARIA M. CHOW

2006

OXFORD
UNIVERSITY PRESS

Oxford University Press, Inc., publishes works that further
Oxford University's objective of excellence
in research, scholarship, and education.

Oxford New York
Auckland Cape Town Dar es Salaam Hong Kong Karachi
Kuala Lumpur Madrid Melbourne Mexico City Nairobi
New Delhi Shanghai Taipei Toronto

With offices in
Argentina Austria Brazil Chile Czech Republic France Greece
Guatemala Hungary Italy Japan Poland Portugal Singapore
South Korea Switzerland Thailand Turkey Ukraine Vietnam

Published by Oxford University Press, Inc.
198 Madison Avenue, New York, New York 10016

www.oup.com

Library of Congress Cataloging-in-Publication Data

Music in American religious experience/edited by Philip V. Bohlman, Edith L. Blumhofer,
Maria M. Chow.
p. cm.
Papers from a conference held at the U. of Chicago, Apr. 22–24, 1994 (p.).
Includes bibliographical references and index.
ISBN-13 978-0-19-517303-1; 978-0-19-517304-8 (pbk.)
ISBN 0-19-517303-1; 0-19-517304-x (pbk)
1. Music—Religious aspects—Congresses. 2. United States—Religious life and customs—
Congresses. I. Bohlman, Philip Vilas. II. Blumhofer, Edith Waldvogel. III. Chow, Maria M.
ML2911.M87 2005
201'.678'0973—dc22 2005052304

9 8 7 6 5 4 3 2

Printed in the United States of America
on acid-free paper

Foreword

Martin E. Marty

One book is about one thing, at least the good ones are. That sentence paraphrases an idea of Eugen Rosenstock-Huessy, a profound if maverick thinker of the recent past. Every doctoral dissertation writer, every proposer of a book she intends to write, and every publisher who sends me a manuscript to appraise gets to hear that line.

Sometimes I get asked, or I ask myself: What about the phone book? It is about many things. The encyclopedia or the dictionary? A catalog? Response: Phone books are full of many names, but it is names that give it its "one thing" integrity. We know exactly what an encyclopedia or a dictionary is "about," and catalogs get filed with other catalogs for particular, focused kind of use.

After those simple cases, take the harder ones. Think of biographies that never get the biographies into focus. The novels that seem to have a plot but let their paragraphs meander. (A plotless novel *can* be about one thing.) The book that sets out to make a point and stick to it, but whose author unwittingly builds ambiguity into its theme. (A nonfiction work *can* be devoted to ambiguity and still successfully be about one thing, if wittingly.)

The most difficult kind of book to be about one thing is the anthology, symposium, or collection, especially if it is the printed version of a conference or a *Festschrift*, an honoring work by students of their senior mentor. The temptation at conferences is to let people unload ideas they already had, ideas that could somehow be made to seem coherent when put between covers. But they aren't. The temptation at *Festschrift* time is to empty the desk drawers and unload an essay that someone else rejected, or one that the author was always going to finish, but hadn't—and only more or less finished now.

Those four paragraphs were a long wind-up for a simple pitch or, more appropriately for this work, a long prelude for a short theme. That theme: This book on music and America and religion acquires its distinctiveness by focusing on *experience*. It takes whole libraries to deal with music or religion, with music and religion in America. What the editors and authors here aspire to do is to hear religious music in the United States and locate it in the experience of citizens who sing and pray, worship and march.

We historians can deal with music or religion as a set of ideas, as intellectual history. Or we can deal with institutions, as social history. This collection is a form of cultural history, thinking of culture as James Axtell does: "Culture is an idealized pattern of meanings, values, and norms differentially shared by the members of a society, which can be inferred from the non-instinctive behavior of the group and from the symbolic products of their actions, including material artifacts, language, and social institutions" (Axtell 1981, 6).

When scholars deal with "meanings, values, and norms," they have to see how these are "differentially shared," for example, by singers and hearers, organists and congregations, hymners and hummers and those put off by the hummer in the next cell or the hospital bed. Such scholars pay attention to the signals given by people who do not know they are giving them. Thus hymn-singers think it is "natural" for adults to erupt in group song, seldom thinking how idiosyncratic such an act is. Millions who sing hymns in congregations never sing outside the shower; at best they mumble impatiently during the National Anthem at a Little League game. In this book, the authors pay attention to the instinctive doings of "less natural" things by fellow-citizens. And they are alert to the symbolic meanings of what goes on, the sounds as they are fashioned and appropriated, and the settings as well. In short, the *experience.*

The differential sharing in this book is particularly rooted in different ethnic experiences, some of them readily and conventionally shared—many non-blacks have long been familiar with some forms of African American music—but non-Chinese know little about the Chinese contexts and non-Native Americans have to reach far or be members of a select group to demonstrate or recall familiarity with Native American sacred sound. In this "one thing" book, the authors narrow the subject somewhat to the ethnic experiential context.

In his chapter on the musical panorama of American religious experience coeditor Philip V. Bohlman sets the scene by concentrating on an often overlooked element in musical experience, especially of religious sorts, where the accent is on congregating and congregations. He takes on the difficult topic of individualism, of which Americans are reputed to have plenty, and follow the lead down the paths of idiosyncratic and unfamiliar musical expression. I have to be in the 0.00053 per cent of readers who have ever heard of "Alfred Ira" Grimm, who comes up in the Bohlman chapter. I was at the tail tail-end of the German American hearership and readership who had some Alfred Ira stories read to us by my father in the late late-end of the *Abendschule* culture Bohlman mentioned. We probably took our Grimm experience as normal—not knowing we'd almost never again meet up with others who went through it. Meanwhile, those others were having their own individual, individualist, and individualizing experiences.

There is no reason to detail response to the subsequent chapters, since only Bohlman's accent on individualism seems to complicate the plot of this people-centered, peoples-centered work. Don E. Saliers discusses what we might call a mainstream or mainline experience, that of the production and appropriation of new hymnals, especially for Protestants. But tens of millions of Americans are no closer to that subculture than they are to the Tibetan fastnesses of the Dalai Lama; indeed, if they frequent bookstores they may be closer to the Dalai Lama than Anglican or Wesleyan hymnody. So white Protestant and, sometimes, Catholic hymn-singing enclaves become one more of the subcultures, the sets of "differential sharers."

From there on in we have nothing but clear focus: on Maine Wabanakis; Old Regular Baptists—who are not the Baptists "down the street," unless you live in streets near hollows and byways; women—not an ethnic group but one whose differential sharing of cultural symbols receives special attention these years; early American evangelicals—who used to be seen at the center of the commonly shared national myth but are now a group among the groups; German Americans—"my tribe," the largest non-English ethnic group and the most hidden, most blended-in; African Americans—about whom others knew, but knew too little; Chinese Americans—who do not all look alike or sound alike to those who pursue the "inner diversity" of their communities; Muslims and Islamic women—new singers down the block, in the experience of others; traditional Jews—who don't "sound" like the assimilated ones others know best.

That sentence, having grown to near-page length, is merely a device to signal the diversities and surprises that await and will inform and, I think, delight those who have ears to hear, eyes to follow, and hearts to co-experience.

I won't keep you any longer, trusting the authors, who know what they hear or heard, and pass on their experience.

WORK CITED

Axtell, James. 1981. *The European and the Indian: Essays in the Ethnohistory of Colonial North America*. New York: Oxford University Press.

Acknowledgments

When music expresses American religious experience, the one becomes the many, the voice of the individual joins with the chorus of the community. Similarly, this book grew from the ideas and exchanges of a few inspired individuals to the collective expression of many musicians and ensembles, scholars and students, religious communities and academic organizations. *Music in American Religious Experience* would be impossible without this inclusiveness and cooperation, and accordingly, we owe a considerable debt of thanks.

In many ways, we owe our first and last debt to James W. Lewis, Executive Director of the Louisville Institute for the Study of Protestantism and American Culture. At a conference of theologians and sacred musicians in Louisville in March 1992, Jim issued a challenge to bring scholars of American religion together to talk about their common interests, but more to the point, then to do something about the need to bring those common interests into dialogue. At every stage of this book's development Jim renewed his challenge, and that very renewal was instrumental in seeing the project through to its completion. We are grateful indeed to Jim and the Louisville Institute for standing so steadfastly by that challenge.

Music in American Religious Experience began its life as a conference that took place at the University of Chicago, April 22–24, 1994. Many organizations made that event a success, not least because so many fine musicians and scholars gathered from throughout the world as a result of generous support. At the University of Chicago we thank the Music Department and the Divinity School. Funding came from the Division of the Humanities, and gracious space was made available by the Franke Institute for the Humanities at the University of Chicago. Generous funding also came from the Louisville Institute for the Study of Protestantism and American Culture, the Eli Lilly Endowment, and the Institute for the Study of American Evangelicals at Wheaton College.

What would a conference about music be without musicians? Eloquently answering that question were the musicians and ensembles who performed during the course of the three days: The Chicago Klezmer Ensemble, the Midwest Buddhist Temple Taiko Group, the Polish Highlanders of Chicago, and the Rockefeller Chapel Choir of the University of Chicago.

In addition to the authors contributing to this book many individuals contributed to the conference in other ways, from presenting papers to chairing sessions to stimulating discussion as respondents. Thanks to Mark Bangert, Bernard O. Brown, David Connell, Michael Fishbane, Samuel A. Floyd, Jr., Philip Gossett, Michael Harris, Mark Harvey, Adina Klein, William Phemister, Anne W. Robertson, Bruce Tammen, and Edward Zimmerman. As always at Chicago, the graduate students in the Department of Music gave tirelessly of their collective time, energy, and ideas. We thank them for being there whenever they were needed.

Music in American Religious Experience has benefited from the wisdom and labors of two fine editors at Oxford University Press. Maribeth Payne, herself a church musician, initially took the book under her wing. During the stages of production, Kim Robinson served as the steward who guided the transformation of manuscript to book. We are indeed very grateful to both. Eve Bachrach, Gwen Colvin, and Lynn Kauppi made production and copyediting truly pleasurable. We are indeed grateful to all of them.

If the choir is at its best after many years of patient rehearsal, we have reason to believe that this book truly will make a contribution to a richer understanding of American religious experience. Its most patient and diligent choristers were our authors, who willingly accepted more than a few editorial transformations and our persistent attempts to transform many religious experiences into a concerted performance that revealed the possibility of an expressive unity. We, the editors, owe much to your patience and the rich resonance of your collective voices.

Philip V. Bohlman, Chicago
Edith L. Blumhofer, Wheaton, Ill.
Maria M. Chow, Hong Kong

Contents

Foreword, v
Martin E. Marty

Contributors, xv

Introduction: Music in American Religious Experience, 3
Philip V. Bohlman

PART I Experience and Identity

1. When Women Recite: "Music" and Islamic Immigrant Experience, 23
Regula Burckhardt Qureshi

2. African American Religious Music from a Theomusicological Perspective, 43
Jon Michael Spencer

3. Medeolinuwok, Music, and Missionaries in Maine, 57
Ann Morrison Spinney

4. Singing as Experience among Russian American Molokans, 83
Margarita Mazo

PART II Liturgy, Hymnody, and Song

5. Hymnody and History: Early American Evangelical Hymns as Sacred Music, 123
Stephen A. Marini

6. The Evolution of the Music of German American Protestants in Their Hymnody: A Case Study from an American Perspective, 155
Paul Westermeyer

7. Singing from the Right Songbook: Ethnic Identity and Language Transformation in German American Hymnals, 175
Otto Holzapfel

8. "When in Our Music God Is Glorified:" Singing and Singing about Singing in a Congregational Church, 195
Judith Gray

PART III Individuals and the Agency of Faith

9. Fanny Crosby and Protestant Hymnody, 215
Edith L. Blumhofer

10. Prayer on the Panorama: Music and Individualism in American Religious Experience, 233
Philip V. Bohlman

11. Women's Ritual Music, 255
Janet Walton

PART IV Congregation and Community

12. *Nusach* and Identity: The Contemporary Meaning of Traditional Jewish Prayer Modes, 271
Jeffrey A. Summit

13. Reflections on the Musical Diversity of Chinese Churches in the United States, 287
Maria M. Chow

14. "Tuned Up with the Grace of God": Music and Experience among Old Regular Baptists, 311
Jeff Todd Titon

15. Aesthetics and Theology in Congregational Song: A Hymnal Intervenes, 335
Don E. Saliers

Index, 345

Contributors

Edith L. Blumhofer is Professor of History and Director of the Institute for the Study of American Evanglelicals at Wheaton College (Illinois). She holds a Ph.D. from Harvard and has conducted extensive research on the history of Pentecostalism in North America and on the role of women in American evangelicalism. She wrote the biography, *Aimee Semple McPherson* (1992) and edited *Religion, Politics, and the American Experience* (2002). Her longstanding interest in sacred music is evident in her current book project on the famed nineteenth-century hymn writer, Fanny Crosby.

Philip V. Bohlman is the Mary Werkman Professor of the Humanities and of Music at the University of Chicago, where he also serves as chair of Jewish Studies. He is an ethnomusicologist with particular interest in the intersections of music and religion. He has published widely on music and revival, pilgrimage, Jewish music, and sacred music in the shaping of American and European modernity. His most recent books are *The Music of European Nationalism* (2004) and *"Jüdische Volksmusik"—Eine mitteleuropäische Geistesgeschichte* (2005). *Jewish Music and Modernity* is forthcoming from Oxford University Press.

Maria M. Chow is a native of Hong Kong, and she took her B.A. from the Chinese University of Hong Kong. Her M.Div. thesis (Yale University) was a study of Lutheran hymnody in Hong Kong, and her Ph.D. dissertation (University of Chicago) is a study of the modern discourse on music and its impact on Chinese national self-identity in the first half of the twentieth century.

Judith Gray is Coordinator for Reference Services at the American Folklife Center of the Library of Congress. Her curatorial and publishing projects have ranged across a vast landscape of folklife and traditional culture in the United States. They include exhibits on local and regional history, and have developed resources for the respect and maintenance of American cultural resources. She has stewarded the rerelease of early recordings of Native American music. An ethnomusicologist who studied at Wesleyan University, she is also an active gamelan musician in Washington, D.C.

Otto Holzapfel teaches Folklore and Scandinavian Studies at the University of Freiburg im Breisgau. He has served in various capacities as a scholar and archivist at the Deutsches Volksliedarchiv in Freiburg, including the head of textual studies, Director until 1996, editor of the *Jahrbuch für Volksliedforschung,* and editor of two monograph series, *Studien zur Volksliedforschung* and *Deutschen Volkslieder mit ihren Melodien.* He has published widely on folk song and ballad, Danish and German identity, mythology, and music and religion. Among his many publications are *Religiöse Identität und Gesangbuch* (1998) and two volumes coedited with Philip V. Bohlman, *The Folk Songs of Ashkenaz* (2001) and *Land without Nightingales* (2002).

Stephen A. Marini is Professor of Religion at Wellesley College, where he teaches broadly in the fields of American religion and ethics. He combines research interests in religion in revolutionary America and the sacred arts in America, both of which are reflected in his book publications, such as *Radical Sects of Revolutionary New England* (1982) and *Sacred Song in America* (2003). He is also the founder and singing master of Norumbega Harmony, a choral ensemble specializing in early American psalmody and hymnody.

Martin E. Marty is the Fairfax M. Cone Distinguished Service Professor Emeritus at the University of Chicago, where he taught in the Divinity School, the History Department, and the Committee on the History of Culture from 1963 to 1998. One of the most prolific and influential scholars on religion in North America, he has published more than fifty books, among them the three-volume *Modern American Religion* and *Righteous Empire,* which won a National Book Award. His lifetime achievements have been recognized by awards from all sectors of American public culture. Currently, he is writing the book, *The Mystery of the Child,* for a project he codirects at Emory University.

Margarita Mazo is Professor of Music at the Ohio State University, from which she received the Distinguished Scholar Award in 1999. A graduate of the St. Petersburg Conservatory, she specializes in Russian vernacular and art musics, with publications on ritual and popular songs, sacred music, musical life in post-Soviet Russia, and Igor Stravinsky. As a field researcher, she initiated the comparative research and representation project on music in cognate communities residing in Russia and the United States that serves as the basis for her contribution to this volume. Currently, she is working on a project in cognitive ethnomusicology, focusing on music, the body, and emotion.

Regula Burckhardt Qureshi is Professor of Music and Adjunct Professor of Anthropology and South Asian Studies at the University of Alberta, where she also serves as Director of the Centre for Ethnomusicology and the Indian Music Ensemble. Her research concerns itself with music and community in Islam, and her publications include the edited volumes *The Muslim Community in North America* (1983) and *Music and Marx* (2002). Her *Sufi Music of India and Pakistan* (1986; 1995) is the classic study of *qawwali,* the traditional and popular music of South Asian Islam.

Don E. Saliers is W. R. Cannon Distinguished Professor of Theology and Worship at the Candler School of Theology, Emory University, where he is also Director of the Master of Sacred Music program. His current research centers on liturgy and culture, and on method in liturgical theology. His many books include *Worship and Spirituality* (1984) and *Worship as Theology* (1994), and he is coauthor of *Human Disability and the Service of God* (1998) and *The Conversation Matters* (1999).

Jon Michael Spencer (newly named Yahya Jongintaba) was formerly a professor at several American universities. He holds a Ph.D. in music, and his master's degree is in theology. His many publications examine the broader questions of theomusicology, especially the intersections of expressive behavior and the sacred in African American music. Currently, he is founder of and teacher at the International Uhuru School, located in the Kilimanjaro region of Tanzania.

Ann Morrison Spinney is Assistant Professor of Music and Irish Studies at Boston College. She has taken degrees in music performance, historical musicology, and ethnomusicology from Oberlin Conservatory, Northwestern University, and Harvard University. Her research broadly concerns the music of Native Americans and First Nation people of the American Northeast and the Canadian Maritime provinces, and she brings particular attention to issues of language and translation in expressive culture. Currently, she is assisting with the reclamation of field recordings by the Passamaquoddy Tribe.

Jeffrey A. Summit is Associate Professor of Music at Tufts University, where he also serves as Rabbi and Executive Director of the Hillel Foundation. His research focuses on the relation of Jewish community to history and expressive behavior, as well as performance and improvisation in Jewish liturgical music. His *The Lord's Song in a Strange Land* (Oxford University Press, 2000) received the Musher Prize from the National Foundation for Jewish Culture. Most recently, he compiled and annotated the CD *Abayudaya: Music from the Jewish People of Uganda* for Smithsonian Folkways Recordings.

Jeff Todd Titon is Professor of Music and Director of the Ph.D. program in ethnomusicology at Brown University, and a Fellow of the American Folklore Society. His research employs interdisciplinary and multimedia approaches to many repertories and practices of American music, including the blues, white and black music in the Southern church, and performance at public festivals. Among his many books are *Powerhouse for God* (1988) and *Give Me This Mountain* (1989). He is currently completing work on a multimedia DVD containing sermons preached by the Rev. C. L. Franklin, father of Aretha.

Janet Walton is Professor of Worship at Union Theological Seminary in New York City. A pianist, she has combined concerns for music and worship in her teaching and research, additionally focusing on the social contexts of music and worship. She is the author of *Art and Worship* (1988) and *Feminist Liturgy* (2000), and with Lawrence Hoffman she coedited *Sacred Sound and Social Change* (1992). Currently, she is writing a book on improvisation and congregational worship.

Paul Westermeyer is Professor of Church Music at Luther Seminary in St. Paul, Minnesota, where he is also Cantor and Director of the Master of Sacred Music program with St. Olaf College. Throughout his career he has been active as a practicing church musician and scholar of hymnody. Twice an editor of *The Hymn,* he was named a fellow of the Hymn Society in the United States and Canada in 2004. He has published many monographs on hymnody, the roles of the church musicican, and music and justice. His most recent book, *Let the People Sing: Hymn Tunes in Perspective,* appears in 2005.

Music in American Religious Experience

Introduction: Music in American Religious Experience

Philip V. Bohlman

Singing "America"

The 1778 setting of William Billings's hymn, "America," leaves little room for equivocation. America is expansive, stretching from "East to West," from "Pole to Pole," and singing praise unto the Lord renders the sacred landscape all the more expansive. The sacred boundaries of America in the hymn only add to the expansiveness, for they are the skies themselves, indeed, the heavens, if we take Billings to mean that the praise echoing from human choruses as "his Praise," God passing musical judgment on a land singing "with one accord." "America" is a hymn about sacred landscape; or more specifically, a landscape made sacred through and by song.

By 1778 there was little doubt that William Billings meant the song's sacred dimensions to underlie its political message. As the first American-born composer to enter the canon of American music history, Billings took an English hymn tradition and consciously transformed it into an American tradition, musically and textually. In Billings's choral works, the sacred and the political did not simply overlap. Their differences diminish and eventually disappear in a discursive process mediated by music. Singing with one accord united Americans as a nation no less than as a congregation. Music emerged and continues to emerge as an agent of mediation between the sacred and the secular, between the religious and the political, and between the mythical and historical imagination of America itself. It is that agency of music to motivate and mediate the diverse formations of American religious experience that provides the common subject of this book.

The position of William Billings (1746–1800) in American music history is virtually inseparable from a rhetoric of "firsts" and "beginnings." Music historians regard Billings not only as the first native-born composer, but the first composer in America whose music and achievements stretched beyond his own lifetime (see Crawford 1993). Billings learned his musical craft in America, as a singer and later choir director in Boston's South Church. He was a professional musician, and his active involvement in singing schools—themselves a visible and influential form of community-formation through sacred music—enabled him to devote sufficient time to composing that his complete works contain some three hundred compositions (see Billings 1981). Musically and historically, Billings stood at a crossroads on the American sacred landscape. Religious experience is no more inseparable from his musical upbringing than from his political coming-of-age. As a church composer he burst into the public sphere at a critical moment in history, making the music he and his contemporary composers created at once both American and religious.

Religious music in the United States lies at the borders between myth and history, sacred time and secular time. Religious and cultural historians draw upon these borders for the tropes with which they calibrate the different histories that together represent America. The tension between musics inside and outside America has often turned around the distinctions between myth and history. Prior to the sacred written traditions of the first colonists from Europe there were only the sacred oral traditions of Native Americans. Literacy in America—or rather, American literacy in America—"begins" with the publication of the *Bay Psalm Book* (1640), the first book of any kind published in North America, whose capacity to symbolize beginnings remains undiminished until today (Krummel 1998). The temporal dimensions of American religious musics constantly allow for new beginnings. New immigrants bring new musics that are themselves—more often than not in American music historiography—sustained the longest within religious contexts. The very possibility of multicultural musics in America depends on the capacity of ethnic communities to establish themselves and to return to their beginnings when musical repertories are in need of revitalization and authenticity.

Beginnings are renewable, through the revival of authenticity and through the genealogies of hymnals or the oral traditions that weave liturgies into the constantly unfolding sectarianisms of American religious experience. American Jewish liturgies, for example, are fundamentally unified through ritual time

FIGURE 1.1. William Billings's "America" (1778)

but, also, constantly woven into different forms and into different movements within American Judaism (see Summit in this volume). In American Protestantism sacred music history unfolds as a series of renewed beginning, whether through revival movements or the penchant ceaselessly to rethink and revise hymn books and prayer books.

The renewal of beginnings is not only an act of authenticating. It also expresses a profound, unremitting uncertainty about music's position in American religious experience. It asks again whether the music of American religious experience is theologically music at all, whether the sacred and the aesthetic are mutually exclusive. William Billings, the first American composer, was subject to this uncertainty; so, too, is every American raising her voice in the daily practices of American religious experience. If American religious experience accrues to historical and political zones of uncertainty, music—the multifarious sacred practices that the essayists in this book examine—marks and intensifies that experience. Music may mediate the uncertainty of American religious experience. Music may mollify or exacerbate the uncertainty. Sacred music necessitates new beginnings and arrests the path of change stretching beyond the horizons of authenticity. Whatever its eventual impact, music is omnipresent in American religious experience, and its agency in the transformation of religion in America is immediate and palpable.

Metaphors, Tropes, and the Musical Language of American Religious Experience

Music crowds in upon America's sacred landscape, filling it constantly, as if to abhor the vacuum of its expansiveness. The differences, even the cacophony of multifarious voices, metaphorically fill the vast spaces of American religious experience as if it were a single congregation. Charles Ives's "The Collection" (fig. 2) captures the spirit of this paradox of a vast sacred space into which music crowds as if it had no place to stretch out and resonate. Like William Billings, Ives enjoys pride of place as an unequivocally American composer, and historically he assumes a foundational position in the emergence of American modernism. Composed in 1920, "The Collection" represents the landscape of a specific sacred space, the village church, and sacred meaning accrues to the space through the voices that fill it. The voices fill that space together and apart, consonantly and dissonantly. They insist on their unity, rejoicing that "Jew and Gentile join in praise," but when the organist, the soprano, and the village choir conclude "with one unified voice," it is anything but unified. The sonic uncertainty of "The Collection" is striking, and it depends on our

FIGURE 1.2. Charles Ives's "The Collection" (1920)

imagination of old hymns jumbled together in the physical space between the covers of a hymn collection, and on our willingness to tolerate the independence of individual voices that insist on their own spaces and rights in the choir. "The Collection," its diverse parts notwithstanding, is William Billings's "America" writ small.

Religious metaphors are transformed by music to acquire agency in the construction of America. The diversity of these metaphors in the following essays is considerable, yet the significant ways in which many emerge again and again speak to the ways in which music participates in the narration of America (see the essays on place in Stokes 1994, and Feld and Basso 1996). Religious song in America insists upon the possibilities of instantiating time and place. Protestant hymns, whether evangelical, Calvinist, or Lutheran, bear place names, which function quite differently from those in European predecessors. In his hymn and anthem collections from the late eighteenth century, William Billings consciously creates a canon of American songs by giving the hymns American place names, therefore distancing them from the European traditions, which had their own place names. In *The New-England Psalm-Singer* of 1770, the America in the hymn "America" evokes a different sense of place from the Europe in the hymn "Europe" (see Billings 1981, 1: 40–41, 316–19). American hymnody takes over the direct reference to place, but intensifies its geographical signification, which affords music the metaphorical power to give the sacred landscapes of America both historical and geographical dimensions.

Metaphor crowds in on sacred song in America, filling it with individual, local, denominational, and national meanings. As with the voices of the village choir, these metaphors coexist, sometimes in harmony, more often not. The essays in this volumes have drawn widely upon such metaphors, which in turn draw attention to the fact that they together address American religious experience in the singular but represent American religious experience in all its diversity.

One of the most predominant metaphors in the essays, particularly significant because of the historical unity it evokes, is the image of music and *the sacred journey.* Metaphors of places far away or of borders determined only by nature or the journey of life abound in American sacred music. In the earliest music histories of sacred repertories, the sacred journey takes the form of *exile* and *exodus,* whereby North America is the Promised Land, the refuge from history's or life's travails. *Pilgrimage,* too, enters American song repertories in countless forms, no less with late twentieth-century immigrant communities than at the time of the so-called Pilgrim Fathers. *Diaspora,* so much a trope of cultural studies on the eve of the millennium, has historicized sacred song throughout American history.

The America of much sacred song is utopian, therefore it is hardly surprising that different variants of the metaphor of *utopia* appear again and again in the repertories investigated in this volume. The *promised land* is surely the most widespread variant of the utopian metaphors. The religious history of North America is replete with utopian movements, each of which charts the sacred landscapes in distinctive ways. For the Hutterites of the Canadian prairie provinces, for example, their utopian communities appear in song as if they were in an "ark on God's ocean" (see, e.g., Holzach 1982). In most repertories, however, it is the land that is sacred, and through continuous reference to the *sacredness of the land* itself, America undergoes sonic reification.

Central to the power of music to instantiate American religious experience is its ability not only to represent but in fact to unify *community*. The religious community assumes other metaphorical forms, notably that of the *family*. Sacred music, it follows, ensures the reproduction of that family, thereby providing through performance the agency through which the religious community's genealogy unfolds (see, e.g., Hinks 1986). The personal possession of prayer and songbooks is just the most obvious form of music's reproductive capacity in the community. *Ritual,* not least when articulated with liturgical song in American Catholicism and Judaism, also ensures the reproduction of the community through performance. Historically, American religious experience has been characterized by the proliferation of communities, which in turn has necessitated the generation of new religious repertories, both to nurture new members in the sacred family and to rein in the propensity to proliferate in order to prevent a population explosion.

Music *encodes the sacred language* and therefore also contributes critically to the sociolinguistic basis of American religious experience. As a linguistic system, sacred music depends on the *dialectic* between written tradition, notably hymnody and the textuality of religious song, and oral tradition, usually liturgy and ritual. The extensive nature of written traditions, such as the countless songbooks published in every religion and denomination, creates the illusion of *authenticity,* song texts whose sacred authority is unassailable. The authenticity of song texts, however, is more often than not illusory, as the essays in part 2 of this book illustrate. Just as prayer books and hymnbooks anchor tradition in the word, they also become sites for change and struggles over change. Sacred song texts respond to changing communities and the changing definitions of community, hence making them also symbols for *hybridity* and *syncretism,* whose presence in the music of American religious experience is undeniable.

Change, nonetheless, fails to follow predictable paths across the sacred musical landscapes of North America. Even as change seems to move forward along the historical path as a means of accommodating new immigrant groups or shifting ideologies, its momentum depends on *historicism* and *revival,* as if to brake the free fall of American history. American religious communities celebrate familiarity in music, and they often take recourse in the "old way" of singing. In most religious communities music exerts a type of conservative influence that allows the community to contextualize the present through the sonic bulwark of the past.

Issues of *history and time* are fundamentally linked to music in American religious experience. The songs everyone in the congregation knows codify a shared historical narrative, allowing the congregation to perform itself as community. Ritual practice (or the performance of sacred time) overlaps with the musical narration of the past (or the performance of historical time). Religious music, woven into the everyday by congregational practices, constantly provides different ways of entering and exiting the experiences of American history and metaphorically proffering them sacred significance.

Singing of the Ancestors

Scholars of religious and musical studies have a long tradition of surveying the musical and religious landscapes of the American experience. The discourses growing from the genealogy of these scholarly ancestors bear witness to the special character of religious experience in America. Virtually all religious scholarship devoted to music, for example, is sectarian and denominationalist. Hymnodists and liturgists have turned with philological zeal to the definition and creation of sacred repertories that would not yield a set of fundamental musical texts and ritual practices for each denomination or movement, but would shore up the religious community. Rare is the volume of song or prayer in the United States that is not the product of years of painstaking scholarship and philological debate (see, e.g., the chapters by Bohlman, Holzapfel, and Summit in this volume).

Musical scholars, in contrast, have more often employed scholarly approaches that effectively separated religious music from religious experience, thereby secularizing sacred music and redeploying it in a secular rather than sectarian history. The ideological reasons for such strategies are all-too-obvious, which is to say that they derive from the American obsession with maintaining separation of church and state. The impact on the ontology of music, however, is more often overlooked or simply avoided. The sustained discourse of Americanist musicologists to lay the groundwork for American music history by identifying a canon of hymns and hymn composers, for example, frequently maps these on American political history (the War of Independence) rather than on American religious history (the Great Awakening) (see Temperley 1998). Sacred music is rendered as mere music.

A third set of voices has historically joined the discursive counterpoint representing sacred music in America. We might call that set of voices congregational or democratic; we interpret it as "the folk" or as the egalitarian community. Whatever we call it, that set of voices arises from those, who perform the sacred music of the United States and locate the music in their everyday practices. At a very fundamental level, Americans take the responsibility for their sacred music into their own hands. They may vote literally for the music they claim as their own—for example, accepting or rejecting a new hymnal or prayer book with new songs or inclusive language—or they may vote figuratively, that is, with their feet, forming breakaway congregations or establishing new movements in which the music does the cultural work they deem most important (see Summit 2000).

Methodologically, the third set of voices poses a special problem for musical and religious scholars, for it further challenges the tendency to objectify music as either text or context, musical or ritual practice. More significantly for the present volume, the third set of voices illumines a neglected middle ground, the borderlands between sectarianism and the unstable territories opened by the pragmatic insistence on separating church from state. These territories and the voices that issue from them form the subjects of the essays in this volume.

From its conception *Music in American Religious Experience* has endeavored to provide a forum for a diverse collective of scholarly approaches. Broadly speaking, about half of the authors writing here most frequently study and write about religion; about half are musicologists or ethnomusicologists, writing usually about music. Institutionally, there is also a balance between those teaching in seminaries or religious studies programs and those teaching in music departments. Such distinctions notwithstanding, all the authors engage in the practices of religious music in one way or another, actively at certain stages in their lives and careers, passively at other stages.

The essays in this volume therefore approach religious music in America along quite different paths, but they are unified at moments when the paths intersect. Such moments of intersection insist that the sacred musics of different religions be examined together as American religious experience. The critical question is not that differences disappear, but rather that differences fail to silence the musical practices that connect religious music so profoundly to a multitude of everyday experiences. The essays contribute distinctive and contrasting perspectives to the book by not privileging one practice over another, but by insisting that the singularity of individual musical practices forms a crucial counterpoint with the singularity of American religious experience as a whole. We believe that the book occupies a pivotal position in the transformation of historical dissonance into palpable possibilities for consonance.

The "Singularity" of American Religious Experience

In early discussions about this volume the editors and authors struggled mightily with the nature of "American religious experience," specifically with the problem of its singularity and plurality. There was never any question that Americans had many different religious experiences. Nor was there any question that the extraordinary diversity of these experiences was itself something characteristically American. Ultimately, however, the essays in the book concern themselves far less with the extraordinary than with the everydayness of religion in America. The issue here is not that all Americans are religious at all times—a case neither the practicing nor the nonpracticing would make—but rather that religion implicates itself everyday in the lives of all Americans.

The emblems of singularity appear again and again in the liturgical traditions and hymnody that Americans use to engage with their religious experience. That singularity is evident in the *locus classicus* of gospel blues (fig. I.3), Thomas A. Dorsey Jr.'s "Precious Lord," which begins this section. The "father of gospel blues," Thomas Dorsey wove a variety of hymn traditions, black and white, into the fabric of American hymnody (see Harris 1992). Dorsey's great gift was the ability to draw out the most distinctive and compatible elements from different Protestant traditions, those elements that lend themselves to synthesis and syncretism. Dorsey also perceived new possibilities for opening up the performance practice that had long anchored text-bound hymnody to the pew, and to achieve this end he turned to the improvisatory practices of African American vernacular music, especially the blues. The singularity of the gospel blues, therefore, derived from the power of synthesis, of singing in a unified voice and performing in a congregational body. The congregational metaphors of singularity notwithstanding, the real power of Dorsey's hymns was their emphasis on singularity itself, the individual, "tired" and "worn," being led "through the storm, through the night."

The essays in this volume represent American religious experience as diverse, polyvocal, and contested, yet historically singular and audible in the chorus singing of American religious experience. They narrate different histories and therefore interpret the sacred journey across the sacred landscape of North America in different ways. In each essay we find that American re-

FIGURE I.3. Thomas A. Dorsey Jr.'s "Take My Hand, Precious Lord"

ligious experience is fundamentally communitarian, that it depends on the ways music shapes and bounds communities of believers. It is characteristic of this singularly American form of communitarianism that the individual never disappears, and that musical practice is inseparable from the agency of individuals, be they composers or liturgists, missionaries or hymnal publishers, prayer leaders or feminist activists. Both tolerance and intolerance drive American religious experience, which therefore implicates sacred music within and outside politics, within and without the nation. Sacred music in America constitutes one of the most fundamental and sustained discourses in counterpoint with American history.

The contrapuntal discourses emerge in some of their most distinctive forms in part I of the volume, "Encounter and Ethnicity." The complexity of the volume's theme itself is stated from the outset in Regula Burckhardt Qureshi's opening chapter. Questions not only of religious meaning but ontological and musical meaning spin out from the practices of Muslim women, whose encounter through the celebration of *mīlād* we view through the experiences of an insider and participant. Critically, we believe, these questions of music and religious experience in Islam take their place as a central theme, in the present and as a stretto, rather than occupying the periphery, as they so often do in studies that treat American religion and music historically, hence teleologically. As if writing as an historian-composer, Jon Michael Spencer follows with a chapter that theorizes theomusicology as a new genre of fugal discourse. Spencer shifts the voices of African American music to the historical center, and in so doing he makes the most powerful claims for a fundamental sacredness. Spencer calls for a rethinking of the center, and he equivocates not in the least about the possibility that there is a sacred core in all American musics and all African American musics, the recognition of which empowers African American history in critical ways. Ann Morrison Spinney and Margarita Mazo move from Spencer's claims for a core to new considerations of the margins. Their two essays do not offer convenient explanations of encounter and ethnicity, for in neither case, the Wabanaki in colonial North America and the American Russian Molokans, does ethnicity unfold as a stage naturally following encounter. Instead, we witness the ways in which encounter may actually have undermined the possibilities for synthesis in Native American sacred traditions. The Molokans, among whom Mazo has conducted fieldwork in both Russia and North America, may more accurately use sacred music as a means of resisting ethnicity.

The essays in the second part lay the groundwork for song as the urtext in histories of American religious experience. For Stephen Marini hymnody and history are inseparable, and his essay illustrates the extent to which they are mutually constitutive. Evangelical hymns, forming an historical canon already in colonial America, cut across denominational boundaries, appearing again and again in each generation of hymnal and hymnbook, but also exhibiting a remarkable appeal that fails to diminish in generation after generation of worshipers. Paul Westermeyer and Otto Holzapfel initially conceived their essays as a pair, as two different perspectives on the same historical tradition of German American hymnody. Westermeyer's American perspective, further informed by his theologian's sensibilities, leads him to an exegesis of evolution, in which German American hymns undergird and participate in change. Holzapfel's German perspective led him to a reading of German American hymnals that he sees as a radical departure from the expected treatment of ethnic change. German American hymnody, according to Holzapfel, quickly abandoned its Germanness, but historically this did not make a difference. Far more important was the deeper sense that the right songs were more important than the right ethnicity. The sense of rightness only strengthened the function of hymnody to juxtapose religious and ethnic experiences. In the congregational experiences given thick description by Judith Gray, exegetical knowledge is fundamental to musical and vocal metaphor. The counterpoint of metaphors in Congregational hymnody is both textual and musical, again a case of different voices mutually constitutive of communitarianism in American life.

The essays in part 3 turn attention from the texts of American religious music to those, who give voice to those texts, individuals and the agency of faith. In her study of Fanny Crosby, Edith Blumhofer ponders just what it was that made Crosby the most celebrated author of hymn texts in the nineteenth century. It can hardly be doubted that Fanny Crosby "stood out" as an extraordinary individual, but the question remains if it was for this reason that Crosby's texts had such mass appeal. Crosby's hymns, in essence, contained something for everyone, allowing her countless followers to crowd in on the landscape of American Protestant hymnody. Philip Bohlman examines less populist personalities, whose impacts on American Lutheran and Jewish traditions, however, were no less pivotal. The contributions of the individual, Bohlman suggests, are pivotal precisely because they are not isolated, rather they determine the topography of a much larger panorama of American sacred history. Janet Walton takes women and worship as points of departure, but ultimately raise much more complex questions about the meaning of music in worship. For the women in Walton's study, music becomes a vehicle for extending the meaning of ritual so that it expresses a vast complex of feminist issues. Together, music and feminist subjectivity forge new facets of faith, and in so doing Walton illustrates one of the fundamental tenets of this book, that music propels American religion ceaselessly along new and different paths.

Individuals act in concert in American religious experience, and the essays in the final part of the book provide four case studies of congregational and communitarian histories. Jeffrey Summit's case study of *nusach* illustrates the ways in which American Jewish congregations take an abstract concept and make it their own. *Nusach* musically embodies Jewish history at many different levels, but it still lends itself to the interpretation of individuals as they worship and sing. *Nusach* at once celebrates diversity while revealing the possibility for unity among American Jewish communities at a very profound level. Maria Chow looks at diversity from quite another perspective, for Chinese American churches confront a distinctive set of problems when developing a common liturgical and hymn tradition. The commonality of their communitarianism necessarily comprises compromise. Common repertories must admit exception, but exception, in turn, complicates the relation of a given congregation to larger bodies of Chinese Christian hymnody. Drawing upon extensive ethnography among Old Regular Baptists, Jeff Titon interprets the American communitarian experience yet another way. Music itself does not provide a form of cultural glue that binds Old Regular Baptists together, and Titon cautions us from facile assumptions about what sacred music really is. Faith and the closest relation with God demand a deep level of experience, and it is individualized forms of music-making that achieve experience for the Old Regular

Baptists. In his concluding essay, Don Saliers illumines the path returning to the mainstream of American Protestantism. Rather than suggesting with his study of the *United Methodist Hymnal* that the mainstream of American Protestantism is homologous with an all-encompassing American religious experience, Saliers shows that hymnody succeeds not by closing down the possibilities for resistive theological stances and individual decision-making, but by empowering them with alternatives. Hymnody and sacred song, if indeed aesthetically symbolic of a congregational whole, are most effective when enhancing the individual's capacity to locate herself on the sacred landscape of America.

Experiencing America Religiously through History's Ethnographic Present

The strains of "Amazing Grace" rumble along, dirge-like and unfamiliar, a sharp contrast to the video projections of the Romanian translations, white on a blue background and flanking the altar in front of the Philadelphia Church of God on Chicago's Northside. The small jazz ensemble and the two women songleaders, or "cantors," dressed in close-fitting chenille dresses, pull the Romanian American congregation through the song on a Sunday night in late March 1998 as Lent draws closer toward the Holy Week and Easter. The performance of "Amazing Grace" is a translation at many levels. It's not just the text that must be rendered in translation, but also the charismatic form of American Pentecostalism, which has long served as a model for Romanian Pentecostalism, but at the Philadelphia Church of God is also perceived as though projected only darkly through a lens. When the Romanian American congregation sings "Amazing Grace," its faith seems not to fit, still foreign and still mystified by what translation to American religious experience demands of it.

Singing "Amazing Grace," however, is only one moment in the three-hour service, the third of the day for the Philadelphia Church of God. In this midwestern urban church, attended almost entirely by recent immigrants from Romania, music maps and remaps American religious experience on the very landscape of its large sanctuary. In the left wing of the sanctuary sits the large choir, mostly women in an age group from about thirty to sixty, though with clusters of high-school girls as well. The repertory of Philadelphia's choir is Romanian choral music, Protestant in the broadest sense and owing its historical tradition more to the influence of Hungarian Calvinism on Transylvania and other regions of western Romania.

Imnurile
Bucuriei

Editia a 2-a

Lăudați pe Domnul de jos de pe pământ...
împărați ai pământului și popoare toate,
voivozi și toți judecători ai pământului, tineri
și tinere, bătrâni și copii!
Să laude Numele Domnului!
Căci numai Numele Lui este înălțat; măreția
Lui este mai presus de pământ și ceruri.

Psalmul 148:7-13

COLECȚIE DE CÂNTĂRI DUHOVNICEȘTI
PENTRU BISERICILE ROMÂNE EVANGHELICE

FIGURE I.4. Romanian hymnal from Chicago's Philadelphia Church of God

Facing the choir, in the right wing, is a large brass band, an ensemble of perhaps thirty musicians, some with instruments from Chicago band programs, others with instruments that bear witness to the instrumentarium of military bands of an older, Habsburg era, for example, the helikon, a tuba-like instrument whose sound anchors the band, but with a much gentler timbre than American counterparts. The band, despite the predominance of junior-high and high-school musicians, punctuates the service with a repertory that few American mainstream Protestants would recognize, not least because it is a palimpsest of Romania's own nineteenth- and twentieth-century histories of changing political loyalties and cultural influences.

With Romanian traditions flanking the altar and the congregation, the center of this sacred musical landscape becomes the site for the most extensive forms of cultural translation. The small jazz ensemble does not really play jazz, though it does its best to inject a bit of swing into the gospel hymns. More important, some of Philadelphia's best young musicians play in the jazz ensemble, and when they play for a church service, they display the success they have enjoyed in the public sphere, not to mention the fact that they have not strayed from the Pentecostal flock, for they are willing to share their talents in the church of their parents and grandparents. Similarly, it is the raised extension of the front of the altar that serves as a stage for young parishioners, who perform from the art-music repertories of the eighteenth and nineteenth centuries, on this evening a Mozart piano quartet, a movement from a Haydn cello concerto, and a selection of Verdi arias.

The congregation sings from its own hymnals, piled high on the pews (see fig. I.4). The hymnal is quite literally Philadelphia's "own," for it is published in suburban Hanover Park, and Philadelphia is by far the largest Romanian Pentecostalist congregation in the Midwest. The hymnal, too, serves the congregation as a vehicle for translation. The texts mediate between a Romanian religious experience and an American religious experience, although, as we have seen already, the Romanian religious experience of Pentecostalism takes as its model the American religious experience. Women in black village dress, whose humility in public leads them to occupy only the pews at the back of the sanctuary, take comfort in the Romanianness of the hymnal, while their children and grandchildren, more eager to be in close proximity to the service's charismatic aspects crowd the front pews, celebrating the elements of Americanness that the publishers have introduced into the hymnal. On this March evening in 1998, the congregation of the Philadelphia Church of God lifts its voice in song, a voice responding in its full counterpoint to American religious experience and a voice possible because of a sanctuary whose complex musical landscape accommodates the difference paths traveled by Romanian Americans toward that experience.

This introduction began with an historical moment, and it concludes with an ethnographic moment. Throughout the book that follows historical and ethnographic moments form the complex counterpoint that constitutes and resonates as American religious experience, not just in the past but also in the present. There is little evidence to suggest that the balance between historical and ethnographic moments will shift, and that their counterpoint will diminish in its complexity. Encounter and ethnicity will continue to mark American religious experience, and new congregations and communities will continue to proliferate. In the twenty-first century, the publication of new prayer and songbooks continues unabated, and individual musicians seek out new prospects for the agency of faith, responding to each the successive journeys across the face of America's sacred landscape. Music continues to crowd in upon American religious experience, on a Sunday night in Chicago or in the hymnody of America's first composers. As crowded with music as American religious experience may become, it is perhaps most remarkable that there will always be room for more voices to enrich the counterpoint and to fill out the choir.

WORKS CITED

Billings, William. 1981. *The Complete Works of William Billings*. Ed. by Hans Nathan, et al. 4 vols. Philadelphia and Boston: The American Musicological Society and the Colonial Society of Massachusetts.

Crawford, Richard. 1993. *The American Musical Landscape*. Berkeley: University of California Press.

Feld, Steven, and Keith H. Basso, eds. 1996. *Senses of Place*. Santa Fe: School of American Research Press.

Harris, Michael W. 1992. *The Rise of Gospel Blues: The Music of Thomas Andrew Dorsey in the Urban Church*. New York: Oxford University Press.

Hinks, Donald R. 1986. *Brethren Hymn Books and Hymnals, 1720–1884*. Gettysburg, Penn.: Brethren Heritage.

Holzach, Michael. 1982. *Das vergessene Volk: Ein Jahr bei den deutschen Hutterern in Kanada*. Munich: Hoffmann und Campe.

Ives, Charles E. 1958? *Sacred Songs*. New York: Peer International Corporation.

Krummel, D.W. 1998. "The Bay Psalm Book Tercentenary, 1698–1998." *Notes* 55 (2): 281–87.

Stokes, Martin, ed. 1994. *Ethnicity, Identity and Music: The Musical Construction of Place*. Oxford: Berg.

Summit, Jeffrey A. 2000. *"The Lord's Song in a Strange Land": Music and Identity in Contemporary Jewish Worship*. New York: Oxford University Press.

Temperley, Nicholas. 1998. *The Hymn Tune Index: A Census of English-Language Hymn Tunes in Printed Sources from 1535 to 1820*. 4 vols. Oxford: Oxford University Press.

PART I

Experience and Identity

1

When Women Recite: "Music" and Islamic Immigrant Experience

Regula Burckhardt Qureshi

Goal and Domain

This chapter focuses on the religious musical sphere "other" to the much televised public worship of men in mosques: the domestic world of the family where Islamic identity is forged through recitation practice that also serves to build the immigrant community from inside out. Of necessity founded in personal participation, this research implicates me as: (1) A quasi-insider by kinship—a longstanding active member of the South Asian community in Edmonton, Alberta. (2) As a professional voyeur-interpreter—longstanding researcher and ethnomusicologist. And (3), fusing both identities, as a longtime performer of Muslim devotional hymns. Such enmeshments require me to be responsible to my partners and accountable for my own experience in the process of probing metaquestions and theorizing practices.[1]

In a religious community so strongly marked by gender separation, being female offers me an obvious ethnographic opportunity to focus on women's experience. Yet I seize this opportunity for two compelling reasons. On the one hand, there is the pragmatic need to transcend the public, male exterior face of Islamic practice in part because this face has congealed into a conventional, sterotypical image that inhibits the ability of Muslims to invite social contact or affective empathy among other North American communities. On the other hand, most importantly, women and their world of personal piety and social connections are inseparable from the significant role of recitation in Muslim immigrant life.

The women's perspective I examine in this chapter is situated in the domestic sphere that women control and manage: home, the extended family, and the circle of friends. Intimate, safe, predictable, and supportive, the domestic sphere is the familial domain its entire membership (not only women) call *apnā*, "their own," where one belongs as a positioned individual, and is the source of one's religious beliefs and practices. My focus on recitation within this context is a move toward profiling a significant dimension of Muslim religious life in the West where women hold agency. In doing so, my intent is to convey a sense of how South Asian women in North America jointly make this religious life happen, using the power of "music" to preserve religious traditions as well as to transform them in the light of new understanding.

I argue that in South Asian Muslim practice, music's multiple effects play a central role in nurturing individual piety and in directing it into an act of participation in order to create an experience that is at once spiritual and communitarian. I further argue that the fusion of devotion and participation in the practice of musical recitation rearticulates an earlier, historically situated response of South Asian Muslims to the Western appropriation of public space. This current rearticulation differs from the previous one in that today both the domestic matrix and the performative character of the practice of musical recitation are being renegotiated in the face of the global articulation and expansion of a mosque-based Islamic metapractice.

Islam in Practice: Public/Private, Male/Female

Islam is a religion with a strong exterior appearance. The mosque with its distinct architectural style, the call-to-prayer (*adhān*) emanating from it, and the fivefold daily prayer ritual are a consistent and universally present combination of visual and auditory statements in the public sphere. The statements embody a divine verbal message that is universally accessible in the Qur'an. The fundamental principles in the divine verbal message are linked to a simple set of rules governing religious practice. Believing in the principles joins all Muslims in a universal Islamic community, the *ʿumma*; practicing the rules together joins individual believers into particular congregations centered in the mosque.

The quintessential manifestation of a local Muslim presence is rows of prostrate men submitting to God—the term "Islam" can be glossed as "submission"—in prayer to the melodious cantillation of the divine Word of Allah in Arabic. How Islam is practiced musically among women and in the home, on the other hand, is not accessible to outsiders. Yet Islam is very communitarian as a religion. For it to settle within the Western public sphere is not easy. Thus in the context of a Western lifestyle, nurturing the culturally particular, personal practice of Islam has assumed crucial importance for Muslim immigrants generally. As a result, in the North American diaspora, notwithstanding the usual male-dominated image of Islam, the participation of women and the family in musical recitation has formed a crucial focus for creating a community of religious experience for first-generation Muslim immigrants and their children.

But Why Music?

Why should music have such an important role in a religion that values it so negatively? The fact is that musical sound plays a highly significant role in articulating the singularly verbal message of Islam, both in its universal quranic form and also in the form of vernacular devotional poetry. What expresses Muslim identity, or experience or faith, is a dynamic of living communication through words being sounded and heard—not "disenchanted into pure medium" (Devji 1991): The words of the quranic message; words that explain and interpret the message; words that praise God and his messenger; words that convey the believer's submission, the literal meaning of "Islam." Presenting these words musically renders the message more articulate and intense, as well as acoustically and aesthetically compelling. Indeed, musical recitation is integral to Islam's essentially oral approach to religious texts.

The term that Muslims have used to designate this vocal style since the Prophet's time is "reading," not "singing," meaning that to articulate verbal sounds is at the same time to apprehend their (religious) meaning. The gloss "music" is therefore strictly speaking inappropriate; its use here signifies the generic presence of a sound idiom that is culturally, and religiously, defined.

Musical sound bound to the Word is ubiquitous in the religious practice of South Asian Muslims and is protected by a complete conceptual separation from all non-religious music, especially music performed on instruments. The ways in which South Asian Muslims manage musical sound through the religious rule system are highly complex and creative. They reveal deep sensitivity to music's "significant effects;" a dual sonic power that is at once intimately individual and broadly social. To elaborate this, the musical sound heard by a community may bear different meanings for the individuals while communicating messages that are collectively shared among the community. In an instant, the sound of music creates, in those who experience it, bonds that are as deep and intimate as they are broad and universal. The bonds are deep and intimate because they do not commit themselves to a single spatial requirement and leave the personal, interior domain unviolated in the experience. Yet they are broad and universal because the very experience of the musical sound is public, shared, and exterior. In short, the social nature of the religious musical experience, underrated in much musical scholarship, is deeply intertwined with its personal, individual character in a highly significant way.

The Practice of "Musical" Recitation

How do South Asian Muslim women harness this dual power of music in their recitation practice? As first-generation immigrants, they have brought with them the memories of a rich and diverse religious soundscape that comprises two categorically distinct styles. The first is quranic cantillation following an Arabic musical model (*qir'at*), which is the Islamic vocal idiom *par excellence* associated with male ritual practice at the mosque. At home quranic cantillation is performed informally and individually by both men and women. Upon the birth of a child, for example, the first message to reach the ear of a newborn infant comprises the words of the Islamic creed, the *kalma* or *shahādā*,[2] recited by a senior woman of the family. At night or after the early morning prayer, a grandparent may also recite from the Qur'an. Most important, during Ramadan, the month when Muhammad's revelation was completed, the entire Qur'an is recited.

The second style consists of vernacular hymns chanted predominantly in devotional assemblies dedicated to principal religious figures of Islam. Assemblies of this kind have traditionally been convened at home, and also as public events; they are not associated with the mosque. A lead reciter, usually with a supporting group, is invited to present a series of hymns to an audience of devotees, who respond in specific ways to the religious listening experience. The performance style of each assembly enhances the religious text and expresses the spiritual-emotional experience it evokes in the listeners.

From the distinct types of ritual-musical events ("a formal procedure in a religious observance"), I focus on the one that is most universally practiced among South Asian Muslim women, the *mīlād*.[3] This assembly celebrating the birth of the Prophet Muhammad is held primarily during the month of Rabī-ul-Awwal, most auspiciously on the actual birthday (12 Rabī-ul-Awwal), but it may also be held to mark auspicious events, such as moving into a new house or the arrival of a daughter-in-law from Pakistan. Hosted at home by families, *mīlād* is particularly a women's event and in common parlance people even call it "women's *qawwālī*," in contrast to the all-male singing of Qawwali at Sufi assemblies. Singing at *mīlād* sometimes involves all participants. Among Sunni Muslims especially, everyone is familiar with the well-known hymns; anyone attending a *mīlād* can join in the congregational refrain passages if they feel like it. For girls and women this is the only approved way of expressing musicality and regaling an audience with musical beauty. Indeed, women, as well as men, also informally recite *na't*, or hymns to the Prophet, before any appropriate listeners.

As shown in the outline of a *mīlād* sequence in table 1.1, a lead reciter with a small supporting group presents hymns in praise of the Prophet alternating with prose passages that relate to the birth of the Prophet, his life, and his divine verbal message. A brief Arabic praise-litany (*durūd*) provides continuity between the segments; it is intoned by the reciting group and often by the audience as well. Like all religious events, the *mīlād* begins in the name of God with *hamd*, a hymn in His praise, and ends with an intercessory prayer (*du'ā*) intoned by the leader, followed by a silent recitation of the quranic *Sūrā-e-fāteha*. The audience listens quietly, but for the final hymn, the *salām* or salutation to the Prophet, all stand in respect for God and join in reciting the Arabic refrain that frames the Urdu verses.

Musically, *mīlād* hymns evoke feelings of both devotion and exultation: devotion through melodic simplicity; exultation through rising melodic movement and sustaining the high pitches (see example 1.3). Participating in a *mīlād* conveys an experience of veneration and submission before the most exalted

TABLE 1.1 *Mīlād*: Standard Recitational Format

( ) = optional	
(*qir'at*	quranic recitation; chanted by any competent participant)
hamd	hymn in praise of God; chanted by performing group, intoned by leader
na't	hymn in praise of Prophet;
riwāyāt	message about life and teachings of Prophet; spoken or chanted by leader
(*durūd*	litany; chanted by performing group, audience may join in)
na't	(one or two) chanted by performing group member(s), sometimes also by individual from audience
(*durūd*	chanted by performing group, audience may join in)
(*riwāyāt-durūd-na't*	sequence repeated one or more times)
riwāyāt	concluding message describing the Prophet's birth
salām	salutation to the Prophet; verses chanted by leader, Arabic refrain by all participants; everyone stands to show respect
du'ā	intercessory prayer, chanted or spoken by leader
sūrā-e-fāteha	recited silently, palms raised in supplicatory gesture

personage in Islam, and a deep affection for his humanity. *Mīlād* directly links this experience with the Prophet's divine message of the Qur'an. The universally chanted *salām* and *durūd* in the *mīlād* (examples 1.2 and 1.4) explicitly use the Phrygian mode, the mode that is privileged in formal *qir'at* recitation and in the call to prayer (see example 1.1).

Being a medium of expressing both personal-devotional and canonical-universal aspects of meaning in *mīlād* texts, music casts the verbal composite within a familiar tonal idiom that embodies both their semantic and formal properties. Such familiarity, much like that experienced by Protestants in the melodies and tonal idiom of Lutheran chorales, is not confined to specific tunes of *salām, durūd,* and *du'ā,* but extends to the general style of hymn tunes making every utterance recognizable and easily comprehensible. In addition, a structural homology between poems and their musical setting reinforces the predictable temporal unfolding of the performance event.

Vernacular devotional recitation, a collective yet deeply internalized voice, has, for at least a century, been a special locus of middle-class South Asian religious experience both for and practiced by women. This special locus covers the language of the poem as well, in spite of the fact that the poem may be composed by men (as is *Mīlād-e-Akbar*). As our examples show, their language is direct, heartfelt, even unsophisticated and unadorned, but is at the same time studded with liturgical Arabic and classical Persian phrases that are revered for sounding canonical even when they are not literally understood.

Mīlād in the Immigrant Milieu

The paramount need of the Muslim South Asian immigrating to Canada and the United States, either individually or with their families, was to build personal communities among fellow South Asian Muslims by seeking common identity. Mediated by shared language and regional lifestyle, Islam has been a major determinant of individual and group identity among these immigrants in Canada. More importantly, it has offered an ideational foundation and a rich set of practices that help them, in response to the uncharted exigencies of life in the West, to articulate clearly their presence in Canadian society.

Shared religious practice centered around recitation, above all devotional assemblies, has been intimately tied to the process of building community from inside out, that is, starting with the individual household. In the South Asian Muslim community one invites for a devotional event at home the members of one's family "circle," which consists of various relationships: ties among women and among men, ties among generations, ties among adults and children, and ties between families in a region. These ties yield personal communities with life revolving around weekend socializing in each other's homes by sharing a meal (dinner). The informal socializing and food sharing within the personal communities affirm the centrality of the family as the center of an expansive private space. Embedded in the social life of the expansive private space are the religious assemblies of the South Asian Muslim immigrants.

Women are in charge of the social life of the personal communities. Since *mīlād* events are home and family based, they, too, are organized and carried out by women. Among the South Asian Muslim immigrant community, expert reciters are scarce within the community; therefore, *mīlād* reciters are usually drawn from one's personal circle. Anyone who is competent, confident, and willing to contribute could assume the role. Listeners are relatives and personal friends, including children.

In the 1960s and 1970s, the early years of limited immigration,[4] the South Asian community was smaller and younger and held *mīlāds* that included entire families, forming mixed assemblies of men and women. In the earliest years of the immigrant community, men were both listeners and reciters. They were particularly called upon to recite an introductory passage of quranic chant. Occasionally, a competent male reciter would even be asked to contribute a hymn. In the last decade or so, however, there has been a shift away from this practice because of the immigrant community's growth, due in part to the increased influx of senior family members sponsored under the Family Reunification scheme. To show respect to the older women who are not accustomed to mixed socializing, there has been a shift to all female *mīlāds* and toward gender segregated socializing generally. Figure 1 shows a recent *mīlād* with women only, held around an extended family of four generations, with the grandmother of the hostess reciting a prayer.

To convey a sense of participation in such a recitation event, let us attend a *mīlād* convened during the month of Rabī-ul-Awwal by an Edmonton family to celebrate the birth of Prophet Muhammad. The intentionally ample selection of textual-musical examples is intended to show the very special blend of formal reverence and personal devotion that marks *mīlād*.

This *mīlād* was held in 1979 on a Sunday afternoon and concluded with an early dinner for forty to fifty guests. Both men and women attended, along with mostly young children.

The men sat in separate rooms and conversed until the *mīlād* recitation started. As soon as most of the guests had arrived, the hostess, being one of the few in the community with the competence to lead a *mīlād* recitation, asked several others who could chant to join her on the low settee (*chauki*) in the living room (fig. 1).

As everyone gathered their focus on the *mīlād*, the host requested one of the male guests to recite from the Qur'an, whereupon the women present covered their heads with their scarf or sari. All listened reverently as he enunciated the hallowed words with melodious intonation (*khushilhani*) while remaining seated in his place among the men.

The lead reciter then took a standard recitational guidebook entitled *Mīlād-e-Akbar*[5] out of its special cloth covering and began the *mīlād* recitation by intoning a *hamd*, a hymn in praise of God, the proper way to begin any task, especially the task of celebrating the birthday of God's Prophet. She held the book open, enabling her partners to read the verses with her while chanting. Moving to another page, she now selected a well-known *na't* in praise of the Prophet. Throughout, the other reciters followed her recitation in unison or responsorially, using a strong voice to chant a familiar text and melody, or reciting more cautiously when following an unfamiliar hymn. To illustrate the collaborative interaction between lead-singer and accompanists that characterizes *mīlād* recitation, musical example 1.1 shows the opening *na't* recited in a standard responsorial style. The talented leader intones each new verse line in a fluid melismatic style until it leads into the refrain-like monorhyme in Arabic that is picked up and repeated by the supporting group; this gives the leader time to take a breath before the next line.

All concluded this first hymn segment with the most widely used *durūd*, which was recited twice. The same brief praise litany concluded each hymn segment (musical example 1.2) leading on to the *riwāyāt* section of spoken recitation.

TEXT (Urdu)
Subhānallāh, subhānallāh
Yeh shams-o-qamar, yeh arz-o-samā, subhānallāh subhānallāh
Har rang meṅ hai jalwa terā, subhānallāh subhānallāh

Maiṅ dar dar tujh ko dhūndh phir ā, lekin bek ār hu ā phirn ā
Shairag se tujh ko pās milā subhānallāh subhānallāh

Translation
Praise be to God, Praise be to God!

You have made the sun and the moon, the earth and the heavens: Praise be to God, Praise be to God!
In all of these is Your reflection: Praise be to God, Praise be to God!

I searched for You at every door, but these were fruitless wanderings
I found You closer than my jugular vein: Praise be to God, Praise be to God!

MUSICAL EXAMPLE 1.1 *Hamd* (hymn in praise of God)

MUSICAL EXAMPLE 1.2 *Durūd* (litany in praise of the Prophet)

TEXT (Arabic)
Sallallāhu alaika yā Rasūlallāh
Wasallim alaika yā Habībāllāh

Translation
May you have the blessings of God, O messenger of God
May you have the peace of God, O Lover of God

What then followed was one of several *riwāyāt* from the *Mīlād-e-Akbar* that recount the marvelous situations and events that led up to the Prophet's birth. These were interspersed with passages that convey the moral and uplifting messages of Islam, highlighted by relevant episodes from the Prophet's life. Following each prose episode the leader, together with the other reciters, selected and intoned perhaps as many as three hymns from their book. Then they once again repeated the *durūd* to give the hostess/lead-reciter time to select and prepare the declamation of the next *riwāyāt* passage. In the subsequent hymn segments, the hostess also invited two male reciters from outside the group to present a *na't*; one of them was the Qur'an reciter. Both were asked to address the listeners in front of the reciting group.

The final *riwāyāt*, as is customary, was an episode that led the listeners up to the Prophet's birth, but the Prophet's qualities as a messenger of God continued to be the main focus. Praise to God for this event found fervent expression in the verses of the *na't* chosen for the final hymn segment, a favorite,

MUSICAL EXAMPLE 1.3 *Na't* with part of *shahādā* as refrain

TEXT	
Refrain (Arabic):	Allāh Allāh Allāhū, lā ilāhā illā hū (2x)
Verse 1 (Urdu):	Āmina bībī ke gulshan meń āī hai tāza bahār (2x) Parhte haiń sallallāh-o-alaihu waśallam dar-o-dīwār, Nabījī
Refrain:	Allāh Allāh Allāhū, lā ilāhā illā hū (2x)
Verse 2:	Bārā Rabī-u-Awwal ko woh āe haiń durr-e-yatīm (2x) Awwal-o-ākhir, zāhir-o-bātin ban kar ghafūr-o-rahīm, Nabījī
Refrain:	Allāh Allāh Allāhū, lā ilāhā illā hū (2x)
Verse 3:	Jibraīl āe jhūlā jhulāe, lōrī de Rahmān (2x) Sōjā sōjā ai rahmat-e-ālam dō jag ke sultān, Nabījī
Refrain:	Allāh Allāh Allāhū, lā ilāhā illā hū (2x)
Translation	
Refrain:	God Is, there is no God but He
Verse 1:	In the garden of revered Amina a new spring comes (2x) The whole house is resounding "May God's blessing and peace be upon you, O Prophet!"
Refrain:	God Is, there is no God but He
Verse 2:	On the 12th of Rabī-ul-Awwal the priceless jewel has arrived First and last, apparent and hidden, forgiving and merciful you are, O Prophet
Refrain:	God Is, there is no God but He
Verse 3:	Gabriel comes to rock the cradle and there are lullabies from God Sleep, sleep, you blessing to the universe, you ruler of the two worlds, O Prophet
Refrain:	God Is, there is no God but He

which includes part of the *shahādā* in its refrain: "Allāh Allāh Allāhū, lā ilāhā īllā hū" (musical example 1.3).

Following the lead of the reciters, everyone then stood for the recitation of the *salām* that concludes every *mīlād* and is the most familiar of all *mīlād* hymns. As the lead-reciter intoned the opening line, participants joined in chanting the opening verse as a refrain, which addresses the Prophet with salutations and praise. The reciter chanted the subsequent verses, each verse alternating with the participants' refrain. Recitation of the *salām* in unison concluded the *mīlād* (see musical example 1.4).

On concluding the *salām* everyone was seated and the lead-reciter intoned *du'ā*, the fervent outpouring of personal prayer that complements the canonical *namāz*. She read a moving rhymed *du'ā* from the *Mīlād-e-Akbar*, intoning it in its own traditional reciting tune familiar to all (musical example 1.5). The rest

MUSICAL EXAMPLE 1.4 *Salām: Ya Nabī Salām Alaikā*

TEXT (Arabic):	
Refrain:	Yā nabī salām alaikā Yā rasūl salām alaikā Yā habīb salām alaikā Salawāt-ullāh alaikā
Verse 1 (Urdu):	Fakhr-e-Ādam, fakhr-e-Hawwā Fakhr-e-Nūh, fakhr-e-Yahyiā Fakhr-e-Ibrahīm-o-Mūsā Fakhr-e-Ismaīl-o-Īsā
Refrain:	Yā nabī . . .
Translation	
Refrain:	O Prophet, Peace be upon you O Messenger of God, peace be upon you O Lover of God, peace be upon you May the blessings of God be upon you
Verse 1:	Pride of Adam, pride of Eve Pride of Noah, pride of Job Pride of Abraham and Moses Pride of Ismail and Jesus
Refrain:	O Prophet . . .

MUSICAL EXAMPLE 1.5 *Du'ā* from *Mīlād-e-Akbar*[6]

TEXT (Urdu)
Mōminō waqt-e-rahmat-e-rab hai
Ab woh māngō jo dil ka matlab hai

Sab ko rabb-e-ghafūr detā hai
Hai woh dātā zurūr detā hai

Yuń karō arz ai karamwāle
Hāth phailā rahe haiń gham wāle

Translation (first 3 verses)
O believers, this is the time of God's mercy
Now ask for what your heart desires

God, the Forgiving One gives to all
He is the Giver, he will surely give

Humbly request him thus: O beneficent God,
We who suffer extend our hands to You

of the assembly listened to her quietly without adopting a demeanor different from normal deportment in a secular situation. Now, to join in the prayer, all present turned their palms upward, in the universal Muslim gesture of supplication that the hymn itself invokes.

After the *du'ā*, a silent recitation of the quranic *Sūra-e-fāteha* concluded the *mīlād*, whereupon everybody resumed normal socializing, and a festive meal was soon laid out to conclude the event.

The all-female *mīlād* of more recent years are of course similar in formal ritual terms. Returning the event to a completely female domain, however, has created something of a shift in dynamics with religious as well as social effects. Most immediately evident is a return to a conservatism that prevailed in South Asia a generation ago and earlier. For one, deference to respected elders—mothers-in-law and grandmothers who are now present—has resulted in an acceptance of their model of religious event, especially its deportment. This becomes particularly desirable in the context of socializing small children and young girls, a process in which these elders are actively involved (fig. 1.1). Also, the religious domain is traditionally considered the elders' territory, especially since in the management of North American secular life deference to elders has of necessity to be compromised.

The conservatism generated by the tendency to return to the South Asian religious past is not only reinforced but also paralleled by the new kind of radical conservatism associated with the recent trend of pan-Islamism. This neo-conservatism reinforces gender segregation. It appeals directly to the younger generation and has helped make women's assemblies not only religiously but also socially appropriate. On the one hand, the all-women meal enables a hostess to invite more people into her personal communities; it has become a socially desirable opportunity in the midst of expanding personal circles brought by the growing numbers of immigrants from South Asia. On the other, mothers, in particular, welcome Islamist influence as a means to strengthen religious socialization among the younger generations.[7] In short, inviting only women to a *mīlād* and a meal has become a new social norm among the South Asian Muslim immigrants.

Recitation and an Islamic Domestic Sphere

From a purely North American perspective, the phenomenon of South Asian Muslims who protect their religious tradition from outside influences is a typically preservationist response of immigrants to an alien environment. But how this process has become situated in the domestic sphere and through the

FIGURE 1.1. Family *mīlād,* four generations; first *mīlād* in the granddaughter's new home (Edmonton, Canada, Rabī-ul-Awwal 1976)

agency of women in the first place bears further exploration, especially in the present climate of a public orthodoxy of Islam. In this connection, it is instructive to consider the historical context of Muslim devotional practices in South Asia. In their research on Muslim reformism in British India, Barbara Metcalf (1984) and Faisal Devji (1991) have focused attention on the "privatization and feminization" of Islamic practice, following British colonization of the once Muslim public domain. In a similar vein, Sandria Freitag, pointing to "the expansion of a 'devotional' idiom to cover a range of reconstructions of the self and the collectivity," articulates the tension between public and private spheres in colonial South Asia (Freitag 1991, 3). Simply put, the Islamization of the domestic sphere in South Asia through Muslim recitation practices, especially devotional assemblies like *mīlād*, is a response to the British control of a public arena. In contrast to the public arena in which native subject communities were marginalized and privatized (Devji 1991), the Islamized domestic sphere creates a locus for men and women to maintain Islamic religious life.

The implications of these antecedents are deeply suggestive. The first, obvious implication is that the first immigrant generation's response has indeed been to draw from their own socialization in South Asia and to activate the same pattern of focusing religious life in the home. Less obvious, but more specifically relevant to the dynamic of the North American situation is the implication that we have here a parallel Muslim response to what may be collectively termed a non-Muslim, Western-dominated public sphere. The North American public domain, too, structurally separates religious from secular public processes. It is ethnic, not religious identity that forms the basis for community identity within the publicly much-supported arena of multiculturalism, at least in Canada. The intense focus on private, feminized religiosity has therefore been appropriately adaptive, offering these immigrants an established South Asian way of dealing with a new kind of foreign or outside sphere.[8]

Reorientations: Western Adaptation of Islamism?

If this has been the initial immigrant response of South Asian Muslims, two recent shifts in recitation practice suggest a religious reorientation that more directly addresses itself to the situation in North America, but in conjunction with the powerful model offered by the Islamic movement.

The first shift is toward a kind of recitation assembly held within the same domestically based circles of participants but having a structure fundamentally different from the *mīlād*: the *qur'ānkhwānī* (Qur'an recitation). Unlike the *mīlād*, *qur'ānkhwānī* is a distinctly nonperformative assembly. Its goal is to invoke blessings and benefice by means of reciting the complete text of the Qur'an. Participants are invited to join in reciting portions of the text until the entire Qur'an is completed. Note that reciting the entire Qur'an is a traditional South Asian practice upon someone's death; what is new here is that *qur'ānkhwānī* is especially convened for a wider range of occasions, often as a replacement of *mīlād*. In a *qur'ānkhwānī* assembly women and men gather in separate rooms, each taking up the recitation of a different section of the Qur'an, made available in the form of separately printed Qur'an segments (*pāra*).[9] Everyone present recites simultaneously and soundlessly for himself or herself, even while visibly mouthing each word. This recitation requires neither spatial nor temporal management, although there is informal coordination between reciters so that each text portion is recited only once. In addition to *qur'ānkhwānī*, a second assembly of quranic recitation also recently introduced is the *āyat-e-karīmā*[10] ("verse of mercy") in which a particularly efficacious verse invoking God's mercy is recited collaboratively 125,000 times.

The dual recitation trend exemplified by these two assemblies, a trend also emerging in Pakistan, suggests a turn away from vernacular devotional texts to scriptural Arabic and to manifestations of a more orthodox Islamic universalism. The setting and management of both assemblies remain fundamentally the same as for *mīlād* assemblies. What is performatively different is the absence of protagonists within the ritual itself, reducing the prominence of women as reciters, although they remain grounded in the domestic, private sphere managed by women.

This difference between *mīlād* and the nonvernacular of recitation assemblies is significantly linked to textual content and voice: Vernacular hymns speak in the voice of South Asian Muslims, and although *mīlād* texts are authored mostly by men,[11] they are composed to express the faith in the words of women who have made them their own. In contrast, the revealed text of the Qur'an is the word of God through the voice of the Prophet, to be articulated in accordance with appropriate skill and training. Articulating it to others requires intellectual and recitation skills that are normally acquired only by men. Very few women take on the role of Qur'an reciter before an audience. In this respect, it is worth noting that many South Asian women are well integrated into the workforce, but they maintain a traditional role both at home and among friends. Overtly, the outside and inside spheres do not mix. Nonetheless, women's outside experience offers not only a foil against which the inside is set, but also a choice of alternative means of managing things inside.

Recitation in the Mosque

Even though recitation and religious life remain deeply intertwined with the growing importance of the domestic sphere, South Asian Muslims increasingly appear to be negotiating a public, mosque-based identity through mosque associations and activities that include recitation assemblies.[12] The mosque-based identity is becoming more and more pan-Islamic, buttressed by the effective outreach of pan-Islamic organization, especially toward the now grown children of the immigrant generation. From a women's perspective, we ask ourselves if this signals another reformist movement (see Metcalf 1992, Al-Azmeh 1993), this time moving toward orthodoxy, with men retaking charge of a more public Islam, and of control over women.

This question draws attention to the recent second shift in religious practice of South Asian Muslims, something that is notable and unheard of in South Asia: the participation of women in recitation assemblies held at the mosque. Of the various recitation assemblies, *qur'ānkhwānī* offers the best fit with mosque tradition; it can be appropriately carried out in the main space for prayer by men and in the corresponding women's enclosure. Besides *qur'ānkhwānī, mīlād* assemblies, addressing the Prophet, not God, and in the vernacular, not in Arabic, are conducted in the basement of the mosque with partitions separating men and women. The basement is also the place where everyone partakes of the food offered after the recitation by the individuals or family "hosting" the occasion.

That women are involved in managing these events even in the mosque can be attributed to the shared meal that is an integral part of all of them. In a creative adaptation of North American church basement activity, women are bringing the domestic sphere into the mosque. They do so, however, clearly under the ideological and actual control of men. The significance of this trend becomes obvious if one considers, in comparison, such centers of minority Muslim worship as the *Shi'a imāmbārā* (or *imāmbārgah*) or, even more so, the *Isma'ili jamā'tkhāna* where women, and thus families, participate in complementary roles as fully as men, so that for these Muslims their centers have become truly a community space.

In spite of such an unprecedented shift, however, the mosque is also the locus of control in the name of Islamic fundamentalists. In Edmonton, this becomes manifest through strict segregation of the sexes, even in the nonreligious space of the basement, and through demands for women to be clothed in a more explicitly Islamic style than that of customary South Asian clothing.[13]

Implications

When the two shifts in the religious musical practice of the South Asian Muslims—quranic recitation in the domestic space and women's participation in recitation assemblies at mosque—are viewed as immigrant experience, what implications do they have for women? As to the first shift, what is the multiple dynamic behind the increased prevalence of the participatory, soundless, leaderless gathering of Arabic recitation? Does it signal a movement toward silencing a particularistic, South Asian "local" voice, a movement toward the loss of difference, toward a "violence of abstraction"?[14] Or does it signal a movement toward reinforcing the more generic Islamic teachings that immigrants can make available to their growing children in North America? One of the keys to these questions is the global impact of orthodox pan-Islamism, which is variously acknowledged by members of Islamic communities. The growing preference for *qur'ānkhwānī* not only in the Diaspora but also in South Asia testifies to the impact.

Other motivations point to a specifically North American adaptation: The nonperformative assembly of *qur'ānkhwānī* strikingly reflects the South Asian immigrants' experience of a voluntary association between individuals who share a bond of religion and community but otherwise live autonomously. The bond between them is activated by nothing but mutual goodwill, leaving behind the ties of dominance and dependence that characterized the more hierarchical social relationships in the South Asian homelands. The *qur'ānkhwānī* assembly accurately represents this reality where everyone's voice is speaking, but no one dominates, a clear contrast with the *mīlād* model which projects dominance, submissions, and temporal-spatial coordination within the group.

As to the second shift, it is being observed that after a generation of residence in the West, Muslims are beginning to engage more specifically with their particular reality in North American public space and thus the issue of public self-representation assumes greater priority for them.[15] Does this imply that Muslims are becoming responsive to the generalized North American notion of public religion, or to the highly specific one held by the Islamic movement? Perhaps to both: Islamist organizations offer a model of self-representation that is adapted to existing within, but also to challenging the Western world order, but it is an exclusivist model that requires conformity. Aziz Al-Azmeh (1993), in situating that model within the historical context of Islamic reformist movements, points to the continuity of an essentially reactive motivation to Western dominance, whether emulative or oppositional. He argues that the movement's overtly oppositional stance toward the West should not obscure the fact that its ideological practice and goals operate on a premise that has more than a little in common with nineteenth-century European idealism, a utopian ideology of universality and power driving an organized conformism that is designed to assert a powerful presence vis-à-vis the West and its agents.[16]

Ritual religious practice is a central site for articulating the premise of uncompromising universality, for transcending the local and particular. Returning all recitation to the quranic is clearly a move in this direction. Carrying out such recitation in silence expresses compliance with voiceless participation in an abstract community. At the same time, the silent assembly of recitation also articulates, and constitutes, a community of voluntary collaboration among equals submitting to a single, superior authority—another foundational premise of the Islamic movement.

Many South Asian Muslim women and men choose to say "yes" to both premises. At the same time their practice also continues to reflect their own personal inclination, their family inheritance and regional-cultural style. The fact that recitation assemblies remain a prime context for Qur'an recitation is itself an affirmation of those influences. Qur'an recitation has not superseded but has become integral to the established format of the assembly. Put another way, the recitation assembly is being adapted to the recitation style of *qir'at*, but side-by-side it also continues to be practice in the old performative form of *mīlād*.

Similarly consistent with inherited tradition is the adaptation of recitation assemblies to the locale of the mosque and thereby to the nonprivate religious center of Islamic practice. In bringing their assemblies to the mosque, women, supported by male members of the community,[17] connect the familial with the ritual, enrich the canonical ritual with personal devotion and bring familial sharing to the formal religious experience. But mosque events also show women's willingness to submit their particular way of experiencing religious texts to the generalized, normative notions that increasingly guide mosque leadership today.

On balance, what this situation affirms is a diversity of choices open to South Asian Muslim individuals and families in Canada and the United States. Fundamentalist claims to exclusive authority notwithstanding, Islam continues to have no "church," and no canonical spiritual authority. South Asian Muslim women operate with men within a process of achieving consensus that is, and will remain, ongoing. Women give voice to that process through recitation, sounded and soundless, not in single tone, but in a rich polyphony of religious devotion and submission, of personal and canonical Islam, through the centrality of its words.

NOTES

1. Special thanks go to Saleem Qureshi, Amera Raza, Siddiqa Qureshi, Atiya Siddiqui, Yasmeen Nizam, and Anisa Khatib and most of all to Yasmeer Nizam for sharing the photo of her grandmother at her family *mīlād.*

2. The *shahādā* consists of the simple, powerful sentence: *Lā ilāhā liallā Muhammad al-Rasūlallāh* (There is no god but God and Muhammad is his Prophet). *Kalma* is the term current in South Asian usage.

3. Also widely and intensely practiced among Shi'a Muslims is the *majlis*, commemorating the martyrdom of Iman Husain, the Prophet's grandson.

4. Canadian immigration laws were liberalized in 1967, replacing the quota of one hundred immigrants from each South Asian country per year. The early 1980s saw a further sudden increase of South Asian Muslims emigrating as refugees from East Africa.

5. Written by Khwaja Muhammad Akbar Warsi (Akbar Warsi n.d.), this is the most often used of such guidebooks containing the texts of many hymns, numerous short prose sermons, and texts for intercessory prayers.

6. Titled *munājāt*, the poem has thirty verses.

7. This differs from predominant parental responses to Islamization for their children among middle-class professionals in South Asian itself, Pakistan included.

8. The alien flavor of that sphere is tellingly embodied in the term *ghair* (foreign, outsider), which Urdu speakers use to contrast with *apnā*, the private, inside sphere.

9. For these recitation purposes the Qur'an is divided into thirty portions (*pārā*) in a readily available magazine format.

10. The verse contains the words of Jonas praying to God from the belly of the whale (Qur'an 21.86–7).

11. The *Mīlād-e-Akbar* is an obvious example; for an outline of the reformist milieu that produced this kind of literature, see Metcalf (1990) and Thanvi (1990).

12. During the last decade the number of mosques has been growing, thanks to community efforts and also to support from several Arab Muslim countries.

13. Head covered with no hair showing, sober, covering clothing.

14. An evocative phrase borrowed from Sayer (1986).

15. At a Social Science Research Council-sponsored conference entitled *Making Space for Islam* this point emerged as central in contributions and discussions (see Metcalf 1996).

16. It has also been pointed out that in Muslim countries Islamist movements target primarily their own Westernized governing elites (Al-Ashmawy 1989).

17. This expression is not meant to be sexist but to evoke the ubiquitous presence of husbands, brothers, or fathers; there are very few single women not closely tied to a man.

WORKS CITED

Akbar Warsi, Khwaja Muhammad. n.d. *Mīlād-e-Akbar*. Delhi: Ratan.

Al-Ashmawy, Muhammad Said. 1989. *L'Islamisme contre I'Islam*. Paris: Edition la découverte; Cairo: al-Fikr.

Al-Azmeh, Aziz. 1993. *Islams and Modernities.* London: Verso.

Devji, Faisal Fatehali. 1991. "Gender and the Politics of Space: The Movement for Women's Reform in Muslim India 1857–1900." In Sandria Feitag, ed., *Aspects of the Public in Colonial South Asia. South Asia.* n.s., 24, no.1, 141–54.

Freitag, Sandria, ed. 1991. *Aspects of the Public in Colonial South Asia. South Asia.* n.s., 24, no.1.

Metcalf, Barbara Daly. 1984. "Islamic Reform and Islamic Women: Maulana Thanawi's *Jewelry of Paradise.*" In Barbara Metcalf, ed., *Moral Conduct and Authority,* 198–95. Berkeley: University of California Press.

———. 1990. "Introduction to the Bihisti Zewar" in Ashraf 'Ali *Perfecting Women.* Trans. and commentary by Barbara Daly Metcalf, 1–38. Berkeley: University of California Press.

———. 1992. *Heavenly Ornaments.* Berkeley: University of California Press.

———. 1996. *Making Muslim Space in North America and Europe.* Berkeley: University of California Press.

Thanvi, Ashraf 'Ali. 1990. *Perfecting Women.* Trans. and commentary by Barbara Daly Metcalf. Berkeley: University of California Press.

2

African American Religious Music from a Theomusicological Perspective

Jon Michael Spencer

I have been studying black music seriously since my undergraduate and graduate school years, but my earliest *research* of black music commenced when I decided that my interests necessitated supplementing my training in music with training in Christian theology. I made the decision thinking that if the creators of black sacred music were Christians who drew from their life experiences as interpreted through the biblical lens, it would be difficult for one to acquire a more informed re-reading of their music without anchoring the message of their music in the Bible. The spirituals and the black preaching out of which many spirituals were spontaneously created clearly called for the integration of theology or a spiritual archaeology into the general field of musicology.

In my research on black preaching, I found that a perspicuous correlation existed between black preaching and the spiritual, in that a substantial number of spirituals evolved most probably via the preaching event of black worship. Although it is likely that slave preachers would work at composing pleasing combinations of tune and text to later teach their spirituals to their congregations, it is perhaps more probable for spirituals to have come from extemporaneous sermonizing that crescendoed little by little to intoned utterance. This melodious declamation, delineated into quasi-metrical phrases with formulaic cadence, was customarily enhanced by intervening tonal response from the congregation. Responsorial iteration of catchy words, phrases, and sentences resulted in the burgeoning of song, to which new verses could be contemporaneously adjoined. Spirituals created in such a manner were sometimes evanescent, no doubt, while favorable creations were probably remembered and perpetuated through oral transmission.

This information was deducible by combing the manuscript pages of plantation diaries, journals, and correspondences and the ex-slave narratives systematically collected during the 1930s. But to address authentically the musicality of black preaching would require me to extend my inquiry beyond the limitations of the intellect to a realm approximated by human participation in religion and mysticism. As theologian William C. Turner Jr. says in his foreword to my book on the musicality of black preaching, *Sacred Symphony: The Chanted Sermon of the Black Preacher* (1987):

> The dominant forces in American culture, greatly influenced by the Enlightenment and the rise of modern science, offer little support for a form of preaching infused with the mystical potency of music. Perceived by teachers of preaching and authors of homiletical texts as an aberration of Christian orthodoxy, this peculiar style of delivery is considered to be a vestige of 'folk religion.' (Turner 1987, ix)

In *Sacred Symphony* I was able to do, on the one hand, the historical and musicological work of documenting the musicality of black preaching from antebellum times and, on the other hand, the ethnomusicological work of collecting, transcribing, and theoretically analyzing contemporary instances of musical black preaching in order to show the continuity of this tradition. But I was not yet able to pursue the spiritual archaeology that, even in my neophyte theological thinking, was implicit in the musicality of black preaching. So I asked Turner to write a foreword to *Sacred Symphony* that plumbed the theological depths of black preaching. Turner did so and identified three ways of understanding the musicality of black preaching as religious. He spoke of this musicality as kratophany, as oppugnancy, and as glossa. On the musicality of black preaching as kratophany, he wrote:

> Within the Black Church tradition, preaching is truly a manifestation of power or a "kratophany." As in a theophany, which is a manifestation of deity, some object is present which opens to the transcendent while simultaneously being rooted in empirical reality. With a theophany, the object may be a tree or a stone, as in African traditional religions, while with preaching, the kratophany is spoken word and rendered gesture. Further, within the context of the cul-

> ture that sustains black preaching, there is no modality more indicative of the presence of deity, power, and intrusion from another order than that of the preached word circumscribed by musicality. In a stalwart way, music is one of the instruments bridging the chasm between the world of human beings and God who speaks to them through preaching. Music in black preaching establishes a direct link between the spirit within the preacher, the word that is uttered, and the worshiping congregation. It operates beneath the structures of logical discourse and produces a captivating effect upon the hearer. (Turner 1987, x)

Turning to the musicality of black preaching as oppugnancy, Turner stated in his foreword to *Sacred Symphony*:

> The presence of music within the African world view corresponded to the oppugnancy African-American slaves had toward the world. To Africans, music was "numinous": it was the property of the deities and it manifested the most primal force in life. As a structuring principle for all reality and an inner force that yielded life and unity, music moved the community backward, away from the reality of the present into the time of the deities. The same atavistic influence operated upon the adherents to Afro-Christian faith. The content and musicality of black preaching moved hearers away from the history that had unleashed terror upon them.
>
> The direction of black preaching itself has never been away from the world of oppression and poverty. . . . Only through perpetuating their quarrel with history while simultaneously sidestepping its terror could they forge a positive identity for themselves. Homiletical musicality and the songs which that musicality produced correspond with the content of the message of black preaching as a "gesture away from history"—an affirmation of the atavistic, the primal, and the world God has truly willed. (ibid., x-xi)

Finally, Turner addressed the musicality of black preaching as glossa, writing:

> In black religious folklore there is also the notion of "moaning so the devil won't know what you are talking about." Conversely, the Spirit prompts and discerns such inarticulate speech (glossa) and grants interpretation of the same.
>
> Hence, the music of black preaching can be understood as a sort of "singing in the spirit," for there is a surplus (glossa) ex-

> pressed in music which accompanies the rational content (logos) enunciated in words. The logical portion is contained in the structure of the sermon and the form of its constituent songs. For the glossal portion, the preacher becomes an instrument of musical afflatus: a flute through which divine air is blown, a harp upon which eternal strings vibrate. In attaining this height of musicality, "the preacher has come." (ibid., xi-xii)

In writing his foreword to my book, Turner demonstrated to me early on in my theological training the importance of integrating theology into musicology in researching black sacred music. With pursuing a deeper understanding of the spirituals themselves as my next endeavor, I decided I should follow Turner's paradigm and apply to my analysis of the spirituals tools gleaned from formal theological training. My models were the published version of Henry Hugh Proctor's 1894 Yale Divinity School BD thesis titled "The Theology of the Songs of the Southern Slave" (1907), Howard Thurman's *Deep River* (1945) and *The Negro Spiritual Speaks of Life and Death* (1947), and James H. Cone's *The Spirituals and the Blues* (1972b). Later I added to this list two unpublished essays of historian Earl E. Thorpe. While teaching history full-time and studying theology part-time during the early 1980s, Thorpe wrote two exemplary essays: "African Americans and the Sacred: Spirituals, Slave Religion and Symbolism" and "Slave Religion, Spirituals, and C. G. Jung." The former was written for a course Thorpe took on "Myth and Symbols" with Duke Divinity professor H. B. Partin, a former student of the historian of religion, Mircea Eliade. The latter essay is the product of Thorpe's integration of musicology, theology, and psychology in an effort to comprehend the mindset of the enslaved Africans in America and the psychological matrix of the South that was responsible for the conditions that produced the spirituals.

In the latter essay, Thorpe begins by saying that his theoretical goal is to substantiate that Jung's psychoanalytical theories comprise a viable tool for deciphering the deepest feelings and unconscious beliefs of the Africans enslaved in America (Spencer 1991, 7–10). He says that just as Jung's principal purpose for psychotherapy was not to transport patients to an unattainable state of happiness but to help them acquire a mechanism for perseverance in the face of suffering, so did the enslaved seek to attain a similar state of mind. Thorpe suggests that the spirituals revealed evidence of the possession among the Africans enslaved in America, thus bearing comparison to the mental health and spiritual wealth sought by Jung's patients. By no means simply an opiate, insists Thorpe, the religion manifested through the spirituals carried the enslaved to an essential stage of mental well-being. Pointing as an example to Jung's belief that prayer reinforces the healing potential of the unconscious, Thorpe says the creators of the spirituals also had faith in the power of prayer and that many of the spirituals were actually the enslaved praying aloud. While in psychotherapy patients tell the physician all about their anxieties, in the spirituals the enslaved told God all about their troubles. Thorpe's approach to the spirituals led him to Paul Tillich's theorizing of the strikingly analogous relationship between theology's concern for personal salvation and psychotherapy's methods of mental healing: They both are "therapies" of grace that involve the overcoming of guilt and estrangement (Tillich 1959, 143–45).

My understanding of the therapeutic implications of Thorpe's research on the spirituals would come later in my theological education. Initially I was simply impressed by James Cone's treatment of the spirituals from his purview as a liberation theologian. I found Cone's theology to be a distinct advancement over Henry Hugh Proctor's treatment of the spirituals as emblematic of "noble Christian sentiment," perfect in their biblically based doctrines about God, Christ, the Holy Spirit, angels, Satan, the Christian life, and eschatology. I also found Cone's theology to be a distinct advancement beyond the imperceptibility of such white scholars as Robert Gordon. In a 1932 essay on the spirituals, Gordon showed an unwillingness or inability to recognize not only the originality of the spirituals but to recognize that they were inherently songs of liberation:

> The entire concept of spiritual slavery, of the bonds and shackles of sin, of Pharaoh and Moses, and the Red Sea . . . is to be found expressed in minute detail in any number of hymns of demonstrable white origin, often in the identical words used by the negro in his spirituals. On the other hand, the total number of cases in all the known spirituals of the negro in which we can be certain that he refers to physical and not to spiritual slavery can almost be counted on the fingers. Among them are, of course, "No More Auction Block for Me," "No Driver' Lash in de Heaben, O Lord," and a very few others.
>
> I do not mean to imply that the negro did not often see in such white songs the possibility of a double meaning, that he did not in his own mind apply whatever he adopted from these songs to physical, as well as spiritual, slavery. But he did not himself create any body of song on his enslaved condition.
>
> He found in white hymns, as commonly sung, fully developed ideas concerning spiritual slavery, the Last Judgment, and the joys of Heaven. These he used as a basis of song building. . . . In no case

> did he change greatly the basic concept, present it from any new point of view, or introduce to it any new philosophy. He reexpressed the borrowed concept in his own way. (Gordon 1932, 217)

Gordon evidently projected the heroic David and Samson types into the New Testament to interpret the Old Testament liberation dramas with a then-current understanding of Pauline hermeneutics.

Since Cone was able to see through the mask of Christian fake morality and piety and realize that the spirituals had picked up and showed the urgency of that prophetic strain of the biblical text that mandates the oppressed be set free, I decided I should formally study liberation theology. In doing so, I discovered that the slave narratives fully corroborated Cone's liberationist reading of the spirituals and of the biblical source from which the theology of the spirituals came. For instance, Solomon Northup, in his autobiographical *Twelve Years a Slave,* wrote that if we could only know the secret thoughts of the enslaved, thoughts never uttered in the hearing of whites, we would find that ninety-nine out of every one hundred of the enslaved were intelligent enough to understand their predicament and to cherish freedom as passionately as all other human beings (1968, 158). Frederick Douglass, in his autobiographical *My Bondage and My Freedom,* stated similarly that every tone in the spirituals was a prayer to God for deliverance from slavery (verifying Turner's notion of musicality as oppugnancy), and that a keen observer might have detected in songs about being "bound for the land of Canaan" that the enslaved were not first interested in going to heaven but in reaching the North (1969, 99, 279).

Cone's reflections helped me see that in their spirituals the enslaved were literal in their interpretation of the Old Testament liberation events. When they sang "Go Down, Moses," for instance, they were thinking about liberation in this world and thus singing with real anticipation:

> When Israel was in Egypt's land
> Let my people go,
> Oppressed so hard they could not stand,
> Let my people go.
> "Thus spoke the Lord," bold Moses said,
> Let my people go,
> If not I'll smite your first born dead,
> Let my people go.
>
> (Refrain)
> Go down, Moses,
> 'Way down in Egypt land,

Tell ole Pharaoh,
Let my people go.

Although being physically "let go" was the ideal attainment of liberation for the enslaved, Cone also argues that the freedom they sang about included but did not depend on historical possibilities (1972, 67). He uses the spiritual "Oh Freedom" to make his point:

Oh Freedom! Oh Freedom!
Oh Freedom, I love thee!
And before I'll be a slave,
I'll be buried in my grave

Cone explains:

> Here freedom is obviously a structure of, and a movement in, historical existence. It is black slaves accepting the risk and burden of self-affirmation, of liberation in history. That is the meaning of the phrase, "And before I'll be a slave, I'll be buried in my grave." But without negating history, the last line of this spiritual places freedom beyond the historical context. "And go home to my Lord and be free." In this context, freedom is eschatological. It is anticipation of freedom, a vision of a new heaven and a new earth. Black slaves recognized that human freedom is transcendent—that is, a constituent of the future—which made it impossible to identify humanity exclusively with meager attainment in history. (Cone 1975, 66)

Looking through this very same hermeneutical lens provides us with one way of interpreting the many "train" songs that are found in the repertory of the spirituals. On the one hand, the real-life liberating activity of the Underground Railroad seems to be thematized, but on the other hand there also seems to be an inclination toward not holding liberation to historical possibilities. One such "train" spiritual had the enslaved singing that the "same train" that carried away their mothers and sisters would "be back tomorrow." Everyone was encouraged to pack their bags in preparation, for though the train was due on the morrow it could pass through any night:

Little black train is a-comin'
Get all your business right;
Go get your house in order,
For the train may be here tonight.

My formal study of liberation theology was helpful in allowing me to see how it is possible to move from the Bible as canonical source of authority to liberation theology. But to follow Cone's arguments also necessitated that I study formally the Old and New Testaments. The study pushed me beyond an uninformed literalist reading of the Bible as a volume comprised of a homogeneous history, doctrine, and theology. As a result, I was able to take interpretive control over the Bible, the kind of interpretive control that enabled Paul Tillich to fashion his theology of culture and to begin reconciling aspects of our humanity that are not strange to one another but have been estranged from one another (Tillich 1959, 29). Thus, what black biblical scholar, Vincent Wimbush, says of the importance of black Christians gaining interpretive control over the Bible became, in my estimation, equally true for the scholar interested in researching black sacred music: "Needed are both a defense from alien, imperialistic hermeneutical constructs (and with them symbols, concepts, rituals, social orientation) and the capacity to assume control over, to evaluate critically, and advance their own traditions. . . . Critical facility for the historical study of both the self, viz., the Afro-Christian tradition, is required for self-defense and self-criticism, as well as the capacity for the construction of a more affirming, indigenous hermeneutic built on the tradition" (1989, 144–45). Wimbush concludes that liberation may initially require "exegetical room" (ibid., 152). This comment reinforced my sense that formal study of the Old and New Testaments was important to my ability to understand and do liberation theology.

To be sure, research into black sacred music, music that has always been under the canonical authority of the biblical tradition, is also needful of "hermeneutical control" and "exegetical room." Without this "control" and "room" our conclusions about the meanings of the spirituals, meanings that Cone has proved to be masked, would be both incorrect and egregiously biased like Robert Gordon's interpretation of the spirituals, or merely sanitized like Henry Hugh Proctor's interpretation. With this "control" and "room" and the almost certain discovery that there is no historical, doctrinal, or theological homogeneity in the Old or New Testament, comes the possibility that a spiritual archaeology of music can excavate more freely and much more deeply.

The first consequence of my learning the Bible and taking "hermeneutical control" over it is that I was better able to follow Cone's liberationist reading of the spirituals. The second consequence was that I was able to follow Cone's argument for the likeness between the spirituals and the blues. This comprised my earliest impetus to push my scholarship beyond the research of sacred folk music to include secular folk music. I was able to corroborate through my own research Cone's contention that the early blues were neither irreligious nor anti-religion. I was able to accomplish this in part with the help of Nicholas Cooper-Lewter's and Henry Mitchell's idea that there is a natural "soul theology" in the black community, a natural law that is inherent to the cultural expressions of the black community (Mitchell and Cooper-Lewter 1986, 4). The substance of this soul theology comes from the hymns, spirituals, gospel songs, and anthems of the church, as well as from the blues outside the church (ibid., 17–18). This natural "singing system" is ultimately one in which the folk of the soul community maintain a wholesome existence free of external (professional) therapy because their intuitive selection of songs that provide them with the internal nourishment and nurturing they need (ibid., 4, 167). So, it is not important that the people of the "soul community" be able to theologize with orthodox constructs, but rather that they demonstrate a firm belief in God through their ability to cope with all of life's experiences (ibid., 4). Neither is it an issue as to whether the core theological beliefs of the "soul community" are even verbalized. Often either articulated incompletely or left unarticulated, say Cooper-Lewter and Mitchell, core beliefs and foundational attitudes are the operative opinions of the people about God (ibid., 3). In short, a worldview that serves as a means of emotional balance is itself a theology (ibid., 6).

Eventually being able to push beyond the research of Cone and of Cooper-Lewter and Mitchell, I discovered that the blues were not only religious in the broadest sense of the word, but their lyrics revealed blues singers to have drawn directly from the mythologies, theologies, and theodicies of the Judeo-Christian tradition, together with a mix of African religious retentions (Spencer 1993). More specifically, the folk blues, as I found, are replete with mythologies revealing blues singers' religious thought on the origin and description of evil; it is a kind of music that is theological and talks about evil in folk theological language; and it posits lay or popular theodicies that reconcile the seeming incongruity of evil existing in a world believed to be created and ruled by a good God.

It was as a result of my study of the blues that I began to develop the discipline of theomusicology. Since theomusicology evolved out of my musicological study of the blues, I have argued that the musicological discipline is inadequate in showing the momentous profundity of black music. The questions and concerns arising from my study of the blues were not historical-musicological questions about style periods, or ethnomusicological concerns about human behavior or musical skill in performance. In other words, those questions and concerns, to which I gave priority in the development of theory, were not historical or social scientific, but rather indigenous religious questions and concerns—vital questions and ultimate concerns coming directly from the "soul community." The questions that the blues had me ask of them—questions that necessitated the development of a disciplinary perspective that would permit them—derived from the fact that the blues are not "evil," as

Cone, Cooper-Lewter, and Mitchell had realized, but are rather characterized by a synthesis of the sacred and the profane. That is to say, the blues were characterized by a synchronous duplicity—the meshing of seeming opposites. This synchronous duplicity made the blues representative of the worldview that music scholars have long acknowledged as typical of black culture. Thus, I began to look at the blues as a paradigm for black cultural criticism and scholarly analysis.

As this scholarship being fashioned through the integration of musicology and theology led me to literary study, I found that Houston Baker had also taken the blues to be a repository of potential theory for the interpretation and criticism of black culture, particularly that culture's literature (Baker 1984, 1–14). Henry Louis Gates, Jr., as I also found, had selected as his repository for an indigenous black literary theory the black trickster known as the Signifying Monkey, who, depersonified and theorized, is the equivalent of the rhetorical artifice of signifying (Gates 1988, xix–xxviii). Through my theomusicological research into the blues, however, I found that Baker's and Gates's sources of indigenous black theory—the blues and the black trickster—are one and the same. That is to say, one can trace a direct lineage from the African tricksters, with whom Gates commences his genealogy toward theory, to the black tricksters whose characters entered the lyrics of the blues, where Baker commences his search for theory. From there one can further trace the lineage into the personages of blues singers themselves, who emulated the tricky figures about whom they sang, and onward into the genealogy of black music-makers spawned from the aesthetic of the bluesman paradigm. Briefly I will extrapolate this lineage.

In black folk-heroic literature, trickster personalities were fashioned and refashioned out of the conscious and unconscious needs of blacks to "act bad" and "talk back" before the guardians of the South's slavocracy. The badman figure, whose heritage lies in the African trickster, was one of the tricksters who has captured the folk imagination of blacks since the 1890s. This figure has become a part of the "folk" or "soul theology" of blacks because of his uncanny ability to outsmart whites and even the devil. Within the trickster tradition, the badman and other figures of wit and guile—such as Tar Baby and Brer Rabbit—became a means of maintaining emotional balance and a wholesome existence for blacks. In the trickster transmitted in their trickster tales, ballads, and blues, and later rhythm and blues, blacks saw an emulative model of behavior. Thus when badman heroes appeared in the lyrics of the blues, it was generally the blues singer himself, as protagonist in his own songs, who was portrayed as the "baddest." So attractive and cathartic were these self-portrayals that the badman-lives of song became the badman-lives of daily life. This bears out the folklorist John Burrison's observation that "narrative impulse," the need to tell story or listen to story that structures experiences and imagination into plot, is one of the traits that makes people human (Burrison 1989, 1). The folk theology of the trickster and the core theological beliefs of the folk, or foundational attitudes operative among the folk, require the story to be intelligible. The story or narrative then becomes a model for lives to be lived.

Narrative impulse is also one of the traits that make people religious. For example, blues singers who portrayed themselves as divine lovers were embodying the story of the sexually prolific African trickster, who was both malevolent and benevolent, disruptive and reconciliatory, subhuman and superhuman, sexual and spiritual. Yet as the mythology surrounding the famous country bluesman, Robert Johnson, illustrates, prolific sexuality and deep spirituality—in his case, voodoo spirituality—form a synchronous duplicity. Like the black preacher, also an heir to the tradition of the trickster's rhythms, Johnson's singing, often but a protracted moan to which words were attached, was as sexual as it was spiritual. Regardless of the blues singers about whom we are talking—Charlie Patton, Leadbelly, Memphis Minnie, Peetie Wheatstraw, or Rubin Lacy—all embodied the mythology, lived the story, and could trace their lineage of synchronous duplicity back to the African trickster.

The same is substantially true of the heritage of the black preacher, whom the blues singer had always criticized in self-defense as being no different from himself, particularly when it comes to loving women. To hear it told in the context of Southern jokelore is really to hear it told by the blues singer. In one story, a "colored" preacher called a meeting after his first service at a new church. Using it as an opportunity for himself and the congregation to get to know and understand one another, he asked everyone who loved the Lord to sit on one side of the church and everyone who loved wine and women to sit on the other side. One man did not budge but looked rather puzzled. When the preacher inquired as to the problem, the man explained that he did not know what side to sit on because he loved the Lord but also wine and women. The preacher responded, "Well, son, you jest come up here in de pulpit wi' me. You's been called t' preach" (Burrison 1989, 176).

Humor aside, I believe that the momentousness in the music that black preachers and blues singers created may be a direct consequence of the synchronous duplicity they embodied. Jung's concept of "the Self"—the archetype of wholeness whose nature is to unite opposites—offers one possible analogy that is perhaps appropriate, for Jung studied the trickster figure in American Indian lore and was on a search to comprehend the holistic nature of the cosmos (Jung 1956, 195–211). The archetype of "the Self" requires that human beings integrate into their consciousness all that belongs to its essential wholeness but which the consciousness has rejected and repressed, such as so-called evil (Sanford 1988, 129–30). That black music seems to embody the capacity to permit wholeness in black lives is precisely because black music-makers and music-making contexts naturally blur and even obliterate the boundaries Western culture has erected between alleged opposites—the spiritual and the sexual, good and evil, and so forth. To integrate into our consciousness all that belongs to its essential wholeness, but which the consciousness has rejected and repressed, permits us, for instance, to appreciate Charlie Spand's most righteous declaration in his "Back to the Woods Blues": "Just as sure as the good Lord sits in the heaven above, now your life ain't all pleasure unless you be with the one you love."

The contexts that yield declarations like the one above are contexts that exist in the betwixt-and-between spaces of repressively structured societies. The communitas that breaks in through the structural cracks of liminality, at the edges of marginality, from beneath inferiority, and from above spirituality, is what actually blurs or obliterates those boundaries. I surmise that the power that black people are able to generate corporately in those spaces within, beneath, beside, and above suppressive structures of society—those spaces that "the Self" is able to forge for rhythmic ritual—is the same power that the traditional music-makers of the black folk genres, from the black preacher to the blues singer, were able to glean through the embodiment of the trickster personality in "soul theology."

As my research disclosed this kind of ideation and theory that seemed to offer a systematic means of excavating the momentousness of black music and of probing its meanings, it simultaneously cast revealing light on the limitations of traditional musicology, which have accepted the traditional Western boundaries between alleged opposites. As the allegedly irreligious blues came to be viewed as religious in the new light cast upon it by my spiritual archaeology, that same light turned upon traditional sacred music and revealed it to be religiously cosmetic, if not in fact religiously sham. Only someone who has lived the blues life is privy to the religious process of human maturity. As former blues singer, Reverend Rubin Lacy, says, church music tended to lack this vantage point:

> The blues is just more truer than a whole lot of the church songs that people sing. Sometimes I think the average person sings a church song just for the tune, not for the words. . . . But the blues is sung not for the tune. It's sung for the words mostly. . . . Now you get out here to sing a church song about "When I take my vacation

> in Heaven." That couldn't be the truth. That's a lie in the church, because a vacation means to go and come. You don't take a vacation in heaven. But now if you're playing the blues, you say "I never missed my water 'til my well went dry." That's the truth. . . . That's the difference in a church song and the blues. (Evans 1967, 13)

Thus, traditional sacred music may be doctrinally correct from the perspective of organized religion, but it is not anthropologically, sociologically, or psychologically reflective of a people's religious beliefs and behaviors in the real world. Human beings are not the holy people of moderation that traditional sacred music portrays, but are in reality people of extremes—love and hate, peace and war, life and death. If we really want to understand what the masses of black people are thinking religiously, we cannot turn solely, if at all, to the music of institutional religion in which provisional answers to the vital questions and ultimate concerns are already doctrinally predetermined. We must look to the musics that flourish outside the domains of institutional religion, in places where there is a more candid and authentic religious discourse, no matter how profane those places and discourses may appear to be, no matter how incompletely articulated those core beliefs may be. If we look to the musics that flourish outside the domains of institutional religion, I believe what we will find will permit us to begin to reconcile the "alleged opposites" of which I have been speaking, those aspects of our humanity that seem strange to one another but which have been estranged from one another.

WORKS CITED

Baker, Houston A., Jr. 1984. *Blue, Ideology, and Afro-American Literature: A Vernacular Theory*. Chicago: University of Chicago Press.

Burrison, John A., ed. 1989. *Storytellers: Folktales and Legends from the South*. Athens: University of Georgia Press.

Cone, James H. 1972a. "Black Spirituals: A Theological Interpretation." *Theology Today* 29, 1 (April), 54–69.

———. 1972b. *The Spirituals and the Blues: An Interpretation*. New York: Seabury.

———. 1975. *God of the Oppressed*. New York: Seabury.

Douglass, Frederick. 1969. *My Bondage and My Freedom*. New York: Dover.

Evans, David. 1967. "The Rev. Rubin Lacy" (interview). *Blues Unlimited* 43 (May 1967), 13–14.

Gates, Henry Louis, Jr. 1988. *The Signifying Monkey: A Theory of Afro-American Literary Criticism*. New York: Oxford University Press.

Gordon, Robert W. 1932. "The Negro Spiritual." In Augustine T. Smythe, et al., eds., *The Carolina Low-Country*. New York: Macmillan.

Jung, C. G. 1956. "On the Psychology of the Trickster Figure." Postscript to Paul Radin. *The Trickster: A Study in American Indian Mythology*. London: Routledge and Kegan Paul, 195–211.

Mitchell, Henry H., and Nicholas Cooper-Lewter. 1986. *Soul Theology: The Heart of American Black Culture*. San Francisco: Harper and Row.

Northup, Solomon. 1968. *Twelve Years a Slave*. Sue Eakin and Joseph Logsdon, eds. Baton Rouge: Louisiana State University Press.

Proctor, Henry Hugh. 1907. "The Theology of the Songs of the Southern Slave." *Southern Workman* 36 (1907), 584–92, 652–56. Repr., *The Journal of Black Sacred Music* 2 (Spring 1988), 51–64.

Sanford, John A. 1988. "The Problem of Evil in Christianity and Analytical Psychology." In Robert L. Moore, ed., *Carl Jung and Christian Spirituality*. New York: Paulist, 109–30.

Spencer, Jon Michael. 1993. *Blues and Evil*. Knoxville: University of Tennessee Press.

———. 1991. *Theological Music: Introduction to Theomusicology*. Westport, Conn.: Greenwood.

Thorpe, Earl. E. 1980? "African Americans and the Sacred: Spirituals, Slave Religion and Symbolism." Unpublished paper.

———. 1980? "Slave Religion, Spirituals, and C. G. Jung." Unpublished paper.

Thurman, Howard. 1945. *Deep River: An Interpretation of Negro Spirituals*. Mills College, Calif.: Eucalyptus.

———. 1947. *The Negro Spiritual Speaks of Life and Death: Ingersoll Lecture*. Harvard University, 1947. New York: Harper & Brothers.

Tillich, Paul. 1959. *Theology of Culture*. Ed. by Robert C. Kimball. New York: Oxford University Press.

Turner, William C., Jr. 1987. "Foreword." In Jon Michael Spencer, *Sacred Symphony: The Chanted Sermon of the Black Preacher*. Westport, Conn.: Greenwood, ix–xii.

Wimbush, Vincent L. 1989. "Biblical Historical Study as Liberation: Toward an Afro-Christian Hermeneutic." In Gayraud S. Wilmore, ed., *African American Religious Studies: An Interdisciplinary Anthology*. Durham, N.C.: Duke University Press, 140–54.

3

Medeolinuwok, Music, and Missionaries in Maine

Ann Morrison Spinney

Maine is part of the territory occupied by Wabanaki peoples and their ancestors for the past twelve thousand years. In the Algonquian languages of its original inhabitants, the northeastern-most portion of North America is called "dawn land," *Wabanakik*; and the people who live there "people of the dawn," *Wabanaki*. At the turn of the present century, five nations represented the Wabanaki culture group: From east to west they were the Mi'kmaq, Maliseet, Passamaquoddy, Penobscot, and Abenaki, often called St. Francis Abenaki after their principal community. Figure 3.1 shows present-day reserves and reservations, and other places mentioned in this article, superimposed on the historical territories, which include northern New England and the Canadian Maritime Provinces.

In the seventeenth century, Maine was part of the territory that the French called *Acadie* (Acadia) and to which they sent traders and missionaries. After Membertou, an influential Souriquois (Mi'kmaq) leader, and his family converted to Catholicism in 1610, missionization took off in this area. Several Catholic orders participated; there were also Protestant ministers included in some early trading expeditions and colonies. The Catholic missions were most successful, but the results were a syncretic blending of traditional Wabanaki culture with the new European Catholicism. Despite four centuries of European Christian influence, contemporary Wabanaki people still have their own unique style of Catholic practice.

In this chapter, I examine specific aspects of Catholic religious ceremony, beliefs, and practice that were congruent with indigenous Wabanaki ceremonies and spiritual practice.[1] The specific qualities of ceremonial elements such as music seem to have been important vehicles for Wabanaki acceptance and absorption of Catholicism. Furthermore, the history of interaction between the two cultures suggests that the practice of Catholicism may have been one means employed by Wabanaki people to preserve some of their traditions. This is a view found among Wabanaki Catholics themselves. In Wabanaki Catholic music, we can hear the history of interaction.

During the process of missionization, the significance of similar elements could have been fluid, and not assigned to one or the other cultural system. The terms of religious faith, and by extension the practices that express them, seem too slippery to be completely controlled, even by the Catholic Church. Therefore, it seems most accurate to acknowledge Wabanaki Catholicism[2] as a syncretic expression of both Native and European cultural systems, a combination with a unique dynamism—and tension. The standard view expressed by outside scholars, the majority of whom have been Protestant, that conversion to Catholicism was the first step the Wabanaki people took toward losing their traditional culture may account for culture loss, but it fails to explain why Catholicism has remained viable for many Wabanaki persons.[3] Such explanations denigrate the conscious choice that many have made to remain Catholic even while participating in traditional cultural activities. Perhaps "conversion" is a bad term with which to frame discussion: It glosses over the possibility that the decision of the seventeenth-century Wabanaki ancestors to become Catholic was motivated by a complex web of reasons.[4]

The adoption and subsequent maintenance of Catholic religious practice by Wabanaki peoples has had significant political ramifications over the last four centuries, of which their leaders were arguably quite aware. Conversion was certainly a means of cementing alliance with the French and gaining access to their trade. Membertou used this as one means of gaining political ascendancy in the region. The political aspects of Catholicism among Wabanaki peoples have been much discussed by scholars, while few have focused on other implications (aesthetic, spiritual) of actual ceremonial practices. When these are also considered, the similarities between the two religious systems present multiple opportunities for "slippage." Ritual actions could have functioned in both worlds.

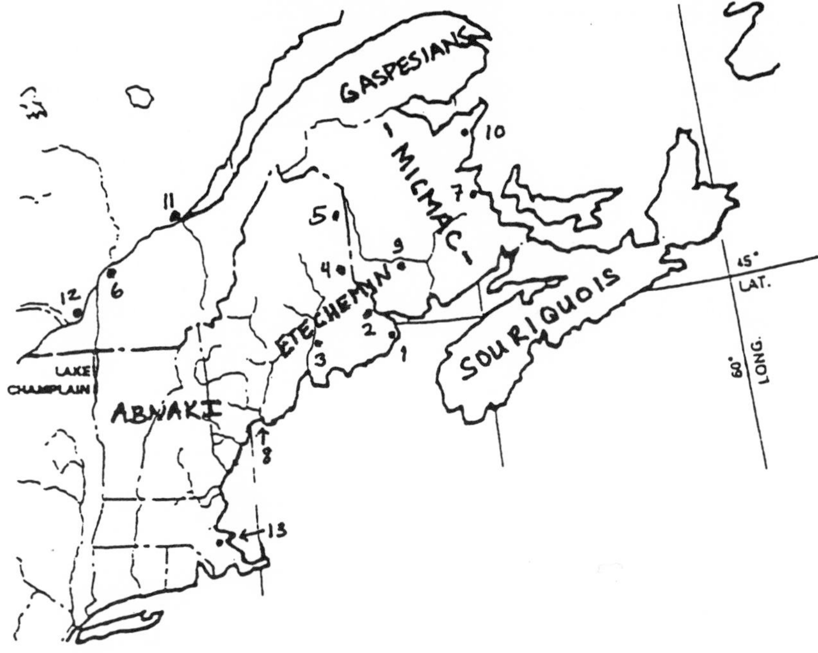

FIGURE 3.1. Wabanakik

1. Pleasant Point Passamaquoddy Reservation
2. Peter Dana Point Passamaquoddy Reservation
3. Indian Island Penobscot Reservation
4. Houlton, Headquarters of Houlton Band of Maliseet
5. Presque Isle, Headquarters of Aroostonk Band of Mi'kmaqs
6. St. Francis Abenaki Reserve
7. Big Cove Mi'kmaq Reserve
8. Hockamock Bay/Kennebec River
9. Frederiction, N.B.
10. Tracadie
11. Québec
12. Montréal
13. Boston

Wabanaki Culture

It is appropriate to speak of the Wabanaki peoples as a group because historically they have shared many significant aspects of culture. Their languages are very similar and are grouped together as a subset of the Algonquian group.

The culture hero, Koluskap (Klu'skap, Gluskabe, etc.), is common to all. The ancestors of the present-day Wabanaki nations were often united politically and many ceremonies were and are celebrated as intertribal events as part of these alliances. All accounts indicate that they also had similar religious and spiritual practices at the time Christian missionaries came to them in the seventeenth century.

Demarcating the domain of "religious experience" in present and past Wabanaki culture is problematic because not only do attitudes that European-Americans would call "religious" permeate the daily lives of modern Wabanaki people, there is also a tendency in our current "new age" climate to find immanent spirituality in every aspect of Native American cultures. Many Native people regard this as one more instance of outsiders projecting essentialized ideas of what it means to be "Indian" onto people descended from the First Nations of America. During the last four centuries of cultural interaction between Wabanaki, Franco-, and Anglo-American peoples, religious practices have necessarily spilled over into social and political realms.

Involvement of Catholic Church in *Wabanakik*

It must be acknowledged that individual Wabanaki relationships with Catholicism have long been polarized. The majority of Wabanaki people today are Roman Catholic, yet many resent the church for very good reasons. Viewed in historical perspective, the Catholic Church has taken what can only be described as an ambivalent stance toward Native culture, some policies displaying antagonism, some broad tolerance. The church's representatives also have displayed a range of individual attitudes above and beyond those of the institution in their dealings with Wabanaki people.

Initially, the missionaries sent to the Wabanaki from Europe allowed a certain amount of mixed cultural practice by their catechumens. This was necessary in order to establish rapport. Where they saw congruence between Native practices and their own, they attempted to show that their way was better and should be adopted. A core Wabanaki cultural attitude is tolerance, and the historical record reveals a keen interest in new technologies (e.g., iron kettles were quickly adopted; see Denys [1675] 1908, 399, 471); today, closed-circuit TV and computer programs are widely employed for cultural activities and entertainment. On their side, however, the priests were also not incapable of a relativist perspective. Consider this summary statement by Fr. Pierre Biard, missionary in Acadia during 1611–13:

> But now if we come to sum up the whole and compare their good and ill with ours, I do not know but that they, in truth, have some reason to prefer (as they do) their own kind of happiness to ours, at least if we speak of temporal happiness, which the rich and worldly seek in this life. For, if indeed they have not all those pleasures which the children of this age are seeking after, they are free from the evils which follow them, and have the contentment which does not accompany them. (Biard [1616] 1897, 3, 135)

Priests and *Medeolinuwok*

Biard's testimony gives weight to the idea that the missionaries found some aspects of Wabanaki life worth preserving. However, the missionaries' social functions and goals placed them in direct conflict with the traditional spiritual leaders, called *aoutmoin* in the historical accounts, *buoin* in modern Mi'kmaq (Erickson 1978), *medeolinuwok* (plural; singular, *medeolin*) in the Passamaquoddy-Maliseet and Abenaki languages (Speck 1919). The current anthropological designation for such a leader is "shaman."[5] As Robert Conkling (1974) has noted, both Catholic priests and Wabanaki shamans possessed charisma (personal in the shamans, official in the priests) and both attempted to control the powers of good and evil.

The similarity between priest and shaman engendered coexistence as well as antagonism. According to missionary accounts, traditional Wabanaki spiritual practices coexisted with Catholicism overtly until well into the eighteenth century, never entirely disappearing (Eckstorm 1945). Furthermore, when analyzing the roles missionary priests historically played in Wabanaki communities, some priests seem to have accepted being cast in traditional roles.

After converting to Catholicism, some Wabanaki bands[6] moved to mission settlements, but many continued their seasonal migratory lifestyle, spending winters hunting inland and summers on the coast, sometimes accompanied by missionaries. The role of the missionary priests in the Wabanaki bands and nations suggests that the adoption of Catholicism by many Wabanaki people did not mean that they abandoned traditional ways of life, but rather were synthesizing the two systems. In many cases, the priest was treated as a *medeolin* or a leader (*sakom*). They were consulted on the occasions of removal to hunting territories, hardship, sickness, or war, and their rhetorical skills—the crucial qualifying characteristic of a *sakom* according to Lescarbot—were employed in making alliances and negotiating with colonial powers and other First Nations.[7]

In the context of the Intercolonial Wars, some French priests who assumed command of Wabanaki bands became notorious as war leaders. The most infamous is Sebastien Râle, who was killed when the Abenaki village of Norridgewock was sacked by an English raid in 1724. While French historians claimed him as a martyr, English writers blamed him for inciting the Abenaki against them.[8] The Abbé Maillard, missionary to the Maliseet and Mi'kmaq in New Brunswick and Nova Scotia, had a similar reputation of leading war parties against the English.[9] Despite the obvious mythologizing inspired by English mistrust of both French and Native peoples, it appears from their own accounts that these priests assimilated to Native culture to a remarkable degree even as they were attempting to change it. Arguably, they fulfilled the Wabanaki ideal of a spiritually powerful war leader, rather than the European ideal of a cleric.[10]

Priests were included as celebrants in the important Wampum Ceremonies of the Wabanaki Confederacy. The Confederacy was a coalition of First Nations formalized at the beginning of the eighteenth century but based on earlier alliances.[11] Priests were called upon to offer Blessings during some of the ceremonies and participated along with the other men in some activities such as choosing leaders (Williamson 1832, 495–98).

Priests also clashed with traditional leaders, particularly over the question of secular schools in Native communities and the role of the state and provincial Indian agents, who were often Protestant and sometimes missionaries themselves. Such clashes were the cause of rifts in the Penobscot and Passamaquoddy nations in Maine in the eighteenth century, which led to the establishment of a Passamaquoddy settlement at Peter Dana Point (Motahkomikuk). In the Penobscot community it led to controversy over the tribal governor and the temporary formation of two factions, the Old Party (loyal to a governor excommunicated and deposed for adultery, and interested in secular schools) and the New Party (loyal to the priest).[12]

As acculturation and assimilation became more desirable goals of the dominant European-derived culture, the church became less tolerant of even nonreligious expressions of Native identity such as speaking local languages in parochial schools.[13] However, since the 1960s the church has participated in the revitalization of Native cultures. The Diocese of Maine coordinated sales of baskets and other traditional arts, bussing artisans to events in Boston and Bar Harbor, and sponsoring the public "Indian Day" at Sipayik Passamaquoddy Reservation. The church reinstated or developed liturgies in local languages, and recently it has consented to incorporating various other elements of Native cultural practice into its rites as well. Cynics might note that this serves the purpose of keeping Catholicism active among people becoming more and more dissatisfied with the European culture they have absorbed or been forced to accept. Yet many of the "nativistic" elements in the liturgy have historical precedents going back hundreds of years and are not new responses to the threat of apostasy.

Contemporary Catholic Practice at Sipayik

Elements of traditional spiritual practice never entirely disappeared from Wabanaki culture, and today many are observably blended into Catholic practice. A Catholic Mass I attended at Sipayik (Pleasant Point Passamaquoddy Reservation) in 1993 illustrates this blending. The occasion was part of the Annual Gathering, also called Ceremonial Day, held since 1965. Intertribal summer gatherings are a traditional part of the Wabanaki yearly cycle,[14] although in some places, among them Sipayik, they have been recently revamped. As in the past, alliances are confirmed, marriages already performed in church are celebrated in the traditional ceremony, and there is much socializing and politicking.

The church at Sipayik is called St. Ann's, after the patron saint especially revered by all the Wabanaki. As Christ's maternal grandmother, she fits well with the special esteem accorded this position in Wabanaki culture. The church has been renovated a number of times; the stained glass windows depicting sainted and blessed personages date from the early twentieth century. Notable among them is Blessed Kateri Tekakwitha. Each window is crowned with the figure of an eagle with its wings spread, a symbol used officially by the Passamaquoddy Tribe. Beadwork and embroidery in traditional Passamaquoddy designs, notably the double-curve motif, decorate the sanctuary, altar, and statuary.

Mass has been part of the official program of the Ceremonial Day since the first "Indian Day" in 1965. The event originally began under the auspices of St. Ann's Church and the Diocese of Maine as a fundraiser, like a church fair. It was also intended from the first to help educate non-Native people about Passamaquoddy culture. In 1993 Mass was listed as one of the Sunday morning options, but the service was so crowded there were many standing a. the back of the church. In addition to drawing more from the local Native community, there were many visitors from other First Nations. The majority of Wabanaki people are still nominally Roman Catholic, and special Masses (Christmas, Easter, installation of the Tribal Governor and Council) tend to be well attended at Sipayik.

The opening hymn accompanying Father Paul McCarty's approach to the altar was sung, in the Passamaquoddy language, by a woman accompanying herself on a small hand drum.[15] She regularly sang at Masses, sometimes leading songs from the hymnal *Glory and Praise* or other devotional songs that had been translated into Passamaquoddy. As Father McCarty led the congregation through the liturgy in English, he used the Passamaquoddy word *Nialetch,* "so be it," in place of "Amen." The Lord's Prayer was said in Passamaquoddy, using a translation that is several centuries old.

A feature of this Ceremonial Day Mass was the presence of three men who had been leading the most important ceremonies around the Sacred Fire outside and were there referred to as "Medicine Men." When Father McCarty went around the congregation giving the Sign of Peace, these three men also fanned out and went around to those assembled, shaking hands and saying, "Megwetch," an Algonquian word meaning "Thank you." This was the same action and word with which they had marked completion of the lighting of the Sacred Fire at the opening of the Gathering. At the height of the Eucharistic Sacrifice, as Father McCarty invoked the Holy Spirit and lifted the bread and wine, the body and blood of Christ, these men also lifted their arms aloft as he did. Such congregational participation in the eucharistic prayers is not uncommon in many parishes in the United States. However, the actions of these men seemed significant because no one else participated in this manner, and they observed the same style of group leadership in their non-church ceremonies. At Sipayik, communion is usually offered and received in Passamaquoddy; but the presence of many outsiders mandated the use of English—a common language—for this occasion.

In the Mass, the sharing of power in words and actions demonstrated what the hymn sung in Passamaquoddy voiced: a mixing of European and Native American religious cultures. The liturgical language incorporated Passamaquoddy—and by extension Algonquian—concepts, while the style of musical performance was distinctly Native American, and identifiable as Passamaquoddy by the relaxed vocal tone and text-driven rhythm.

This Mass might seem to include an extraordinary liturgy, taking place in the context of the Annual Gathering and including many outsiders. Precedents for the inclusion of identifiably Native American elements in Catholic rites in this Passamaquoddy community, however, are numerous, and in this respect this particular community is not unique among the Wabanaki nations. The coexistence of indigenous practices within Wabanaki Catholicism has created a polyvalent liturgy, which is simultaneously a spiritual experience, and, by declaring cultural and religious identity, a political action. It is also a multicultural performance,[16] in which the European and Wabanaki systems seem to be in dialogue. To explicate the multiplicity of meanings this modern Passamaquoddy Mass presents, it is necessary to consider specific elements of practice within the historical context.

Musical Style

The use of heightened speech—chanting and singing—for its spiritual efficacy by both the European Roman Catholic and the Wabanaki traditions facilitated mutual understanding of ceremonial practices. The similarity of Wabanaki musical style to Catholic plainchant was remarked on by Catholic and later Protestant observers.[17] Wabanaki people refer to their traditional music as "songs" (in English) because it is all sung; there is a general Passamaquoddy term for "songs" (*lintuwakon*) but not for "music." Likewise, the missionaries employed only vocal music. Wabanaki musical style is characterized by an open relaxed vocal quality, an *ambitus* within a comfortable singing range, text-based rhythm, close intervals, and clearly staged phrase structures. Eugene Vetromile, a missionary to the Wabanaki communities in Maine in the mid-nineteenth century, noted that his congregations invariably preferred plainchant or broken chant to singing in harmony (1858, [1]). Although harmonized Protestant hymns have entered the Catholic liturgy since Vatican II, many Wabanaki congregations still prefer to sing the melodies alone and without accompaniment. At Sipayik only a few leaders sing, a performance style that corresponds to the way traditional songs are performed. Although everyone sings the same line, individual voices stand out, in a kind of competitive combination that is also typical of non-church ceremonial and social singing.[18] That the traditional Wabanaki and Catholic ceremonial practices should share musical styles seems significant, given the other possibilities for church singing; harmonizing is admired, but it has not been adopted.[19] This suggests that church and traditional ceremonial practices use vocalization in similar ways, and that harmony is just too different to qualify for such use.

The first impressions Europeans and Wabanaki had of each other's music were not always positive. Father Biard described a musical encounter on the Kennebec River in 1611 in which a French exploring party met a group of Almouchiquois (Abenaki) men investigating the French presence. While the Abenakis held council on the riverbank, singing songs suitable for such a serious occasion, the French sang the *Salve Regina*, *Ave Maris Stella*, and other hymns on board their ship to counteract the effect of the Abenakis' singing. Neither party could understand the content of the other's songs, but both seem to have understood their power. The French finally turned to imitating the Abenakis' songs, thinking themselves very clever; but the next day the Abenakis, having observed the French mockery, guided the ship into the shallows of Hockomock Bay and left them stranded (Biard [1612] 1896, 2, 36–39).

Style of Liturgical Speech

The overall style of liturgical speech—using special ceremonial words not used in everyday life, and chanting and singing delivery—had affinities to Wabanaki styles of ceremonial singing and chanting. Contemporary Wabanaki ceremonial chants use words that are glossed as "chant words" by elders and singers; they are apparently archaic and are specifically associated with the ceremonies. This is not quite the same as using the Latin language, but it is remarkably similar from the point of usage.

The common idea of special, powerful words seems to have encouraged Wabanaki use of Catholic formulae even before conversion. In his *History of New France* Marc Lescarbot described how he heard the word "alleluia" used in a song sung in Membertou's cabin in 1606:

> Having made the usual exclamation, they began another in these words: Tameja alleluya tameja douveni hau hau hé hé. The tune thereof was: Sol sol sol fa fa re re re fa fa sol fa sol fa fa re re. I listened closely to this word, alleluya repeated many times; and could make nothing else of it. (Lescarbot [1618] 1914, 106)

Lescarbot wrote the melody down in solfège syllables, the first transcription of any Wabanaki music.[20] Concerning the word "alleluia," there is no reason to doubt Lescarbot's ears; indeed, Ruth Holmes Whitehead has suggested that Membertou had probably picked up the word from the priests as one conveying particular power and was using it for its efficacy, as he would have used Mi'kmaq "words of power" (Whitehead 1991, 26). No translation for the other syllables has been possible, unless as Whitehead suggests "douveni" is "tu veni." "Hau" and "he" might be emphasis syllables, such as those added at the end of Wabanaki ceremonial song phrases. At the time Lescarbot made his observations (1606–7), Membertou had been partially catechized by the priests who accompanied the trading expedition.

Treatment of Sickness

The Catholic missionaries practice of chanting and praying over sick people and the laying on of relics closely paralleled the practices of the Wabanaki shamanic healers. The similarities in practice are evident from the priests' own descriptions. Father Biard, the first Jesuit missionary to reside among Mi'kmaq people, wrote of the efforts of the traditional healer to cure a sick man:

> [H]aving studied his patient, [he] breathes and blows upon him some-unknown enchantments. . . . If he sees after some days that notwithstanding all his blowing the evil does not disappear, he finds the reason for it according to his own ideas, and says it is because the Devil is there inside the sick man, tormenting and preventing him from getting well; [and] he must have the evil thing, get it out by force and kill it. . . . [T]he Juggler [sic; i.e. shaman or healer[21]] hides a stick in a deep hole in the ground, to which is attached a cord . . . after various chants, dances and howls over the hole, and over the sick man . . . little by little uncovers the stick, which . . . by hard pulling is torn out, bringing with it some rubbish, which the charlatan has fashioned to the end, such as decayed and mouldy bones. (Biard [1616] 1897, 3, 118–21)

When Membertou's son fell sick in 1611, Biard wrote to his superiors "we put upon the sufferer a bone taken from the precious relics of the glorified St. Lawrence, archbishop of Dublin in Ireland . . . at the same time offering our vows for him, and then he improved" (Biard [1612] 1896, 2, 18–19). Note that the healer focuses on an evil spirit, which he drives out (exorcises), whereas the priest focuses on a good spirit, which he invokes into the presence of the sick man to strengthen him. Both, however, use an external object as the locus of the spirit they deal with; and both use heightened speech to effect their contact with the spirit.

Missionaries, as well as traders, began traveling from trading posts into the interior of Wabanaki territories. The most immediate effects of the first European contacts with Native peoples were devastating—they introduced European diseases against which the Wabanaki had no immunities. Estimates of how many died during the period of first contact have varied widely, but it is now generally accepted that tens of thousands perished.

Ironically, these epidemics helped convince many Wabanaki to abandon their traditional religious and medicinal practices and follow the religion the French priests preached. Many Native religious leaders and healers were stricken, while the priests were not—being Europeans, they had the antibodies Native people lacked. In both Wabanaki and French Catholic belief systems sickness was understood as a manifestation of evil. Thus, if someone survived, he or she appeared to have more spiritual power than the evil causing the sickness.[22] Furthermore, the French Catholics preached a religion in which death was viewed as the way to a greater life. This might have helped make sense of the devastation for Wabanaki people as well as for the missionaries. Both cultures included belief in an afterlife, but it is not apparent that the traditional Wabanaki idea of death was an exalted state, merely a different state of existence in a different place.[23]

Political Aspects of Wabanaki Catholicism

The Wabanaki bands and nations had been allies of the French in the Intercolonial ("French and Indian") Wars, led in some cases by their priests as discussed above. When the French were banished and their influence suppressed in 1763, the new Anglo government offered Protestant missionaries to the Wabanaki nations as part of their treaty. Declining this offer, the Wabanaki leaders recognized that to the Europeans, professing a particular faith implied certain political alliances. They told the English that had they been introduced to Protestantism earlier: "We should have embraced it and detested the religion which we now profess, but now being instructed by the French we have promised to be true to God in our Religion" (Leger 1924, 74).[24]

In 1764, Penobscot leaders met with the leaders of Maine and Massachusetts, asking for freedom to perform Catholic rites, but they were refused a priest. The evidence is that they continued in the Catholic practices they had been taught from memory (see below); but Wabanaki leaders did not stop trying to obtain priests for their communities. Only two days after the Battle of Bunker Hill—the start of the American War of Independence—Chief Orono and other Penobscot *sakomak* arrived at the Provincial Congress in Cambridge, Massachusetts to ask for a priest in exchange for their alliance against the British (Leger 1924, 116). One year later, *sakomak* of the Mi'kmaq and Passamaquoddy did the same (ibid., 125). Thus priests, who were in some cases erstwhile war councilors, were important enough to be used by Wabanaki political leaders as bargaining points.

As the Colonies could do nothing to meet these requests during the War, Catholic rites were performed in Wabanaki communities following indigenous methods of oral transmission.[25] In 1797, Rev. John Cheverus marveled at the singing of the Requiem Mass by the Passamaquoddy congregation at Sipayik in the very same manner as French Catholics, "with the correct singing of the Kyrie and the responses at the Preface" (Cheverus to Carroll 1797, quoted in Leger 1924, 138). Cheverus had been sent as envoy from the newly ensconced American Bishop John Carroll to visit the Wabanaki living in Maine and Acadia.[26] The priests often had a native assistant, called a *nutonan*, who assisted with catechumenal training and other duties in his community. Since the priests were usually assigned to more than one community, they moved around, and a resident liaison was needed. It has been suggested that the *nutonan* may have fulfilled even some liturgical functions of a priest in his absence, especially after the French cession (Erickson 1980, 87–88 n. 33); whether they administered the sacraments is an open question.

The Thomas Kyrie Manuscript

A representation of a Kyrie movement on a manuscript page in the collection of the New Brunswick Museum provides a glimpse into the mix of oral traditions and Catholic practice during this time (figs. 3.2 a, b).[27] On the verso of this leaf are words written in a similar hand and ink, and although the leaf is obviously a scrap (a circle was cut out of the bottom center), every available area on both sides is judiciously used, and the two could be related. The text on the verso seems to be in the Maliseet-Passamaquoddy[28] language but only fragments are recognizable; it could be a prayer, words to a devotional song, or a catechetical excerpt.[29]

Vincent Erickson identified the Etienne Thomas who signed under the Kyrie as a Maliseet man living in the vicinity of Fredericton, New Brunswick (Erickson 1980, 81). Erickson's discussion of the Kyrie Manuscript focused on the linguistic features, from which he concluded that the writer probably learned to spell at a Protestant mission school, but must have had some exposure to French and Latin writing systems as well as to English (ibid., 82). Erickson raised the possibility that the writing was either learned from or written for a *nutonan*, one of the priests' native "helpers" (ibid., 88). From the overall format of the Kyrie Manuscript, it is reasonable to assume that the writer's exposure to musical notation was from Catholic chant books. There are no staff lines, and the syllable underlay is not specified in the Kyrie representation, but it gives the shape of the melody using similar symbols and layout. If this were written by a person who already knew the chant, perhaps it served as a mnemonic aid. It could also simply have been a representation that had sentimental or spiritual value (see the discussion of hieroglyphics, below).

An annotation on the margin of the verso states that the Kyrie Manuscript was purchased "from an old French Indian" in 1816 (it was acquired by the Museum in 1965). Between 1793, when Etienne Thomas may have been in

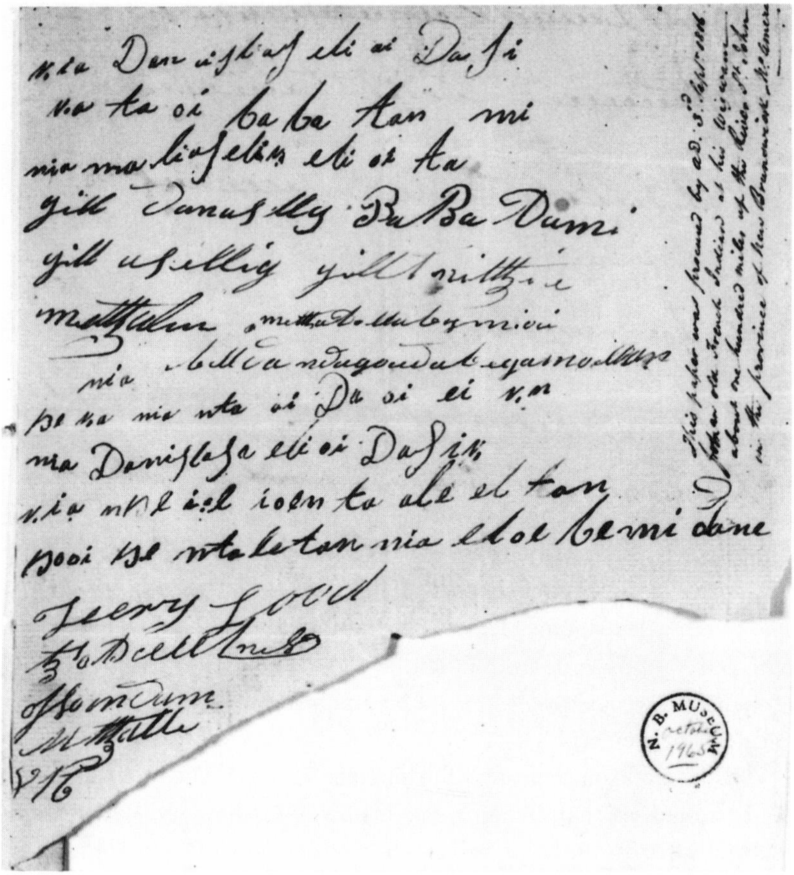

FIGURE 3.2a. The Thomas Kyrie Manuscript page 1

school learning to write, and 1816, the services of Catholic priests in Wabanaki territories were completely disrupted. The conclusion of the American Revolution in 1783 necessitated establishing a completely new Catholic infrastructure in North America; resident priests were not sent back to Wabanaki territories until 1799 (Leger 1924). If ever written documents were needed as mnemonic aids to carrying on Catholic rites in the Northeast, it was during this time.

After the US bishops took over the administration of the Maine missions, special arrangements were made with the Bishop of Québec to get French-speaking priests for the Penobscot and Passamaquoddy-Maliseet. This arrangement was continued well into the nineteenth century. These priests had access to several centuries of Francophone Catholic resources for their Wabanaki congregations.

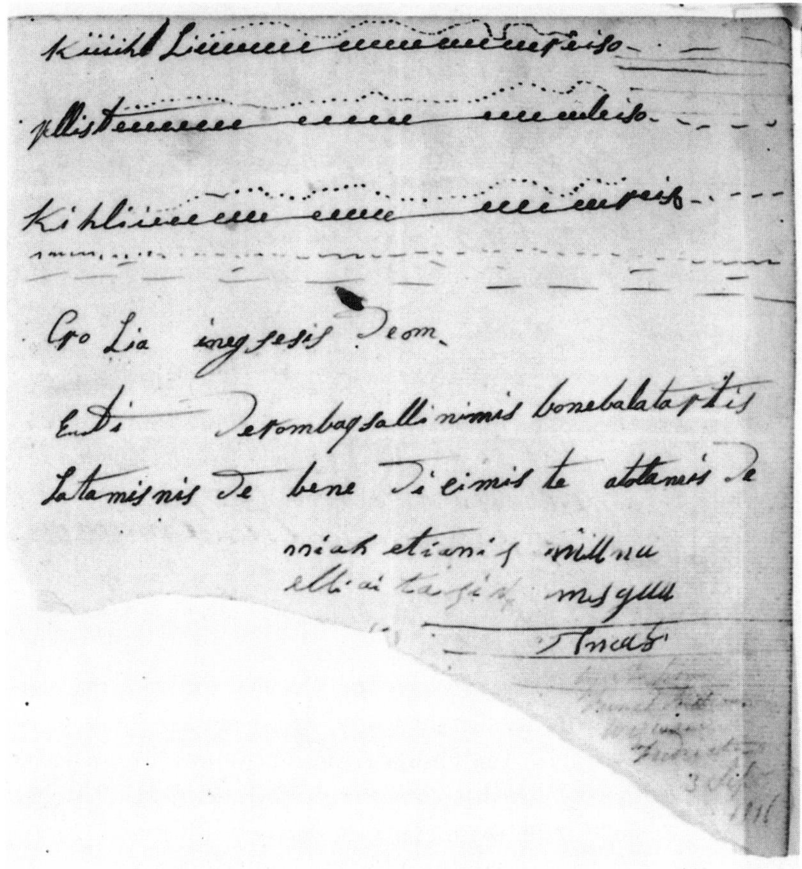

FIGURE 3.2b. The Thomas Kyrie Manuscript page 2

Music in the Jesuit Prayer Books

French Jesuit missionaries who worked in Acadia—among the Abenaki in Québec and Maine, and the Passamaquoddy and Maliseet in Maine, New Brunswick, and Nova Scotia—wrote catechisms, books of prayers, and what amount to *libri usuali* in the local languages.[30] Their manuscript books provide glimpses—albeit somewhat refracted—of what Wabanaki Catholic services were like during the tenure of their missions. The books were in some cases passed down from one priest to another at the same post, and it is not certain who contributed what. Furthermore, music is notated only sporadically, so it is often hard to tell what tunes were employed for the chant texts.

Eugene Vetromile, the last traveling missionary priest to the Wabanaki communities in Maine, drew on the liturgical materials used by his predecessors in his several liturgical books including *Ahiamihewintuhangan: The Prayer Song* (1858).[31] Some of the sources he used are in the collection of the Maine Historical Society in Portland; they include the manuscript "Father Demillier's Prayerbook," which was probably the work of several people.[32] This manuscript contains prayers, formulae, liturgies, and chants in old (but very good) Abenaki and Passamaquoddy dialects.[33] Demillier served at Sipayik and other Native communities in Maine. Another contributor to the manuscript may have been Father Romagné, who also served both Penobscot and Passamaquoddy congregations.[34]

Vetromile published some of these materials combined with similar items from sources from Abenaki, Mi'kmaq, and Montagnais missions. Unquestionably, Vetromile had several motives in publishing his books. His position as missionary in Maine was threatened by increased state involvement with Native affairs and a dispute between the Jesuits and the diocese. He clearly enjoyed his post: There is even a photo of him decked out in furs with parishioners at Sipayik.[35]

The contents of *The Prayer Song* are unfortunately a very mixed bag. Vetromile admits in the Preface that though he was inspired to "preserve some National airs" he was "obliged to substitute several new tunes" (Vetromile 1858, [1]). Most of Vetromile's melodies do not fit the stylistic profile of Wabanaki songs, nor of Catholic chant. For example, the *Gloria* for Christmas (Vetromile 1858, 31) begins like the popular song "The Mexican Hat Dance."

The texts Vetromile published, however, follow the Demillier manuscript, and more important, some are maintained in oral tradition today. I have already noted the use of the Lord's Prayer at Sipayik in the Mass. Vetromile's liturgical books were ostensibly for use by Wabanaki Catholic congregations; the prayer book *Alnambay Uli Awikhigan* especially was a prized possession of Wabanaki families in the twentieth century. Most contacts noted that they were used mnemonically, however, not actually "read."

Burial Hymns

The selections that Vetromile presented in *The Prayer Song* also reflect Catholic rites and ceremonies that were of special importance in native communities. There is a Christmas liturgy (*Nipayimiyamok*, "praying all night"). The Mass for the Dead (*Alameskewank N'pinwak*) is included. The song *Wasis Metchinet* (Vetromile 1858, 41), a song commemorating the death of a baby, reflects the highly valued traditional practice of Death and Burial songs.[36] According to seventeenth-century French sources, Wabanaki funeral songs were a significant part of indigenous burial rites. The songs even impressed the French missionaries, although they disapproved of the burial ceremonies as a whole (Biard [1616] 1897, 3, 126–35; LeClercq [1691] 1910, 218–19). The genre of burial songs today has special emotional potency for some Passamaquoddy people. Basket-maker Mary Gabriel told an interviewer that, although she knew someone who sang these songs, "I never wanted to learn because it was so sad for me" (Gabriel, interview). Beyond the haunting melodic qualities of these songs, their connection with the death of elders in Wabanaki communities evokes more than a personal tragedy: The elders are the repositories of culture. The musical style of the song Lillian Gabriel recorded for the same interviewer (transcribed in fig. 3.3) combines elements of Catholic religious music and Wabanaki song style: limited ambitus, pure vocal quality with some slides, a flowing text-based rhythm. The phrase structure follows a typical Wabanaki scheme, although it is not uniquely Wabanaki: balanced phrases, dividing the

Passamaquoddy Burial Hymn
Northeast Archives, NA 1621

Sung by Lillian Gabriel
Recorded by Debbie Brooks
Transcribed by Ann Morrison Spinney

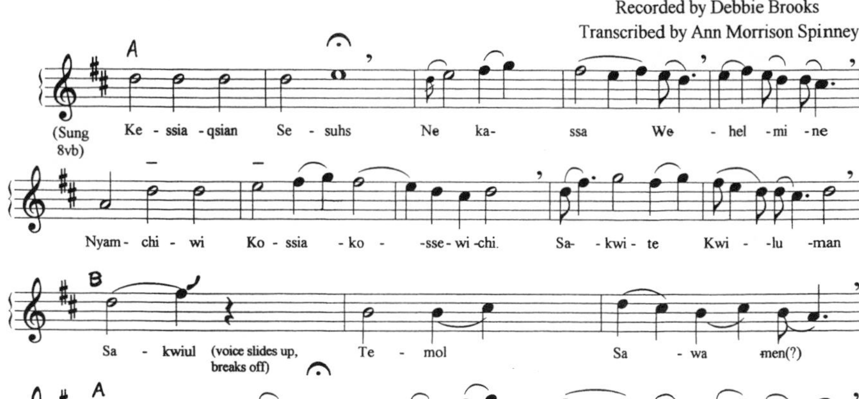

(The text is a prayer for departed souls. It is a Passamaquoddy version of one in Vetromile 1856, 214.)

FIGURE 3.3. Passamaquoddy Burial Hymn

song into a higher-pitched first section (A) and a second lower-pitched section (B), returning to the first to end. The text is a prayer for departed souls; it is a Passamaquoddy version of one for All Souls' Day published by Vetromile (1856, 214).

Death and Burial songs are still used at wakes and visiting hours in the Passamaquoddy communities (for transcriptions, see Morrison [Spinney] 1996). The songs are translations of rosary prayers and the Requiem Mass; the texts are nearly identical to those given in the Demillier ms. and Vetromile's texts. The melodies seem to be adaptations of standard chant tunes to the syllables of the Passamaquoddy language. They have even been recorded on cassettes, so that if someone is not available to lead the singing, they can be played.

Franciscan Use of Mi'qmak Hieroglyphs

The prayer books written by Franciscan missionaries in Mi'kmaq hieroglyphs are further examples of an indigenous technique combined with European Catholicism as a means of supporting religious practice. Père Chrestien LeClercq claimed in 1677 to have adapted the hieroglyphs he used for catechizing Gaspesian (Mi'kmaq) people from a pictographic code he saw children using (LeClercq [1691] 1910, 131). The pictographic writing may have had wider use; mnemonic symbols were used in the wampum belts that were shared among Wabanaki nations.[37] LeClercq's copies of the Lord's Prayer and Catechism were on handwritten sheets called *Kignamotinoer*. In 1738, the Abbé Maillard claimed to have improved and expanded LeClercq's system (Ganong in LeClercq [1691] 1910, 29), producing similar manuscript sheets for use in catechizing. Maillard's manuscript pages were preserved in special boxes like the mnemonic wampum historical records and passed down within families.

The manuscripts were intended for private instruction, and there were no attempts to notate liturgical songs until the missionary Charles Christian Kauder encountered Maillard's system in 1860 at the Mi'kmaq community of Tracadie. Kauder arranged for an edition of the catechism, with additional prayers and hymns, to be typecast and printed in Vienna. This was done under the auspices of the Leopoldinenstiftung, an Austrian charitable organization dedicated to funding Catholic missionary work among German-speaking immigrants and First Nations people in North America. Kauder seems to have made a further extension of the hieroglyphic system to accommodate the new material he included. Unfortunately, he did not include musical notation in his book. Over five thousand pieces of type were cast for the hieroglyphs alone—musical notation would probably have been too expensive.

Most "hymns" included in Kauder's book are not devotional but pieces for the Mass and Offices and were likely meant to be sung to the tunes in standard use. The shipment of books was sadly lost at sea, and only a few proof copies survive. However, a new edition was printed with subtitles in French and Latin at Restigouche, Québec in 1921. Some Mi'kmaq elders can still read it, and others know the symbols of specific prayers.[38]

The Mi'kmaq hieroglyphic system was apparently not extended to other Wabanaki tribes for catechizing, perhaps because the Mi'kmaq language is the most distinct of the culture group (Maliseet-Passamaquoddy being two dialects of the same, and closely related to the Abenaki dialects, e.g., St. Francis, Norridgewock, Penobscot). However, copies of the hieroglyphic prayers are prized in other communities for their symbolic value—they have been transcribed in artistic wall hangings, and have been used in beadwork.

Toward the end of the Vienna edition, a "Gesang für den Regen" (Song for Rain) appears between the office hymns *Te Deum* and *Benedictus* (1866 [3], 202–3). This same piece—the hieroglyphs are identical—appears in the Restigouche edition in the same context with the Latin title *Rorati Coeli* ("Drop down dew ye heavens from above, and let the skies pour down righteousness") (Kauder 1921, no. 447, [n.p.]). It makes sense to assume that this is indeed *Rorati Coeli*, placed as it is in the context of the other two hymns; all three have similar multiple functions in both Office and Mass Proper.[39] Was the German title given by Kauder as an attempt to make the Latin rites intelligible in what Kauder imagined were local terms, a rain dance? Or was it perhaps an acknowledgment that the two religions share a concern with controlling the awesome powers of nature? Underlying the Christological interpretation of this text is an association with Christ's birth. Advent is a season celebrating the promise of fertility as well as salvation.

Conclusion

The examples I have presented here are merely highlights from the four centuries of syncretism between Wabanaki traditions and Catholicism. I have intentionally chosen from different Wabanaki communities, partly to emphasize the similarity across this culture group and partly to reflect the paths of the missionaries who traveled between them. Specific congruencies between Wabanaki and Catholic religious practices may have made conceptually moving between the Catholic and traditional systems impossible for ecclesiastical authorities entirely to control. An action such as praying over a sick person, chanting "Alleluia," or singing a Death Song could have meaning in both. The process of formulating meaning continues in this living tradition, especially today, as the style of liturgies is more open to local influences since Vatican II.

Music's role in facilitating this cultural encounter has been crucial. The stylistic affinities of the Catholic chant with indigenous ceremonial music allowed room for local interpretation, as shown in the burial hymns. Because Wabanaki congregations were without resident priests for much of the period after the French cession of Canada, they had to rely on traditional techniques of oral transmission to preserve their Catholic rites. The use of native languages is more problematic—they were not used continuously in the churches, but were in most cases reinstated after Vatican II.[40] Lastly, professing Catholicism proved to be politically advantageous to Wabanaki peoples, helping them to maintain political autonomy and a separate identity after the colonial period.

In addition to stressing the syncretic nature of Wabanaki Catholicism, I have deliberately avoided focusing my discussion on Catholic practice as primarily political, cultural, or spiritual—one thing or another. That it can and has been all of these is the source of its efficacy for Wabanaki people. At times, the Wabanaki nations have used Catholicism for pragmatic political ends, while individuals continued to exercise interpretive control over their spiritual experience through ritual actions that had multiple significances.

The complex history of the political, spiritual, and aesthetic interactions between Wabanaki and European Americans is recorded in the Wabanaki Catholic liturgical music. The voices of both *medeolinuwok* and missionaries are there; and today, both still inspire Wabanaki spiritual life.

NOTES

1. The research for this paper was undertaken with the support of a Paine Travelling Fellowship from the Department of Music, Harvard University as part of my doctoral dissertation project.

2. In using this terminology I am following the lead of Mildred Milliea, who described "Mi'kmaq Catholicism" as she remembered it in her community of Big Cove, New Brunswick (Milliea 1989). It captures the essentially syncretic character of many modern Wabanaki persons' Catholicism and, as I shall argue, the character of their ancestors' practice as well.

3. See Speck (1940), Bock (1966), Wallis and Wallis (1953).

4. See Kenneth Morrison's discussion of the complex symbolic processes in the neighboring Montagnais people's conversion to Catholicism (1990). See also John and Jean Comaroff's study of Christianity in Africa (1991) for another study of the complex cultural processes glossed over by the word "conversion."

5. There is some confusion over these terms; modern sources use *buoin* (also *buowin*) in discussing the Jesuits' *aoutmoin* (Whitehead and McGee 1983, 54; Leavitt 1985, 35). Speck (1919) equates *buwin* [*sic*] with *medeolin*, although some writers translate *medeolin* as "witch" rather than shaman (Prince 1899). I use *medeolin* (an orthographic normalization of Speck's version) here only because it is appropriate for the majority of the cultures discussed. Of these terms, none is used so consistently as to correspond perfectly to the anthropological categories of shaman (person using good power), sorcerer (person using evil power), and witch (supernatural person). As priests and, later, white doctors took over the roles of the shaman, the practice of indigenous healing methods could have been recast as something to be feared. See Eckstorm 1945 for examples of persons whose powers were regarded with mixed fear and respect.

6. A band is a smaller political organization than a nation; it may be based on family relations (as in a Family Band; see Speck [1915]), or based on location, as in the contemporary Aroostook Band of Mi'kmaqs.

7. The example par excellence of this role is Père Gabriel Druillettes, who appeared before the Confederation of New England Colonies on behalf of the Wabanaki in 1650 and 1651 (A. H. Morrison 1984). He made an unsuccessful attempt to persuade the English to support the French and Wabanaki in their defensive wars against the Iroquois; the English allied with the Iroquois.

8. Some Native people have suspected that he was a double agent and delivered the Abenakis up to the English to massacre. Kenneth Morrison (1974) argues that he was simply a political realist, who tried to negotiate on behalf of the Norridgewock village for the best treatment from both English and French.

9. A captured letter supposedly written by Maillard to French authorities describing his life with the Mi'kmaqs and Maliseets—like one of the Jesuit *relations*—was printed as a pamphlet in London with commentary that disparages Catholic rituals as akin to the "savage" native lifeways (Maillard 1758). Robert Conkling's discussion of French missionaries in the Northeast provides several other examples of priests who acted as sakomak (1974).

10. Given European religious history of the sixteenth and seventeenth centuries, there could have been some models for the heroic role.

11. It has recently been formally reconstituted, though ceremonies were continued in individual communities. My dissertation (Morrison [Spinney] 1997) includes an extended study of this ceremonial complex.

12. Eckstorm 1945, 194–97. See also Morrison (Spinney) (1997, 60–61).

13. See Isabel Knockwood (1992) for a personal account of treatment of Mi'kmaq children in Catholic boarding schools in Canada. According to members of the Sisters of Mercy—the order assigned to teach school on the Passamaquoddy Reservations in Maine since 1879—the decision to enforce "English only" was taken with the support of Native parents, who felt it would advance their children's prospects.

14. According to my contacts, the Wampum Ceremonies were often celebrated in these summer gatherings.

15. Drums are used at Sipayik St. Ann's on special occasions with dispensation from the Bishop. Hymns are regularly sung in Passamaquoddy, and more translations continue to be made.

16. I am using this term "performance" in its anthropological sense here, fully aware that many Native people object to its colloquial associations with Vaudeville and Wild West shows.

17. Vetromile 1858, Preface [n.p.].

18. I have discussed this striking kind of unison and related it to Wabanaki political structure in my unpublished paper "Unisons and Unity" (1995).

19. When I first visited Pleasant Point I was told a professional church musician had just been there, giving a workshop on choral singing that aroused little interest. There was only a small electric organ in the back of the church, not used except for this workshop. It is curious that singing in harmony is much admired; when singing at St. Ann's, I added a descant to "Amazing Grace" and always received compliments. Furthermore, the multi-part psalmody of a group led by Congregational missionary Elijah Kellogg attracted many Passamaquoddy people in the 1820s, but did not lead them to convert (Erickson 1985).

20. It is curious however, that the solfège transcription of this and other songs only appears in the third edition of Lescarbot's *Histoire*; he was perhaps competing with Jean de Léry, who included Brazilian songs, also in solfège, in the later editions of his report on his trip to Brazil (de Léry [1585] 1990, 248, n. 13).

21. French writers called shamanic healers *Iongleurs* and English writers, "jugglers." Their use of this term was probably politically motivated; I have discussed the multiple significances of this term (Morrison [Spinney] 1997b).

22. One Passamaquoddy person, who wishes to remain anonymous, made this point to me as the reason her ancestors converted to Catholicism.

23. Nicolas Denys, who held various government positions in the French colony of Acadia in the mid-seventeenth century, was one European who discussed Native peoples' concepts of death. In his *Description and Natural History of the Coasts of North America (Acadia)*, he reported on an extended debate between Europeans and Native people over the traditional practice of burying implements with dead persons for their use in the next world. A Gaspesian man showed Denys that a rusted metal kettle (a valued trade item) "no longer has any sound, and . . . no longer says a word [i.e. it did not reverberate when struck] because its spirit has abandoned it to go to be of use in the other world" (Denys [1672] 1908, 440).

24. The original source for this quote is James Phinney Baxter, ed., *The Baxter Manuscripts*, Documentary History of the State of Maine, 2nd ser.(Portland: Maine Historical Society, 1889–1916) 10, 94.

25. Mildred Milliea (1989, 263) notes that the congregation of Big Cove, New Brunswick had no resident priest in the early twentieth century, and the Chief and elders led performances of the Mass and other rites.

26. Acadia was the region northeast of the Kennebec River. The final boundary between Maine and New Brunswick was not agreed upon until 1842.

27. New Brunswick Museum, Archives. Indians of New Brunswick, Box I, shelf 5, Maliseet Song. Caption: "Song by a half-literate person signed Henry Hood" (this refers to the other side). I am grateful to the Museum for permission to reproduce it here.

28. The two political groups share the language; there are dialect differences.

29. I am very grateful to Passamaquoddy Elder David A. Francis for his translation, and his assistance in analyzing the manuscript. For more on Passamaquoddy-Maliseet devotional songs, see Morrison (Spinney) (1996).

30. I have discussed these sources in more detail (Morrison [Spinney] 1996, 1997). What is presented here is a summary.

31. A similar volume is his *Alnambay Uli Awikhigan: Indian Good Book* (1856), a prayer book with catechism. He also separately published excerpts from both works, a history of the Abenakis and various other bits and pieces.

32. There are several handwritings evident. I am grateful to librarian Nicholas Noyes for his patience with my long examination of this manuscript.

33. I am grateful to Pauleena MacDougall and David A. Frances for their comments on the languages.

34. A prayerbook by Romagné published in Boston in 1834 was listed in J. C. Pilling (1891).

35. In the collection of the Waponahki Museum, Sipayik. I am grateful to Joseph A. Nicholas and David A. Francis for allowing me to study the collections there.

36. This identical song is also found in the manuscript *Father Demillier's Prayerbook*, Maine Historical Society, Coll. 114, p. 28. Musical notation is penciled into the manuscript.

37. See also David L. Schmidt, Murdena Marshall, *Mi'kmaq Hieroglyphic Prayers: Readings in Noth American's First Indigenous Script*, Halifax, Nova Scotia: Nimbus Pub., 1995, (1995, 4–5). The Wampum belts were mnemonic prompts for the oral Wampum Records, and recorded alliances and other political events with symbols woven out of blue and white shell beads. Even marriage arrangements were so symbolized. Ganong (in LeClercq [1691] 1910, 32) says the Protestant missionary Silas Rand did not use the hieroglyphic system and disparaged it in his *Legends of the Micmacs*.

38. See Schmidt and Marshall (1995) for a discussion of the history and use of the hieroglyphs in Mi'kmaq communities.

39. According to the *Liber Usualis*, "Rorate Caeli de super, et nubes pluent justum" (Isaiah 45: 8) is the Introit for the Fourth Sunday of Advent. The Vespers hymn for the vigil before; it is also one of "Varii Cantus in Tempore Adventus" (various chants for Advent).

40. At Sipayik only in the 1970s; by 1993 only a few portions were performed in Passamaquoddy. A complete Mass in Maliseet was published at Tobique, New Brunswick in 1990; unpublished versions are available in some Mi'kmaq parishes.

WORKS CITED

Baxter, James Phinney, ed. 1889-1916. *The Baxter Manuscripts*. Documentary History of the State of Maine, 2nd ser. Portland: Maine Historical Society. Quoted in Leger 1924, 74.

Biard, Pierre. [1612] 1896. *Lettre au R. P. Provincial, à Paris. Port Royal, Janvier 31, 1612*. In Thwaites, 2: 3–55.

———. [1616] 1897. *Relation de Nouvelle France.* In Thwaites, 3: 21–283; 4: 7–165.

Bock, Philip K. 1966. *The Micmac Indians of Restigouche: History and Contemporary Description.* National Museum of Canada, *Bulletin* 213; Anthropological Series No. 77. Ottawa: National Museum of Canada.

Comaroff, Jean, and John Comaroff. 1991. *Of Revelation and Revolution: Christianity, Colonialism, and Consciousness in South Africa.* Vol. 1. Chicago: University of Chicago Press.

Conkling, Robert. 1974. "Legitimacy and Conversion in Social Change: The Case of French Missionaries and the Northeastern Algonkian." *Ethnohistory* 21 (1): 1–24.

Denys, Nicolas. [1672] 1908. *The Description and Natural History of the Coasts of North America (Acadia).* In William F. Ganong, trans. and ed., *The Publications of the Champlain Society*, Vol. 2. Toronto: The Champlain Society.

Eckstorm, Fannie Hardy. 1945. *Old John Neptune and Other Maine Shamans.* Repr., Orono: University of Maine at Orono Press, 1980.

Erickson, Vincent O. 1978. "The Micmac Buoin, Three Centuries of Cultural and Semantic Change." *Man in the Northeast* (Spring/Fall) 15/16: 3–41.

———. 1980. "The Thomas Kyrie Manuscript." In William Cowan, ed., *Papers of the Tenth Algonquian Conference,* 79–91. Ottawa: Carleton University.

———. 1985. "Passamaquoddies and Protestants: Deacon Sockabason and the Reverend Kellogg of The Society for Propagating the Gospel." *Man in the Northeast* (Spring/Fall) 29: 87–107.

Father Demillier's Prayerbook. [n.d.]. Manuscript, Maine Historical Society, Portland, Coll. 114.

Gabriel, Mary, and Lillian Gabriel. [n.d.]. Interview by Debbie Brooks. Northeast Archives of Folklore and Oral History, University of Maine, Orono, Tape 1621.

Ganong, William. 1910. "Introduction" to *Nouvelle Relation de Gaspesie* by Chrestien LeClercq. Toronto: The Champlain Society.

Kauder, Christian. 1866. *Buch das Gut, enthaltend den Katechismus, Betrachtung, Gesang.* Vienna: Staatsdruckerei.

———. 1921. *Sapeoig Oigatigen tan tetli Gomgoetjoigasigel.* Restigouche, Quebec: The Micmac Messenger.

Knockwood, Isabelle. 1992. *Out of the Depths: The Experiences of Mi'kmaw Children at the Indian Residential School at Shubenacadie, Nova Scotia.* Lockeport, Nova Scotia: Roseway.

Leavitt, Robert. 1985. *The Micmacs.* Markham, Ontario: Fitzhenry & Whiteside.

LeClercq, Chrestien. [1691] 1910. *Nouvelle Relation de Gaspesie.* Toronto: The Champlain Society.

Leger, Mary Celeste. 1924. *The Catholic Indian Missions in Maine, 1611–1820. Publications in American Church History.* Vol. 8. Washington, D.C.: The Catholic University of America.

de Léry, Jean. [1585] 1990. *History of a Voyage to the Land of Brazil, Otherwise Called America.* Trans. by Janet Whatley. Berkeley: University of California Press.

Lescarbot, Marc. [1610] 1896. *La Conversion des Sauvages.* In Reuben Gold Thwaites, ed., *The Jesuit Relations and Allied Documents.* Vol. 1: 49–113. Cleveland: Burrows Brothers.

———. [1618] 1914. *Histoire de la Nouvelle-France.* 3 vols. Trans. W. L. Grant. *Publications of the Champlain Society*, Nos., 1, 7, and 11. Repr., New York: Greenwood, 1968.

Maillard, C. S., Abbé. 1758. *An Account of the Customs and Manners of the Mickmackis and Maricheets, Savage Nations . . . from an Original French Manuscript-Letter . . . to Which Are Annexed, Several Pieces, Relative to the Savages, to Nova Scotia and to North America in General.* London: Printed for S. Hooper and A. Morley.

Milliea, Mildred. 1989. "Micmac Catholicism in my Community." In William Cowan, ed., *Actes du Vingtième Congrès des Algonquinistes*, 262–66. Ottawa: Carleton University.

Morrison, Alvin H. 1984. "Black Robe in Boston: Rare Man/Rare Moment." In William Cowan, ed., *Papers of the Fifteenth Algonquian Conference*, 193–200. Ottawa: Carleton University.

Morrison (Spinney), Ann. 1995. "Unisons and Unity." Unpublished paper delivered at the annual meeting of the Society for Ethnomusicology in Los Angeles.

———. 1996. "Christians, Kyries, and *Kci Niwesq*: Passamaquoddy Catholic Songs in Historical Perspective." *European Review of Native American Studies* 10 (2, Fall): 15–21.

———. 1997. *Music That Moves between Worlds: Passamaquoddy Ceremonial Songs in the Cultural History of the Northeast.* Ph.D. diss., Harvard University.

———. 1997b. "Going for the Juggler: Colonial European Reactions to Algonquian Shamans." Unpublished paper delivered at the annual meeting of the American Musicological Society in Phoenix.

Morrison, Kenneth. 1974. "Sebastien Racle and Norridgewock, 1724: The Eckstorm Conspiracy Thesis Reconsidered." *Maine Historical Society Quarterly* 14 (2, Fall): 76–97.

———. 1990. "Baptism and Alliance: The Symbolic Mediations of Religious Syncretism." *Ethnohistory* 37 (4, Fall): 416–37.

Pilling J. C. 1891. *Bibliography of the Algonquian Languages.* Washington, D.C.: Government Printing Office.

Prince, John Dynely. 1899. "Some Passamaquoddy Witchcraft Tales." *Proceedings of the American Philosophical Society* 38: 181–89.

Speck, Frank. 1915. "The Family Hunting Band as the Basis of Algonkian Social Organization." *American Anthropologist* 17: 289–305.

———. "Penobscot Shamanism." American Anthropological Association, *Memoirs*, 6: 239–88.

Thwaites, Reuben Gold, ed. 1896–1901. *The Jesuit Relations and Allied Documents.* 73 vols. Cleveland: Burrows Brothers.

Vetromile, Eugene. 1858. *Ahiamihewintuhangan (The Prayer Song).* New York: E. Dunigan & Bro.; James B. Kirker.

———. 1856. *Alnambay Uli Awikhigan: Indian Good Book.* New York: E. Dunigan & Brother.

Wallis, Wilson D., and Ruth Sawtell Wallis. 1953. "Culture Loss and Culture Change among the Micmac." *Kroeber Anthropological Society Papers*, 1953 (8–9): 100–29.

Williamson, William D. 1832. *The History of the State of Maine [1602–1820]*. 2 vols. Hallowell, Maine: Glazier, Masters & Co.

Whitehead, Ruth Holmes. 1991. *The Old Man Told Us: Excerpts from Micmac History, 1500–1950*. Halifax, Nova Scotia: Nimbus.

Whitehead, Ruth Holmes, and Harold McGee. 1983. *The Micmac: How Their Ancestors Lived Five Hundred Years Ago*. Halifax, Nova Scotia: Nimbus.

4

Singing as Experience among Russian American Molokans

Margarita Mazo

"You do not need to tell me who is singing, I know these are Molokans!" exclaims a younger Molokan in Los Angeles.[1] For the first time in his life he is hearing the singing of his brothers in the Molokan faith from Russia on a tape that I recorded three months earlier, in the summer of 1989. Singing is a keystone of the Molokans' self-identity. It epitomizes Molokan religious experience and social life to such an extent that most adults in the community consider the continuity of their singing a critical factor for their survival as Molokans.[2] Furthermore, the Molokans believe that singing, as a channel of direct communication with God, has the power of evoking the Holy Spirit. So critical is singing for the Molokans' faith that they call "the Molokan religion a singing religion" (James Samarin 1975, 6).

Understanding why singing is so crucial for the perpetuation of the Molokans' faith and culture among the Russian American Molokans may come only within a larger framework that addresses their history and the phenomenon called Molokanism. In this article, Molokanism is understood as a cultural, social, rhetorical, and cognitive continuum formed out of tightly entwined religious concepts and worldviews; the continuum serves as the Molokan conceptual universe in which singing is an integral part and takes on specific meanings and significance. Diversity of individual interpretations notwithstanding, Molokanism is approached here as a domain of collective meaning and symbolic order.

Molokanism is little known even to specialists of Russian religion, history, or culture.[3] To present Molokanism in a comprehensive way while limiting the discussion to a manageable scope, I have chosen to focus on its specific cognitive aspects, which I consider most fundamental both to the Molokans' musical practices and to musical signification in their communities. The repertory of Molokan religious singing consists of several hundred psalms[4] and spiritual songs. A comprehensive analysis of this repertory is not my concern here. Nor do I explore the broader question of how Molokan singing is related to other Russian musical traditions, although these relationships are compelling.[5] Instead, by teasing out the issues behind the salient characteristics of performance practices of psalms and songs, I situate the collective experience of Molokan singing within their conceptual universe. My goal, therefore, is to offer an interpretive framework that shows their singing as a unique and powerful collective experience, recognizable as such by the Molokans themselves and by any outsiders.

Needless to say, the collective experience and the experiences of the individuals are completely interdependent, if not altogether inseparable. Anyone willing to approach a living culture as a dynamic, complex, and dialectic phenomenon is confronted with this multidimensional dilemma. The dilemma emerges as he or she strives to integrate conceptual abstractions with specific individual experiences, to address the Bakhtinian "self/other" relationship, and to articulate deeply interdependent cognitive views, social constructions, and cultural notions. During field research in various Molokan communities, this dilemma became particularly prominent. Revealing a strong predisposition for self-reflection, most of the people who generously spent time talking to me were mainly interested in constructing the meaning of being a Molokan in general and decontextualized ways, using an endless number of biblical passages as the ultimate validation of their points. As our relationships grew closer, I realized that such abstract discourse is part of daily life for many Molokans, particularly men, and not just a rhetorical screen to demarcate a distance from me, a person from the outside and secular world.

One of the Molokan rhetorical ideals is unanimity in everything, from communal affairs to private family life. Yet, Molokan everyday life is different. Their cognitive views resonate with vividly different individual attitudes and opinions as well as highly intense personal relationships. This intensity expresses itself through intimacy, but also through potent tensions, manifested in arguments and debates that permeate Molokans' communal and personal life. As a result, separateness, in the sense of individual interpretations of Molokanism, is strong among the Molokans. At the same time, the inner tension created by diversity on the personal level may have been largely responsible for the survival of Molokanism. Drawing on the individual interpretations and concerns of valued and devoted members, Molokanism is continually reaffirmed and redefined through ongoing construction of negotiated meaning (see Flower 1994). This process becomes a particularly potent instrument of change through situated rhetoric in structured religious or social contexts. Such negotiation is all the more significant in view of the fact that for individual Molokans, imbued as they are with profound moral convictions and religious beliefs, there can be only one truth in any argument. It is precisely the process of constructing negotiated meaning, in my opinion, that assures flexibility of this single truth to new challenges and secures its ability to bear relevance to an ever-changing world. In brief, strong individual opinions and concerns of the respected members of the community create among the Molokans an inner tension that may have largely been responsible for the community's perpetuation and survival.

Molokans are very private people who do not seek attention from outsiders. Not every one of them believes that their singing, let alone their religion, should be studied by the *ne nashi* (those who are not one of us). I am fortunate that many members of the Molokan community not only have endorsed my intellectual inquiry about their singing, but also have generously shared with me their gifts, knowledge, and convictions. It is my hope that the choices I make in the following discussion lie within the bounds of a mode of representation that does not betray their confidence and trust.

By Way of Historical Introduction

Molokans are members of a small religious denomination originally called "Spiritual Christians."[6] As part of grassroots protest movements in rural Russia of the eighteenth century, Molokans dissented from the main Orthodox Church in the 1760s. The sobriquet *molokane* (milk drinkers, plural of *molokanin*) was given by outsiders.[7] The precise number of Molokans living around the world is not known, and the exact roots of their pilgrimage are not well documented, but the largest settlements are in Russia and the United States. The number of Molokans residing in the former Soviet Union varies in different sources from fifty thousand to two-hundred thousand. About twenty thousand live in California, and several thousands in Oregon, according to the latest data (Magocsi 1996, 57).

Like the Dukhobors (spirit fighters), a sect from which the Molokans branched out, the Molokans sought religious freedom from the Russian Orthodox Church and economic independence from state-imposed poverty through establishing a self-governing and egalitarian brotherhood. To this day, communal energy is considered to have more spiritual power than the spiritual energy of any individual.

Because of their resentment toward the Orthodox Church, the Molokans, like other Russian sectarians, were outlawed by mainstream society and were severely repressed throughout their history in Russia, where the autocracy and the Orthodox Church were inseparable. In 1805, Molokans submitted a written petition to Czar Alexander I, and three Molokan spokesmen were called to present their case in front of the Czar and twelve senators. They explained their beliefs, described the hardships that they had been subjected to for their faith, and begged for the Czar's protection.[8] A large group of Molokans from central Russia was soon resettled, on the Czar's order, in the area along the river *Molochnye Vody* near Crimea, in the Tavricheskaya province, where a large Dukhobor settlement had already existed since 1801 (Livanov 1872, 2:95–8). The Molokans were conscientious objectors. During the 1830s, they accepted Czar Nicolas I's offer to receive a fifty-year exemption from mandatory military service in exchange for their relocation from central and southern Russia to the Russian Empire's new frontier in the Caucasus mountains and Transcaucasia (Moore 1973, 19; Izmail-Zade 1983, 55). After the law allowing exemption from military services expired, their further petitions to be excused were denied. In conjunction with the millenarian prophecies of impending doom, many Molokans migrated further south and east to central Asia and Siberia. By the turn of the century, a large number of Molokans, led by the prophesies, had settled beyond Russia's borders, in Turkey, Persia, Germany, Australia, and other parts of the world (see Livanov 1872; Klibanov 1982; Moore 1973; Izmail-Zade 1983). In the United States the first Molokan settlers arrived in the Los Angeles area in 1904–05.[9]

There are currently three main Molokan groups both in Russia and in the United States: *Postoyannye* (Steadfast), who claim not to have changed the original doctrine and order of worship; *Pryguny* (Jumpers), who, under a condition of communal ecstasy and mystic solidarity, seek a direct manifestation of the Spirit, whose embodiment may come in jumping, prophesizing, and speaking in tongues; *Maximisty*, who branched out from the Jumpers and revere the teachings of the late nineteenth-century prophet Maxim Rudometkin as much as they revere the Bible. A new branch of Molokanism, currently emerging in the United States, is a group of *Reform* Molokans, who has yet to be mentioned in the literature. I have worked with all four groups, although my experience with the *Maximisty* has been limited, particularly in the U.S., as they are almost entirely closed to outsiders. Each group refuses to yield regarding separatism and independence. The differences among them are marked by a wide variety of issues, ranging from doctrines, liturgical practices, and ways of interacting with the outside world to family relationships. Internal disagreements further caused the three main groups to split into smaller units, each believing it strictly follows "the form prescribed by the founders of our denomination" (Berokoff 1987, 195). In reality, forms of practicing Molokanism are numerous and vary from church to church and even from individual to individual.

The Role of the Spiritual

The Molokan faith is syncretic, being an amalgamation of the two Testaments, the teachings of their forefathers, and folk beliefs commonly found in Russian villages. Furthermore, it exhibits an obvious bond with Russian mysticism through its emphasis on a highly personal relationship with God. In this connection, the Molokans are akin to some earlier Russian sectarians, who believed in the direct indwelling of God in men and women. This doctrine became particularly widespread in Russia during the eighteenth century, when "contacts with the West brought into Russia sectarian Protestant ideas along with Western secular rationalism" (Billington 1970, 179). Molokanism also incorporates certain aspects of Jewish religious mysticism and some elements of Jewish communal service and dietary laws into their fundamentally Christian doctrine.

Regardless of the religious and cultural integration that it manifests, Molokanism is basically a Russian movement that grew out of cultural models of Russian peasantry but has evolved into unique forms. The Molokan conceptual universe is deeply mystical yet thoroughly rationalistic. A favorite Molokan expression offers valuable insight into this duality: Live and sing "by the spirit and by the mind."[10]

Although Molokans seek a high quality for their earthly life, probably stemming from their effort to build an independent and self-sufficient spiritual community in preparation for Christ's kingdom on earth,[11] material symbols have little significance in their religious life. Like other Russian sectarians, Molokans completely abandoned the Russian Orthodox Church. They did so by rejecting all ecclesiastical hierarchy, rituals, the calendar of feasts and fasts, and all material attributes pertaining to Russian Orthodoxy, including the most sacred of the sacred, the icon and the cross. They believed only in what they consider as internal spiritual aspects of Christianity, accepting only the symbolic essence of religious sacraments. Salvation accrues through faith alone, Molokans claim, not in the church's ritualistic celebration of sacraments made as "objects of human artistry." "The Lord is the Spirit," and the ultimate enlightenment of "receiving the Spirit," the Molokans believe, comes through experiences unfathomable by the senses and logic (Dogmas, 12–3). It is not to be sought in the material world, but only in the spiritual world through communal worship "in spirit and truth." Such a notion of spiritual and communal power, which is the key issue in Molokan self-identity as a group, is nicely summed up by their original name, *Spiritual* Christians.

The functioning and perpetuation of Molokan spiritual life transpire entirely within the community, with the exception of using the Bible, that is, "God's word," as their major source of spiritual nourishment. For Molokans, not unlike for fundamentalist Christians, the Bible has become not only the theological foundation of their beliefs, but also a lens through which they view, interpret, and gauge everyday life. Molokan interpretation of the Bible is largely associative and metaphoric rather than literal. The Molokans use this approach to find in the Bible guidance for practically any need, from interpretations of doctrinal concepts to explanations of their name, song structure, or the most pragmatic daily activity. Interpretation through analogy and metaphor becomes a favorable rhetorical instrument in any Molokan discourse.

Support System—*Zakon*

Molokans, like many other confessional groups, have established a whole order of life to separate themselves from *ne nashi*. Living in a state of consciousness affected by their perpetual separation from mainstream society, whether in Russia or elsewhere, Molokans were forced to take charge of their own lives, both spiritual and physical, in an orderly way. As Young has pointed out, in seeking to provide individuals with "a secure refuge against doubts, uncertainties, and conflicts, which rage outside the sect," their communal life has become highly structured (1932, 273). They call this order of life "our *zakon*," literally, the law. In a more inclusive way, however, Molokan unwritten *zakon* refers to a distinct and self-sufficient maintenance system responsible for the stability and well-being of the community. Through a system of privileges and obligations, restrictions and prohibitions, this self-imposed *zakon* governs not only pragmatic matters, from behavioral codes to sociocultural institutions, but also spiritual issues, including values, worldviews, and the relationship between humanity and God. Molokan singing too is regulated by *zakon*.

Today, many young and middle-aged Molokans consider their *zakon* to be "too hard, too strict and too demanding." Their struggle to live by the highest standards of *zakon* reveals the unbridgeable disparity between the realms of the doctrinal ideal and earthly necessities. At the same time, to fulfill its function as a guardian of Molokanism, *zakon* must be tolerant enough to accommodate and reconcile the inconsistencies of individual needs and internal tensions. Thus, a continuous dialogue of competing interpretations is supported by *zakon*. As frequent and heated as Molokan debates over *zakon* are, they are essential venues for individuals to construct and negotiate its new meanings. Understanding the significance of Molokan commitment to verbal discourse is important for our purpose here, as it helps build a conceptual framework for understanding Molokan singing. In Molokan teachings, singing exists only in the unbreakable unity with *slovo,* the word. "Music could never be an art. It [is] a form of speech," according to one Molokan singer (James Samarin 1975, 65).

The Role of the Verbal

While many closed communities are keen about self-reflection through words, the Molokans demonstrate an especially strong proclivity toward verbal expression. In aspiring to give their inner life a rational order, they devote great effort to constructing their ideas and experiences through verbal language. Molokan verbal discourse is dynamic, not reducible to specific categories and forms. Instead, it has generated a web of rhetorical situations corresponding to various occasions and contexts, including communal worship, training sessions, and private discussions. In this light, it is not by chance that Molokans have a strong tradition and history of practicing rhetorical discourse. They greatly appreciate the ability to articulate and develop one's thoughts in an orderly fashion and consider it a special gift from God. To utilize this gift fully, and motivated by the utmost respect for the written text, the community has produced a profusion of books containing creed, prayers, and songs through which they have systematized and rationalized their thoughts and beliefs.[12] Some Molokans have even published their personal discourses on spiritual matters individually. It is significant, in the context of our discussion, that the very first publication of dogmas had a chapter "On singing," and the first publication of *The Molokan Prayer Book* included a list of psalms to be sung at every communal function and ritual.

The distinct expressions and terms of Molokan verbal discourse are adopted from colloquial Russian language. Through metaphoric use these casual expressions and words have been either modified or refined in such ways that their connotations can no longer be easily articulated, but instead bear unique symbolic meanings. In a sense, they have become semiotic symbols. One does not have to search hard for these symbols of concepts and experiences that the Molokans themselves have singled out to denote their cognitive universe. It is enough to listen to the American Molokans who do not understand Russian. For the sake of preserving the symbolic meanings of these Russian expressions and terms, they use them without translation.

The Communal Worship and "Church Jobs"

Sobranie, translated here as "communal worship," literally means assembly of people.[13] The structure and communal nature of Molokan *sobranie* determines the ways in which singing is conducted. The service is guided by *prestol,*[14] a relatively large leadership group of experts. This is an all-male group of which each person is chosen by the Spirit or on the basis of his gift from God to carry out a particular function during *sobranie,* that is, a specific "church job." Church jobs manifest an order, based on a recognition of different gifts from God. The church jobs are the *presviter* (presbyter, minister), *besednik* (a discussant, commentator and interpreter), *pevets* (a singer), *skazatel'* (here, a reader or an announcer who prompts the psalm's text to a singer), and *prophet.* Only singers and prophets can be both men and women, but even if recognized for their gift from God, the women are not part of the *prestol* and sit separately (see fig. 4.1).

Although all church jobs are necessary for conducting a proper service, their makeup is elaborately hierarchical, and the hierarchy is maintained rather strictly. Church jobs also define the ways in which singing reflects the social fabric of the community. Each church job, with the exception of the prophets, is overseen by a *starshiy* (the head person), whose seniority in the hierarchy can be irrespective of age. A further ranking within each church job is based on various factors, including age, knowledge, skills, memory, wisdom, personal predisposition or God's gift, professional training, and *revnost'* (literally "jealousy," but in Molokan use means eagerness to acquire the expertise and to perfect the skills for the job).

The structure and communal nature of the Molokan *sobranie* in part determines the social make up of the community, and the church job hierarchy largely defines an individual's social status. Each job is a lifetime commitment and requires special expertise. Transmission of professional knowledge and skills is secured by formalized educational institutions and teaching processes specific to each church job. The job of *pevets* is considered one of the most difficult and requires many years of training.[15]

Holders of the jobs are all volunteers; Molokans seek direct contact with God in such a way that they reject the idea of intercession by paid clergy. Each

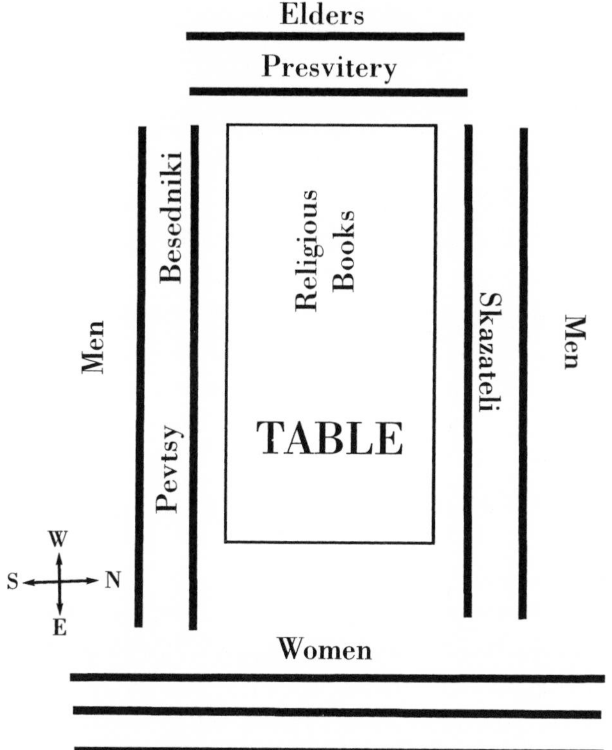

FIGURE 4.1. Molokan *Sobranie* seating arrangement

person is expected to contribute to the spiritual life of the community by contributing his own energy, thus helping build the communal spiritual power during *sobranie.* There are also no paid musicians. Musical instruments are not allowed, for they are considered objects of human artifice.[16] As far as singing is concerned, *sobranie* comprises only a cappella choral psalms and spiritual songs.[17]

"The order of service is simple," notes Pauline Young when describing the *sobranie* (1932, 32).[18] Indeed, *sobranie* does not contain any elaborate liturgical acts. Stripped of the effects of bright and solemn costumes, icons and frescos, lighting and incense, Molokan *sobranie* takes place between bare white walls with backless wooden benches. The only props are religious books on top of a plain rectangular table covered with white cloth. In rejecting all visual attributes of Orthodox religious service, however, *sobranie* has given different aural forms of verbal and non-verbal communication crucial roles in channeling spiritual energy among the worshiping community. As a result, even if the service order of *sobranie* is considered "simple," the ways in which its sonic aspects are pursued and managed are immensely intricate. The *sobranie*'s sonic aspects, once the dynamic relationships of all aural forms are considered, tellingly reflect rational order in Molokan spirituality.

Traditionally, *sobranie* consists of two parts. The first part includes several repetitions of a cycle consisting of a *beseda* (literally, a talk or a dialogue; but here a discourse, a special rhetorical situation and a kind of sermon by a *besednik*) and singing a *posalom* (old-Russian for *psalm*, both versions of the word are in current use), that is, singing a scriptural passage from the Russian version of the Bible, corresponding with, but not identical to, the King James Version. The cycle begins as the *presviter* who leads the service signals to the *starshiy besednik* to choose a *besednik* for the first *beseda*. The *besednik*'s task is to select and read a biblical passage and then interpret it in the light of the community's current concerns, using his specific gift and skills of discourse.[19] There follows the singing of a psalm. The process involves intricate interaction within the hierarchy of the entire *prestol* and the congregation. In brief, the singing can begin only after the *presviter* has given a signal to the *starshiy pevets*. The latter, in turn, assigns one of the *pevtsy* to select and lead a psalm. The selected *pevets* then becomes the main figure in the singing of this psalm. Meanwhile, the *starshiy skazatel'* assigns a *skazatel'*, whose responsibility is to recognize instantaneously the psalm, promptly find the text in the Bible, and call out a short passage that will be fitted to the melody by the *pevets*.

How melodic is the prompting of the *skazatel'* depends on the local school and personal talent, but his intoning must never disturb the mood of singing. The visual contact between *pevets* and the *skazatel'* is secured by the seating order; they are located across the *prestol* (see fig. 4.1). The job of *skazatel'* is to work in perfect coordination with the *pevets*, timing the reading and choosing the length of the prosaic text exactly as the particular *pevets* requires. If the *pevets* does not know the biblical passage from memory, a smooth performance largely depends on the *skazatel*'s skills. Note that an important characteristic of an experienced *pevets* is his ability to line up the words to the melody in a meaningful manner, so that the congregation can follow him. As the assigned *pevets* sings, other *pevtsy* support him, building the multivoice texture, appropriate for the local style.[20] The entire congregation participates in heterophonic singing *za sledom* (literally, "following one's footprints," here to follow the *pevets*). Then the *beseda*-psalm cycle repeats as many times as the *presviter* requires.

Ideally, the entire *sobranie* is unified by a theme, "the golden thread," to use a Molokan expression, that runs throughout the service. The interpretive commentary on a biblical passage read by a *besednik* does not stop with the end of his *beseda*. It continues in the succeeding singing of a psalm. The job of the *pevets*, thus, is not only to lead the singing *per se* but also to respond to the *beseda* and select an appropriate psalm instantaneously. Specific religious holidays or specific secular occasions certainly call for particular topics of the *beseda* and for particular psalms, but in a regular Sunday *sobranie,* the choice of the topic depends, to a large degree, on the first *besednik.* Sustaining the golden thread thus depends on the cooperation of all members of the *prestol* and their continuous concentration throughout *sobranie,* as they do not know in advance who is going to be called to officiate the next component of the service. Clearly, all church jobs require special expertise; all jobholders must be extremely knowledgeable of the scriptural text and have proficient skills in their particular duty. That is to say that the hierarchical nature of the "church jobs," while seemingly incongruent with an egalitarian community, is in fact indicative of a community that reveres order and also values equally the use of specific gifts from God to maintain order.

The climax of the *sobranie* falls in the second part, which consists mainly of the communal prayer proper, formed by the combination of various prayers. Before the second part begins, all the benches in the service space are quickly removed. The congregants stand throughout this part of the service. Thus, in contrast to the first part, where the *presviters, besedniki, skazateli, pevtsy,* prophets, male congregants, and, separately, female congregants all occupy well defined spaces, the communal prayer proper has all the congregants gathered in a conceptually and physically different space. Through their movement into this space, it is as if all the petitioners in the prayer were stripped of their professional and social positions to form a united body before God.[21]

Public, communal prayers offered either by a *presviter,* or by a *presviter*-assigned individual, must be perfectly memorized and recited so that everyone is able to hear him clearly. In contrast, other members of the congregation intone their individual prayers privately and spontaneously (the sonic form of the communal prayer will be discussed later). Concluding the *sobranie* is a symbolic communion ceremony accompanied by singing.[22] Subsequently, one more short prayer is recited and one more psalm or song is sung for the closure of the *sobranie,* traditionally forming the end of the Steadfast service. At the end, several additional spiritual songs may be sung; these can be started by women. In the Jumper churches, "spiritual jumping," under the influence of the Spirit, often occurs at this moment, although *deistvie* (acting in the Spirit manifested by raised hands, stomping feet, or other bodily gestures) may have occurred at any moment earlier. Prophecies may also take place at any time, with utterances in a tense and harsh voice as well as speaking in tongues.[23]

It should be clear from the above description that *sobranie* unfolds both "by the Spirit and by the mind." While spontaneity and flexibility of the choices made by the experts play an important role, the *sobranie* relies on the professional knowledge and skills of the experts, who work in dynamic relationships within the overall design predetermined by the *zakon*.[24] Ordinarily, as far as I have been able to observe, any deviation from this general structure occurs only under special circumstances and as an exception that needs to be justified and negotiated. The construction of negotiated meaning thus becomes an important instrument for introducing necessary transformations or deviations from this order, specifically at the moments when certain individuals or the entire community undergo some drastic changes or stress.

The Power of Singing

The *sobranie* involves different aural forms or sound modalities:[25] speaking, reading, sermonizing, praying, singing, and prophesying. Each *sound* modality has a distinct paralinguistic profile marked by specific tempo, volume, intensity, timbre, pitch contour, and duration. For Molokans, all aural forms used in *sobranie* are based on the Scripture, God's word. And "God's word is made of sound," teaches one of the spiritual leaders of the Fresno community. Yet the symbolic power of the different forms of God's word is not the same. It seems that for Molokans, the power of God's word consists not only in the meanings or contents of the word, but also in the *sound* modalities through which it is delivered. Of all the modalities on the *sound* continuum of *sobranie*, singing is attributed with a particularly great power. God's word, when sung, occupies a remarkably high point in the service in the eyes of the congregants.

Many religious communities recognize the enormous symbolic power of singing in engendering collective experience. Some of them in fact privilege participation in the communal act of singing so much that they seem to show little concern for the technical and expressive quality of the actual singing. It is not so for the Molokans, for whom singing can either stifle or vitalize the *sobranie*, and "good" singing is crucial. They even have the concept of "a quality singer," although its precise definition is not easy to construct. "Singing brings man to God," many Molokans say, and a "poor" performance during the *sobranie* might prevent the congregants from reaching a spiritual state where they could communicate directly with God.

Singing as a source of spiritual power is a common discourse among the Molokans: "Singing is to melt the heart, and then your heart opens itself to God's word. Singing reveals the word of God to man." In their universe, singing thus is not only inseparably bound to God's word, but also has the power to make the work of the Spirit tangible and directly accessible for people. The connection of singing and spiritual energy is not simply an abstract theological notion written down in the creed and used in rhetorical situations; it is a very actual and personal experience, one of the most valuable experiences of Molokan worship today. A number of skilled leaders say that it is singing, more than anything else, in which they engage during the *sobranie*, in order to communicate with the divine. In the act of communicating with the divine, singing is indispensable:

> First, the singers start singing, and this will bring us the spirit, *but not before the singers start singing.* God says: "If you want me to tell you something, call the singers, and then I will speak the word to you." We sing to praise God, and if He wants to announce something to us, He will do this through our singing." (emphasis added)

It appears that in the context of the *sobranie*, "God's word" is understood as a metaphor for the "presence of the Holy Spirit." Liturgical singing is the primary instrument in building up the presence.[26] Thus, sanctity does not reside in the psalms and spiritual songs as such, but rather in the instance when the psalms and songs are sung.[27]

Undoubtedly, singing is an act of the divine for Molokans, whose image of heaven is impregnated with singing: "All those who have earned their access to heaven sing. There [in heaven], they do not work, neither do they eat; they only sing." Yet while Molokan singing is a divine act, not least because it channels the work of the Spirit in guiding the selection of psalms and songs in the *sobranie*, it is at the same time a rational act. There is abundant evidence that Molokans sing as much "by the mind" as "by the spirit." First of all, many Molokan psalms are highly complex, demanding sophisticated musical skills; they are also impossible for the congregation to sing without the competent leadership of the *pevtsy*. Second, the rationality of Molokan singing is manifested in the thematization of their psalms. A number of Molokan psalms are occasion-specific. These psalms are divided into various categories on the basis of their message. There are psalms to console, to beseech, and to give thanks; there are also psalms for funerals, weddings, birthdays, and house warming. Out of more than a thousand psalms in the community's collective memory, however, only a few share a common theme to make them suitable for the same occasion. In choosing a psalm, it is necessary to match the psalm's message with the golden thread of the *sobranie*. Choosing a psalm proper for an occasion is of great importance; it is a task left to the *pevtsy*—the ones with the greatest gift in this area of expertise among the community.

All its unique Molokan features notwithstanding, the sonic in the *sobranie* has a function shared by the sonic in similar ritualized contexts in other cultures: to induce a truly communal experience among the congregants. In the words of one Molokan, "[Through] singing, the Spirit comes to other people [. . .] so everyone will be united." This function also produces a coalescence of the emotional and the rational, a process clearly manifested in the performance of the skillful *pevtsy*. In singing during *sobranie*, the *pevtsy* have to be fully in control—appropriately detached—at all times in their response to various ritualized situations, without becoming too excited or involved (Mazo 1990, 119–20). Arguably, it is precisely the sense of communal unity created through synergetic states of many different individuals during singing that contributes to the emotional intensity and potency of the worship.

Transformations of Singing during *Sobranie*

The communal worship styles of the Steadfast and Jumpers are not exactly the same. Accordingly, their singing also differs in certain ways. If both psalms and spiritual songs are essential for the Jumpers, the Steadfast Molokans allow songs in worship only after the *sobranie* proper has ended, if there is any singing at all.

During the *sobranie* of the Jumpers, when physical manifestations of God's blessing are sought, appropriate singing helps the participants achieve a religious trance-like state they call *deistvovat'* (literally, "to act," but used by Molokans in a sense of "being in the Spirit"). The works of the Spirit bring changes in the physical behavior of the individual congregants and induce the jumping that gives the group its name. Although prophetic ecstasy and *deistvie*, the definitive assurances of the community's spiritual vitality in the eyes of the Jumpers, can occur any time, they often commence during singing and cease as soon as singing stops. Moreover, according to one Molokan singer, singing has always been used for the attainment of *deistvie*. This duality of spontaneity induced by divine inspiration and mediation controlled by one's professional singing skills is not perceived by the Jumpers as a contradiction: "Music has never been held in greater honor, nor cultivated with more judgment and high artistic sense, spiritually speaking, than at the time when a song properly sung arouses the prophet to ecstasy." For this singer, "To prophesy meant to sing, and there is little doubt that Isaiah, Jeremiah, and others uttered their prophecies in song" (James Samarin 1975, 68 and 65).

An experienced observer can anticipate the approach of *deistvie* from changes in the singing. Musical patterns become more fixed, easier to recognize and predict, thereby drawing less attention to themselves; they are meant to pave and adorn the road toward taking part in the congregants' most significant trance-like experience. In my observations, the communal *deistvie* is not connected with what a musicologist would select as the most powerful melodies. On the contrary, they are the "simplest" ones, consisting of one laconic pattern repeated over and over with accelerating tempo, swelling volume, and growing intensity of sound. Molokans call this type of singing *udarítel'noe* (from *udarénie*, "emphasis," or "accent"), a term that eludes precise definition but can be loosely rendered as percussive, accentuated, forceful, and emphatic. Unlike psalms at the beginning of sobranie, *udaritel'noe* singing is syllabic, it is not smooth, but rather staccato-like, with frequent and forceful breathing.[28] The character of musical prosody also changes in *udaritel'noe* singing; the accentuation of every beat-syllable becomes more and more intense, thereby transforming the melody's metric pattern into a throbbing one-pulse meter. The speed and the rhythm of jumping, as far as I could observe, concur with the pulse of the song. "We want the Holy Spirit, that is why there is rhythm," says an elder woman, "jumping and rhythm are related." I have never observed any significant deviation between the voices, either in melodic contour or rhythm. The participants breathe and sing as one, and their individual energies completely synchronize and become one synergetic whole.

The spiritual life of the Steadfast Molokans is less apparent to an observer, but here, too, singing intensifies during the service through increasing the voices' volume and intensity and gradually raising the pitch level. In both denominations, the climax of the service, the communal prayer, is a complex sonic whole: a prayer recited by the *presviter* sounds simultaneously with the personal prayers of all the others. These individual petitions to God blend into a single multivoice communal moaning, in which individual voices are hardly perceptible. Careful listening, however, reveals that most often the individual petitions are expressed in a form close to Russian village lament (dirge or keening), in which melodic recitation is mixed with tears and sobbing, sometimes even wailing.[29] As during other village rituals that use simultaneous laments (e.g., funerals and weddings), all participants employ the same melodic formula, although each renders it in an individual way. As with village laments, these individual prayers occupy the border of musical, paramusical, and paralinguistic expression. The application of laments during the communal prayer becomes conceivably more comprehensible if one keeps in mind that lamenting, not unlike such prayer, brings a cathartic feeling of relief.[30]

The instability of pitch in laments is one of the important indicators of the performer's emotional involvement. Similarly, in Molokan psalms sung during the first part of *sobranie*, before the communal prayer, the pitch level is usually unstable and rises within each psalm.[31] After the communal prayer, of which the prayer-lament is a prominent component, the local pitch level becomes more stable, or even entirely stable. The particulars of the pitch level certainly vary from case to case, but I observed this general tendency during many Molokan services, both in Russia and the United States.[32] The process of "praying" or "petitioning," here often with lamenting, helps to bring out an outburst of extreme emotional intensity, and as a result, the state of catharsis is achieved. Thereafter, the pitch level becomes more stable.

During the first part of the ritual, before the prayer, each *sound* modality is temporally well defined and can be isolated from the others in a sequence: reading followed by a discussion, pronouncing, and singing. Later, at the climactic moment of the service, distinct *sound* modalities become compressed in the ritual's metaphorical time and space. This is to say that the boundaries between separate modalities become ephemeral as the sounds of the "public" prayer, singing, and private prayers-laments fuse into one sonic whole. It is worth repeating that we have already observed a consolidation of all the congregants in the physical space of the Molokan *sobranie* as well.

Molokan Psalms: Transmission, Formal Features, and Performance Practices

Molokan oral history preserves many legends and stories about Molokan singing and singers. According to the legends, the early forefathers of the Molokans devoted great attention to seeking special forms of songs and approaches to singing. As one legend goes, Semen Uklein, the preeminent founder of Molokanism, sent special messengers all around Russia and to Cossack villages to listen to local songs and collect good ideas for Molokan psalms.[33] Indeed, Molokan singing exhibits various kinds of subtle and obvious ties with folk song. Molokan singing of psalms, nonetheless, has evolved into completely unique forms.

The transmission of Molokan singing relies on a combination of oral and written forms. Words of psalms and songs are, as a rule, transmitted as written texts. Psalm texts themselves comprise actual printed scriptural passages. Texts of spiritual songs are usually written down as soon as they are composed (or given to the individual believer by the Spirit) and then distributed as written poems. The text of a spiritual song can be created (or given) with or without a melody, but the melodies of both psalms and songs are always transmitted orally. While songs are still being actively composed, only one small group of singers in the Stavropol' area in South Russia, as far as I know, "is working" on psalm melodies, that is, composing new melodies or adapting existing melodies for different scriptural texts. The names of the creators of Molokan psalms and songs usually are not announced and are known only to a closed circle of people. Because the psalms and songs are both the source and the manifestation of the communal power, they are considered to be something belonging to the entire community.

Before addressing the way in which Molokan psalms function within oral transmission, a brief examination of their salient musical characteristics is in order. In a 1911 study, Evgeniya Linyova[34] offered the earliest and still the most comprehensive published discussion of the general characteristics of Molokan psalms:

> The singing is very broad and melodious. Under the influence of the dignified, flowing style arises a deep religious feeling, not ascetic or gloomy, but gladsome, full of life. Very remarkable is the form of the musical period. The text of the psalms is not rhymed, and this necessitates a very long musical period, quite as long as the corresponding verse. The working-out of such broad melody, which passes a complicated design of free-voice parts, necessitates a very gradual crescendo and a complete absorption of the singers in the musical and ideal contents of the psalm. (Linyova 1911, 188–89)

Sung directly to nonrhymed scriptural passages, psalm melodies have to accommodate prose phrases of different lengths and accent patterns. This results in their exceptionally elaborate formal structures and asymmetrical phrases, some of which can be repeated as many times as the particular text passage requires.

Figure 4.2 presents a comparison of two analytical transcriptions of the same psalm, sung by two Russian and two American lead *pevtsy*.[35] The visual alignment of the transcriptions reveals that regardless of all the differences, these are two versions of the same melody. The melody is "difficult," according to the singers. Indeed, the intricacy of this melody is not easy to grasp at once. Yet this makes their similarity striking, especially considering that the melodies have been orally transmitted separately thousands of miles apart for almost a century. In 1990, when I recorded both melodies, these Russian and American performers had never heard or seen each other; there had been no contacts between these two communities for many decades. This fact brings up an important and fascinating question of stability in oral transmission, though this discussion cannot be undertaken here.

The spatial layout of the transcriptions in figure 4.2, with the similar melodic gestures aligned vertically, also reveals how the melody as a whole evolves through repetition and subtle variation. The melodic building blocks, expanded or constricted in various ways, are almost never repeated exactly. The design of this melody is certainly very complex, but, like other psalms, it has its own

II. California Singers Only

♩ = 40 Zapev

Ya ska- za - l sa. . . (a) - - - - l sa - - m se - be ya pri

I. Stavropol Singers (St. I)

♩ = 60 **Zapev**

Ya

II. California Singers (Ca. II)

po - lo -

St. I

ya (a) s - ka - (a) - - - za -

Ca. II

vi - - ne ne dnei

St. I

(a) - - l p - ri po - - - - (o) - lo - vi - - ni d - ne i mo... mo - ikh I ya do...

Ca. II

mo - - j - - - - kh do... do - l - zhen i ya jd - i i - va

St. I

do - l - zhe

Ca. II

ti vo vo

St. I

(e)- n i... i - d - ti vo v - ra... vra - ta

Ca. II

vo vo ya vo vra -

St. I

ya - pre - i - s- po-d-nei

Ca. II

ta ya pre - i - s- po-d-nei

specific logic, making the melody recognizable in various performances and in various local styles.

Many psalm melodies, like the one in figure 4.2, show strong links with *protyazhnaya* songs (long-drawn-out),[36] the most elaborate and melismatic form of Russian village song, even though Molokan psalms are different in many respects (cf. fig. 4.3).

Like *protyazhnaya*, the psalm's melody is characterized by aperiodic construction; both begin with a solo *zapev* (song's opening), a melodic gesture whose tonal content and overall shape determine the unfolding of the entire melody. Both are sung at a slow tempo, with the melody stretching out the text through extensive melismata. In both, the melisma is not a mere decoration; rather it is such an integral part of the melody that removing it will virtually destroy the melody's musical sense and unity. The syllables are not only lengthened, but also may be repeated, the vowels transformed, and particles and exclamations added, so that the sung text becomes almost incomprehensible. Yet contrary to what one might expect, when performed properly, the melismata, in spite of the various kinds of "interruptions," contribute to rather than disturb the song's artistic coherence. As in folk *protyazhnaya*, they endow the psalms with "a quality that fascinates by its freshness and power" (Lopatin 1956, 96). *Protyazhnaya* is known in many local styles. The style known in many local traditions in the South Russian and Cossack regions as singing with a *podgolos*, a solo upper voice with an elaborate melodic embellishment (see fig. 4.3), is particularly similar to a large group of Molokan psalms.

In spite of all the variations in performances, Molokan *pevtsy* insist that many "difficult" psalms, as the one in figure 4.2, require extensive memorization: "You must learn the melody and sing it exactly the same, every time. You cannot cut something or add something, and if you do, you can easily turn the melody into a different psalm, lose it altogether, and confuse everybody." Many psalms are built from similar melodic gestures that are varied slightly or substantially and put together in different ways; it is indeed easy to see how one can "lose" a psalm. In addition, unlike in *protyazhnaya*, the text alignment in psalms is not fixed, but varies in each stanza and each performance, depending largely on communication between the *pevets* and the *skazatel'*. The melody has to be so familiar to the *pevets* that he may concentrate on fitting

FIGURE 4.2. *Ya skazal pri polovine dnei moikh* (I Said in the Cutting Off of My Days.) Isaiah 38:10. Comparison of a Russian and American versions of the psalm recorded in 1990.

FIGURE 4.3. Don Cossack *protyazhnaya* song transcribed by Alexander Listopadov in 1900 in a Don Cossack village Yermakovskaya (Listopadov, 1906, 214).

the prose in a sensible way, permitting other *pevtsy* and the congregants to follow him comfortably.

Accordingly, oral transmission of psalm melodies is more formalized than in folk song practices, with more conscientious memorization and less improvisation. This is not to say that improvisation is excluded from the performance of the psalms and every interpretation is "exactly the same" in the sense of written music. In comparison with Russian folk song, however, the boundaries of freedom in each performance appear to be closer to the regulations of written tradition and are confined to nonformal properties. Conforming to the rules of oral transmission, each singer has his own version of the melody, but my recordings of the same psalm by the same singers show an unusual degree of stability over a period of five years. The psalm transmission process, then, reflects how the overall Molokan *zakon* perpetuates itself. If we take this parallel a step farther, one may argue that the liturgical performance of the psalms, with its hierarchical relationships between all participants and its intricate design, appears as a small-scale replica of the dynamic relationships between the components of the *sobranie* and Molokan spiritual universe at large.

Comparison of American and Russian Singing

Molokans, always conscious of their own history, are fascinated to hear the singing of their brothers living across the ocean. I asked American Molokan singers to comment on psalms and songs recorded from their counterparts in Russia. In response, they often connect the differences in singing with differences in their life. Commenting on the singing of spiritual songs (not psalms), one prominent singer said, betraying his everyday life in Los Angeles through his reference to freeways:

> We sing a song as we live our life. We are rushing, and it is not right, because the Molokan singing is sad, sorrowful. In Russia we were in need, and we sang sorrowfully. But we have everything and don't need a thing. We jump on freeways, rush and run for money. And this is how we sing. . . . We should sing to melt the heart, but we sing to do the jumping.

Later, commenting specifically on a practice of singing psalms (not spiritual songs), he added:

> They lessen the *kolyshki* [roughly, "swaying"; a term of American Molokans to indicate melisma], and here we expand the *kolyshki*. . . .

> We sing like our costume, lace on top of lace on top of lace, with a lot of *kolyshki.*

Comparing the singing of the same psalm by *pevtsy* from Russia and California in figure 4.2 may serve as a testimony to what he said. The American melody appears to be an extended version of the Russian one. The American version is slower and longer. It is even more melismatic, melodically elaborate and free ("lace on top of lace, with a lot of *kolyshki*"). Structural augmentation comes through large- and small-scale procedures, particularly salient in the addition of new melodic phrases at strategic points of the melody (see an elaborate melodic phrase as a new *zapev* by the Californian singers in figure 4.2).[37] The similarity between the American and Russian versions of a psalm is not always as self-evident as in figure 4.2. Many, however, are recognizable, particularly if a psalm has a unique melodic or rhythmic gesture (e.g., the octave leap downward before the cadential phrases in figure 4.2).

American *pevtsy* often comment on the voice quality of their Russian counterparts. Having a nice, "beautiful" timbre is not as crucial for Russian "quality *pevets*" while an American "quality *pevets*" must have "a good voice." It is not by chance that many notable American Molokans have recordings of famous singers in their homes (Chaliapin, Lemeshev, Sobinov, Caruso, Lanza, Pavarotti). Neither is it accidental that American *pevtsy* who attended music classes in American public schools became interested in taking professional voice lessons in order to acquire some of the vocal techniques and vocabulary of classical musicians. This naturally has influenced both their manner of singing and vocal production, making them quite distant from the "folk manner" and "harsh voices" of traditional *pevtsy* in Russian villages.

Keeping Russian Melody versus Russian Language

If we compare the way Russian and American singers handle the verbal text, we find a picture somewhat different from their handling of melody. While lining up the words to the melody after the *skazatel',* Russian *pevtsy* exhibit more freedom. They may change some words, omit or modify others, repeat some syllables, and finish the melodic stanza not necessarily at the same point as the *skazatel'.* American *pevtsy* approach the text with more restraint than their Russian brothers. This is understandable, since for many singers Russian is no longer the language they know best.

For third-generation American Molokans, Russian has become only the language of the ritual, like Latin or Hebrew in other liturgies. Young people do not understand it and cannot participate fully in the service. Still, until recently, maintaining the Russian language, at least as the language of religious rites, and, on a broader scope, of Russian culture, was an untouchable and a highly sensitive issue. Conducting *sobranie*, at least partially, in Russian has been perceived as part of the Molokan *zakon* itself, and while English has been acceptable for *beseda* in some churches, prayers and psalms must be in Russian.

Today, many among the third- and fourth-generation American Molokans identify themselves as Russians, even though disparity between the two cultures is sharply sensed: "The Russian mind is different from the American one." Moreover, for the majority of American Molokans, the Russian language is thought to be an essential component of doctrine itself. Russian Baptists, Pentecostals, and Adventists living in the United States convert their service into English much more easily, and the loss of the language does not necessarily cause the weakening of their self-identity. For the Molokans, keeping the Russian language is apparently so crucial that they refuse to compromise even in the face of serious consequence: A number of younger people who do not understand the service and are not able to follow it gradually distance themselves from the church. The issue of the interrelations between religious, ethnic, and cultural matters is much debated in the community, and the opinions vary even within one family.

Among several strategies that the American Molokans have adopted, one is very radical and deserves mention, especially because it has never been recorded in the literature as far as I know. A small group of young families in Oregon, who call themselves a Reform Molokan Church, following the path of other religious groups in United States, changed the language of the entire *sobranie* into English. The Oregon group is fighting in their own way to keep memory and culture alive, trading the language for the spiritual survival of Molokanism. The rhetoric about the significance of Russian is quite different in this church. For its members, the inseparability of ethnic, cultural, and religious matters is no longer an issue:

> Some people think Molokan is a nation; it is not. If you are a Molokan, you're only a Molokan because of the religion. [If] you join into this religion, into this church, then you are a Molokan. It is not a certain kind of a people or a certain race of people. You could be a Molokan. To be a Molokan you, first of all, have to receive Jesus Christ. That makes you a Christian. To be a Molokan, when you join our church, you agree to abide by the by-laws. Then you are a Molokan.

Negotiating and redefining the meaning of some fundamental concepts of Molokanism by the members of the Reform church is presently very much in progress. The rhetorical discourse of the young leaders of this church promotes flexibility, an inclusive and accommodating approach that allows people with very different backgrounds to feel comfortable, thus manifesting an important departure from traditional rhetoric of the *ne nashi*. It may be too early to reach definitive conclusions, but as far as I know, conducting the entire *sobranie* only in English has been rigorously followed. During our conversations, the leaders would use Russian words freely—particularly those related to spiritual and religious matters: *Presviter, pevets, skazatel', beseda, byt' v dukhe,* and so on—just like American Molokans in all other churches. In the formal setting of *sobranie,* however, even these have been translated as a matter of principle.

Singing is no exception: Psalms and songs are sung in English. At the same time, remarkably, Reform Molokans use only Russian melodies. Converting the sung portions of the Molokan service into English requires that they solve some technical difficulties. The strategies chosen for songs and psalms have been different. The lead singers say that the conversion of psalms to English, contrary to what one would expect, has been a relatively easy matter. Figure 4.4 illustrates this process by overlapping transcriptions of the same melody sung by the same singer of this church in Russian and English.[38]

In the English version, neither the structure of the melody nor the melodic details are changed. The singers do subject the English text to some of the procedures borrowed directly from a characteristic treatment of the text in Russian psalms. One can identify at least three such procedures. First, they extend certain syllables with long melismata. Second, they add vowels or semivowels into clusters of consonants, like "bre-th(e)-ren(e)" or "da-r(e)-k(e)-ness," even if this makes the English words sound quite awkward. Third, they inserted non-lexical syllables—"yo," "ya," "ah," "oh," and so on—into the text. Lining up these additional syllables with the melody and distributing the entire text over the melody coincide strikingly with the Russian version, in spite of the differences of structure or meaning in the English language. As a result, if there were a notion of a musical accent, their English singing can be said to have a strong Russian accent.

FIGURE 4.4. *No vy brat'ya ne vo t'me* (But You Brethren, Are Not in Darkness), 1 Thessalonians 5:4. The psalm, sung in Russian (top staff) and English (bottom staff) by the same singer, was recorded in 1990.

♩ = 78 Zapev
(ye) No (ah)
♩ = 80
(a) Bu - - - (u)t
(ye) (ah) (oh) (ah) (ah) no vy (ah) (yeh) (a) (oo)
(u) (ah) (yeah) (ah) bu - (u)t you (ah) (ah) (ye)(ah ah)
(ah) (yeh) (oh) (ah) (ay)(ah)(ye) vy bra... (ye) (ah) (oh) (a) (a) no- vy b- ra - ti - ya
(oh) (ah) (ah)(yeh)(ah) (ah) (ah)(ye)(ah)(ah)(ah) bu - (u)t you (ah) (yeah) (oh) (ah) bu- (u)t you bro- th(e) - re -
(ah) (ah) (a) (a)
- n(e) (ye) (oh) (ah) (yeah) (ah)
(ya) (ye) (a) (ye) (ah)
(ah) (ye)(ah) (ah) are not (ye) (ah)
(ye)(ah) (ah) (ay) (ye)(ah)(ay)(a) (ye)(ah) ne vo- ti - me.
(a) (ah) (ah) (ah)(ye)(ah)(ah) are not (ah) (ye) (oh) (ah) are not in da- r(e)- k(e)- ness.

Handling songs has been more difficult. At the beginning, the Reform Molokans decided to keep the melodies unchanged and to manipulate the text to fit them:

> I think that when I adapt a song [from Russian into English] I do it so that the English words fit the melody. That's the primary concern. I retain the biblical thought, so that I don't deviate from that. . . . When I adapt a song, I just make it [the English text] fit the tune that has been already established.

A year later, the same singer came to distinguish the process of "adaptation" from that of "translation:"

> My preference is no longer to take a set of words and adapt them to the established tunes. My preference from now on is to translate the words exactly. . . . But if I come up with new words, I am also to come up with a new tune as well.

The very existence of the group of Molokans who take issue of translation into English to such extremes has generated immense friction in the community, deepening their separatism even further. Often, the members of the Reform church are shunned even by their parents, who believe that converting the sung texts to English causes their children to cease being Molokans. In the early 1990s, when I first visited the Reform group, there were only a few members, certainly not enough to declare the church to be officially functioning. Less than a year later, there were about thirty-five people during a regular Sunday service, and they have officially registered the church.

Resettling the Culture

Regardless of their different histories and living conditions during the twentieth century, Molokans in both Russia and the United States are undergoing a similar spiritual development. In both countries, they make a serious effort to preserve Molokanism and keep the younger generations within the tradition. In both countries, albeit in rather contrasting ways, Molokans feel threatened by the dynamics of contemporary life. If in Russia and the USSR Molokanism had to withstand religious and ideological repression, in the USA the pressure comes, above all, from the gradual loss of language and new economic and cultural orientations.

Continuity of living space is often considered an issue of cultural conservation. For any culture, migration—change of living space—is like uprooting a plant into a different soil. But for several Russian confessional groups (Old Believers, Dukhobors, and Baptists), living in diaspora has also been a factor that has stimulated the preservation of culture, no matter where the groups settle. Throughout their numerous migrations over the last two centuries, Molokans have thus far been able to negotiate a balance between preserving the old and creating the new. Molokans welcome an opportunity to borrow a melody and make any tune they like into their own song to praise God, at either religious gatherings or social occasions. Hit songs of all kinds, including songs from Soviet films and popular American songs, have landed in their repertory: "Amazing Grace," "It's the Last Rose of Summer," "Clementine," and "Red River Valley," just as "*Korobochka*," "*Kogda b imel zlatye gory*," and "*Na zakate khodit paren'*" have provided melodies for favorite spiritual songs. Émigré culture is often characterized as operating between two poles: memory on the one side and adaptation on the other. Among Molokans it is usually singing that fills in the continuum: A traditional psalm melody ensures continuity with the past, while composing and learning new songs link the past with the present.

Any small cultural enclave is unique, and often a single factor can change its practices drastically. A critical mass of people and the sufficiency of their singing repertory, for example, may be crucial for the survival of the Reform Molokan group. Most recently, one major change has affected the American Molokan community at large. As a result of new politics in Russia, the Americans were able to reestablish connections with their historical brethren. Singing together is always a high point of their meetings, and a cassette with recorded psalms and songs is one of the most precious gifts.

Molokans and village communities in Russia, no doubt, share many historical links. Many outer signs may serve as an example: An American Molokan man who wears a specially tailored shirt with a rope-like belt (granted, made from silk threads); a woman whose head must be always covered with a shawl (granted, made from lace); or one who speaks in a distinctly rural South Russian dialect and keeps in the closet a handwritten notebook with charms, almost identical with charms circulating all over rural Russia (granted, written down in Latin characters). Perhaps even more important, the spiritual life of Russian peasants prior to World War II, unlike that of the city-dwellers, was not a separate sphere of their daily life. Faith for these peasants was a way of living, permeating every aspect of daily life. Molokans, through their understanding of religion as a syncretic entity with no compartmentalization between life and faith, are closely tied to other peasant communities in Russia. The modern world leaves less and less space to such non-compartmentalized living for Russian Molokans, and even less so for their American brothers and sisters.

The Molokans, however, have always been distinct from other peasant communities in Russia. There is evidence that many Russian peasants had a rather limited knowledge about Christianity as a religious doctrine and often were not particularly interested in learning this side of religion (Mazo, 1991). The icons and *dukhovnye stikhi* (spiritual verses, songs with religious subjects sung outside the church) were often the peasants' most typical sources for knowledge of Christian creed.[39] In contrast to the Russian peasantry, perhaps because of their status as outcastes and oppositionists, practically all Molokan men and many women have knowledge, sometimes in-depth knowledge, of the Molokan doctrine and the Bible. This is one of the requirements of the unwritten *zakon*.

By Way of Conclusions

Obviously, in order for Molokanism to survive, the *zakon* has to be open for interpretation and allow some flexible readjustments to keep a balance not only with the needs of the individuals and their ever-changing physical environment, but also, in view of their pilgrimage, with the socio-cultural environment. Most Molokans prefer not to discuss the issue of change and modern adjustment with outsiders. Instead, they emphasize that the *zakon*, carefully guarded by the elders, is still strongly observed in the community,[40] even though many complain that "it is getting harder and harder to comply with." Opinions, however, vary. Those who consider a strict observance of the *zakon* to be necessary for the survival of Molokanism are opposed by some younger voices saying that without adequate flexibility Molokanism cannot compete with the advances in modern society.

No doubt, the inner dynamics of Molokanism contain opposing tendencies. In Molokan ideal reality, the community's life is oriented toward history and tradition; historical events that took place in a distant past are recounted continuously and what happened to Molokan forefathers is relevant directly to the present, at least rhetorically: "We live and pray exactly as our forefathers did." New features are introduced slowly and seemingly imperceptibly through the process of constructing the negotiated meaning. Some Molokans in Russian villages, for example, still refuse and forbid their children to watch television while many are among the first to use cars, tape recorders, and other modern technologies. In contrast, American Molokans do not object to any technology on ideological grounds. On the whole, Molokan communities appear to be open to anything in the outside world that can be useful for spiritual and economic prosperity. In Russia, it is perhaps not by chance that the Molokans were quick to take advantage of the new political and economic freedoms. It is perhaps also not a coincidence that most of the Molokan newcomers to the United States love what they call "the American way of living," with its dynamic necessity to make choices constantly and quickly, importance of personal prosperity, and respect for professional skills. Yet, the response to the environment in most Molokan communities can be described as one with a centric orientation: quickly responding to modern advantages but strictly warding off outsiders. Molokans do not encourage inviting *ne nashi* to their gatherings; most often, their beautiful and powerful singing is not known even to their neighbors. Will the new generation want—and will it be able—to continue "living in the world without being a part of it," as an old Molokan saying suggests? Experiences of other ethnic and religious communities in the United States offer no single answer.

I sit at the festive table with the Molokans gathering for the house-warming ritual that will secure the well-being of a young family in its new, very American, house in Whittier, a very American town in the greater Los Angeles area. I am overwhelmed by the feeling that I have already seen it all just a few months ago, in a small South-Russian village near Stavropol', at the foot of the Caucasus Mountains. The entire order of the *sobranie* and the following feast seem the same as there. The hostess brings in a ten-inch tall, round loaf of freshly-made bread with a salt shaker on top of it; men and women are clothed in the same light colors and patterns as in Stavropol'; all the men have long beards. The meal unfolds through distinct courses, and their order is familiar as well: Tea, borscht, lamb stew, fruit compote, with pieces of bread spread all over the table, not on plates but directly on the table cloth. The room, with long parallel rows of tables and benches, is filled with familiar and dignified singing. The language one hears, however, is not just Russian; women's dresses and men's shirts are made from much more expensive fabrics than in Russia; as far as I can see through the window, the street is packed with American cars of all models. After a while, the singing too appears to sound somewhat different from what I heard in Stavropol'. I still find it astounding to be in the heart of the most American urban setting and in a world that at this moment appears so strikingly Russian and Molokan.

Postscript

Completed in 1994, this article imparts a particular moment in Molokan history as well as a particular moment in the history of ethnomusicological studies. It also reflects a certain point in my own experience as a scholar. Certainly, the communities have changed since that time, new issues have come forth, and much has changed in my own interpretive thinking.[41] Several scholars, including myself, have since published new works on Molokan culture and music. Nevertheless, to preserve the historical perspective of this study, no significant revisions have been undertaken during the final preparation of this article for print, and no references have been added to research published since 1994.

NOTES

1. Most of the people I interviewed requested that their names not be used in print. Throughout this article, field interviews are cited in quotation marks but without personal attribution.

The article is based primarily on field research between 1989 and 1994 in Russia and the United States as part of a larger research and representation project on Russian cognate cultures. The project focuses on cultural continuity and change under different social and cultural conditions. I gratefully acknowledge support from the Office of Folklife and Cultural Studies at the Smithsonian Institution and Director Richard Kurin, Russian Research Institute for Cultural and Natural Heritage (Moscow) and Director Yury Vedenin, Russian Ministry of Culture, and the Center for Studies on Russian Folklore in Moscow. In 1990 I invited Dr. Seraphima Nikitina, a linguist from the Institute of Language Studies at the Russian Academy of Sciences, to join the project. Our collaborative work on an article about the verbal components of Molokan culture has mutually enriched our understanding of field data. I thank the graduate students in my seminars on Russian music at Ohio State University for their stimulating responses to my research. A particular acknowledgment goes to Margaret Bdzil, Kathy Gruber, and Vladimir Marchenkov for translating into English some parts of my field interviews, and Deborah Andrus, Todd Harvey, Olga Velichkina, and Deborah Wilson for transcribing some of the recorded melodies. Olga Velichkina also worked as my assistant in 1989 field research in Russia. I am indebted to Andrey Conovaloff, who introduced me to the Molokan communities in California and Oregon and helped throughout my first field research there. Most of all, my deep gratitude goes to many individual Molokans in the US and Russia, who invited me to their homes, shared with me their personal libraries and recordings of the best Molokan singers, past and present, and who welcomed me to their services.

2. This comes forth in an overwhelming number of field interviews both in Russia and USA. It also echoes prominently the response from one of the most respected Molokan elders of the Los Angeles community interviewed by the American ethnomusicologist Linda O'Brien-Rothe. When asked what a Molokan is, he responded, "A Molokan is a person who sings the psalms." He then elaborated, "When Molokans no longer sing the psalms in their services, they would cease to be Molokans" (1989, 1).

Every observer who had visited Molokan communities commented on the power and importance of their singing. However, only two works published prior to 1994, contain specific studies of Molokan singing. In 1911, Linyova was the first to publish transcriptions of Molokan songs and psalms. The next study, by Linda O'Brien-Rothe, appeared only in 1989.

3. For the history of Molokanism and Molokan ways of life in the English language see Young (1932), Dunn (1983), Klibanov (1982), Moore (1973), and Morris (1981). The current article does not incorporate works published after 1994.

4. "Molokan "psalm" is sung on a scriptural passage selected from any part of the Bible, and not necessarily only from "The Book of Psalms." Thus, the Molokan repertory of psalms numbers in the hundreds.

5. Connections between Molokan singing and Russian village and urban songs are multifaceted and need to be explored in a broader context of Russian musical traditions. In this way, Linda O'Brien-Rothe's work is pioneering (1989). Notwithstanding its limitations, which are largely due to the overall lack of scholarly information on Russian folk song outside Russia, she revealingly traces some melodies of spiritual songs to well-known popular songs and other published sources.

6. Many American Molokans resent being called a sect. In Russian, *sekta* (a sect) is any religious group that has dissented from the mainstream Orthodox Church. Only *starovery* (Old Believers), who also left the mainstream church, but maintained the old order of Russian Orthodoxy, are not considered to be part of Russian *sektanstvo* (the whole body of religious dissenters).

7. Three interpretations of the origins of the name Molokane exist in Molokan lore, all three connected with the Russian word *moloko* (milk). According to the first, the outsiders called them *molokane* because they did not observe the prohibition by the Orthodox Church to consume milk (among other non-vegetarian products) on Wednesdays and Fridays, as well as during numerous longer fasts. The second dwells on a metaphorical meaning of "drinking milk" and refers to the Molokans' reading of the Scripture, the "spiritual milk." The third interpretation connects the name with the river *Molochnye Vody* (Milky Waters), along which some Molokan groups were relocated in the early nineteenth century.

8. An account of the meeting with Alexander I and the text of this document have been carefully preserved in Molokan self-published books. It was first published in Livanov 1872, 1:3–14.

9. For a concise and powerful account of Molokans' pilgrimage, see Berokoff (1987), one of the first settlers and a prominent elder of the American Molokan community. Thanks to William John Berokoff for giving me his father's book.

10. This expression was first recorded by Seraphima Nikitina in the Stavropol' region.

11. The Molokan concept of the New Millennium, similar to that embraced by other Russian sectarians and many prophetic Protestants of the seventeenth century, is not equally strong among different Molokan denominations.

12. The first publication of the creed appeared as early as 1865, *The Confessions of Faith of the Spiritual Christians called Molokanye*, the second in 1905, *Foundations of the Molokan Doctrine*. Since 1912, prayer books, songbooks, and books of doctrine have been published and reprinted in multiple editions and translations. So far, *Molokan Songbook* has been published in five editions. Many of these publications, except the earliest ones, are available in Molokans' private libraries, which have also collected all

available materials on Molokan history. Practically every Molokan house also has a collection of audiotapes with Molokan singing. A full bibliography on Molokans' own publications and private collections has yet to be compiled. Compared to publications by other Russian schismatics, the number of those by the Molokans is impressive. This fact alone is telling about the importance of verbal expression and literary discourse in this culture.

13. In Molokan use, the word *sobranie* also refers to all congregants of a particular church, as well as the building in which the service is conducted.

14. Russian word *prestól* has two meanings: a throne and a church altar. The Molokan usage of the word *prestol* refers primarily to a group of leaders, who during *sobranie* sit *pri stole* (literally, at the table), that is, sit at the ceremonial table. (See fig. 4.1.)

15. For American *pevtsy* (plural of *pevets*), the initial selection process starts at *spevka*, a singing practice session open to the entire community and led by an experienced *pevets*. Those who have special *revnost'* to learn psalms are further trained by an expert *pevets*, usually on a one-to-one basis. Once appointed, a *pevets* spends all his free time practicing and learning new repertory from whatever source he can find; he always seeks an opportunity to listen to the *pevtsy* of different churches. *Spevka* is an American institution; some Molokan communities in Russia adopted it only recently.

16. Such a prohibition of musical instruments is similar to the practice of the Russian Orthodox Church. Note that in spite of their denunciation of the Orthodox Church, Molokans have retained some other characteristics of Orthodox singing as well: Many local congregations still use only unison singing; professional singers are only men; only choral music is allowed.

17. According to *zakon*, adult Molokans are not supposed to sing anything else. Before marriage, they can to some extent sing and dance with non-Molokan youth, but this is to stop after marriage. In reality, however, older men and women know Russian secular songs of various genres, including dance songs (without dancing); some women even play musical instruments. Young American Molokans rarely know this secular repertory, but many love and know various types of non-Molokan music. The present article focuses only on liturgical forms of Molokan singing, that is psalms and spiritual songs, and the words "Molokan singing" refer to these two categories only.

18. Young's study of early Molokan settlers in Los Angeles, including their beliefs, notions, customs, and ways of adjustment to a new social life, remains one of the most sensitive and perceptive.

19. Molokan *besedy* (plural of *beseda*) are genuine examples of folk hermeneutics. They show a great variety of local schools and individual styles in the interpretation of the Bible, and many of them are conducted on the highest level of the oratory art.

20. The multivoice texture of psalms is always heterophonic, although it varies depending on local styles. In some, the singing is aiming at a unified sound of unison (San Francisco *sobranie*, for example). In other styles the texture often includes a *podgolos*, literally "a voice below other voices," but it is usually the highest voice, above all others. *Podgolos* is a single voice that sings the most melismatic and intricate variation of the melody (see fig. 4.2). There are still other styles of Molokan multivoice

singing, but a discussion of local schools and styles of Molokan singing is beyond the scope of this essay.

21. Such use of the ritual space is markedly different from the practice of the Orthodox Church, which always separates the spaces of the clergy and the congregation.

22. This part of *sobranie* is called *poklonénie* (from *poklon*=to bow) or *tselovanie* (from *tselovat'*=to kiss), a symbolic act of unity in spirit and faith. The congregants form a line that moves toward the *prestol.* Passing the *prestol* table, they leave a small donation; they then line up into a circle, bowing to each other and kissing on the mouth. Both *poklonénie* and *tselovanie* are Old Russian words. The entire episode is accompanied by singing.

23. For a description of the Jumpers' service as well as other types of the *sobranie* see Young (1932, 30–47).

24. The *sobranie* structure is so well-ordered, that it can be represented through the following formula, in which "B" stands for *beseda,* "PS" for performance of psalm, "PR" for a prayer by a *presviter* or another officiating person, "prs" for individual prayers by the congregants, and "S" for song: $(B + PS)^x + (PR/prs + PR + PS + \{S\}^y)$.

25. The term "*sound* modality" here is a modification of Crystal's "religious modality" (Crystal 1976). The term incorporates the meaning of a Russian word *zvukovóy* (roughly, "made of sound"), used by some Molokan leaders to impart one of the meanings of God's word. Henceforth I will use *sound* in place of *zvukovóy* and *zvukovóye.* It will appear in italics when used as a technical term, not to be confused with a regular meaning of the word "sound."

26. According to the doctrine, singing is "To prepare God's people for works of service in order to build up the body of Christ" (Dogmas 1912, 162).

27. This is why no recording is normally allowed during the *sobranie.* Moreover, Molokans often ascribe failure and trouble in life to fault committed in singing during the *sobranie.* Once during the wedding of his son, my friendly host "arrested" my tape recorder "just in case," explaining that recording during the ritual could have negatively influenced his son's marriage. If his son's marriage went wrong, he would never forgive himself for allowing a tape recorder into the ritual.

28. Judging from my own attempts to recreate *udaritel'noe* singing, a brief voiced inhalation is followed by a forceful exhalation on the ensuing note; exhalation is accompanied by a spasm-like movement of the diaphragm. The whole utterance appears to be similar to gasps in crying and laughter. See Mazo (1994b), where this type of breathing is examined as a paralinguistic characteristic of emotional vocalization.

29. In many areas of rural Russia, lamenting or crying with words and melody, both structured in a certain way, is not only a necessary component of a ritual but is also a conventional form of individual expression of frustration, grief, unhappiness, and similar psychological and emotional states. Each local tradition determines the formal and idiomatic aspects of a lament's melody and text, such as the overall form of a lament, patterns of the structural units, melodic and rhythmic idioms, and the use of conventional motives and verbal formulas. The local tradition also regulates, to a large degree, the body movements, as well as the role, placement, and even volume

of the sobbing and wailing "acceptable" in lamenting. At the same time, each lament is unique, a true poetic and melodic improvisation, spontaneous and personal as well as structured within the limits established by local tradition (Mazo 1994a).

30. Such use of Russian laments has never been previously reported in the research literature. In Russia, there is also a strong tradition of funeral and remembrance laments, but only a few women in the United States still know them. For analysis of one lament by a Molokan woman in Russia, see Mazo (1994b).

31. Sometimes the pitch level rises significantly, up to the sixth or even higher.

32. I do not have contextual recordings of the *sobranie* in California. Californian Molokans have never allowed me to record during the service, even though they welcome my presence among them.

33. Only one name of early psalm composers has survived: Gregoriy Skovoroda (1722–1794). He was one of the celebrated Ukrainian philosophers in the late eighteenth century, but his exact contribution to the composition of Molokan psalms is not known (Kudrinsky 1898, 43).

34. Evgeniya Linyova was the first Russian ethnomusicologist to make phonographic field recordings in the 1900–1910s. Her cylinder collection includes psalms and songs of Russian sectarians living in Tiflis and Vladikavkaz areas. The collection is housed in the Phonogram Archive of the Institute of Russian Literature (Pushkinskii Dom) in St. Petersburg. So far, her three transcriptions have been the only known published sources on Molokan psalms.

35. Note that the very top staff in figure 4.2 is the opening phrase of the Californian version only; the phrase does not exist in the Russian version at all. The rest of the melodies align well, as the subsequent notational systems demonstrate. Version I (top staff of each system) is a recording of two male singers in the Stavropol' area in Russia (marked St. I), version II (bottom staff of each system) is of male and female singers in the greater Los Angeles area (marked Ca. II). Version II is transposed by a minor third down to facilitate the comparison. Todd Harvey made the initial skeleton transcription; Margarita Mazo made a detailed transcription and the analytical layout presented here.

In addition to presenting the two versions in parallel, the transcription layout shows how similar melodic phrases and gestures are woven into a long and complex stanza of this psalm. The melodic stanza is constructed by combining the melodic gestures in different ways, varying, omitting, extending and constricting them, changing their order, and the like. Here, the related gestures and phrases from various segments of the stanza are aligned vertically. The continuity of each melodic version can be restored by following the respective staves from left to right and sequentially from top to bottom.

36. The term is borrowed from folk terminology. Following an interpretation of Feodosii Rubtsov, one of the founders of Soviet ethnomusicology, Russian scholars began to use the term to designate a particular form of Russian folk song. For a discussion of this issue in English, see Zemtsovsky (1980); Mazo (1987, 37–43, 64–73). Like Molokan psalms, *protyazhnaya* exists in several distinctly different categories.

37. While numerous small-scale elaborations of a melodic gesture occur at any point, an addition of a new melodic unit in American versions, as in figure 4.2, usu-

ally occurs at strategic structural points of the melody. This bears out one of Leo Treitler's ideas about the role of melodic beginning and ending in chant transmission. Specifically, in support of his model of melodic formulas, the identical distribution of the words in the cadential phrase in both Californian and Stavropol' versions in figure 4.2 is worth noting.

38. Deborah Wilson made the initial skeleton transcription. Margarita Mazo made the detailed transcription and analytical layout presented in figure 4.4.

39. Still today, Russian words *khristianin*, "a Christian," and *krest'yanin*, "a peasant," are phonetically almost identical and in the past were sometimes interchangeable.

40. A comparison of field observations with earlier accounts of Molokan life in the United States indeed shows a great continuity (see Young 1932).

41. A remarkable event took place in the summer of 1995 in Washington, D.C. during the American Folklife Festival produced by the Smithsonian Institution. As part of the program "Russian Roots American Branches: Music in Two Worlds," a group of Steadfast Molokans from the Stavropol' area in Russia met with a cognate religious group residing in San Francisco. The festival was a powerful experience for everyone involved, first of all for the participants, but also for the audience, including Washington tourists, those who just passed by "the Russian" stage, and those who came every day and listened to Molokan singing with rapt attention.

WORKS CITED

Berokoff, John K. 1987. *Molokans in America*. 2nd ed. Buena Park, Calif.: Stockton Trade.

Billington, James. 1970. *The Icon and the Axe*. 2nd ed. New York: Vintage.

Confessions of Faith . . . 1865. *Confessions of Faith of the Spiritual Christians called Molokanye. By members of the sect*. Geneva, n.p.

Crystal, David. 1976. "Nonsegmental Phonology in Religious Modalities." In William Samarin, ed., *Language in Religious Practice*, 17–23. Rowley, Mass.: Newbury.

Dogmas and the Prayerbook . . . 1912. *Izlozhenie dogmatov i molitvennik istinnykh dukhovnykh khristian Molokan (sekty imenuemoy "staro-postoyannymi molokanami")*. Compiled by N. M. Anfimov. Izdanie Yakova Pavlovicha Burtsova I Ivana Yakovlevicha Tomilina. Tiflis: "Trud." Published in English as *The Summary of Dogmas and the Prayerbook with Traditional Worshipping of the Spiritual Christians Molokan (by name the sect) "Old-Constant Molokans."* Translated by Elders of the Church Journal Committee, 1975–1890, San Francisco, Calif. Edited and Published by Sheridan Molokan Church, Sheridan, Calif., 1982.

Dunn, Ethel, ed. 1983. *The Molokan Heritage Collection*. Vol. 1 of *Reprints of Articles and Translations*. Berkeley: Highgate Road Social Science Research Station.

Flower, Linda. 1994. *The Construction of Negotiated Meaning: A Social Cognitive Theory of Writing*. Carbondale: Southern Illinois University Press.

Foundations of the Molokan Doctrine. 1905. *Izlozhenie dogmatov istinnykh dukhovnykh khristian Molokan*, 1905. Astrakhanka, Russia: n.p. Repr. in English, "Molokane" in *Encyclopedia of Religion and Ethics*. Vol. 2, 341–42. Ed. by James Hastings. New York.

Ismail-Zade, D. 1983. "Russkie poseleniya v Zakavkaz'e v 30[kh]-80[kh] godakh XIX veka." *Voprosy Istorii* 11(1976), 18–31. Trans. as "Russian Settlements in the Transcaucasus from the 1830s to the 1880s" in Dunn 1983, 51–77.

Istoriya dukhovnykh khristian molokan. 1979. *Istoriya dukhovnykh khristian molokan*. San Francisco: First Russian Molokan Church.

Klibanov, Alexander. 1982. *History of Religious Sectarianism in Russia (1860's–1917)*. Ed. Stephen Dunn, trans. by Ethel Dunn. Oxford: Pergamon.

Kudrinsky, V. F. 1898. "Filosof bez sistemy." *Kievskaya Starina* 60 (1898), 35–63.

Linyova, Evgeniya (Eugene). 1911. "Psalms and Religious Songs of Russian Sectarians in the Caucasus." *International Musical Society Congress Reports*. London, 1911:187–201.

Listopadov, Alexander. 1906. "Narodnaya kazach'ya penya na Donu. Donskaya expeditsiya 1902–1903 gg." In *Trudy Muzykal'no-etnograficheskoy komissii*. (Works by Musical-Ethnographic Commission), vol. 1, 159–218. *Izvestiya Obsbcbestva Lyubiteley Estestvoznaniya, Antropologii i Etnografii*, no. 113. Moscow 159–218.

Livanov, Fedor Vasil'evich. 1872. *Raskol'niki i ostrozhniki;*. 3 vols. St. Petersburg: n.p. 1872. Trans. as *Schismatics and Convicts*. Chapters on Molokans and Dukhobors were reprinted by the Molokans of San Francisco community in one volume as Livanov, Fedor. *Istoriia dukhovnykh khristian molokan*. San Francisco: First Russian Molokan Church, 1979. Trans. as *History of Spiritual Christians Molokans*.

Lopatin, Nikolai, and Vladimir Prokunin. 1956. *Russkie narodnye liricheskie pesni* [Russian Folk Lyric Songs]. Ed. V. Belyaev. Moscow: Gos. Muzykal'noe izd-vo.

Magocsi, Paul. 1996. *The Russian Americans*. New York: Chelsea House Publishers.

Mazo, Margarita. 1994a. "Wedding Laments in North Russian Villages." In Margaret Kartomi and Stephen Blum, eds., *Music Cultures in Contact*, 20–40. Basel: Gordon and Breach Science Publishers.

———. 1994b. "Lament Made Visible: A Study of Paramusical Features in Russian Lament." In Bell Yung and Joseph S. C. Lam, eds., *Theme and Variations: Writings in Honor of Rulan Chao Pian*, 164–212. Cambridge, Mass., and Hong Kong: Music Departments of Harvard University and Chinese University of Hong Kong.

———. 1991. " 'We Don't Summon Spring in the Summer': Traditional Music and Beliefs of the Contemporary Russian Village." In William C. Brumfield and Milos M. Velimirovich, eds., *Christianity and the Arts in Russia*, 73–97. Cambridge: Cambridge University Press.

———. 1990. "Stravinsky's *Les Noces* and the Russian Village Ritual." *Journal of the American Musicological Society* 43, no. 1. (Spring 1990): 99–143

Mazo, Margarita, 1987. *A Collection of Russian Folk Songs*. Introduction. In Malcolm Brown, ed., *A Collection of Russian Folk Songs*, 1–82. Ann Arbor, Mich.: UMI Research Press.

Molokan Songbook. 1986. *Sionskiy Pesennik Stoletnyago perioda Khristianskoy Religii Molokan Dukhovnykh Prygunov v Amerike*; 5th ed. Los Angeles: United Molokan Christian Association (YMCA). (The date of the first edition is not known; 2nd ed. 1950; 3rd ed. 1958; 4th ed. 1964.)

Moore, Williams. 1973. *Molokan Oral Tradition: Legends and Memorates of an Ethnic Sect.* Folklore Studies 28. Berkeley: University of California Press.

Morris, Richard A. 1981. "Three Russian Groups in Oregon: Comparisons of Boundaries in a Pluralistic Environment." Ph.D. diss., University of Oregon.

O'Brien-Rothe, Linda. 1989. *The Origins of Molokan Singing.* Vol. 4, *The Molokan Heritage Collection.* Berkeley: Highgate Road Social Science Research Station.

Prokhoroff, William. 1978. *Maxim Gavrilovich Rudometkin "King of Spirits," Leader of New Israel (Molokans).* Sacramento, Calif: Image Printing.

Samarin, Edward I. n.d. "Russian Spiritual Christianity (Molokanism): 'Come Ye Out From Among Them and Become Separate.'" Unpublished manuscript.

Samarin, James J. 1975. *The Hieroglyphics of Mystery and Meaning.* Cudahy, Calif.: n.p.

Spirit and Life . . . 1947. Dukh I Zhizn'. Kniga Solntsa. Bozhestvennye izrecheniya nastavnikov I stradal 'tsev za Slovo Bozhie, Veru Iisusa I Dukh Svyatoi Religii Dukhovnykh Khristian Molokan-Prygunov, 3rd ed., corrected by the Brotherly Union of the Spiritual Jumpers and augmented by an essay on religion. Los Angeles: *Dukh I zhizn',* 1947; 1st ed: Ivan Samarin, ed. Dukh I Zhizn', Los Angeles: n.p.: 1915; 2nd ed. Los Angeles: n.p. 1928.

Young, Pauline. 1932. *The Pilgrims of Russian-Town.* New York: Russel & Russel.

Zemtsovsky, Izaly. 1980. "Russian Folk Music." In Stanley Sadie, ed., *The New Grove Dictionary of Music and Musicians.* Vol. 19, 388–97. London: Macmillan.

PART II

Liturgy, Hymnody, and Song

5

Hymnody and History: Early American Evangelical Hymns as Sacred Music

Stephen A. Marini

The hymns and spiritual songs of the evangelical Protestant tradition are the most widely used spiritual and ritual texts in American history. Sacred lyrics like "All Hail the Power of Jesus' Name," "Amazing Grace! How Sweet the Sound," "Jesus Lover of My Soul," and "When I Survey the Wondrous Cross" have been sung, preached, and prayed by millions of Americans since the eighteenth century. In weekly worship, revivals, youth services, and camp meetings; at conferences, conventions, and colleges; and in the family circle, these hymns have been rehearsed in an unending round of living oral tradition. Since the Anglo-American Great Awakening two and a half centuries ago, the poets and composers of the evangelical tradition have created literally tens of thousands of hymn texts and tunes. The perennial popularity of these hymns establishes them as a critically important and characteristic expression of American religiousness.

Hymns performed vital functions for the evangelical denominational families in the new republic: The Baptists, Methodists, Presbyterians, Congregationalists, Reformed, and Disciples of Christ, who constituted the preponderant majority of early American Protestants. For all evangelicals, hymn singing was a primary vehicle of the numinous, the very wind of the Spirit itself. Singing, hearing, or praying upon hymn texts frequently mediated the regenerating moment of "the new birth," evangelicalism's most characteristic form of spiritual experience. Hymnody also played a crucial role in the development of revivalism, the distinctive ritual mode of the evangelical movement, and in shaping its institutional ideals of the gathered church and the mission society. Hymns also served evangelicals as educational media for children, aids to prayer for adults, homiletic devices for preachers, and literary material for poets and novelists. In all these ways, hymnody furnishes a unique, vast, and largely untapped resource for interpreting the early American evangelical tradition.

This chapter is a first effort to utilize hymnody as an interpretive lens to understand early American evangelicalism as a religious culture. What can we learn from these texts and tunes that amplify our understanding of evangelicalism as a cultural reality in post-Revolutionary and Antebellum America? The most important recent response to this question has been that of Nathan Hatch in his book, *The Democratization of American Christianity* (1989). Hatch identifies hymnody as a vital part of mass religious culture created for and dictated by "the sovereign audience" of the early American republic. His view stresses the popular nature of evangelical sacred song and the unprecedented availability of texts and tunes supplied by singing schools and an avalanche of publication.

Hatch is correct about the popularity and availability of evangelical hymnody, but his view of its content is inadequate. He has chosen to emphasize the anticlerical and democratizing elements in evangelical hymnody, found in the lyrics of dissenting sects and in the laicizing effervescence of revivalistic performance. My own study of evangelical hymns, however, shows anticlericalism and laicization to be little more than trace elements. These minor textual elements were thoroughly overwhelmed by the hymnic expression of evangelicalism's most powerful and characteristic beliefs, institutions, rituals, and spirituality. If we are adequately to assess the significance of hymnody in the religious culture of early American evangelicalism, it is this religious content, presented through the hymn's complex literary and musical form, that must become the central focus of our inquiry.

Hymnals and Hymnody

Before proceeding to that inquiry, however, two preliminary evidentiary questions must be addressed: How did early American evangelicals learn and use hymns? And how may we determine which of their hymns were the most religiously significant? The answer to the first question is to be found principally in the hundreds of hymnals, most of them "worded" (words only), published by American evangelicals from the mid-eighteenth century through the

Civil War. This protean genre of hymnic publication constitutes an immense and virtually unused resource for the interpretation of the religious culture of the early American republic. How were these books of hymns designed and what religious intentionality attended them? What lessons did editors mean to teach to singers and readers of these hymnals?

The archetypes for early American evangelical hymnody were set by Isaac Watts (1674–1747), the great English Congregationalist poet and theologian. Watts's two most important and influential hymnic works were *Hymns and Spiritual Songs* (1707, 1709) and *The Psalms of David Imitated in the Language of the New Testament* (1719). These two titles became the unquestioned poetic masterworks of early American evangelicalism, running to more than twenty-five printings each in North America alone before 1800. Watts divided *Hymns and Spiritual Songs* into three parts: "I. Collected from the Scriptures. II. Compos'd on Divine Subjects. III. Prepar'd for the Lord's Supper."[1] By this classification Watts differentiated his hymns into poetical renderings of biblical texts, Christian doctrine, and ritual practice.

In his preface to the second, canonical, 1709 edition, Watts outlined the nature and purpose of his hymnic "composures":

> The greatest part of 'em are suited to the general State of the Gospel, and the most common Affairs of Christians: I hope there will be very few found but what may properly be used in a religious Assembly, and not one of 'em but may well be adapted to some Seasons, either of private or of public Worship. The most frequent Tempers and Changes of our Spirit, and Conditions of our Life are here copied, and the Breathings of our Piety exprest according to the variety of our Passions, our Love, our Fear, our Hope, our Desire, our Sorrow, our Wonder and our Joy, as they are refin'd into Devotion, and act under the Influence and Conduct of the Blessed Spirit; all conversing with God the Father by the new and living Way of Access to the Throne, even the Person and the Mediation of our Lord Jesus Christ. (Bishop 1962, liii)

Such an aggressively experiential approach to sacred poetry justified "hymns of human composure" written on any scriptural text, doctrine, or spiritual state. Watts took advantage of this amplitude by grouping his hymns into extremely broad categories; his was clearly not an attempt to present a systematic theology through hymnody. Likewise, his *Psalms of David* undertook an ambitious poetic agenda but eschewed an explicit theological one. For Watts, the language of the Psalms limited the full effectiveness of Christian praise because as Old Testament texts they did not specifically refer to the Christian gospel. Watts grounded his poetic adaptation of the Psalms in Athanasius's aphorism that "he who recites the Psalms is uttering them as his own words, and each sings them as if they were written concerning himself" (Booth 1981, 127). It was because Christians sing the Psalms "as if they were written about ourselves" that Watts proposed by poetic paraphrase to "imitate" the Psalms "in the words of the New Testament."[2] As with his original hymns and spiritual songs, Watts undertook no major theological classification of the "imitated" Psalms.

It was John Wesley, not Isaac Watts, who pioneered the doctrinally-based evangelical hymnal. Wesley, the founder of Methodism, used the hymns of his brother Charles and those of many other early British evangelicals as a central element in the liturgical and devotional life of his followers. Editor of both worded hymnals and sacred music publications, Wesley knew whereof he spoke in offering what was to become the classic definition of the evangelical worded hymnal in his preface to *A Collection of Hymns for the Use of the People Called Methodists* (1780):

> [This hymnbook] is large enough to contain all the important truths of our most holy religion, whether speculative or practical; yea, to illustrate them all, and to prove them both by Scripture and reason. And this is done in a regular order. The hymns are not carelessly jumbled together, but carefully ranged under proper heads, according to the experience of real Christians. So that this book is in effect a little body of experimental and practical divinity. (Hildebrandt and Beckerlegge 1983, 73–74)

Wesley's definition of the hymnal as a guide to religious experience and moral theology was widely shared by early American evangelicals, but in the new republic his definition, and his hymns, took on a polemical character. Wesley's Arminian theology of human freewill and Christian perfection met relentless opposition from evangelical Calvinists, the largest religious constituency in early America, most of whom were rooted in the Calvinist theology of the great Massachusetts Congregationalist Jonathan Edwards. Calvinists and Arminians engaged in epic theological struggles during the Great Awakening (1726–1755) and the Second Great Awakening (1799–1830). It was in service of those great intellectual and spiritual conflicts that the hymnal became a medium of doctrinal instruction in the early republic.

While the evangelical denominations in America shared many fundamental beliefs, they were also communions who had preserved their historic Reformation particularities in their transit to America. During the Awakenings, evangelical denominations were both allies in the common cause of the new birth and competitors in recruiting converts to their own gathered churches.

Hymnals tended to serve the latter agenda. Like Wesley's 1780 *Collection of Hymns*, early American evangelical hymnals were edited by individuals or committees who selected the hymn texts and presented them in a particular order reflecting their particular communion's theological tenets. These classification schemes varied widely from denomination to denomination and offered to the evangelical public competing ways of understanding and singing their faith. They underscore both the doctrinal particularity of denominational hymnals and the larger sense in which hymnody became "a little body of experimental and practical divinity" for all evangelicals.

Hymnals as Denominational Media

Three examples will serve to illustrate this denominational variation in hymn classification, drawn from Timothy Dwight's *The Psalms of David Imitated in the language of the New Testament, and applied to the Christian use and worship.* (1801), Jesse Mercer's *Cluster of Spiritual Songs, Divine Hymns, and Sacred Poems* (1810), and *The Methodist Pocket Hymn-Book. Revised and Improved* (1819) (see table 5.1). These hymnals rank among the most influential in early American evangelicalism, standing as canonical hymnic expressions for three of the largest denominational families in the movement, Congregationalist/Presbyterian, Baptist, and Methodist respectively. Although these hymnals share a number of hymns in common, they organized their texts in significantly different ways. The singer or devotional user would "read" each of these books and their sacred lyrics from a specific theological perspective. Indeed, the same hymn text could carry different significations depending upon which context its denominational hymnal provided.

In the 1719 first edition of *The Psalms of David Imitated*, Isaac Watts supplied Christian titles for each of his metrical psalms, but he published them strictly in the numerical order of the Hebrew Scriptures. Eighty years later—at the onset the Second Great Awakening in America (1799–1830)—Timothy Dwight, President of Yale College, felt free to rearrange Watts's psalms so as to maximize their doctrinal and revivalistic impact. In the event of the Second Awakening, Dwight's reordering in his *New Edition* of 1801 proved to reflect the characteristic theological persuasion of American evangelical Calvinists like his own Congregationalist denomination and their Presbyterian allies. Dwight's version was no longer simply the Christianized rendering of the Hebrew psalter that Watts had originally conceived nearly a century earlier. The *New Edition* had become instead an instrument of evangelism designed to persuade the unregenerate and to comfort the converted.

TABLE 5.1. Hymn classifications of three major early American evangelical hymnals

1. Timothy Dwight, *The Psalms of David Imitated. by I. Watts. D.D. A New Edition* (1801)
1. Character, Actions, Sufferings, and Glory of Christ
2. Creation and Providence
3. Fall and Temptation
4. The Scriptures
5. Invitations of the Gospel
6. The Doctrines of the Scriptures
7. Christian Worship
8. Baptism
9. Lord's Supper
10. Times and Seasons
11. Time, Death, Resurrection, Judgment, and Eternity
2. Jesse Mercer, *The Cluster of Spiritual Songs*, 3rd Edition (1810)
1. Christ
2. Christian
3. Church
4. Death
5. Faith
6. God
7. Gospel
8. Grace
9. Jesus
10. Judgment
11. Invitation
12. Prayer
13. Redeemer
14. Religion
15. Sinner
3. William McKendree, et al., eds., *The Methodist Pocket Hymn-Book. Revised and Improved* (1819)
1. Awakening and Inviting
2. Redemption, or the Grand Atonement in the Death and Passion of Christ
3. Seeking Pardon of Sin, and Justification by Faith
4. Sanctification of Believers, or Gospel Perfection
5. Christian Union, and Gospel Fellowship
6. Christ Our Passover, or the Lord's Supper
7. Keeping the Sabbath-Day
8. On Backsliding
9. For Preachers of the Gospel
10. For the Spread of the Gospel
11. Morning and Evening
12. Social and Family Worship

TABLE 5.1. (continued)

13. Prayer and Watchfulness
14. Reading the Scriptures
15. Temptation and Affliction
16. For the Rulers
17. On Death
18. On Judgment
19. Additional Hymns
20. Resurrection
21. Ascension

Dwight's edition began with the identity and ministry of Christ rather than the nature and attributes of God, traditionally the first rubric of systematic theology. Only after introducing Christ's "character, actions, sufferings, and glory" did Dwight turn to the doctrines of creation and fall, both of them tinged with the characteristically evangelical Calvinist theological emphases of his grandfather Jonathan Edwards. Having presented the ministry of Christ and the predicaments of human sin, Dwight offered an extensive treatment of the scriptures as the definitive source of saving truth. Three additional sections explicated the ritual practice of reborn Congregationalists in worship, baptism, and the Lord's Supper, before Dwight completed the theological architecture of the *New Edition* with groups of psalms addressing time, eternity, and the Last Judgment.

Dwight's arrangement of Watts's psalms marked a revolution in American evangelical hymnody. In exchanging Watts's original canonical ordering of the psalms for a dramatic presentation of evangelical beliefs, Dwight demonstrated the growing impact of revivalism and popular theology on evangelicalism in the new republic. Positioned somewhere between the biblical record and the propositions of systematic theology, American evangelical beliefs had assumed their own significant form by the turn of the nineteenth century. The Yale President engraved that pattern onto the Wattsian psalm corpus and transmitted it thereby to a generation of Congregationalists and Presbyterians after 1801, the same year in which the two denominations signed a Plan of Union designed to improve their mutual position in the burgeoning Second Great Awakening.[3]

Jesse Mercer's famous *Cluster of Spiritual Songs* (Mercer 1810) represents a radically different approach to hymn classification. The first great hymnal by a southern Baptist, Mercer's *Cluster* eschewed any explicit narrative or argumentative organization for its hymns, opting instead for a topic arrangement by alphabetical order. Mercer literally created small "clusters" of hymns according to their principal theological reference, and then published these groupings in the alphabetical order of cluster names. The result of this method appears at first to be simply random: What possible theological sense could be made of the topic sequence "Church—Death—Faith—God?"

But there was in fact an important and characteristically Baptist reason behind the apparent randomness of Mercer's hymn classification. Mercer did not arrange his hymns in an argument for a particular *ordo salutis* because he assumed that singers who used his volume would already be spiritually reborn Baptists and therefore would possess an evangelical theology of salvation. Put differently, Mercer organized his hymnal for a converted and gathered communion of Baptists. His audience, therefore, owned an "experimental and practical divinity" implanted in its heart by God's Holy Spirit. Given this assumed audience, Mercer conceived his hymnal more as a ritual resource volume than as a body of systematic theology.

Mercer's hymnic strategy exactly paralleled Baptist hermeneutical use of the biblical narrative. Of all American evangelical denominations the most suspicious of systematic theology and most dedicated to rhetorical and isogetical rather than exegetical understanding of scripture, Baptists tended to employ the biblical narrative in small bits to "prove" particular doctrines. Mercer's *Cluster* made hymnody susceptible to this same interpretive method. Just as Baptist preachers reached for appropriate fragments of the biblical text to persuade their congregations regardless of those fragments' narrative or historical context, so Mercer's *Cluster* made it possible for those same preachers to select at a glance whatever hymn text would further the evangelistic effort. If preachers and people already knew the theological script, then the hymnal, like the scripture, could assume its proper function as a pure expression of true religion.

If Dwight's *New Edition* presented a hymnody ordered by doctrinal imperatives and Mercer's *Cluster* offered a sort of theological dictionary in verse, then *The Methodist Pocket Hymn-Book* articulated a sense of evangelicalism rooted primarily in the experience of the believers' community. Derived from Wesley's 1780 *Collection of Hymns*, the hymn classification of *The Methodist Pocket Hymn-Book* focuses, even more relentlessly than Wesley's, on the believer's path to salvation and sanctification and the saved community's practice of worship, mission, devotion, and spiritual union. Such an emphasis was not surprising coming from William McKendree of Virginia, veteran Methodist itinerant who was ordained bishop by Francis Asbury in 1808, and under whose signature the 1819 edition of *The Pocket Hymn-Book* was issued.[4] In recounting his own conversion experience, McKendree wrote of Methodist itinerant John

Easter's preaching, "He never indulged in metaphysical discussions, and rarely in doctrinal expositions. His themes were repentance, salvation by faith in Jesus Christ, and the Witness of the Spirit" (Hatch 1989, 55). Small wonder, then, that thirty-five years later McKendree's edition of Methodist hymns reflected this characteristic American emphasis on religious experience.

McKendree's hymn scheme stood somewhere between the systematic theological classification of Timothy Dwight and the theological dictionary approach of Mercer. McKendree certainly presented the basic elements of Wesley's evangelical Arminian theology in his classification, but he also incorporated into that general framework a quite specific treatment of Methodist institutions: the closely-knit system of class meetings, itinerant preachers, and episcopal administration that facilitated Methodism's meteoric rise in the early republic. It was not possible for any singer to miss the explicitly Methodist identity of McKendree's hymnal expressed not only in doctrinal teachings but in institutional, ritual, and devotional categories as well.

These three hymnals and their hymn classification suggest that early American evangelicals understood hymnody to be a function of doctrinal teaching and church practice. The texts and tunes gathered into any particular hymn collection were understood to reflect a specific denominational synthesis of religious culture, and the books were used didactically as well as liturgically. In the diverse denominational and sectarian environment of early American evangelicalism, this particularity worked well as an evangelistic device and invited the publication of ever-increasing numbers of hymnals, each designed for a specific audience. This pronounced quality of particularity has in fact restricted historians' use of hymnals. What researchers can find rendered poetically in a hymnal, they can find more fully expressed in denominational theological works, diaries, and institutional records. Hymnals in this sense are ancillary at best to the discovery of a particular denomination's historical identity.

But hymnals may be used in another, more generic way. If in fact a significant body of hymns was shared across denominational boundaries in early America, that corpus of texts should reveal the common ground of evangelical religious culture. Despite its immense diversity, early American evangelicalism was an historically coherent movement with characteristic beliefs, institutions, and rituals (or practices). Far from unimportant, these common qualities were the glue that held together the culture of the early republic's most important religious movement. The hymnal offers a unique and unexplored vehicle for discovering this historically crucial common ground of early American evangelical religious culture.

What Is American Evangelical Hymnody?

In order to make such an inquiry into the common elements of early American evangelical religious culture, it is necessary to give more precision to defining its hymnody. This is a vitally important preliminary step because historians have used evangelical hymnody arbitrarily and impressionistically, with little sense of its formal and historical integrity. There is, in fact, no established canon of texts for American evangelical hymnody. Nearly two million data cards have been assembled in the Dictionary of American Hymnology project at Oberlin College, an aggregate listing of each hymn published in every American hymnal. Eventually this project will provide definitive information on all empirical questions about American hymnody, evangelical or otherwise, but computerization and publication of this vast database will not be available in the foreseeable future.

On the literary side, there is no critical anthology of evangelical poetry at all, either English or American. The closest we have is Donald Davie's *The New Oxford Book of Christian Verse*, an eclectic collection with large sections devoted to Isaac Watts, Charles Wesley, and William Cowper, but lacking any hymn texts by an American evangelical writer (Davie 1981).[5] Over the past century, the discipline of hymnology has supplied many landmark studies on English hymnody, preeminently Louis F. Benson's *The English Hymn* (1915), still the definitive work. Benson established the religious and literary significance of Watts and Wesley beyond dispute and ably traced evangelical hymnody in its British and American developments, but he made no attempt to establish a literary canon for that tradition of sacred lyrics.

A number of close studies of the Wattsian and Wesleyan corpus have appeared since Benson's work, notably Horton Davies's magisterial *Worship and Theology in England* and Franz Hildebrandt and Oliver Beckerlegge's 1983 critical edition of John Wesley's *Collection of Hymns for the Use of the People Called Methodists*.[6] Two of Donald Davie's recent books, *Dissentient Voice* (1982) and *The Eighteenth Century Hymn in England* (1993), have added important historical and critical dimensions to Benson's pioneer work. For specifically American hymnody, however, Henry Wilder Foote's *Three Centuries of American Hymnody* (1940) remains unsurpassed as a narrative of denominational hymn publication in the United States. Despite ongoing hymnological and literary scholarship about evangelical hymnody, a fundamental historical question remains unanswered: What hymn texts were the most religiously significant for evangelicals in the early American republic?

In seeking some remedy for this lack of a literary canon for American evangelical hymnody, I have computerized the first-line contents of 175 historically significant American evangelical hymnals, from John Wesley's 1737 *Charleston Hymnal* (*Collection of Psalms and Hymns*) to the Southern Baptist Convention's *Broadman Hymnal* (1940). From this database of more than 150,000 hymns, my analysis has produced two lists of texts by frequency of publication, one before and one after 1870. My evidentiary basis in this essay is drawn primarily from the literary canon that comprised for the two hundred fifty most popular texts used by American evangelicals before 1870.

Three preliminary remarks about this canon of hymn texts are appropriate before proceeding to consider its composition and meanings. First, I do not wish to defend frequency of publication as the only or even the best criterion for determining the historical significance of hymn texts in theory, but I will defend it as the best method in practice. My goal has been to establish which hymns were most familiar to most antebellum evangelicals, and what texts could be found in their church services, at their revival meetings, and in their homes. Hence, I have used those hymnals that hymnologists agree were most important historically for each major family of evangelical denominations, along with a substantial selection of early tunebooks used in the ubiquitous singing schools of the early republic.

I have aimed principally at reconstructing the historical use of hymns by denominational families, but I have supplemented this data with a generous sample of more ephemeral hymn collections from the evangelical periphery. For a popular form of religious culture like hymnody, I believe that historical use, defined by denominational and commercial publication, is a theoretically adequate, as well as an empirically feasible, criterion by which to establish the significance of hymn texts and their musical settings.

Second, a word about the term "American" as it is used here. Scholars of the early republic will not be surprised to learn that these texts were written principally by British, and not American, authors. Americans began imitating the poetry of Isaac Watts and Charles Wesley as early as the Great Awakening, yet it is nonetheless extraordinary, as shown in table 5.2, that only twelve hymns by nine Americans are to be found among the 250 most popular evangelical hymns in American use during the early national and antebellum periods.

Among the thirty-five most popular in American use before 1860, only one was by an American evangelical, Congregationalist Timothy Dwight's "I Love Thy Kingdom, Lord" (see table 5.3).

By contrast, 73 texts by Isaac Watts appear on the list of 250 hymns, contributing nearly one-third of the entire canon. As table 5.3 shows, five of Watts's hymns rank among the thirteen hymns most published and sung by American

TABLE 5.2 Popular Antebellum Evangelical Hymns by American Authors

Rank/Author	Title	Date
17 Timothy Dwight	I Love Thy Kingdom, Lord	1817
23 Ray Palmer	My Faith Looks Up to Thee	1832
34 Henry F. Muhlenburg	I Would Not Live Always	c1790
38 John Leland	The Day Is Past and Gone	1824
43 Phoebe H. Brown	I Love to Steal a While Away	1824
44 William B. Tappan	'Tis Midnight, and On Olive's Brow	1822
45 Samuel F. Smith	The Morning Light Is Breaking	1843
52a Timothy Dwight	While Life Prolongs Its Precious	1817
52b Willaim B. Tappan	There Is an Hour of Peaceful Rest	1822
56 Thomas Hastings	Gently Lord, O Gently Lead Us	c1840
57 John Leland	O When Shall I See Jesus	1824
61 Phoebe Cary	One Sweetly Solemn Thought	1852

evangelicals; nine of his texts are included in the top 35 hymns. The other most popular evangelical poets in America were also British, including Charles Wesley with 25 hymns on the canonical list (six of them among the top 35), PhilipDoddridge with 13, John Newton with 12, and Anne Steele, James Montgomery, Samuel Stennett, John Cennick with six or more hymn texts.

This vast preponderance of British texts teaches an important cultural fact about early American evangelicalism: It was lastingly dependent on British models, especially in the area of ritual language. Although evangelicalism was vastly more successful in America than in Britain before 1860, evangelicalism in America continued to rely disproportionately on British sources for their hymnic language.

My third and final preliminary comment addresses the theoretical location of hymnody as a religious phenomenon. For our purposes, hymnody may be considered a medium of religious culture—a complex of acts and psychological effects, texts and vocal techniques, group behavior and ritual gestures—that expresses for worshipers the universe of sacred meaning. It is precisely this protean ability of hymnody to express virtually everything about a religious tradition that makes it so valuable as a body of evidence.

But if hymnody is a medium of religious culture, we will also need some agreement on the nature of religious culture itself before proceeding to interpretation. Anthropologist Clifford Geertz's now-classic 1973 definition of "religion as a cultural system" provides helpful guidelines for hymn interpretation:

> A religion is a system of symbols which acts to establish powerful, pervasive, and longlasting moods and motivations by formulating

TABLE 5.3 The thirty-five most popular American evangelical Hymns to 1860 by frequency of publications

Rank/author	Title
1 Edward Perronet	All Hail the Power of Jesus's Name
2 Charles Wesley	Jesus, Lover of My Soul
3 Isaac Watts	Am I a Soldier of the Cross
4a Isaac Watts	Rock of Ages, Cleft for Me
5 Robert Robinson	Come, Thou Fount of Every Blessing
6 William Cowper	There Is a Fountain Filled
7 James Burder	Lord, Dismiss Us with Thy Blessing
8 John Fawcett	Blest Be the Tie That Binds
9 Jilliam Williams	Guide Me, O Thou Great Jehovah
10	
9b Isaac Watts	Joy to the World
10a Isaac Watts	On Jordan's Stormy Banks
10b Isaac Watts	When I Survey the Wondrous Cross
11 John Rippon	How Firm a Foundation
12 Reginald Heber	Holy, Holy, Holy, Lord God Almighty
13a John Newton	Amazing Grace, How Sweet the Sound
13b Reginald Heber	From Greenland's Icy Mountains
14a John Cennick	Children of the Heavenly King
14b John Newton	How Sweet the Name of Jesus Sounds
15a Isaac Watts	There Is a Land of Pure Delight
20	
15b Joseph Hart	Come Ye Sinner, Poor and Needy
16 Charles Wesley	Love Divine, All Loves Excelling
17 Timothy Dwight	I Love Thy Kingdom, Lord
18a Charles Wesley	Blow Ye the Trumpet, Blow
18b Joseph Gregg	Jesus, and Shall It Ever Be
18c Charles Wesley	O, For a Thousand Tongues
18d Charles Wesley	A Charge To Keep Have I
19 Isaac Watts	Before Jehovah's Awful Throne
20a John Newton	Glorious Things of Thee Are Spoken
20b Phillip Doddridge	Grace! Tis a Charming Sound
30	
21a Charles Wesley	Hark! The Herald Angels Sing
2lb Isaac Watts	Salvation! O, the Joyful Sound
21c Isaac Watts	Jesus Shall Reign Where'er the Sun
22a Joseph Bromehead	Jerusalem, My Happy Home
22b William Cowper	O, For a Closer Walk With God

> conceptions of a general order of existence, and clothing these conceptions with an aura of factuality so that the moods and motivations seem uniquely realistic. (Geertz 1973, 90)

While this definition may not find universal assent, it does nicely distinguish some of the most salient functions and attributes of early American evangelical hymnody. Geertz, furthermore, establishes components of a religious culture that break down roughly into the following categories: beliefs, institutions, ritual, and spirituality (1973). Applied to the texts themselves, Geertz's categories may be translated into theological categories that early evangelical editors would readily have recognized: doctrine, the church, worship, and piety. By examining the most popular hymns expressive of these four areas of religious culture, it is possible to develop a new understanding of early American evangelicalism and to gain thereby a new appreciation of hymnody's importance as a medium of religious culture.

Hymnody and the Evangelical Beliefs

Historians have tended to use only the most obvious quality of hymns, their didactic function, in interpreting the evangelical movement. When cited with any critical seriousness, evangelical hymns are usually accompanied by a reference to John Wesley's dictum that his 1780 *Collection of Hymns* was "carefully arranged under proper heads, according to the experience of real Christians. So that this book is in effect a little body of experimental and practical divinity" (see Hildebrandt and Beckerlegge 1983). This doctrinal function represents Geertz's "description of a general order of existence," or what historians of religion call a "myth of origins."

Christianity, like all religions, is constituted by comprehensive mythic narrative that explains the divine source of being, the status of human nature, and the way believers can gain union with the sacred powers. Western Christianity assembled its myth of origins at the seven canonical councils of the church (325–787 CE), which defined Jesus Christ as a divine person, begotten and consubstantial with God the creator, who for the sins of humanity ministered, suffered, died, and rose again to heavenly glory and who will at the end of time come again to judge the quick and the dead according to their acceptance of his teachings. The Protestant and Catholic Reformations of the sixteenth century reappropriated, redefined, and amplified these classic doctrines, especially those regarding the ontological and moral status of human beings and their salvation.

Early American evangelical Protestantism was a unique historical variant of this orthodox core of beliefs. Heir to a combination of Reformation doctrine and Enlightenment philosophy, evangelicalism placed special stress on certain beliefs, particularly "the necessity of the New Birth"—the requirement of a charismatic conversion experience as evidence of true Christianity—and "the gathered church"—the ecclesiastical ideal that all members of the church must experience the New Birth and stand together in separation from the profane world even as they seek to reform it. Despite dramatic and divisive conflicts that often punctuated its antebellum history, American evangelicalism was a remarkably coherent intellectual, social, and spiritual movement whose beliefs found perhaps their most powerful articulation through hymns.

It is no exaggeration to claim that for evangelicals only the Bible itself surpassed the hymnal as a definer of religious beliefs. Before 1830 the vast majority of hymnals were worded. Worded hymnals like Wesley's were carefully organized into theological categories. They often served as the only book besides the Bible that most evangelicals owned and shared. Early American evangelicals learned hymns from infancy, then recited and sang them in a wide array of social, ecclesiastical, and familial contexts wherein their beliefs were publicly expressed and approved.

If evangelical hymnody was indeed, as John Wesley claimed, "a little body of experimental and practical divinity," then it is worth asking just what sort of divinity early American evangelical hymns taught. Some of the sacred lyrics that American evangelicals sang from the Great Awakening to the Civil War articulated doctrinal peculiarities of their own sectarian identity. Nathan Hatch's anticlerical hymn texts, for example, belong to this category of sectarian particularity. But most of early American evangelicalism's sacred song texts were shared across denominational lines. By 1810, major hymn collections and supplements contained poetry of Watts *and* Wesley, Doddridge *and* Cennick. This eclectic accumulation of Calvinist and Arminian hymnic divinity continued unabated through the nineteenth century and beyond.

Nathan Hatch concludes from this theological "blurring" that the doctrinal content of the hymns is not worth close analysis because the hymns were simply poetic and musical expressions of a generic evangelical faith (1989, 34–40). I would argue the opposite: They are important precisely because they *do* articulate a common core of evangelical beliefs in antebellum America. Given the extraordinary competition between Calvinist and Arminian denominations in the late eighteenth and early nineteenth centuries, of which Hatch also writes, the fact of hymn-sharing among these communions indicates that a substantive core of popular doctrines undergirded all forms of evangelicalism. This core of hymnic beliefs must be examined closely if we are thoroughly to understand the evangelical movement as a religious reality.

The evangelical hymnic worldview is grounded in several central beliefs that comprise the drama of salvation: the authority of scripture, the nature and attributes of God, the economy of grace, the Christian life, and the last things. In the hymn canon, one of the most prominently expressed evangelical doctrines is that of biblicism. Popular hymns like John Fawcett's "How Precious Is the Book Divine" (Rank 83) and Anne Steele's "Father of Mercies in Thy Word" (Rank 96) affirmed the finality of scripture as a source of doctrinal teaching. The supreme hymnic expression of this biblicist persuasion is "How Firm a Foundation," an anonymous, universally popular hymn first published in English Baptist John Rippon's *Selection of Hymns* (1787). Ranked eleventh overall, this eleven-syllable-meter hymn invokes in its first stanza the supreme authority of the Bible:

> How firm a foundation,
> ye saints of the Lord,
> Is laid for your faith in his excellent word!
> What more can he say than to you he hath said,
> To you who for refuge to Jesus have fled?

Subsequent stanzas render some of the "precious promises" that Jesus gives to believers in the scripture.

Another central doctrinal concern of evangelical hymnody is the doctrine of God. In this category, the hymns are predominantly and characteristically Christocentric. By far the most popular hymns are about Christ, including the most popular of all evangelical hymns, Edward Perronet's "All Hail the Power of Jesus' Name" (common meter, Rank 1), which begins:

> All hail the power of Jesus's name,
> Let angels prostrate fall.
> Bring forth the royal diadem,
> And crown him Lord of all.

and Charles Wesley's "Jesus Lover of My Soul" (7-syllable, Rank 2), the first stanza of which is:

> Jesus, lover of my soul,
> Let me to thy bosom fly.
> While the nearer waters roll,

While the tempest still is high:
Hide me, o my savior, hide,
Till the storm of life is past;
Safe into the haven guide;
O receive my soul at last.

While numerous early evangelical hymns address the other persons of the Trinity, none of them approaches the popularity of these hymns to Jesus by Perronet and Wesley. William Cowper's 49th-ranked hymn, "God Moves in a Mysterious Way," leads the lyrics addressed to God the Creator while the most popular hymn to the Holy Spirit is Isaac Watts's 52nd-ranked text, "Come, Holy Spirit, Heavenly Dove."

What accounts for this Christocentric hymnic pattern? Any kind of Christianity might be expected to focus on the nature and person of Jesus, but I think there is more involved here. The doctrines of God the Creator and the Trinity were deeply controverted among early American evangelicals. The role of the Holy Spirit, especially in the process of regeneration, was similarly disputed. Such divisiveness did not easily admit of hymns that pleased all parties. On the other hand, Christology, especially the figure of Christ as Savior and Lord, lay at the heart of the evangelical appeal. The extraordinary popularity of "All Hail the Power" and "Jesus, Lover of My Soul" suggests that the most widely used hymns indeed expressed doctrines about which evangelicals were in agreement, rather than in conflict. They could more easily gather around the figure of Christ than either the Calvinist Creator God of deterministic cosmic law or the extreme Holy Spirit doctrines of radical charismatics.

The most characteristic evangelical ideas appear in hymns on the economy of grace. These texts present a familiar Pauline, Augustinian, and Reformed view of sin, atonement, invitation, and conversion. But again there are some surprises in the evangelical pattern. While revivalism is both famed and criticized for its insistence on human sinfulness, there is no major hymn that speaks directly to that human condition. This grim text from Isaac Watts, the best of the lot (C. M., Rank 149), perhaps explains why:

And are we wretches yet alive?
And do we yet rebel?
'Tis boundless,'tis amazing love,
That bears us up from hell.

On the other hand, many popular and powerful texts articulate the evangelical doctrine of the New Birth, most notably John Newton's "Amazing Grace" (Rank 13a), and the characteristic revivalistic invitation to turn to Christ, compellingly expressed in Joseph Hart's lyric "Come Ye Sinners, Poor and Wretched" (8.7.8.7.4.7., Rank 26):

> Come, ye sinners, poor and wretched,
> Come—'tis mercy's welcome hour;
> Jesus ready stands to save you,
> Full of pity, joined with pow'r?)
> He is able,
> He is willing; doubt no more.

Hart's hymn carried the additional significance of creating an archetype for American evangelical invitation hymns. His "Come ye" formula spread widely throughout the world of American evangelical revivals, spawning the appropriation of similar English hymns like Anne Steele's "Come, Ye That Love the Saviour's Name" as well as many American imitations, including Edward Jones's "Come, Humble Sinner, in Whose Breast."

Arguably the most significant single doctrine in all evangelical hymnody, however, was the difficult concept of atonement, the teaching that Christ's suffering and sacrificial death paid God's just penalty for human sin. This doctrine generated no less than three of the ten most popular evangelical hymns—August Toplady's "Rock of Ages" (Rank 4a), Watts's "Alas, and Did My Savior Bleed" (Rank 4b), and William Cowper's "There Is a Fountain Filled with Blood" (C. M., Rank 6):

> There is a fountain filled with blood,
> Drawn from Immanuel's veins;
> And sinners plunged beneath that flood,
> Loose all their guilty stains.

This concentration of extraordinarily popular conversion and atonement texts suggests that the heart of popular evangelical thought is to be found not in abstruse formulations of systematic theology, but rather with the rehearsal and recollection of the economy of grace. These hymns of human sin, Christ's atonement, and the experience of conversion and sanctification constitute nothing less than an evangelical myth of origin, the ritual recitation of what Mircea Eliade called "*illud tempus*" (literally "that time" when the sacred was first made known) the sacred time when evangelical converts experienced a conscious, episodic, often protracted process of spiritual transformation (see Eliade 1959, chs. 1 and 2).

Eschatology, the doctrine of the last things, has always been a central element in evangelical preaching and belief. The unknown terror of life after death, the near approach of Christ's Second Coming and the Last Judgment were used by evangelical preachers from Whitefield and Edwards onward as persuasives to conversion. These elements of the final and future elements of the economy of grace supplied a scenario of fear and uncertainty relentlessly exploited by revivalists and local preachers alike. Indeed Gilbert Tennent, the premier Presbyterian itinerant of the Great Awakening, defined the preacher's task as "thrusting home the nail of terror into the sleeping soul" by threats of eternal punishment for the unrepentant and promises of eternal heavenly reward for believers (Tennent 1967).

Somewhat surprisingly, the leading early American evangelical hymn on death was Margaret MacKay's sentimental 1832 Long Meter hymn "Asleep in Jesus, Blessed Sleep" (L. M., Rank 38):

Asleep in Jesus! blessed sleep,
From which none ever
A calm and undisturbed repose,
Unbroken by the last of foes.

Asleep in Jesus! peaceful rest,
Whose waking is supremely blest:
No fear, no woe, shall dim that hour
That manifests the Savior's power.

This text expressed an antebellum shift in ideas about death from eighteenth-century texts popular in early tune books, like Watts's "Why Do We Mourn Departing Friends" (Rank 91), Wesley's "And Let This Feeble Body Fail" (Rank 99), or John Leland's "The Day Is Past and Gone" (Rank 127), which expressed the insignificance of the body, the fearful unpredictability of death, and the soul's continuing consciousness and activity after death in "Abraham's Bosom." McKay's lyric, on the other hand, depicted death as a peaceful experience of "psychopannychaea," or the sleep of the soul, a controversial doctrine endorsed by Calvin and some Reformation radicals.[7]

It is also surprising to discover that the Last Judgment did not especially attract the American evangelical muse in antebellum times. Despite the millennial and Adventist enthusiasms of the 1840s, it appears that most American evangelicals continued to rely on classic British eighteenth century texts to express the unruly and often confusing tenet of the Second Coming of Christ. The most popular hymnic articulation of the Last Judgment was Charles Wesley's "Lo, He Comes with Clouds Descending" (8.7.8.7.8.7., Rank 31):

Lo, He comes with clouds descending,
Once for favored sinners slain;
Thousand thousand saints attending

Swell the triumph of His train:
Alleluia, alleluia!
God appears on earth to reign.

Like sin and death, the threatening nature of the Last Judgment, though existentially compelling enough to induce powerful revivalistic effects, seems to have received an unenthusiastic if dutiful hymnic reception by antebellum evangelicals. The evangelical vision of heaven, on the other hand, has been far more celebrated in hymns like Samuel Stennett's immensely popular lyric "On Jordan's Stormy Banks I Stand" (C. M., Rank 10a):

On Jordan's stormy banks I stand,
And cast a wistful eye
To Canaan's fair and happy land,
Where my possessions lie.

O the transporting, rapturous scene,
That rises to my sight!
Sweet fields, arrayed in living green,
And rivers of delight.

O'er all those wide-extended plains
Shines one eternal day;
There God the Son forever reigns,
And scatters night away.

This small sample of texts serves to make a large point: Early American evangelical hymnody provided a complete and highly nuanced expression of the movement's religious thought that discloses an inexhaustible fascination with the economy of grace rendered not as doctrinal proposition but rather as mythic narrative. That narrative, ritually sung by millions of American evangelicals, represented the living belief of the dominant religious force in the early republic. The creedal content of that mythic narrative was fundamental to the movement's self-understanding. But the lesson hymnody teaches us is that early American evangelicals overwhelmingly appropriated their essential beliefs through the media of lively metaphor, biblical paraphrase, and experiential poetic narrative of the economy of grace, rather than through the bare propositional logic of systematic doctrinal formulations. The significance of doctrinal content, however, was not diminished thereby. To the contrary, it was heightened by the emotive and narrative power of the hymnic medium.

Hymnody of the Church

The second area of religious culture addressed in evangelical hymnody is that of institutional order, embodied in hymns of the church. For evangelicals "the gathered church" was the institutional corollary to the necessity of the New Birth. Only those individuals saved by grace and spiritually reborn were eligible to enter the covenanted community of believers. Such local communities of believers came to be identified in theological terms with the kingdom of God on earth. New England Congregationalist Timothy Dwight gave classic expression to this evangelical ideal of the gathered church as the divine community in his great hymn, "I Love Thy Kingdom, Lord" (S. M., Rank 17):

1 I love thy kingdom, Lord,
The house of thine abode,
The church our blest redeemer saved
With his own precious blood.

2 I love thy church, O God!
Her walls before thee stand,
Dear as the apple of thine eye,
And graven on thy hand.

The social ideal of evangelical church fellowship in the "kingdom" of the church was consensus, motivated by the common experience of and guidance by the Holy Spirit. Given the extensive history of ecclesiastical conflicts and divisions during antebellum times, however, it is easy to lose sight of the vital significance for American evangelicals of spiritual union in the local congregation. One of the ten most popular of all evangelical hymns, John Fawcett's "Blest Be the Tie That Binds" (S. M., Rank 8) draws the analogy between the congregational fellowship on earth and the union of the saints on high, then details the very human realities that attend life in religious community:

1 Blest be the tie that binds
Our hearts in Christian love,
The fellowship of kindred minds
Is like to that above.

2 Before our Father's throne
We pour our ardent prayers:
Our fears, our hopes, our sins are one,
Our comforts and our cares.

3 We share our mutual woes;
Our mutual burdens bear;
And often for each other flows
The sympathizing tear.

In addition to these metaphors of the institutional church as the kingdom of God and the fellowship of the regenerate saints, early American evangelical hymns of the gathered church focused on believers' commitment to witness and mission in the world, classically expressed in Isaac Watts's immensely popular hymn of the church militant, "Am I a Soldier of the Cross" (C. M., Rank 4):

1 Am I a soldier of the cross,
A follower of the Lamb?
And shall I fear to own his cause,
Or blush to speak his name?

4 Sure I must fight if I would reign;
Increase my courage, Lord!
I'll bear the toil, endure the pain,
Supported by thy Word.

For evangelicals, the agenda of evangelism and moral reform in the United States proceeded directly from their imperative to witness for the faith. Foreign missions, on the other hand, proved to be a far more controversial but increasingly accepted dimension of the evangelical movement in America (see William 1987). American evangelical foreign missions began with the 1806 Haystack Meetings at Williams College in the Berkshire Hills of western Massachusetts, led by an undergraduate named Adoniram Judson. Judson and his Williams colleagues attended Andover Seminary, then set out for the foreign mission field in imitation of William Carey, the pioneer British missionary to Burma. The fame of Carey and Judson swept through Anglo-American evangelicalism after 1815, prompting hundreds of young men and women to join the foreign mission cause. One of them, Reginald Heber, an Anglican bishop in India, wrote the most popular early evangelical foreign mission hymn in America, "From Greenland's Icy Mountains" (7.6.7.6.D., Rank 13b):

From Greenland's icy mountains,
From India's coral strand,
Where Afric's sunny fountains
Roll down their golden sand,
From many an ancient river,

From many a palmy plain,
They call us to deliver
Their land from error's claim.

As the foreign mission cause gained popularity in antebellum America, hymn texts like Heber's became anthems for a fateful religious and cultural crusade upon which American evangelicalism embarked, albeit with uncertain resolve.

Evangelical Hymnody as Ritual Song

Early American evangelicals, like most Christians, would have accepted Augustine's judgment that a hymn is "the praise of God in song." In addition to concision, this definition carries the authority of western Christendom's greatest ancient theologian, one who learned about hymns firsthand from Ambrose of Milan, the founder of Latin hymnody. Augustine's "sung praise" points to the compound form of hymns as words and melody. This combination makes hymns songs, but hymns are not just any kinds of songs. What about this combination of words and melody makes them sacred? Part of the answer involves the fourth and final general dimension of hymnody as a medium of religious culture, its status as ritual action. According to Clifford Geertz, religious symbols are "clothed with an aura of factuality" that makes them "seem uniquely realistic" (Geertz 1973, 90). Hymnody as a mode of ritual expression is capable of producing this "aura of factuality" precisely because it can synthesize the doctrinal, communal, spiritual, and physiological dimensions of worship.

This extraordinary ritual power of hymnody played a central role in the American evangelical movement from its beginning in the Great Awakening. Although evangelicals like John Wesley, as we have seen, emphasized the doctrinal function of hymnody, they along with the continental Pietists should also be credited with the reversal of this hymnic logic. Evangelical hymn writers placed their lyrics at the disposal of religious emotions as a self-conscious strategy to promote the process of conversion. George Whitefield, John Wesley, Jonathan Edwards, Gilbert Tennent, and James Davenport all used hymns successfully in their public evangelism during the Great Awakening. Hymnody has been a staple of evangelical outreach in America ever since.

Whitefield introduced Edwards to the hymns of Isaac Watts and other British evangelicals during his 1740 visit to Edwards's Northampton, Massachusetts congregation. Within a year, Edwards reported that his people "sang nothing else, and neglected the Psalms wholly" (147–49). Edwards also drew a connection between heightened hymn singing and his successful evangelism during the Awakening: "There has scarcely been any part of divine worship," he reported in *A Faithful Narrative*, "wherein good [people] amongst us have had drawn forth, and their hearts so uplifted in the ways of God, as in singing his praises . . . with unusual elevation of heart and voice"(405–406). The journals of evangelical itinerants from the Great Awakening to the Civil War abound with references to hymnic power in revivals and camp meetings, north and south, among women and men, blacks and whites. How such conversions and spiritual renewals were facilitated by sacred song is perhaps the most fundamental historical question posed by early evangelical hymnody.

Certainly part of the answer has to do with the performative nature of singing. Hymns do not flow simply to the rhythms of the spoken word; they also accommodate the human instrument as song. Singing differs from speech. It requires much higher levels of sustained breathing, tone production, vibration of the head and upper body, intensive hearing, and physical energy. When these effects are intensified over time, as was frequently the case with evangelical singing in revivals and in worship, and when they are multiplied by the synergy of many voices, they produce something that can only be termed *ecstasis*. The sacred singer, either alone or in the company of believers, "stands outside" of everyday profane consciousness and experiences the powerful emotional and perceptual transformations of the sacred realm. It was the distinctive genius of evangelicalism to excite and exploit these "religious affections," as Jonathan Edwards called them, as the vehicle of the soul's regeneration and sanctification.

Early American evangelicals appropriated popular Anglo-American musical forms to amplify the affective impact of singing. The first major collection of original sacred song compositions by an American was William Billings's *The New England Psalm-Singer* (1770). Billings, a Boston Congregationalist of moderate evangelical persuasion, adapted four-part plain tunes, fuguing tunes, and anthems from the English country parish tradition to create a new musical vocabulary for American sacred song.[8] Billings drew the preponderant majority of his texts from Isaac Watts and dedicated *The New England Psalm-Singer* to the memory of George Whitefield, who died at Newburyport shortly before the collection was published.

Billings's later works, including *The Singing-Master's Assistant* (1778), *The Suffolk Harmony* (1786), and *The Continental Harmony* (1794), established a canonical style for American musical settings of evangelical hymn texts (see McKay and Crawford 1975, 41–131; Barbour 1960, 1–118). A vast lineage of American singing-school masters followed Billings, creating tens of thousands of choral settings for the hymn texts of Watts, Wesley, and their British and

American imitators (see Britton, Lowen, and Crawford 1990). In literally hundreds of tunebooks published by itinerant singing-masters during the early republic and antebellum periods, the solemn harmonies of plain tunes and spiritual ballads, the spirited refrains and choruses of fuguing tunes and camp-meeting songs, and the folk melodies of tavern, workplace, and family circle combined mightily to enhance evangelical hymnody's success as a ritual medium for raising the emotions of the unconverted as well as of the faithful.

Isaac Watts and his evangelical successors developed a powerfully effective poetical form to achieve their goal of religious subjectivity. Their central achievement was to create a highly emotional rhetoric of religious experience and biblical reference and to capture the breath of singers by casting their words into short, succinct lines. The amount of text a singer can articulate is strictly determined by the amount of breath he or she can muster. The average English-speaking singer can articulate about ten syllables, a half-dozen words, a single sentence or phrase, with each breath. The most-used evangelical hymnic meters reflect this strophic utterance of song by limiting each line to six or eight syllables: Common Meter (8.6.8.6.), Short Meter (6.6.8.6.), and Long Meter (8.8.8.8.).

These are the basic textual and musical elements of evangelical hymnic form, but how does this kind of sacred song work as ritual action? We must remember that the hymns were sung in the context of evangelical worship and revival, where the biblical drama of sin, redemption, and sanctification were pressed upon the assembly through public prayer and preaching. Singing such hymns in this context was an act of *union* for evangelical believers, yet another way of remembering and reenacting the crucial spiritual episodes of their lives. Given the ecstasis *intrinsic* to sacred *singing*, the performance of hymns could and did produce spiritual states analogous to those of one's original conversion experience—the sacred time of one's spiritual origin.

Indeed the heightened charisma of sacred singing can be understood as the ritual effort to return to what Eliade called *illud tempus* (1959). In evangelical terms, *illud tempus* was the individual's experience of regeneration during which individual consciousness and biblical cosmos become one. Samuel Medley's well-known eighteenth-century hymn, "O, Could I Speak the Matchless Worth," (8.8.6.8.8.6., Rank 37c) gave particularly clear expression to this primal ritual experience:

O, could I speak the matchless worth,
O, could I sound the glories forth,
Which in our Savior shine,
I'd soar, and touch the heavenly strings,

And vie with Gabriel, while he sings,
In notes almost divine.

I'd sing the precious blood he spilt,
Our ransom from the dreadful guilt
Of sin and wrath divine;
I'd sing his glorious righteousness.
In which all-perfect heavenly dress
We shall forever shine.

Such highly personal sacred experiences found potent reinforcement in the communal nature of sung spiritual utterance. It is this re-presentation of what believers understood as their common experience of the Holy Spirit that ushered them corporately into what hymnal compilers almost universally characterized as the cosmic harmony attained in sacred singing, the spiritual union of one to all and all to God. For believers and prospective converts, the aural impact of sacred singing and its embodied qualities as word, music, and spirit, could only be experienced religiously as that "aura of factuality" Geertz described as so mysteriously essential to ritual action. Sacred singing is one of the most powerful ways whereby the "general order of existence" described by evangelical theology seemed so "uniquely realistic" that believers could reexperience, and unbelievers could be swept into, the transforming power of the New Birth. Again, Isaac Watts is our best hymnic guide to evangelical praise as ritual song, giving utterance to what he called "heavenly joy on earth" in his widely sung hymn "Come We That Love the Lord" (S. M., Rank 39c):

1 We come, we that love the Lord,
And let our joys be known;
Join in a song of sweet accord,
And thus surround the throne.

3 Let those refuse to sing
That never knew our God,
But favorites of the heavenly king
May speak their joys abroad.

9 The hill of Zion yields
A thousand sacred sweets,
before we reach the heavenly fields,
Or walk the golden sweets.

10 Then let our songs abound,
And every Tear be dry;

We're marching through Immanuel's ground
To fairer worlds on high.

Hymnody as Spirituality

The final constituent dimension of early American evangelical religious culture expressed in its hymns was spirituality. Prayer, meditation, devotion, and reliance on divine providence were the principal spiritual virtues of evangelicals, the foci of the soul's relationship with God. Hymns expressing this characteristic spirituality of the holy life as well as the disciplines of prayer and piety reveal Geertz's "powerful, pervasive, and longlasting moods and motivations" as understood by early American evangelicals. In his book *The Practice of Piety* (1982), Charles Hambrick-Stowe demonstrated the vital importance of the media of piety—psalters, emblem-books, devotional guides—in the spiritual life of seventeenth-century New England Puritans.

No comparable study exists for early American evangelicals, but hymn texts provide an essential source through which the spiritual dimension of their religious life may be understood. To the extent that historians' depiction of evangelicalism has concentrated too much on the head and not enough on the heart, hymn texts offer an important corrective. Consider what James Montgomery said so simply in 1818 about the centrality of prayer (C. M., Rank 35c):

Prayer is the soul's sincere desire
Unuttered or expressed,
The motion of a hidden fire,
That trembles in the breast.

Prayer is the burden of a sigh,
The falling of a tear,
The upward glancing of an eye,
When none but God is near.

Prayer is the simplest form of speech,
That infant lips can try;
Prayer, the sublimest strains that reach
The Majesty on high.

This is about as close as the historian can get to the intimate subjectivity of evangelical prayerfulness. Montgomery's observation that "prayer is the Christian's vital breath, the Christian's native air" tells volumes about the evangelical prayer experience in just two lines.

Devotional hymns, lyrics that express the believer's contemplative relationship with Christ, bring the historian close to the heart of evangelical piety. From Isaac Watts's oft-analyzed 1707 classic "When I Survey the Wondrous Cross" (Rank 10b) to American Presbyterian Ray Palmer's 1830 poem "My Faith Looks Up to Thee" (6.6.4.6.6.6.4., Rank 23b), devotional hymns' selflessness and intimacy with Christ have been the ground of evangelical spiritual of every sort:

My faith looks up to thee,
Thou Lamb of Calvary:
Savior divine,
Now hear me while I pray;
Take all my guilt away;
O, let me, from this day
Be wholly thine.

Closely related to devotion is the strong evangelical stress on divine leading in personal life, what they called providence and perseverance. Based on their belief in the indwelling of the Holy Spirit after the New Birth, evangelicals taught that God would give the regenerate no test they were not able to overcome—the doctrine of perseverance of the saints; and that, in the words of St. Paul, "all things work together for good to them that love the Lord" (Romans 8:28)—the doctrine of divine providence. Protected from the world by providence in their gathered churches, yet empowered by perseverance to change the world itself, evangelicals lived out a double imperative both to separate from and to transform society. This paradoxical attitude promoted a deep spirituality of pilgrimage. In the proto-evangelical literature of late seventeenth-century England, the metaphor of pilgrimage found classic articulation in John Bunyan's epic poem *The Pilgrim's Progress* (1678). A century later William Williams, a Welsh Baptist, gave evangelical spirituality of pilgrimage its definitive hymnic form in his 1772 lyric "Guide Me, O Thou Great Jehovah" (8.7.8.7.4.7., Rank 9a):

1 Guide me, O thou great Jehovah,
Pilgrim through this barren land;
I am weak, but thou art mighty;
Hold me in thy powerful hand:
Bread of heaven,
Feed me till I want no more.

2 Open thou the crystal fountain,
Whence the healing streams do flow:
Let the fiery, cloudy pillar
Lead me, all my journey through:
Strong deliverer,
Be thou still my strength and shield.

The immense popularity of texts like "Prayer is the soul's sincere desire," "My Faith Looks Up to Thee," and "Guide Me, O Thou Great Jehovah" make it plain that hymnody played an essential role in individual evangelical spiritual life. Yet these texts and their role in evangelical religious culture have been largely neglected by historians, as have their most characteristic early American literary forms.

American Evangelical Hymnody as Sacred Medium

Beliefs, institutions, ritual, and spirituality hardly exhaust the functions of hymnody in evangelical religious culture. But they do point us not only toward a more appropriate and complete role for hymnody than historians have usually granted but also toward a newly balanced understanding of the evangelical movement. That new understanding highlights the important beliefs about the New Birth and about Christology—particularly the atonement—as the centerpiece of evangelical beliefs, rather than the time-honored metaphysical focus on Calvinism and Arminianism. One detects in hymnody a significant institutional emphasis on union and consensus in the evangelical idea of the gathered church and its mission, to place over against the predominant image of evangelicalism as an individualistic and privatistic movement.

Hymnody also clearly indicates the fundamental importance of spiritual experience to evangelicalism. While this would appear to be a truism, it does not appear in much historical interpretation, which is uncomfortable dealing with such explicitly stated religious states. The depth and nuance of evangelical prayer and meditation is therefore lost except in biographical accounts. Hymn texts and tunes on spirituality offer a useful way to approach these sensitive matters of interpretation.

Finally, the hymns tell us unequivocally that evangelicals practiced and valued ritual action fully as much as any other religious tradition. This religious reality, too, has been obscured by the traditional generalization that since Luther's attack on the "Babylonian captivity" of the church by priests and prelates, Protestantism has been an anti-ritual movement. This interpretation was not true of Luther and it certainly is not true of evangelicalism, a movement that invented one of the most effective modern religious rituals, the revival. Evangelicals wrote many hymns rehearsing and repristinating the primal ritual of revivalism and its experience of the New Birth. So many evangelical hymns are of such nature and enjoy such popularity that it is not too much to claim that for the evangelicals, worship—traditionally filled with powerful spiritual *singing*, emotional preaching, intense public prayer, and a culminating invitation to "come to Christ"—is literally a ritual recapitulation of the primal revival experience.

Hymnody therefore provides not only a vast array of hymn texts and music texts to be used as expressions of evangelical religious culture, but even more importantly, when they are placed at the center of inquiry as perhaps the most characteristic and influential form of evangelical articulation itself, they reveal a new range of primary *meanings* and significations for America's largest Protestant religious culture. The audible religious culture of hymns and the methods necessary to understand it are of first importance to understanding what religion meant as a lived reality for American evangelicals.

NOTES

1. The only critical edition of this work, superbly executed, is Selma L. Bishop (1962).
2. For Watts's complete program for "renovating" the psalms, see Isaac Watts (1813, 7: 1–23).
3. On the 1801 Plan of Union, see Walker and Nordbeck ([1893] 1991).
4. On McKendree, see Youngs (1830, 388–89).
5. See especially 146–53, 157–72, 191–204.
6. The collection can be found in both Davies (1967) and Hildebrandt and Oliver (1983).
7. See Williams (1962) and McDannell and Lang (1988).
8. For the musicological context of Billings and his early American colleagues, see Temperly (1979 141–243)

WORKS CITED

Barbour, J. Murray. 1960. *The Church Music of William Billings*. East Lansing: Michigan State University Press.

Benson, Louis F. 1915. *The English Hymn: Its Development and Use in Worship*. London: Hodder & Stoughton.

Bishop, Selma L. 1962. *Isaac Watts, Hymns and Spiritual Songs, 1707–1748: A Study in Early Eighteenth Century Language Changes*. London: Faith.

Booth, Mark W. 1981. *The Experience of Songs*. New Haven: Yale University Press.

Britton, Allen, Irving Lowen, and Richard Crawford. 1990. *American Sacred Music Imprints, 1698–1810*. Worcester, Mass.: American Antiquarian Society.

Broadman Hymnal. 1940. *The Broadman Hymnal. . . .* Nashville: Broadman.

Davie, Donald, ed. 1981. *The New Oxford Book of Christian Verse*. Oxford: Oxford University Press.

Davies, Horton. 1940. *Three Centuries of American Hymnody*. Cambridge, Mass.: Harvard University Press.

———. 1967. *Worship and Theology in England*. 5 vols. Plates. Princeton: Princeton University Press.

Davies, Donald. 1982. *Dissentient Voice: The Ward-Phillips Lectures for 190 with Some Related Pieces*. Notre Dame, Ind.: University of Notre Dame Press.

———. 1993. *The Eighteenth-Century Hymn in England*. Cambridge: Cambridge University Press.

Dwight, Timothy. 1801. *The Psalms of David Imitated in the language of the New Testament, and applied to the Christian use and worship. A New Edition, in which the psalms omitted by Dr. Watts are versified by Timothy Dwight*. Hartford, Conn.: Hudson & Goodwin.

Edwards, Jonathan and C. C. Goen. 1972. *The Great Awakening: A Faithful Narrative*. New Haven, Conn.: Yale University Press.

Eliade, Mircea. 1959. *The Sacred and the Profane*. New York: Harcourt, Brace.

Geertz, Clifford. 1973. *The Interpretation of Cultures: Selected Essays*. New York: Basic Books.

Hambrick-Stowe, Charles. 1982. *The Practice of Piety: Puritan Devotional Disciplines in Seventeenth Century New England*. Chapel Hill: University of North Carolina Press.

Hatch, Nathan. 1989. *The Democratization of American Christianity*. New Haven: Yale University Press.

Hildebrandt, Franz, and Oliver A. Beckerlegge, eds. 1983. *A Collection of Hymns for the Use of the People Called Methodists*. Vol. 7. *The Works of John Wesley*. Oxford: Clarendon.

McDannell, Colleen, and Bernhard Lang. 1988. *Heaven: A History*. New Haven: Yale University Press.

McKay, David P., and Richard Crawford. 1975. *William Billings of Boston: Eighteenth Century Composer*. Princeton: Princeton University Press.

McKendree, William, and Francis Asbury. 1819.*The Methodist Pocket Hymn-Book. Revised and Improved*. New York: J. Soule and T. Mason for the Methodist Episcopal Church in the United States.

Mercer, Jesse. 1810. *The Cluster of Spiritual Songs, Divine Hymns, and Sacred Poems*. 3rd ed. Augusta, Ga.: Hobby and Bunce.

Rippen, John, and Issac Watts. 1787. *A Selection of Hymns from the Best Authors: Intended to Be an Appendix to Dr. Watts's Psalms and Hymns*. London: Thomas Wilkins.

Temperly, Nicholas. 1979. *The Music of the English Parish Church*. Vol. 1. Cambridge: Cambridge University Press.

Tennent, Gilbert. 1967. "The Dangers of An Unconverted Ministry." In Sydney E. Ahlstrom, ed., *Theology in America*. Indianapolis: Bobbs-Merrill.

Walker, Williston, ed. 1991. *The Creeds and Platforms of Congregationalism*. With an introduction by Elizabeth Nordbeck. Repr. New York: Pilgrim. Orig. ed., New York: Scribner: 1893.

Wesley, John. 1737. *Charleston Hymnal (Collection of Psalms and Hymns)*. Charles-Town: Lewis Timothy.

Watts, Isaac. 1707. *Hymns and Spiritual Songs*. London: J. Humfreys for John Lawrence at the Angel in the Poultrey.

———. 1709. *Hymns and Spiritual Songs*. 2nd ed. London: J. Humfreys for John Lawrence at the Angel in the Poultrey.

———. 1813. *An Essay Towards the Improvement of Psalmody*. In Williston Walker and Elizabeth Nordbeck, eds., *The Creeds and Platforms of Congregationalism*. vol. 7.

William, R. Hutchison. 1987. *Errand into the World: American Protestant Thought and Foreign Missions*. Chicago: University of Chicago Press.

Williams, George Huntston. 1962. *The Radical Reformation*. Philadelphia: Westminster.

Youngs, James. 1830. *A History of the Most Interesting Events in the Rise and Progress of Methodism in Europe and America*. New York: A. Daggett.

6

The Evolution of the Music of German American Protestants in Their Hymnody: A Case Study from an American Perspective

Paul Westermeyer

As German communities adopted the English language in their worship in the United States, their hymnody and its music were influenced as much or more by Anglo-American currents as by German ones.[1] These communities also sometimes seemed to think that what they did was German when it was essentially Anglo-American. Henry Harbaugh, "Mr. Pennsylvania German," illustrates both of these points. Before getting to the case study of Henry Harbaugh, however, we need to trace what he inherited.

German Antecedents

By 1780 there were more than 200 German Reformed churches in Pennsylvania and nearby states (see Gaustad 1976, 28). Like their German Lutheran compatriots, the German Reformed used European hymnals, especially those from Marburg, Germany, which Christopher Saur reprinted in Germantown, Pennsylvania. The *Neu-vermehrt-und vollständiges Gesang-buch* of 1753 was typical. In good

Reformed fashion, it contained the Psalter in Ambrosius Lobwasser's translation, but, with more freedom than psalters of some other Reformed groups, it also contained 700 "auserlesener alter und neuer Geistreichen Liedern" ("Choice Old and New Spiritually Enriching Songs") which were sung in Reformed churches in the Palatinate and surrounding regions. Some editions, like the one in 1772, added Pennsylvania to the list of regions: "Hessisch-Hanauisch-Pfältzisch-Pennsylvanischen und meheren andern angrätzenden Landen" ("Hessen-Hanau-Palatinate-Pennsylvania and other bordering lands").

The first official American German Reformed hymnal appeared in 1797 with the title *Das neue und verbesserte Gesangbuch.* It relied on its European predecessors in organization and contents—the 150 Psalms were followed by a "Collection" of 700 "alter und neuer Geistreichen Lieder"—and moved in the same pietistic directions (the church year, for example, was less obvious) as its Lutheran counterpart, the *Erbauliche Lieder-Sammlung* of 1786 with which it had 153 hymns in common. Common directions and hymns were not surprising since, on the one hand, denominational boundaries were indistinct at that time and, on the other, the Reformed and Lutheran hymnals were edited by leading Philadelphia pastors who were friends. The pastors even worked together on a joint tune book that was never published.[2] John William Hendel (1740–1798), pastor of the Race Street Church, edited the Reformed book that was nicknamed for him, "Hendel's Gesangbuch." J. H. C. Helmuth (1745–1825), pastor of St. Michael's and Zion, was among the editors of the Lutheran hymnal. Both books enjoyed considerable popularity and were used until 1850 when they were last printed.

Some German Reformed and Lutheran churches shared common buildings called "union" churches. It is not surprising, therefore, that, during the first part of the nineteenth century when confessional boundaries were vague anyway, merger attempts and shared educational endeavors were being discussed by these groups. They bore no fruit, just like Hendel's and Helmuth's tune book. A joint hymnal was published in 1817 in Baltimore, however, by Schaeffer and Maund. Called *Das Gemeinschaftliche Gesangbuch,* it received both German Reformed and Lutheran endorsements. It omitted many classic German chorales, abbreviated or altered others. Although it did not stimulate congregational singing it was a successful commercial venture throughout much of the nineteenth century.[3]

In 1842 the German Reformed published a "hastily-prepared" hymnal (see Dubbs 1885, 355), *Eine Sammlung Evangelischer Lieder,* which was popularly known as the "Chambersburg Hymnbook" because of its place of publication (see Westermeyer 1978, 36–37). It followed Hendel's *Gesangbuch* for part of its organization, but moved in a still more pietistic direction and obliterated the usual Reformed division between psalms and hymns. The preface recognized that the tunes of many psalms and many hymns had become unfamiliar, especially to the young, and sought to rectify the problem with a melody index that suggested alternative tunes. Still, however, the heritage of German chorale melodies dominated the book. For the 673 texts, 212 tunes were suggested, plus four metrical designations. In characteristic fashion no music was printed. Of the 212 tunes, about 120 grew out of—or in the case of psalm tunes like Psalm 42 ("Freu Dich sehr") had been assimilated into—the German chorale tradition. The other tunes were listed in the tune index and, with rare exceptions, were not mentioned with the hymns themselves.

A large number of hymn texts in *Eine Sammlung Evangelischer Lieder* are sung to a small number of hymn tunes. Fifteen tunes were listed for use with ten or more (as many as 79) hymns. Below are with the number of their occurrences. "Wer nur den lieben Gott" topped the list by a large margin.

Eine Sammlung: Tunes Used 10 Times or More

	Tune	Times
1.	Allein Gott in der Höh	18
2.	Alle Menschen müssen sterben	20
3.	Es ist gewißlich an der Zeit	39
4.	Gott des Himmels und der Erden	13
5.	Jesus, meine Zuversicht	13
6.	Liebster Jesu, wir sind hier	12
7.	Mir nach spricht	10
8.	Nun ruhen alle Wälder	27
9.	O Durchbrecher alle	11
10.	O Gott Du frommer Gott	19
11.	Psalm 42 (includes "Freu Dich sehr")	36
12.	Ringe Recht wenn Gottes Gnade	26
13.	Wer nur den lieben Gott	79
14.	Wie schön leuchtet der Morgenstern	10
15.	Zeuch mich, zeuch mich	15

A comparison of this list with two earlier German Reformed hymnals used in this country is instructive. In the 1772 edition of the *Neu-vermehrt-und vollständiges Gesangbuch,* which maintained the Reformed division between psalms and hymns, all but twenty-five of the psalms have their own tunes printed out in musical notation before their respective psalms. Tune names are given for the twenty-five that are not notated. Twenty tunes are used more than once for the psalms, only one as many as four times (Psalm 24), three used three times, sixteen twice. Seven tunes are given in the psalter that are not repeated in the hymnal.

In the hymn section of *Neu-vermehrt-und vollständiges Gesangbuch* there are 700 hymns followed by an "Anhang" ("Appendix") of 30 additional hymns. For the 730 hymn texts 275 tunes are suggested. The tunes are notated more sparingly than those for the psalms, and those that are notated seem to be the least familiar ones. Fifty of the tunes are psalm tunes. The rest are a repository of classic German chorale tunes with some later additions. There are only nine, possibly only eight, tunes repeated more than ten times. Below is a list of the number of their occurrences. Psalm 42 tops the list (39 times), followed by "Wer nur den lieben Gott" (27 times).

Neu-vermehrt Hymnal: Tunes Used 10 Times or More

1. Herr Jesu Christ	10
(may refer to more than one tune)	
2. Liebster Jesu	14
3. Nun freut Euch	15
4. O Gott Du frommer Gott	15
5. Psalm 42	39
(includes "Freu Dich sehr")	
6. Psalm 100	15
(not "Old One Hundredth" which is Psalm 134, used four times)	
7. Wer nur den lieben Gott	27
8. Werde munter	12
9. Wie schön leuchtet	14

In terms of the number of psalm tunes and the number of occurrences of hymn tunes, the 1828 edition of Hendel's *Das Neue und verbesserte Gesangbuch* occupies a position halfway between the 1772 edition of *Neu-vermehrt-und vollständiges Gesangbuch* and the 1842 *Eine Sammlung*. There, nineteen tunes were given for the 150 Psalms, of which only nine were psalm tunes. Of the nine tunes, only three were unique to the psalter; the other six also appear in the hymn section. Most important, the three dominant tunes for the psalms were chorale tunes.

Das Neue Psalter: Tunes Used 10 Times or More

1. Allein Gott in der Höh	17
2. Nun sich der Tag	17
3. Wer nur den lieben Gott läßt walten	11

As regards hymn tune occurrences, the 1828 *Das Neue und verbesserte Gesangbuch* listed 93 tunes for 700 hymns. Nineteen tunes were used with ten or more hymns. As in the 1842 *Eine Sammlung*, "Wer nur den lieben Gott" tops the list, with Psalm 42 not far behind.

Das Neue Hymnal: Tunes Used 10 Times or More

	Tune	Times
1.	Allein Gott in der Höh	26
2.	Alle Menschen müssen sterben	28
3.	Es ist gewißlich an der Zeit	41
4.	Gott des Himmels	10
5.	Helft Gottes Güt' mir	13
6.	Herr Jesu Christ	10
7.	Herzlich thut mich verlangen	14
8.	Liebster Jesu	12
9.	Nun freut Euch	15
10.	Nun ruhen alle Wälder	15
11.	O Gott Du frommer Gott	32
12.	Psalm 8	10
13.	Psalm 38	10
14.	Psalm 42	61
15.	Psalm 100	19
16.	Was Gott thut	11
17.	Wer nur den lieben Gott	67
18.	Wie schön leuchtet	18
19.	Zeuch mich, zeuch mich	14

Collating the above information about the three German Reformed hymnals between 1772 and 1842 yields the following observations:

1. The most popular tunes among the German Reformed were Psalm 42 and "Wer nur den lieben Gott."
2. The psalm tunes had the least staying power. Already in the 1772 *Neu-vermehrt-und vollständiges Gesangbuch* most of them had to be printed out, but there were still 129 of them (125 in the psalter plus four additional psalm tunes in the hymnal). In the 1828 *Das neue . . . Gesangbuch* there were 29—100 fewer (26 in the psalter and three more in the hymnal), and in *Eine Sammlung* only seven. *Eine Sammlung* did the obvious by collapsing what remained of the psalms into the hymns.
3. The repertoire of tunes from the church's German tradition diminished and became less well-known. In the 1772 *Neu-vermehrt* there

> were 282, in the 1828 *Das neue . . . Gesangbuch* 96 (this count may be higher because tunes were not given for many hymns), and in the 1842 *Eine Sammlung* about 120. Not only did the number decrease, but the better-known ones, like "Wer nur den lieben Gott," were used for more texts. With *Eine Sammlung* the English scheme of metrical designations was introduced along with an attempt to suggest alternate tunes from the English environment.

By the middle of the nineteenth century, then, psalm singing as a separate entity was pretty much lost for the German Reformed, and even the more popular traditional German chorale tunes were being forgotten.

Philip Schaff, the foremost nineteenth-century American historian, at mid-century was teaching at the German Reformed seminary in Mercersburg, Pennsylvania. In 1855 the Synod requested that he chair a committee and prepare a new German hymnal. A hymnological expert who the year before had been in Germany and had learned about the revival of classical German hymnody, Schaff was prepared for the task. He viewed the *Gemeinschaftliches Gesangbuch* as "beneath all criticism" (Schaff 1869, 241). Faced with it and the unsatisfactory "Chambersburg Hymnal" (*Eine Sammlung*) that never entered the life blood of the denomination (see Dubbs 1885, 355), he provided the German Reformed church in 1859 with an alternative, his *Deutsches Gesangbuch* (see Westermeyer 1978, 84–86). It recovered the chorale heritage and balanced the use of tunes, stimulated congregational singing, and was printed in large and pocket editions at least fifteen times until 1916.

The 540 hymns in Schaff's *Deutsches Gesangbuch* called into play 195 tunes. Of those only three were not from the German chorale heritage. Many of the tunes were used more than once, obviously. But the popularity of certain tunes was different, and so was the proportion of the number of times the new popular tunes are used. "Wer nur den lieben Gott" was only used five times and Psalm 42 ("Freu Dich sehr"), six times. "Wie schön leuchtet," the "Queen of Chorales," topped the list by appearing 25 times, followed by "Wachet auf," the "King of Chorales," sixteen times, as opposed to 79 times for "Wer nur den lieben Gott" and 36 times for Psalm 42 in the "Chambersburg Hymnal."

Below is the list of tunes used ten or more times in the 1874 edition of Schaff's *Deutches Gesangbuch*.[4]

Deutsches Gesangbuch: Tunes Used Ten Times or More

	Tune	Times
1.	Herr Gott, Dich loben alle wir	10
2.	Herzlich thut mich verlangen	12
3.	Jesus, meine Zuversicht	14
4.	Nun ruhen alle Wälder	14

5. O Du Liebe meiner Liebe 12
6. Vom Himmel hoch, da komm ich her 13
7. Wachet auf, ruft uns die Stimme 16
8. Wie schön leuchtet der Morgenstern 25

The strong presence of "Vom Himmel hoch" and "Wachet auf" on this list indicates the influence of the classical and confessional chorale revival. Schaff was not unconcerned about what German Reformed folk in the United States had been singing, so Psalm 42 and "Wer nur den lieben Gott" were not omitted, but Schaff was clearly intent on making a course correction and restoring some balance.

English Antecedents

While this activity in the German language was going on, the needs of the increasingly English-speaking German population did not go unnoticed. In 1830 the German Reformed Synod adopted an English hymnal. Called *Psalms and Hymns*, its standard revised edition appeared in 1834 (see Westermeyer 1978, 34–35). The book was reprinted until 1868. The German and Reformed characteristics of this hymnal were minimal. Formally one could tell it was Reformed because it retained the traditional division into psalms and hymns. But there was virtually no clue to its Germanic association. The English evangelical tradition overwhelmed it. Of the 299 entries for the 150 Psalms (many of the psalms were divided into parts), 169 were by Isaac Watts. Of the 520 hymns that followed the psalms, 100 were by Watts. The leading contributors of hymns after Watts were Philip Doddridge with 37, Anne Steele with 36, John Newton with 24, Charles Wesley with 20, Benjamin Beddome with 12, William Cowper with 12, John Fawcett with 8, and Elizabeth Scott with 6. Watts and these other English evangelical authors accounted for 49 percent of the texts. Most of the remainder of the texts were by other eighteenth-century writers in the same style. There were only four or five translations from the German, and not from the classics of the German chorale heritage. One was by Johann Hertzog, two by Wesley of Gerhardt, and one by Nicholaus Zinzendorf. (The possible fifth is Wesley's "Hearts of Stone, Relent, Relent," if it is a translation.)

Psalms and Hymns was typically a book of texts, but unlike the "Chambersburg Hymnal" and other German hymnals, it did not give tune names with the hymn texts. It used the English system of metrical designations, most of which were the meters Watts used: Short Meter, Common Meter, and Long Meter—60 of the first, 348 of the second, and 302 of the third. The tunes that accompanied these hymns came therefore from the English heritage, not the more varied German metrical tradition. In short, the hymnal essentially obliterated the German chorale tune heritage along with the German chorale texts.

It should be noted that the German Reformed were not unique in what they were doing as they adapted to their English-speaking environment. Their Lutheran compatriots published in 1828 a comparable English hymnal called *Hymns Selected and Original* (see Westermeyer 1978, 33–34). It was printed until 1864. Their top ten contributors also came from the English evangelical tradition and were remarkably similar to the ones in *Psalms and Hymns*: Isaac Watts with 197, Anne Steele with 49, Charles Wesley with 49, Philip Doddridge with 43, John Newton with 38, James Montgomery with 31 (he had five in *Psalms and Hymns*), William Cowper with 26, Samuel Stennett with 18, John Fawcett with 12, and William Beddome with 11. The Lutherans also dropped tune names and included the usual English metrical designations in a breakdown not unlike that of *Psalms and Hymns*: 76 were Short Meter, 329 were Common Meter, and 329 were Long Meter.

Characteristically the Lutherans included more hymns and had a bit more regard for their heritage. They chose a total of 1024 texts, 30 of which were translations from the German. In a table at the back of the book they gave the German texts of the 30 German hymns with 35 tunes, including alternatives. The alternatives were also from the chorale tune heritage, not from Anglo-American sources. Here are the tunes and the number of times they are cited.

German Tunes in *Hymns Selected and Original* (1828)

	Tune	Times cited
1.	Ach Gott, vom Himmel sieh darein	1
2.	Allein Gott in der Höh' sei Ehr	1
3.	Auf, auf! Ihr Reichsgenossen	1
4.	Aus tiefer Noth Ruf ich zu dir	1
5.	Befiehl' Du Deine Wege	1
6.	Das Brünnlein quillt	1
7.	Der Tag ist hin, die Sonne gehet unter	1
8.	Der Tag ist hin, Mein Jesu	1
9.	Dies irae, dies illa	1
10.	Ein' feste Burg ist unser Gott	1
11.	Erhalt uns, Herr, bei Deinem Wort	1
12.	Es ist das Heil uns kommen her	3
13.	Es ist gewißlich an der Zeut	1
14.	Gott ist getreu, der über meine	1
15.	Gott ist getreu, der über meine	1
16.	Gott ist getreu, sein Herz	1
17.	Gott ist getreu, sein Herz, sein Vaterherz	1
18.	Hast Du, denn, Jesu, Dein Angesicht	1

19. Herzlich thut mich verlangen	1
20. Ich habe nun den Grund gefunden	1
21. Jesus nimmt die Sünder an	1
22. Jesus meine Zuversicht	1
23. Jenen Tag, den Tag der Wehen	1
24. Lobt Gott, Ihr Christen, allzugleich	1
25. Lobet den Herrn, den Mächtigen	1
26. Noch sing ich hier aus dunkler Ferne	2
27. Nun freut Euch, lieben Christen	1
28. Nun komm der Heiden Heiland	1
29. O daß ich tausend Zungen hätte	1
30. O Ewigkeit Du Donnerwort	1
31. O Haupt voll Blut und Wunden	1
32. O heil'ger Geist, kehr' bei uns ein	1
33. Sollt ich nicht meinem Gott nicht singen	1
34. Wenn ich, o Schöpfer, Deine Macht	1
35. Wer weiß wie nahe mir mein Ende	1
36. Wie schön leucht uns der Morgenstern	1
37. Von Gott will ich nicht lassen	1

There are probably 35, not 37, tunes since numbers 14 and 15 almost certainly refer to the same tune, as do numbers 19 and 31.

The Lutherans did not quite obliterate the chorale tune heritage as the Reformed did, even though 30 translated German hymns with 35 chorale tunes is not a high percentage for a volume of 1024 texts, especially when classic tunes like "Wachet auf" and "Vom Himmel hoch" are missing or when a tune name like "Wie schön *leucht uns*" (the title of a text which the German Reformed also used, referring to the same tune as "Wie schön leuchtet") indicates pietism's erosion of the heritage.

Henry Harbaugh

Henry Harbaugh[5] was born into the flux of this period—on October 28, 1817, the year *Das Gemeinschaftliche Gesangbuch* was first published. From German Swiss and Palatinate ancestry, Henry was the tenth child of George and Anna Harbaugh who lived in a stone house next to a creek at the Pennsylvania-Maryland border, four miles south of Waynesboro, Pennsylvania. There Henry grew up, drinking in the Pennsylvania German life around him.

In August of 1836, not quite nineteen, he left home for the "promised land" of Ohio like many of his contemporaries. He settled in the area of Massilon, Canal Dover, and New Hagerstown, Ohio. There he worked for a house builder and a builder of machinery, taught school for three winters, attended the New Hagerstown Academy for two summers, studied, read, and engaged in lectures and debates. Through his contacts with the Massilon church and its choir he quickly became a singing school instructor, and one of the essays he delivered at the New Hagerstown Academy was on "Music."

In the fall of 1840 he left Ohio and enrolled at Marshall College in Mercersburg, Pennsylvania. He stayed there three years, the first at the College and the last two at both Marshall College and Mercersburg Seminary. His course of study was neither normal nor complete, but he was getting older and did not have much money. So he was advised to cut his formal education short and enter the ministry with the study he had completed. In December of 1843 he received a call to two German Reformed congregations in Lewisburg, one of which required German every other Sunday in its services. He was ordained in January of 1844.

After helping to build up the church and dedicating a new building in Lewisburg, he accepted a call to First Reformed Church in Lancaster in 1850. There he presided over the consecration of a new building in 1854, but not everything was peaceful in Lancaster. Harbaugh supported both temperance and the liturgy the denomination was working on, and a majority of the congregation turned against him (though First Reformed eventually became one of the staunchest supporters of the liturgy).

In 1860 he left Lancaster and was called to the fledgling St. John's Church in Lebanon where the liturgy and the church year were greeted with enthusiasm. In Lebanon his leadership helped turn St. John's into a place humming with activity. But he stayed only three years, for in October of 1863 the Synod elected him Professor of Didactic and Practical Theology at the Seminary in Mercersburg. There he remained until his premature death at the age of 50 on December 28, 1867.

Harbaugh, in addition to his work as a pastor and teacher, wrote extensively. He founded the popular monthly called the *Guardian* in 1850, and edited and contributed to it until 1866. He contributed to and briefly edited the more scholarly *Mercersburg Review* where the "Mercersburg" theological and liturgical themes were being hammered out. *The Sainted Dead*, *Heavenly Recognition*, and *The Heavenly Home* were completed by 1853. They concerned life after death. Then he did a series for the *Guardian* on the birds of the Bible, followed by a manual on church membership. During his time in Lancaster, he found Michael Schlatter's journal and translated it. (Michael Schlatter [1716–1790] organized the first German Reformed synod on American soil in 1747 and is for the German Reformed what Henry Melchior Muhlenberg is for the Lutherans.) That led him to write *The Life of Michael Schlatter*, which he followed with two volumes and more called *The Fathers of the Reformed Church*. His devotional book for the young, *The Golden Censer*, was still being used and published as late as 1954.

Whatever else Harbaugh may have done, however, he was known mostly both in and beyond German Reformed circles for his Pennsylvania Dutch poetry. He was even called "Mr. Pennsylvania German" or "Mr. Pennsylvania Dutchman." "Dutch" here is a Low German form of "Deutsch" and refers to the Germans in Pennsylvania of Swiss and Palatinate descent among whom Harbaugh grew up. It includes the more "churchly" German Reformed and Lutherans like Harbaugh himself and his family (his brother David became a Lutheran pastor), the plain or peace people like the Mennonites, and those Germans especially influenced by the Second Great Awakening whom Don Yoder referred to as the "bush meeting" Dutch (1961). Harbaugh was regarded as the most popular of the Pennsylvania Dutch writers (see Gibbons [1869] 1963, 38). Well over a century later, in my lifetime, I have spoken with Germans from Pennsylvania or surrounding states who still remember Harbaugh's poems.

Harbaugh's Pennsylvania Dutch poetry was published posthumously in *Harbaugh's Harfe* (1870). The first entry was "Das Alt Schulhaus an der Krick" which began like this.

> Heit is 's 'xaectly zwansig Johr,
>   Das ich bin owwe naus;
> Nau bin ich widder lewig z'rick
> Um schteh am Schulhaus an d'r Krick,
>   Juscht neekscht an's Dady's Haus. (H. Harbaugh 1870, 13)

Harbaugh himself made a translation.

> Today it is just twenty years,
>   Since I began to roam;
> Now, safely back, I stand once more,
> Before the quaint old school-house door,
>   Close by my father's home. (ibid., 87)

Harbaugh also wrote English poems, not connected to his Pennsylvania Dutch creations (1860). His English poetry included some hymns. He is especially known for the hymn "Jesus, I Live to Thee." In 1861 he included it and four others by him in a hymnal he edited for schools, especially for his Sunday school at St. John's Church in Lebanon. This small hymnbook made a big hit in the denomination and was used at least until 1901. It was called *Hymns and Chants* (see Westermeyer 1978, 86–93). That brings us to our case study.

Harbaugh and Hymnody

In the popular mind the cluster of hymns, devotional writings, hymnal editing, and Pennsylvania Dutch poetry with which Harbaugh is associated has left the impression that he represents or even, as "Mr. Pennsylvania Dutchman," embodies the German hymnic musical heritage as well.

This is not without basis in what might be called a logical expectation, not only related to his representative "Pennsylvania Dutch" character. Harbaugh knew, studied with, and worked closely with the principal Mercersburg theological figures John Williamson Nevin and Philip Schaff. He knew Philip Schaff's work in German hymnody, and we realize this because his *Deutsches Gesangbuch* referred to or actually printed the German chorale tunes (in their isometric versions) with texts, thus reversing the attempt in *Eine Sammlung* to find substitutes.[6] He knew and had access to the German language with its hymns, and could claim the ability to translate German poetry into English.[7] At the point of transition when he lived, he could easily have turned all that into a concern not only for the German chorales of his heritage, but also for the music that goes with them.

But he did not do that, as *Hymns and Chants* amply indicates. *Hymns and Chants*, like the other English hymnals we have encountered, was controlled by the English evangelical tradition. Of its 217 hymns, 62 were by Watts, 12 by Charles Wesley, 11 by Anne Steele, and ten by Philip Doddridge. The English system of meters, not tune names, was used. Watts's three meters dominated the book. If one includes the 15 doxologies and the 217 hymns the count is 87 hymns in Common Meter, 55 in Long Meter, and 33 in Short Meter.

There is barely a trace of the chorale tunes we have encountered: One can assume Harbaugh intended "Herzlich thut mich verlangen" for Gerhardt's "O Sacred Head" (83), and perhaps he had German tunes in mind for some other texts like Gerhardt's "Jesus, Thy Boundless Love to Me" (60) and John Wesley's version of Zinzendorf's "Jesus, Thy Blood and Righteousness" (78). That is not clear.

Two things are clear. First, the only music given in the book came in the last section titled "Chants." The canticles and psalms included in that section were supplied with Anglican chants and instructions for their use.

Second, as to choice of hymn tunes, the tune Harbaugh himself selected for his hymn "Jesus, I Live to Thee" is instructive. In 1861 he taught this hymn to his Sunday school at St. John's in Lebanon, singing it to them with the tune "Lake Enon" with which it has continued to be associated (see Haeussler 1952, 287). "Lake Enon" is a tune by I. B. Woodbury (1818–1858), a blacksmith born in Massachusetts who went to Europe to become an operatic singer. He returned to the United States, founded singing schools in New England, taught in New York, edited, and published. An Anglophile who visited England on several occasions, he composed "Lake Enon" for the English Baptist writer Anne Steele's text "While My Redeemer's Near" (ibid., 289 and 991). It first appeared in 1854 in Woodbury's book *The Cythara* (ibid., 289).

Woodbury's Short Meter tune begins with, ends with, and is controlled by the upward leap of a major sixth. That interval alone tells the tale. The 1894 edition of Schaff's *Deutsches Gesangbuch* "mit Noten" included among its classic German chorale tunes some later German and Anglo-American melodies. But if you count up all the tunes that use the upward leap of a major sixth in that edition, including repeated tunes, the total is 28 out of 550 or about five percent. If you add upward major sixths between phrases, there are nine more, so that the total comes to 37 out of 550 or a little less than seven percent. This tally includes four appearances of "O daß ich tausend Zungen hätte" where the interval is hidden.

If you do a similar count in a book published one year later, *Gospel Hymns Nos. 1 to 6 Complete* of 1895 (Sankey et al. 1972 [1895]), you find a different world. In *Gospel Hymns* 132 of the 705 musical entries (there are 739 hymns in the book, but 34 are only texts), or almost 19 percent, employ the upward major sixth. If you add occurrences between phrases, there are ten more, bring the total to about 20 percent. If you add instances where a perfect fourth is interpolated or where the contour of the phrase is controlled by the upward major sixth, there are another 171 to add to the tally, which brings the total to more than 44 percent.

The upward major sixth is clearly a prominent melodic signature of Sankey, McGranahan, Stebbins, Bliss, and their gospel hymnody. It is not characteristic of German chorale tunes. Harbaugh was therefore calling into play a musical syntax that is related to the American phenomenon of what came to be called gospel hymnody. It is not related to the German tunes of his hymnic tradition. That is, musically, in both the Anglican chant he printed (which, incidentally, *Gospel Hymns* also occasionally included) and in the tune he selected for his most famous hymn, "Mr. Pennsylvania German" used the Anglo-American heritage, not the German one.

This can be explained in different ways. One is to suggest that Harbaugh was confused, as James Hastings Nichols says (1961, 299). He means Harbaugh supported but did not understand the theological and historical work of his mentors Nevin and Schaff. The same thing could be said musically: he mistakenly and unknowingly used the musical syntax of the very revivalism which he himself, and Nevin and Schaff as well, opposed.

Another possibility is that by the time he published *Hymns and Chants* he had sorted things out more clearly, but found himself in a bind. He was the popularizer of Nevin and Schaff's Mercersburg theology, but also identified himself with the Pennsylvania Dutch. If Yoder is right, they expressed their ethnicity primarily in the Pennsylvania spirituals of the "bush-meeting Dutch"—the revivalist German sects like the Winebrennarians and the Evangelical Association that grew out of the Second Great Awakening (Yoder 1961, especially 78–94). Harbaugh clearly avoided the revivalist spirituals, but did not always stick to what we might regard as the logic of his position, for example, by using chorale tunes. Did he think that what he was doing would lead to their gradual reintroduction, but that at his cultural moment that was impossible? Is that what he implied in the "Preface" to *Hymns and Chants* (Harbaugh 1861, xii–xiii; see Westermeyer 1978, 86–93)?

A third possibility is to see the Mercersburg evangelical catholic position as itself mollifying the German tradition, so that among English-speaking people in an essentially English-speaking country the German musical tradition would not be expected to be very strong.

Is Harbaugh Paradigmatic?

All these are interesting and possible reasons for Harbaugh's use of Anglo-American rather than German musical materials. Such possibilities invite further exploration. But they do not concern me here. What intrigues me here is the question of whether Harbaugh was a lone figure, or is he paradigmatic for Germans more generally on the American scene? That is, though perceived it as essentially German, Harbaugh in fact did not invigorate his Germanic heritage as Schaff did with the *Deutsches Gesangbuch*, but introduced music that was Anglo-American. Is that the pattern German hymnic music has taken in the English-speaking American context?

One would have to do many more case studies to demonstrate such a thesis. But a quick look at several German hymnals in the twentieth century at the very least confirms the importance of the Anglo-American heritage.

The *Lutheran Hymnal* of 1941 was produced by one of the most insular German groups, the Missouri Synod Lutherans. A majority of its tunes bear witness to a German heritage. But it is not "all" German, nor as overwhelmingly German as is often thought. With a few exceptions like the *Sanctus* and *Agnus Dei*, the service materials use Anglican chant, not the Gregorian heritage as filtered through Luther, nor the music of Luther's metrical settings from the *Deutsche Messe*, nor something in either of those styles. The hymn tunes are mostly German, to be sure, 62 percent, but the Anglo-American heritage nevertheless accounts for almost 28 percent of the tunes.

The *Hymnal* of the Evangelical and Reformed Church of the same year was prepared for the German Reformed and their partner in merger, the Evangelical Synod of North America, a group of pietistic Lutherans who came from union church attempts in Germany as foes of the Missouri Synod. Here one would expect less German, more English, and a warmer embrace of the adopted culture than the more insular Missouri Synod. But the proportions for a hymnal of German people are still somewhat surprising. Only about 26 percent of the tunes are German, while 41 percent are English and 19 percent American—or sixty percent Anglo-American.

More recently, the *Lutheran Book of Worship* (1978), by the groups that formed the Evangelical Lutheran Church in America (used by some Missouri Synod churches as well), has been perceived as having all German music. Yet fewer than 33 percent of its hymn tunes are of German provenance. If "German" is taken to mean everything that is "Germanic" or "Nordic" and one includes Scandinavian, Polish, Slovak, and Swiss sources in the tabulation (and there is obvious cross-fertilization here so that hard and fast lines are hard to draw), the total is just over 41 percent. That still is lower than Anglo-American sources which total 44 percent of the book.

Qualifications

(1) I have utilized hymnals and the proportions they embody in this study. That obviously is only one piece of the story. Hymnals do reflect a given church's practice, and they do need to be taken seriously; but they also reflect editors' judgments. What a church actually uses from a hymnal may not match the proportions in the hymnal, as different congregations do different things. Actual usage is notoriously difficult to document, especially in the nineteenth century before the advent of service folders. Even in the twentieth century things are not so clear as they may seem.

Missouri Synod churches that sang Anglican chant for the Ordinary of their liturgy Sunday after Sunday, for example, actually utilized a higher proportion of English materials than their hymnal proportions suggest. This was especially true in congregations where Anglo-American hymns were regularly chosen instead of translations of German chorales (as in some congregations on the East Coast) and less true where German chorales were the standard fare (as in some congregations in the Midwest).

(2) It is equally difficult to document that a community perceives something to be German when it is not. I have not attempted to do such documentation here. Like actual usage of hymns and hymn tunes, such careful work would require studies far longer than this one. I have responded instead to my own observations of German people from German Reformed and Lutheran backgrounds in the East and Midwest where this perception appears to have been operative.

I have observed it among educated pastors and lay people, especially in two contexts. The first was in Pennsylvania in the 1960s where the assumption prevailed that singing "Harbaugh's hymn" meant doing a German musical thing.

The second context has been less benign. I noted it in the Midwest a couple decades later. When it became fashionable to sing "ethnic" music for hymns, "ethnic" meaning African American or Hispanic, music in the denominational hymnal was regarded as all German, or, depending on the context, all German/ Scandinavian or Nordic. If one inquired about the specific music the speaker or group had in mind, the reference was usually amorphous but often turned out to mean something English or American like S. S. Wesley's "Aurelia" or Lowell Mason's "Olivet."

(3) Harbaugh's use of the upward major sixth and its relation to gospel hymnody generate two further matters. One is to point out that Harbaugh did not appear to gravitate to the compound rhythms of gospel hymnody that make the rhythmic musical syntax of his hymnal quite different from it. If, as I would tend to argue, rhythm is more central than melody, Harbaugh remains distanced from gospel hymnody.

Second, it should also be asked whether Harbaugh was consciously or unconsciously drawing on eighteenth- to nineteenth-century German sources for the melodic materials to which he gravitated. For example, the tune "Canonbury" which is adapted from Robert Schumann's *Nachtstücke,* opus 23 written in 1839, starts with an upward major sixth, as does the tune for "O Gott, mein Gott" attributed to "Mozart" in the 1894 edition of Schaff's *Deutsches Gesangbuch* (number 41). These matters probably do not negate my point, but they do qualify it.

(4) This story is obviously more complex than the part of it I have isolated for sketchy study in this short article. Any full recounting of the story would need to include which German tunes fell in and out of use and, when the

influence of pietism and the influence of nineteenth-century confessional roots were recovered. One would need to investigate the rhythmic and isometric forms of the chorale tunes that separated the more confessional Lutherans from their less confessional brothers and sisters and from the German Reformed during the course of the nineteenth century. Social factors, too, would be crucial to the story, among them the impact of anti-German fervor during World War I and World War II, and the influence of the many German groups whose religious practices differed entirely from those I have examined in this essay. All of that needs to be included in a careful telling of what Germans did with the music of their hymns in this country.

My point here is not to imply that any of that is unimportant, but to suggest two other things: first, that a goodly part of what some Germans in the United States have done in their hymnic music has been as much Anglo-American as it has been German; and, second, that they have at times perceived to be German what was really Anglo-American. Precisely how important these things are and how they might color our understanding are topics for further investigations.

NOTES

1. This article relies in part on my dissertation (see Westermeyer 1978).

2. See J. H. C. Helmuth's diaries for 5 July 1794, 11 July 1794, and 19 July 1794.

3. Between 1817 and 1851 there were at least 21 printings. At mid-century two further publications were spun off from the first one: *Das Neue Gemeinschaftliche Gesangbuch* received three printings from 1850 to 1871, and the *Neuestes Gemeinschaftliches Gesangbuch* was printed 14 times between 1850 and 1889.

4. The tabulation for other editions, like 1894, differs somewhat from this one, especially for "Herr Gott, Dich loben alle wir," but the overall contours are the same.

5. The sketch of Harbaugh's life here is taken from Linn Harbaugh (1900). The biography is a bit flowery, as one might expect from its time, nonetheless the data are correct.

6. In 1861 G. F. Landenberger compiled an organ book (1861). The title of the organ book refers to the Lutheran hymnal *Deutsches Gesangbuch für die Evangelisches-Lutherische Kirche in den Vereinigten Stäten* (1849). The Lutheran hymnal was the parallel to the Reformed *Eine Sammlung* and was nicknamed "Wollenweber" for its publisher. In 1874 an edition of Schaff's *Deutsches Gesangbuch* was published in which Landenberger provided four-voice settings of the isometric versions of the chorale tunes without the *Zwischenspiele* (see Westermeyer 1978, 37, 101).

7. In addition to the musical interests already mentioned, Harbaugh directed the Reformed Church Choir while a student at Mercersburg Seminary, directed the choir at his first church in Lewisberg, and played the "bass violin" there (see Westermeyer 1978, 107).

WORKS CITED

Dubbs, Joseph Henry. 1885. *Historic Manual of the Reformed Church in the United States.* Lancaster: Inquirer Printing.

Erbauliche Lieder-Sammlung. 1786. *Erbauliche Lieder-Sammlung.* Germantaun: Leibert und Billmeyer.

Deutsches Gesangbuch. 1859. *Deutsches Gesangbuch.* Philadelphia: Lindsay and Blakiston.

Deutsches Gesangbuch für.... 1849. *Deutsches Gesangbuch für die Evangelisches-Lutherische Kirche in den Vereinigten Staaten.* Philadelphia: L. A. Wollenweber.

Gaustad, Edwin Scott. 1976. *Historical Atlas of Religion in America.* New York: Harper & Row.

Das Gemeinschaftliche Gesangbuch.... 1817. *Das Gemeinschaftliche Gesangbuch, zum gottesdienstlichen Gebrauch der Lutherischen und Reformirten Gemeinden in Nord Amerika.* Baltimore: Schaeffer und Maund.

Gibbons, Phebe E. [1869] 1963. "The Pennsylvania Dutch." *Atlantic Monthly* 24 (October, 1869). Repr. as *The Pennsylvania Dutch,* Witmer, Penn.: Allied Arts, 473–87.

Haeussler, Armin. 1952. *The Story of Our Hymns.* St. Louis: Eden.

Harbaugh, Henry. 1870. *Harbaugh's Harfe.* In Benjamin Bausman, ed., *Gedichte in Pennsylvanisch-Deutscher Mundart.* Philadelphia: Reformed Church Publication Board.

———. 1861. *Hymns and Chants: With Offices of Devotion for Use in Sunday-Schools, Parochial and Week-Day Schools. Seminaries and Colleges arranged according to the Church Year.* Philadelphia: Reformed Church Publication Board.

———. 1860. *Poems.* Philadelphia: Lindsay & Blakiston.

Harbaugh, Linn. 1900. *The Life of Henry Harbaugh, D.D.* Philadelphia: Reformed Church Publication Board.

Helmuth, J. H. C. n.d. Diaries are kept at the Lutheran Seminary in the Mt. Airy section of Philidelphia.

The Hymnal. 1941. *The Hymnal: Authorized by the General Synod of the Evangelical and Reformed Church.* St. Louis: Eden Publishing House.

Hymns Selected.... 1828. *Hymns Selected and Original, for Public and Private Worship. Published by the General Synod of the Evangelical Lutheran Church.* Gettysburg: General Synod of the Evangelical Lutheran Church.

Landenberger, G. F., comp. 1861. *Choral-Buch für die Orgel mit Zwischenspielen versehen, und für den vierstimmigen Gesang eingerichtet. Enthaltend: Melodien zu sämtlichen Versmaasen des deutschen Gesangbuches für Evangelisches-Lutherische Kirche in den Vereinigten Stäten, sowie zu denen des deutschen Gesangbuches für die Reformirten Kirche von Philip Schaff, Dr. u. Prof. der Theologie....* Philadelphia: Kohler.

Lutheran Book of Worship. 1978. *Lutheran Book of Worship.* Minneapolis: Augsburg.

The Lutheran Hymnal. 1941. *The Lutheran Hymnal.* St. Louis: Concordia.

Neu-vermehrt-und Vollständiges Gesangbuch. 1753. *Neu-vermehrt-und Vollständiges Gesangbuch.* Germanton: Christoph Sauer.

Das Neue Gemeinschaftliche Gesangbuch. 1850. *Das Neue Gemeinschaftliche Gesangbuch.* New York: Wilhelm Raddle.

Das Neue und Verbesserte Gesangbuch. 1797. *Das neue und verbesserte Gesangbuch*. Philadelphia: Steiner und Kaemmerer.

Neuestes Gemeinschaftliches Gesangbuch. 1850. *Neuestes Gemeinschaftliches Gesangbuch*. New York: Koch.

Nichols, James Hastings. 1961. *Romanticism in American Theology: Nevin and Schaff at Mercersburg*. Chicago: University of Chicago Press.

Psalms and Hymns.... 1834. *Psalms and Hymns for the Use of the German Reformed Church in the United States of America*. Chambersburg: Publication Office of the German Reformed Church.

Eine Sammlung evangelischer Lieder.... 1842. *Eine Sammlung evangelischer Lieder zum Gebrauch der Hochdeutsch Reformirten Kirche in den Ver. Staaten von Nord Amerika*. Chambersburg: M. Kieffer.

Sankey, Ira, et al., eds. [1895] 1972. *Gospel Hymns Nos. 1 to 6 Complete*. New York: Da Capo Press. An unabridged republication of the original "Excelsior Edition."

Schaff, Philip. 1869. "German Hymnology." Trans. T. C. Porter. *Mercerburg Review*, 12, no. 2 (April, 1869), 228–50.

Westermeyer, Paul. 1978. "What Shall We Sing in a Foreign Land? Theology and Cultic Song in the German Reformed and Lutheran Churches of Pennsylvania, 1830–1900." Ph.D. diss., The University of Chicago.

Yoder, Don. 1961. *Pennsylvania Spirituals*. Lancaster: Pennsylvania Folklife Society.

7

Singing from the Right Songbook: Ethnic Identity and Language Transformation in German American Hymnals

Otto Holzapfel

I cannot describe what sort of picture must have come to mind for Alexander Mack when he arrived in the New World with a group of emigrants from West Frisia in 1729. At that moment in history, there were numerous emigrations, most of them religiously motivated. To some degree, there were entire communities that formed new settlements, many of them had previously been cohesive communities gathering about a trusted pastor in the original homeland; there were also different religious communities that sought out German-speaking spiritual leaders in America. In 1727, for example, Pastor George Michael Weiss from the western German Palatinate was sent, and similarly John Peter Miller from Heidelberg arrived in 1730. Michael Schlatter from the Swiss canton of St. Gall came to the New World in 1746, but he was in fact sent by a Dutch synod. Schlatter was to return again to Europe, where he collected money for "the Germans of Pennsylvania" (Sweet 1950, 110; Noll 1992, 71). Denominations mixed with each other in the New World, and when they did so, new denominations took shape. It was also not uncommon for individuals to switch from one denomination to another, perhaps because of geographical and social conditions.

Whereas there were confessional and ideological reasons for the cohesiveness of many if not most Christian denominations in Europe, immigrants to the New World, even when religiously motivated, often left these behind. The process of transforming a European-oriented church into one that met the needs of immigrants in America steadily led to the formation of new denominations, often unfolding over a period of several generations, but nonetheless proceeding with inevitability. The exact path of these transformations is difficult for us to trace, and it is probably the case that we could understand such transformations only as each individual followed his or her own path. It is not my intent, here, to follow individual paths or even illustrate the religious transformation of immigrants with case studies. Instead, I turn to quite a different aspect of music in the immigrant culture of American religious experience, and I shift my focus to another century. I wish to sketch a picture of what religious and denominational options were open to an immigrant to the United States roughly in the mid-nineteenth century. In doing so, I bring us to the height of an immigration wave that affected every area and state in Germany. Unlike in the eighteenth century, the immigration wave in the nineteenth century was only rarely motivated by religion. Far more significant causes for immigration were economic forces or political events, such as the failed Revolution of 1848. The general history of this moment in German American immigration history is well known, and I do not propose here to add any new evidence to the overall history of the period. I should like instead to focus my attention on a rather narrow slice of German American church history, analyzing the presence of music in the German American church at a time when religion was not a primary motivation for immigration, and comparing nineteenth-century church music to the eighteenth century, a time when religion was more important.

My primary evidence comes from the Midwest, which had become the most important goal for German immigrants in the mid-nineteenth century and would remain so well into the twentieth century. Up until World War I the Midwest could boast an abundance of social institutions that fostered "German" musical activities—singing, musical, and sporting societies. Some of these organizations survive even until the present. At mid-century, the Midwest appeared so overwhelmingly German that government officials were reported to have claimed that the region would become a "country within a country" in the near future, that it would emerge as "a new Germany" (Marty 1986, 131). Catholic organizations that gathered in Innsbruck in 1867 organized immigration to Wisconsin, which, according to reports, was already "half German." More and more settlers would choose the fertile regions around the Great Lakes and the Mississippi River, not least because of abundant sources of water, serving as the foundation for expanding agriculture. The Yankees already settled in the region both feared and respected the German agricultural practices, and they inveighed against the Germans with phrases such as, "go ahead and dry it up" (Barry 1953, 26). By the 1880s, the region stretching from Cincinnati to Milwaukee to St. Louis, with Chicago in the geographical middle, came to be known as "the German triangle of the West" (ibid., 26). Abundant and fertile land, not religious freedom, attracted Germans to the Midwest during the first major wave of immigration to the region.

Religion enters the picture only secondarily, and we witness its influence in fragmented forms, for rather than the consolidation of denominational traditions, as witnessed in the eighteenth century, the new immigrant denominations and religious organizations splintered in diverse ways. For a European, the religious structure and polity of the mid-nineteenth-century Midwest is entirely unfamiliar. In contrast to centralized and hierarchical German churches, the American churches rejected central authority. There were numerous debates and discussions about which theological directions provided the "right" way to believe. The various awakenings and revivals, moreover, were not denominationally based, but rather they tended to cut across denominations, indeed, virtually all denominations. These patterns of fragmentation were especially prominent in American Protestantism, and I therefore focus primarily on Protestant churches of the German Americans.

The "right" songbook functioned as a weapon in quarrels over which denomination or church provided the true path toward righteousness. A denomination could display its songs as a sort of sign, with which it advertised its religious wares. It was also necessary for a congregation to find a songbook that possessed practical, communal functions, and the decisions that brought together a community of believers were frequently more practical than theological. The identity of songbooks often had little to do with sacred doctrine. Hence we find books such as the *Deutsches Gesangbuch für die Evangelisch-Lutherische Kirche in den Vereinigten Staaten,* printed by L. A. Wollenweber in Philadelphia in 1849, referred by the name of the publisher, in other words as "The Wollenweber" (Deutsches Gesangbuch 1849; see also Westermeyer 1978, 37). A songbook used by St. Paul's Church of Chicago at the turn-of-the-century bore the name, "Blue Book," like scores of other official books throughout the United States (Fellerer 1935, 132).

In the nineteenth century, the question of whether to publish a new songbook "still" with German songs, or whether it was "already" the moment to print English texts, arose as a point of discussion on an almost daily basis in many synods. The "language quarrel" persists throughout the history of many American churches. Concern over the contents of song texts is secondary in importance. Which songs should be included? Which songs should be excluded, and on what basis? Which melody is correct, and how should the book employ the melody? Should an editor himself prepare the song text, or does the text require reference to an *Urtext,* or original version? What meaning does this have for the ways in which the song is handed down? How does one convince a congregation to accept the changes? Whereas a newly prepared songbook provided the church leadership with an opportunity to undergird unity in the church, it also stirred up negative feelings, for congregations were notoriously conservative in their response to change. There was no absence of similar cases in the Old World, but, there, the larger framework for resistance to change was different, since it generally resulted when the upper echelons of church authority wanted changes that clashed with the more conservative-minded needs of the local congregation.

The language question crescendoed from the middle of the nineteenth century into the twentieth. By World War I, however, it had largely been settled. My comments here largely pertain in the United States to groups other than the Pennsylvania Germans in the East. The usual model for language assimilation recognizes rather quick acceptance of the everyday use of English, with a somewhat slower transition from the church language. Eventually, in the third generation immigrants largely speak English, with at best vague knowledge of German. In the relatively conservative state of Wisconsin, Germans assimilated culturally at a relatively rapid pace after the 1840s, and during the same period German dialects (e.g., "Low German," or *Plattdeutsch*) diminished quickly. Still in the final decades of the nineteenth century, however, Wisconsin was unquestionably "German" in the ways language marked culture.

The situation would appear to be quite different within those groups whose religious life was more or less isolated and intensively ascetic, at least in socio-economic conditions; this allowed them to maintain the German mother tongue as the most idiomatic language. This is the case with the Amish ("Old Order Amish"), the Mennonites ("Old Order Mennonites"), and the Hutterites, who lived in large settlements in the plains provinces of Canada. The Mennonites retained the German language for many years, also in their sacred music. Among their earliest publications to appear in German were *Die Gemeinschaftliche Liedersammlung* (1836), *Der christliche Sänger* (1860), and *Eine unparteiische Lieder-Sammlung* (1860). At the same time, there appeared songbooks in English, such as *A Collection of Psalms, Hymns, and Spiritual Songs* (1875) and *A Collection of Hymns* (1847). It is noteworthy that the English-language songbooks did not initially appear in the areas of intensive German-speaking settlement, but rather in the densely populated and ethnically mixed regions of New York.

The more common language transition in urban centers, which was distinct from rural areas, characterized other churches. In New York's Trinity Church, the sermon was delivered in English already during the time of Mühlenberg, that is, by 1780, and the congregation also sang English hymns from the *Hymn-Book*. In 1807, the church elected to use English as its official language, although the transition to English lasted until at least 1866 (see Jacobs 1912, 327). In 1837, for example, German was emphasized again at the request of immigrant parishioners. The language transition, therefore, took place as a process, and it demonstrated considerable differences from place to place.

The Mennonites began clearly to make their language transition only after the mid-nineteenth century, when the fourth edition of *A Collection of Psalms, Hymns, and Spiritual Songs* (1859) marked what must be seen as an "official" change by placing all the German-language songs in the hymnal's appendix (Benson 1915, 369). A later, expanded appendix nonetheless indicates that the congregations were, in fact, not quite so willing to give up their "old" and German-language songs. Among the songbooks that continued in use within American congregations were *Gesangbuch in Mennoniten Gemeinden für Kirche und Haus* (1901), *Gesangbuch zum Gottesdienstlichen und häuslichen Gebrauch in Mennoniten Gemeinden* (1873), and *Gesangbuch mit Noten* (1936).

Songbooks and church prayer books are among the cultural goods that persist most conservatively in a religious community. So strong is the sentiment for songbooks that parishioners might wage ideological wars with church leaders and church power structure over retaining an older songbook. The linguistic transformation in a songbook unequivocally marked a decisive rupture in the entire communication that connected a community to its church. Despite the adaptive changes through which the everyday language of a community passes, the desire to retain the "old" language of hymns in the songbook remains strong for several generations. The changes in the vernacular notwithstanding, songbook texts in German often do not appear as foreign in any sense, but rather they symbolize "a golden time" or "the old homeland."

In 1935, Karl Fellerer sketched the history of Protestant hymns in the United States. The history begins with "hymnbooks brought from the homeland" and unfolds toward German hymnals produced in the United States. In this way, American congregations sang from hymnals with repertoires shared with one of the synods that had taken root in the New World. I am interested here to discern just when and how the switch to English took place within the much longer transformation process. One of the books that was brought with settlers or later procured by them was the songbook published by Freylinghausen in Halle (1704). The songbook was so popular that in Kuntz's lectures at the end of the Colonial Era in 1773 every student received a copy of it imported from Halle. Fellerer observed that "even today" (1935) a hymnal published in

Württemberg was still being used in Michigan (Fellerer 1935, 120). One of the most widely distributed hymnals was the *Vollständiges Marburger Gesangbuch* (1798), which Mühlenberg used as the basis for his hymnal. We know that the Marburger songbook was reprinted several times, at least in 1770 in Germantown, Pennsylvania.

The development of schools, especially the system of private schools in the United States, exerted a major impact on church history and on the language transition (see Doerris 1986, 258–75). During the 1850s and 1860s, German American schools sprang up in large numbers, especially those founded by the Missouri Synod of the Lutheran Church and by the Roman Catholic Church. One on hand, these schools were a pedagogical response to the great flood of German immigrants in the mid-nineteenth century. The children of the second and third generations, on the other hand, were also expected to attend these schools, even when the German language for them was, as H. L. Mencken personally recalled, "an irrational and crazy language" (quoted in Billigmeier 1974, 130). Such schools, in fact, remained quite popular until the end of the century. In 1887, instruction in German ceased in Louisville and St. Paul; an 1889 law in Illinois ended German-language instruction in that state, and an 1890 law did the same for Wisconsin. In 1873, however, it was possible still to found a school with instruction in both English and German in Baltimore; there is evidence of numerous schools with German-language instruction being established as late as 1900.

By 1917, when the United States entered World War I, German schools increasingly disappeared, not least because of growing and politically-motivated anti-German sentiment. According to Andrew M. Greeley, "World War I signified the end for German Americans" (1974, 113). It surely was the case that World War I brought about a significant change, but even after the war Sunday-school instruction often remained in German, if sporadically so, until 1940 (Rippley 1976, 127). Again we witness that the private domain of religious conviction retained its conservative character far more than do the official domains of the church's communication channels, which, because of their connections to the mainstream, had to demonstrate a willingness to employ English.

Conventional studies overwhelmingly regard "German influence" in quite straightforward terms, and they interpret it very specifically as a component of immigration to the United States. Again and again, Pennsylvania receives emphasis as a type of *locus classicus*. Accordingly, the famous Amish *Ausbund* repeatedly receives attention. The hymnal was first published in 1583 in Schaffhausen and appeared in numerous later additions (1742, 1751, 1767, 1785, etc.) published by Christopher Sauer (Christoph Saur) of Germantown, Pennsylvania. At present it is still in use among the Amish of Pennsylvania. Because the history of the *Ausbund* is well known, it will concern us less here. The literature devoted to the Amish and similarly conservative denominations and churches in the United States is relatively inclusive. To go into depth would only serve to repeat a phenomenon that usually serves as the case-in-point.

Still, virtually every historical summary of the music of conservative denominations fails to take the language transformation into consideration. When noted at all, it is the translation of Martin Luther's "Ein' feste Burg" ("A Mighty Fortress Is Our God") that receives some attention (Foote 1940, 7, 201, 243). There are approximately one hundred English translations of the hymn. As the result of popular belief, it may often seem as if hymns outside Pennsylvania were necessarily in the English language. In my own researches I have seen that this was by no means the case and that the transition into English during the nineteenth century took place with numerous problems and ruptures (Holzapfel 1998). The language transformation in hymnals, in fact, might well be interpreted as a sort of parallel to the general Americanization of German immigrants. At any rate, the available sources call for much more intensive research than they have heretofore received.

At the very least, the language transformation in the German Reformed Church was the result of heated quarrels. That synod, founded in 1863, based itself on the German Evangelical Church Association of the West [*Deutscher Evangelischer Kirchenverein des Westens*]. In 1877 it acquired the name, German Evangelical Synod of North America. English-language hymnals had already been around for some time, with editions in 1817 and 1820, and finally in 1830 the *Psalms and Hymns, for the Use of German Reformed Church, in the United States of America*. That a gradual, de facto language transformation was already underway in the 1830s is evident in the fact that official church documents still appeared in German, but at the same time they appeared in English in some documents used by those who presumably knew only that language (ibid., 108).

Even the Lutheran Church had to endure language battles, whose beginnings can be traced to the mid-eighteenth century, a period of struggle between German- and Swedish-speaking immigrants. Well into the twentieth century, indeed into the 1930s, there appeared numerous opponents to the practices of using German in hymns (Jacobs 1912, 109; Sweet 1950, 201). Over two centuries of struggle just to determine the "right" language for the church! During the nineteenth century, Lutheran synods proliferated: The North Carolina Synod was founded in 1803, the Ohio Synod in 1818, and the Maryland and Tennessee Synods in 1820. Together, these four synods constituted the General Synod, remaining the first and only umbrella organization for Lutheran churches until the Civil War.

One of the most important personalities during the eighteenth century was the Lutheran, Heinrich Melchior Mühlenberg (Americanized: Henry Melchior Muhlenberg [1711–1787]). In 1742 he arrived in Philadelphia from Halle, and like many others at the time, he had been sent to America by August Hermann Francke, a leader in German Pietism. He remained for a brief period in a Salzburg community and then founded the first German synod in 1748. Mühlenberg's activities stretched far beyond Pennsylvania; he sent reports to Halle, and these provided him with further sources of financial support. He wrote many letters and extensive diaries, which were later published. Even when he was on the ship to America, he attempted to preach in English. We know that he was preaching in New York in 1748, and that by 1751 or 1752 he was preaching in both English and German, as well as Dutch, which he learned after immigration.

In a diary from 1751 Mühlenberg observed about New York and other places in Colonial America: "I had but a single copy of an English hymnal. . . . I had to read every verse aloud and sing it for the congregation. The English speakers in the congregation apparently had no prior knowledge of the melodies; accordingly, I chose well-known English melodies that fitted our German texts" (see Gaustad 1966, 95). There are other cases from the eighteenth century in which it appears that the pastor was the only member of an entire congregation who possessed a book containing the church's liturgy and music (Sweet 1950, 40). From my German perspective, the use of the same songbook within an entire congregation symbolically represents the growth of unification and assimilation processes. Whereas it was a matter of necessity in the eighteenth century, it had influenced American popular culture and the American sense of unity by the twentieth, which we witnessed when, for example, President Bill Clinton reflected on an ability to bring about political agreement by observing that "everyone was singing out of the same hymnal" (Clinton 1993).

Settlers in the United States differed from one another according to the situations they left in the Old World and the conditions determining just how they got their start in the New World; these contributed in different ways to their "new" identity. German Lutherans and members of the Reformed churches often came as individual families. Occasionally, they had only limited interest in religion, and establishing a new church, it follows, had to put on hold. Their ethnic identity, at least as it related to religion, was only weakly expressed; the consciousness of being German disappeared relatively quickly in the eighteenth century. Few of these eighteenth-century immigrants, moreover, perceived themselves as having left "Germany," but rather they regarded their cultural past as derived from the independent states within Central Europe: Franconia, Bavaria, Württemberg, and so on.

The situation was different by the mid-nineteenth century, when Lutherans founded Wittenberg College (today, Wittenberg University) in 1845 to serve the spiritual needs of German immigrants to Ohio. In 1851, we might understand that "Wittenberg" had a different, which is to say American, symbolism for German American Protestants. Still, as far as the question of American identity was concerned, it had long before been decided in favor of the English language. Samuel S. Schmucker emerged as a kind of "linguistic guide" for American Lutheranism, and his venue was the journal, *Lutheran Observer.* There was also a contrasting position, also theologically more conservative, whose organ was the *Evangelical Review,* based in Gettysburg, Pennsylvania (see Apel-Birnbaum 1993, 202).

An expressly ethnic consciousness emerging from "German" confessionalism associated itself primarily with the conservative wings of the Lutheran Church, especially the Missouri and Wisconsin synods. These denominations were truly ethnic churches (see Smith 1993, 18, and passim). They were, however, "ethnic" for the first time in the United States and only then on the threshold of the linguistic transformation from German to English, even when the conditions for the transformation may have existed already in the Old World (ibid., 9). As far as ethnic identity in the German church is concerned, the eighteenth and nineteenth centuries differ entirely from one another.

During the course of American history the ethnic church was an important social institution, which demanded considerable care from immigrants and accordingly provided them with considerable support from the day of their arrival in the New World (Doerris 1986, 241–58). The ethnic church provided mutual aid societies, such as the German Lutheran Aid Society (founded 1790) or the Catholic St. Raphael's Society (founded 1871). If the centralized Catholic organizations developed rather later in the history of German immigration, at the time of growing South German settlement, it was nonetheless far more effective than most Lutheran organizations, which according to some accounts appeared "at first quite helpless" (ibid., 247). There are many instances of cooperation, however, that cut across denominational borders, and this, too, is related to the problem of language transformation. In 1787, German Reformed and German Lutherans together founded Franklin College in Pennsylvania (today, Franklin and Marshall College). In 1805 the German Reformed Church permitted English in the worship service (Gaustad 1966, 397). The conservative Missouri Synod established its own "Lutheran Pilgrim House" in New York City, which was open to German Protestants of all denominations and kept its doors open until 1917 (Doerris 1986, 249).

The diverse picture of American denominations and churches, however, should not obscure the fact that there was an everyday existence outside the church, which in turn had relatively little to do with an immigrant's religious affiliation. At least until the first Great Awakening, most Americans belonged to no church whatsoever (Hudson 1981, 58). The German immigrant historian, Donata Elschenbroich, describes the situation as follows: "The immigrant came not so much in search of a 'religious freedom' that freed him or her from the practice of religion, but rather 'through religion' sought greater freedom" (*author trans.*; Elschenbroich 1986, 148). The Great Awakening in the second half of the eighteenth century, therefore, was already permeated by a strong "American" identity, which extended religious dimensions to separation from England and eventually to the War of Independence itself.

In the early immigrant generations we witness quite different responses to the interrelations among religion, freedom, and Americanization. Whereas Heinrich M. Mühlenberg remained quite ambivalent to the American Revolution, leaving Philadelphia and settling in a rural area in order to maintain his "neutrality," one of his sons, John Peter Gabriel Muhlenberg (1746–1807), at first a pastor in the German Lutheran Church, served as a general in the revolutionary army. His other son, Frederick August Conrad Muhlenberg (1750–1801), who was the pastor of Christ Lutheran Church in New York and had to leave the city when the English fleet approached, later became a congressman from Pennsylvania and in 1789 served as the first Speaker of the House in the American Congress. A grandson, William A. Muhlenberg, would play a crucial role in the English Catholic Church, associating himself with the Oxford Movement in 1847.

As the different ethnic denominations and churches consolidated, a growing sense of Americanness became palpable, accompanying the inner transformation of the churches. The more Americanized the churches became, the more they turned toward their own pasts, politicizing and historicizing Christianity in America, and creating a virtual hagiography of saintly founding fathers, such as the Pilgrims. History itself began to reflect sacred legends, and in this way the founding myths of the United States took shape. One of the crucial concepts of American identity is the missionary passion with which settlement of the New World proceeded. A Connecticut election sermon stated that passion quite baldly: "When the Lord shall have made his American Israel high above all nations" (quoted in Hudson 1981, 109). The extreme case of the American national self-consciousness is that of the Mormons (ibid., 193; for a more extensive discussion of American self-consciousness among American Protestants see Marty 1986).

For my considerations here, the period around the mid-nineteenth century has proved to be crucially important. By this time, the desire to integrate dominated most German immigrants, and this led to a relatively quick and abrupt language transformation. In his study of the 1840 *Pennsylvanische Sammlung von Kirchen-Musik (The Pennsylvania Collection of Church Musik),* Philip Bohlman has argued that this bilingual hymnal lends itself to interpretation as a "textbook for German Americanization" (Bohlman 1993). Americanization arose from the texts in such hymnals, hence from the role of language in congregational singing. "The hymnal served as a model for acculturation because one participated in acculturation when singing from it" (ibid., 93). The hymns, moreover, were imbued with a patriotic spirit, and they served musically to represent the optimistic spirit of the American frontier: One praises God in order to build a new life and to learn English. Religion, patriotism, and hymns were contrasting conditions of the same phenomenon during the Second Awakening in the first half of the nineteenth century. Perhaps more than any other group, the Methodists gained from the Second Awakening, which absorbed many of the pietistic elements from the hymns. At the same time, as Philip Bohlman observes, new musical foundations for "ethnic religion" were being laid, and these have remained intact for many groups until the present.

The confessional and denominational issues that distinguished one hymnal from another appear clearly on the book's title page, and they are made even clearer once one looks beyond the title page into the contents. The 1857 *Kirchen-Gesangbuch für Evangelisch-Lutherische Gemeinden ungeänderter Augsburgischer Confession* (lit., "Church Songbook for Evangelical Lutheran Churches, Strictly Adhering to the Augsburg Confession"), whose connections to Luther and German Lutheranism are unequivocal, appeared in the "Verlag der deutschen-evang. Luth. Gemeinde ung. Augsb. Confession" of St. Louis in 1857; in other words, the hymnal would serve one denomination only, not the whole of American German Lutherans. The same hymnal, published in another edition in 1909, had not altered its title at all, which still clumsily specified the American Lutherans for which it was intended, though it by that time relied on the Missouri Synod's Concordia Publishing House. A comparison of texts from both editions reveals relatively little change, affirming the hymnal's conservatism over a period of a half-century.

If the denominational differences between hymnals diminished somewhat over the decades, the concept of a conservative "ethnic church" that adhered to transmitting German texts, however artificial, remained largely intact. This was especially the case in the Lutheran churches of the Missouri and Wisconsin synods, in which the notion that the language of the church must retain its conservative functions survives even until the present. The Missouri Synod continued to serve as one of the most prominent examples of an ethnic church, and within the church the Sunday school was stressed as a particularly conservative institution (Doerris 1986, 266). During the early years of World War I, prior to American entry, many church members of the Missouri Synod attempted to stir up a sort of nationalism in support of Germany, which then had serious repercussions for the church once the United States had joined the allied forces in 1917 (ibid., 238, 294).

The remarkably conservative character, which the Missouri Synod sustains until today, derives in large part from the influence of German immigrants (Luebke 1990, 3–13). C. F. W. Walther founded the Missouri Synod in Chicago in 1847 as the "Deutsche Evangelisch-Lutherische Synode von Missouri, Ohio und anderen Staaten" ("German Evangelical Lutheran Synod of Missouri, Ohio, and other States"). A century later, in 1947, the church took the name by which it is now known, Lutheran Church–Missouri Synod. By about 1906, fully two-thirds of all German-speaking Protestants belonged to the Lutheran church, and from these about one-half belonged to the Missouri Synod. This pattern remained unchanged until World War I; the inception of the language transformation, nonetheless, did not only have political motivations. Assimilation in the second and third immigrant generations naturally played a role. By 1916, only about 11 percent of German-language congregations used German as the official language of the full religious service. By 1925 only half of all churches in the Missouri Synod continued to use German in sermons (Conzen 1980, 419, and passim). In large congregations of Chicago, however, German-language services survived until the eve of World War II.

Soon after his emigration from Germany to the United States, where he served as Professor of Church History at Mercersburg, Pennsylvania, Philip (Philipp) Schaff (1819–1893) described the religious life in America as "puritan and oriented toward New England" (see Noll 1992, 222). During his tenure in Mercersburg, Schaff published a number of significant works that represented the transition from German to English, in both German and English, for example, *Geschichte der christlichen Kirche* (1851) and *The Principle of Protestantism* (1845). He also published a German hymnal, called *Schaffs Deutsches Gesangbuch,* which quickly became very popular in several editions bearing the shortened title *Deutsches Gesangbuch,* "German Songbook" (Schaff 1859; Schaff 1860; Schaff 1876; for more about the Schaff songbook itself, see Westermeyer 1978).

If one compares, for example, Schaff's edition with the aforementioned *Kirchen-Gesangbuch für Evangelisch-Lutherische Gemeinden ungeänderter Augsburger Confession* published approximately at the same time (1857) by the Missouri Synod, it becomes quickly evident just how conservative the latter was. To take one specific example, the version of the hymn, "Mit Ernst, o Menschenkinder," in the 1809 *Altenburgisches Gesangbuch nebst Gebeten* served as the source for the Missouri Synod version, published almost a half century later.

Mit Ernst, o Menschenkinder,	O children of Man, with seriousness
betrachtet diese Zeit,	consider this time,
in der der Ueberwinder,	in which the conqueror,
der Herr der Herrlichkeit,	the Lord of Hosts,
sich äußert seiner Ehr',	expresses himself in his honor,
verläßt den Thron der Freuden	leaves the throne of joy
und kommt, für uns zu leiden,	and comes to suffer for us,
von seinem Vater her.	From his Father.

Further textual comparisons are required in order to verify the extent to which this presumed conservatism extended into German American hymnals. Schaff, in contrast, also drew upon English translations of German hymns, especially those by Catherine Winkworth, who had published an edition of these in 1857, two years before Schaff's hymnal appeared. The high-quality Schaff *Deutsches Gesangbuch* continued in use, at least in part, into the twentieth century, though it did not completely become the preferred hymnal of all German Protestants because it was arguably too esoteric in its historicist plumbing of earlier sources (see Fellerer 1935, 121; and Westermeyer 1980, 94, 204). One could designate several of the hymnals I have described here as not entirely denominational. It would be appropriate, instead, drawing on the concept of an "ethnic church," to describe them as "ethnic hymnals" because of their appeal across the entire ethnic group.

Schaff's own observations are themselves quite telling: In 1854, he wrote in a report to Berlin that the United States was the most religious land in the world. "Daily table prayers and well-attended religious meetings characterized the moral and social life. At that time, Berlin would have 450,000 residents but only 40 churches, which in turn were visited by perhaps only 30,000 worshipers; with 600,000 residents, New York had over 250 churches, and these were usually overflowing with worshipers." One reason for this degree of American religiosity was perhaps the willingness to experiment, which was not hampered by laws. This American religiosity was not limited by restrictions on what was or was not presumably one's own "tradition" (Hudson 1981, 181–83). In such a climate of religious experimentation one of the "traditions" that one could rather easily discard was the German language.

For the present book, it may well be the case that it is not the real ancestry that is most interesting, but rather the following questions: Which degree of ethnicity do the tradition bearers themselves give to a particular phenomenon?

How much weight do they give, consciously and subconsciously, to the maintenance of certain special forms of ethnicity, which is to say, how consciously do they stress and utilize ethnicity? In my opinion these are the more important concerns, if indeed they are less commonly stated than the usual stress on maintaining tradition or on identifying ethnic roots. Previously, emigration research, which obviously dominates European scholarship, has endeavored to unravel the invisible strands of ancestry. If one turns the perspectives toward the problems posed by immigration, however, what emerges is the importance of the ways in which those affected, the immigrants themselves, perceive their sense of belonging in certain objects or appearances, which may differ substantially from the real ancestry.

Accordingly, many church organizations connected to specific immigration groups confront similar questions about how they might have affected German Americans in the nineteenth century. In the 1990s, there is a comparable situation among the approximately 100 different denominations of Chinese churches in the United States, which also demonstrate different relations to successive immigrant generations. Among other denominational affiliations, they belong to the Baptists as well as their own mission congregations, but in the second generation they already have accelerated the incorporation of English texts from the *Pilgrim Hymnal* of the Congregational Church. The previous repertoire, moreover, remains in bilingual settings, and indeed even the English hymns, while still retaining the English melodies, have been translated into different Chinese languages and dialects. Most interesting of all, many of the proudest members of the congregation are firmly convinced that they are maintaining a "Chinese" tradition, and for the most part they are even unaware that these Chinese hymns are the products of translation (see Maria Chow's chapter in this volume). The subjective impression in such cases deserves our attention, and it must be understood as subjectively "correct" and fundamental to the construction of ethnicity and identity, even when it contradicts the objective data.

There is perhaps an additional reason that, after the mid-nineteenth century, the language question about the priority of a German or an English American hymnal was settled in favor of the latter. If one examines the immigration statistics from 1850 to 1880 and then until World War I, it becomes clear that the first two immigrant waves during the period were dominated by Germans and by Protestants, not least because of the failure of the Revolution of 1848 at the beginning of this period. The third major wave, while still predominantly Protestant, had a much greater mixture of ethnic groups, particularly those from Scandinavia and from the Baltic countries. This third wave was by far the most influential on American Protestant identity (Apel-Birnbaum 1993). The total number of hymns that were not German expanded in Protestant hymnals during the third wave. For many of the new Protestant groups it was less a question of producing their own Icelandic, Norwegian, or Finnish hymnals than of concentrating on a common hymnal for all groups. The language for most common hymnals would naturally be English. From the standpoint of the German individual congregation, then, the question of maintaining a German Protestant language for the church became increasingly unimportant.

Carl Ferdinand Wilhelm Walther (born 1811), the theological leader of the Missouri Synod, decided to immigrate to North America in 1839 along with many other families in Saxony. Together with Mühlenberg, Walther was a leading figure in the Lutheran Church in America. Establishing a center in St. Louis, he even believed in maintaining German as a language for the schools. For his hymnal, he took Friedrich Layriz's *Kern Geistlicher Lieder* as a basis. In 1857, the Missouri Synod discussed the need to establish its own normal school for training teachers, and they later relocated it in Springfield, Illinois. The press of the Missouri Synod, the Concordia Publishing House, printed teaching materials in both German and English. Walther's denominational newspaper, *Der Lutheraner,* enjoyed wide dissemination (first published in 1844 as *Walther's Lutheraner*).

In 1847, Walther edited a new hymnal that was designed to replace the great variety of hymnals being used by Lutherans in America since the eighteenth century. To serve this end, Walther used another Layriz hymnal, *Kern des deutschen Kirchenliedes* (published in different editions in the 1840s). In 1857, the Missouri Synod discussed the principles of establishing English congregations that grew out of German mother congregations. Walther agreed with these principles, stating "our fathers' faith was to be preached in our children's tongue," though he himself remained resolutely German-speaking (Steffens 1917, 332). In the Walther tradition, the Missouri Synod adopted and adapted the *Evangelical Lutheran Hymn-Book* (Baltimore) in 1894, and then the Concordia Publishing House published its own English-language hymnals in successive editions in 1912 and 1941, which in turn became the official hymnals of the Lutheran Church–Missouri Synod (Schalk 1965, 43–46).

The transformation to English as a church language took place in different ways for every denomination, and there is no single way to describe the path it followed. For the large Evangelical churches, however, which unified over the course of the eighteenth and nineteenth centuries, one might crudely describe the transformation with the following stages. In the 1750s, the predominant hymnal was the *Marburger Gesangbuch,* either in its imported German form or in American reprints of the German. At the end of the eighteenth century, the German Reformed Church adopted the *Erbauliche Lieder-*

sammlung, and the Lutheran Church adopted *Das neue und verbesserte Gesangbuch*. The first relatively common, that is, interdenominational, hymnal appeared in 1817, namely *Das Gemeinschaftliche Gesangbuch, zum Gottesdienstlichen Gebrauch der Lutherischen und Reformierten Gemeinden in Nordamerika*. The fifth edition of this hymnal, called "Grünsburg" and "Greensburg," contained a preface attributed to, among others, J. Georg Schmucker, whose signature bears the date of 1816. It is at this point that English hymnals begin to serve some German churches, especially *Hymns, Selected and Original* (1828) and *Psalms and Hymns* (1834). Samuel S. Schmucker (1799–1873) drew upon the model of the *New York Hymn Book* (1814) and published his own English hymnal in 1828, *Hymns, Selected and Original, for Public and Private Worship* (see Westermeyer 1978, 32–33). The Anglicization process, therefore, was firmly established in the late 1820s, and it accelerated in subsequent generations.

The concluding stages of the whole pragmatic, yet also ideological, language transformation linger even today. There are still some German hymnals, particularly among the Mennonites and Amish, but the tendency to cultivate German consciously has suffered considerably during the twentieth century, not least because of the political associations resulting from the two world wars. After World War I, for example, the hymnal of the Episcopal Church contained a complement of German hymns designated as "good," which needed to be retained because of their theological significance, but these were in a sense hidden behind the English hymns. By 1940, these German hymns also contained English melody references, as if, in William Reynolds's phrase, to "camouflage" their Germanness (Reynolds 1990, 39). "Stille Nacht," to take the most obvious example, became "Silent Night," as if to deny its German origins and symbolism.

The *Lutheran Book of Worship* of 1978 served in part as a revised edition of the 1941 hymnal, but it also intentionally included some ecumenical grounds for singing with American Catholics in the post-Vatican II era, and it drew heavily on the hymn repertoire shared with other evangelical churches in North America. The questions addressed by the 1978 hymnal were contemporary, in both their social and ethnic significance; the presence and purity of German elements, in fact, was regarded as quite insignificant in comparison with other issues facing a late twentieth-century Lutheran church. Ironically, references to German hymn sources began to be more common again, they served as an index not to a single ethnic church but rather to the full range of different melodic and textual sources, regardless of the denomination. The modern German American tradition, therefore, was historicized as the product of many different German-language traditions.

Whereas previous studies of the "German elements" in the United States arise from patriotic if not nationalistic motivations, the approach I bring to the study of German American hymnody does not rely on the extent to which any given personality may or may not have felt him- or herself to be German. Scholarship during the period of late nineteenth-century and early twentieth-century German imperialism has already attempted to use nationalistic questions to interpret the contributions of the early hymnal editors, such as Christopher Sauer, Philipp W. Otterbein, Jacob Albrecht, Heinrich Melchior Mühlenberg, and Philipp Schaff. My concern here is to use hymnals as a window to perceive changing ethnicity, at the time of a given hymnal's publication and in successive generations. "Ethnic affiliation" itself is relatively less significant than are the reasons for its existence and the impact it has on German American culture. Thus, it seems entirely reasonable that hymnodists and hymnal editors understood their endeavors as American and not as German. The hyphen that appears in the designation, "German-American hymnal," was therefore not a means of emphasizing the Germanness of a sacred song tradition, but rather a means of creatively facilitating its transition to a meaningful Americanness, with all its implications for ethnic and religious identity.

WORKS CITED

Altenburgisches Gesangbuch nebst Gebeten. 1809. *Altenburgisches Gesangbuch nebst Gebeten: Zum Gebrauch bey der öffentlichen Gottesverehrung und häuslichen Andacht.* Altenburg: H. A. Pierer.

Apel-Birnbaum, Gudrun. 1993. "Religions Denominations during the Time of Mass Immigration: Cleveland 1880 to the First World War." *Amerikastudien/American Studies* 38: 415–24.

Ausbund. 1583. *Ausbund, Das ist Etliche Schöne Christenliche Lieder,* etc. *Allen und Jeden Christen, Welcher Religion Sic Seien, Unpartheyisch Last Nützlich.* Schaffhausen.

Ausbund. 1742. *Ausbund, Das ist: Etliche Schöne Christliche Lieder, Wie sie in dem Gefängnus zu Bassau in dem Schloss von den Schweizer-Brüdern, und von anderen rechtgläubigen Christen hin und her gedichtet worden.* Germantown: Christoph Saur.

Barry, Colman J. 1953. *The Catholic Church and German Americans.* Washington, D.C.: Catholic University of America Press.

Benson, Louis F. 1962 [1915]. *The English Hymn: Its Development and Use in Worship.* Richmond: John Knox.

Billigmeier, Robert Henry. 1974. *Americans from Germany: A Study in Cultural Diversity.* Belmont, Calif.: Wadsworth. Minorities in American Life Series.

Bohlman, Philip V. 1993. "Die *'Pennsylvanische Sammlung von Kirchen-Musik'*: Ein Lehrbuch zur Deutsch-Amerikanisierung." *Jahrbuch für Volksliedforschung* 38: 90–109.

Cassel, Samuel K., ed. 1855. *Der Christliche Sänger, eine Sammlung der vornehmsten und gebräuchlichsten Lieder zum Gebrauch des öffentlichen und privaten Gottesdienstes für alle heilsuchende Seelen jeder Christlichen Benennung*. Skippackville, Penn.: Franconia Conference.

Clinton, Bill. 1993. Television Interview. 22 November.

A Collection of Hymns. . . . 1847. *A Collection of Hymns Designed for the Use of the Church of Christ, by John Reist, Minister of the Gospel*. Buffalo, N.Y.: n.p.

A Collection of Psalms. . . . 1859. *A Collection of Psalms, Hymns, and Spiritual Songs, Suited to the Various Occasions of Publish Worship and Private Devotion of the Church of Christ, with an Appendix of German Hymns*. 4th ed. Lancaster, Penn.: John Baer's Sons.

Conzen, Kathleen Neils. 1980. "Germans." In Stephan Thernstrom, ed., *The Harvard Encyclopedia of American Ethnic Groups*, 405–25. Cambridge, Mass.: Harvard University Press.

Deutsches Gesangbuch für *Gemeinschaftliche Liedersammlung, Die, zum allgemeinen Gebrauch des wahren Gottesdienstes aus vielen Liederbüchern gesammelt, und mit einem Inhalt sammt Register versehen*. . . . 1849. Deutsches Gesangbuch für die Evangelische-Lutherische Kirche in den Vereinigten Staaten. Philadelphia: L. A. Wollenweber.

Doerries, Reinhard R. 1986. *Iren und Deutsche in der Neuen Welt: Akkulturationsprozesse in der amerikanischen Gesellschaft im späten 19. Jahrhundert*. Stuttgart: F. Steiner.

Elschenbroich, Donata. 1986. *Eine Nation von Einwanderern: Ethnisches Bewußtsein und Integrationspolitik in den USA*. Frankfurt am Main: Campus.

Erbauliche Lieder-Sammlung. 1786. *Erbauliche Lieder-Sammlung*. Germantown, Penn.: Leibert und Billmeyer.

Evangelical Lutheran Hymn-Book. 1894. *Evangelical Lutheran Hymn-Book*. Baltimore, Md.: Lutheran Publication Board.

Fellerer, Karl Gustav. 1935. *Das deutsche Kirchenlied im Ausland*. Münster i.W.: Aschendorff.

Foote, Henry Wilder. 1940. *Three Centuries of American Hymnody*. Cambridge, Mass.: Harvard University Press.

Freylinghausen, Johann Anastasius. 1704. *Geist-reiches Gesang-Buch. Den Kern Alter und Neuer Lieder*. Halle: Waysenhaus.

Gaustad, Edwin Scott. 1966. *A Religious History of America*. New York: Harper and Row.

Das Gemeinschaftliche Gesangbuch. . . . 1817. *Das Gemeinschaftliche Gesangbuch, zum gottesdienstlichen Gebrauch der Lutherischen und Reformirten Gemeinden in Nord-Amerika*. Baltimore, Md.: Schäffer und Maund.

Die Gemeinschaftliche Liedersammlung. . . . 1836. *Die Gemeinschaftliche Liedersammlung, zum allgemeinen Gebrauch des wahren Gottesdienstes aus vielen Liederbüchern gesammelt, und mit einem Inhalt sammt Register versehen*. Berlin (Kitchener), Ontario: H. W. Peterson.

Gesangbuch in Mennoniten-Gemeinden. . . . 1901. *Gesangbuch in Mennoniten-Gemeinden für Kirche und Haus*. N.p.: Mennoniten-Gemeinden West Preussens.

Gesangbuch mit Noten. . . . 1936. *Gesangbuch mit Noten.* 1st ed., Berne, 1890; 15th ed. Philadelphia.

Gesangbuch zum Gottesdienstlichen . . . 1873. *Gesangbuch zum Gottesdienstlichen und Häuslichen Gebrauch in Mennoniten Gemeinden.* Philadelphia.

Greeley, Andrew M. 1974. *Ethnicity in the United States: A Preliminary Reconnaissance.* New York: John Wiley & Sons. The Wiley Series in Urban Research.

Harbaugh, Heinrich von. 1870. *Harbaugh's Harfe, Gedichte in Pennsylvanisch-Deutscher Mundart.* Ed. by B. Bausman. Philadelphia, Penn.: Reformed Church Publication Board.

Holzapfel, Otto. 1998. *Religiöse Identität und Gesangbuch.* Berne: Peter Lang.

Hudson, Winthrop S. 1981. *Religion in America: A Historical Account of the Development of American Religious Life.* New York: Scribner.

Hymns Selected. . . . 1828. *Hymns Selected and Original, for Public and Private Worship. Published by the General Synod of the Evangelical Lutheran Church.* Gettysburg: General Synod of the Evangelical Lutheran Church.

Jacobs, Henry Eyster. 1912. *A History of the Evangelical Lutheran Church in the United States.* American Church History 4. New York: Christian Literature.

Luebke, Frederick C. 1990. *Germans in the New World: Essays in the History of Immigration.* Urbana: University of Illinois Press.

Lutheran Book of Worship. 1978. *Lutheran Book of Worship.* Minneapolis, Minn.: Augsburg.

Marty, Martin E. 1986. *Protestantism in the United States: Righteous Empire.* New York: Scribner's.

Das neue und verbesserte Gesangbuch . . . 1814. *Das neue und verbesserte Gesangbuch.* 5th printing. Philadelphia: G. and D. Billmeyer.

Neu-Vermehrt und Vollständiges Gesangbuch. 1753. *Neu-Vermehrt und Vollständiges Gesangbuch.* Germantown: Christoph Saur.

Noll, Mark A. 1992. *A History of Christianity in the United States and Canada.* Grand Rapids, Mich.: Eerdmans.

Pennsylvanische Sammlung. . . . 1840. *Pennsylvanische Sammlung von Kirchen-Musik/ The Pennsylvania Collection of Church Musick.* Harrisburg, Penn.: Wyeth.

Pilgrim Hymnal. . . . 1931. *Pilgrim Hymnal.* Boston: The Pilgrim Press. 8th ed. 1962.

Psalms and Hymns . . . 1834. *Psalms and Hymns for the Use of the German Reformed Church in the United States of America.* Chambersburg: Publication Office of the German Reformed Church.

Reynolds, William J. 1990. "The Hymnal 1940 and Its Era." *The Hymn* 41 (4), 34–39.

Rippley, LaVern J. 1976. *The German Americans.* Boston: Twayne.

Schaff, Philipp. 1845. *The Princples of Protestantism as Related to the Present State of the Church.* Chambersburg, Penn.: Publication Office of the German Reformed Church.

———. 1851. *Geschichte der christlichen Kirche: Von ihrer Gründung bis auf die Gegenwart.* Mercersburg, Penn.: Philip Schaff.

———. 1809. *Altenburgisches Gesangbuch nebst Gebeten: Zum Gebrauch bei der öffentlichen Gottesverehrung und häuslichen Andacht.* Altenburg: H. A. Pierer.

Schaff, Philipp. 1859. *Deutsches Gesangbuch.* "Probe-Ausgabe," or "Prepublication edition." Philadelphia: Lindsay und Klakiston.

———. 1860. *Deutsches Gesangbuch: Eine Auswahl geistlicher Lieder aus aller Zeiten der christlichen Kirche für öffentlichen und häuslichen Gebrauch, Taschenausgabe.* Philadelphia: Lindsay und Klakiston.

———. 1876. *Deutsches Gesangbuch: Eine Auswahl geistlicher Lieder aus allen Zeiten der christlichen Kirche für kirchlichen und häuslichen Gebrauch.* Philadelphia: Lindsay und Klakiston.

Schalk, Carl. 1965. *The Roots of Hymnody in the Lutheran Church–Missouri Synod.* St. Louis: Concordia.

A Selection of Psalms. . . . 1847. *A Selection of Psalms, Hymns, and Spiritual Songs.* Harrisonburg, Va.: Joseph Funk, David Hartman, and Joseph Wenger.

Smith, Timothy L. 1993. "Religion and Ethnicity in America." In Martin E. Marty, ed., *Modern American Protestantism and Its World: Historical Articles on Protestantism in American Religious Life.* Vol. 8, pp. 3–33. Munich: K. G. Sauer.

Steffens, Diedrich Henry. 1917. *Doctor Carl Ferdinand Wilhelm Walther.* Philadelphia: Lutheran Publication Society.

Sweet, William Warren. 1950. *The Story of Religion in America.* New York: Harper.

Eine Unparteiische. . . . 1860. *Eine Unparteiische Lieder-Sammlung.* Lancaster, Penn.: John Baer's Sons.

Vollständiges Marburger Gesang-Buch. . . . 1798. *Vollständiges Marburger Gesang-Buch, Zur Vbung der Gottseligkeit.* Marburg and Frankfurt am Main: H. L. Brönner.

Westermeyer, Paul. 1978. "What Shall We Sing in a Foreign Land? Theology and Cultic Song in the German Reformed and Lutheran Churches of Pennsylvania, 1830–1900." Ph.D. diss., University of Chicago.

———. 1980. "German Reformed Hymnody in the United States." *The Hymn* 31: 89–94, 96, 200–204, and 212.

8

"When in Our Music God Is Glorified": Singing and Singing about Singing in a Congregational Church

Judith Gray

Brian Wren, the contemporary British hymnodist, has defined hymns as "song(s) of faith sung by a group of people" that ideally "unify the singers, not merely in fellowship but in faith. . . . Hymns, as corporate, sung statements of faith, hope, seeking and praise, can *empower* people, by putting their faith into memorable, beautiful, repeatable language" (1986). The important aspects of hymnody, according to this definition by one involved in its creation, are unification through mutual participation, expression of faith, and empowerment. (And notice the stress on *language* rather than on music.) But what happens in ministers' studies and music directors' offices during the week and in the pews and organ loft on Sundays? How is such a theory of hymnody turned into practice?

Hymnody is generally attuned to and reflects the church year, but it is typically less constrained than liturgical observances attached to given days. The scope of songs available within a congregation for corporate expression includes not only the "official" collection of the church (the hymnal in the pew), but also the familiar songs from the early years of each member, newly composed hymns, and secular songs adopted because of contemporary significance. A church could conceivably draw on this whole historical, contemporary, and personal range of hymns. But, as we shall see, the potential corpus is much broader than the sum of the choices actually made.

Hymnody decisions occur on both denominational and on individual church levels, perhaps especially so in a denomination as self-conscious about issues of unity and diversity as the United Church of Christ (UCC). The UCC was formed in 1957 from the merger of the Congregational Church with the Evangelical and Reformed Church; these churches of English and German background are found primarily in New England and the upper Midwest, respectively. The UCC motto is: "That they may all be one." But such professions of unity are always balanced against recognition of local diversity. This is particularly true of the Congregational side of the merger—a descendant of the English Free Church tradition. One of Congregationalism's main characteristics was the assertion of local autonomy over against larger hierarchical units of church polity. In other words, individual churches had the right to govern themselves. Then and now, there are no bishops, although there are associations, national boards, and the like.

UCC churches often seem to attract people raised in other traditions, perhaps especially those of conservative background seeking a more liberal church home. This may be because the UCC is covenantal rather than creedal: Historical testimonies of faith such as the Apostles' Creed are not understood as tests of faith for present members. Joining is a matter of saying, "I promise to walk with God and these people," rather than "I believe in this and this and this."

Thus the UCC's history, structure, and ideology promote the establishment and maintenance of diverse congregations with independent histories, theologies—and, of course, potentially broad musical backgrounds—situations where factors of choice are localized but also visible against the shared heritage.

Musically the shared heritage for the Congregational side of the UCC is the *Pilgrim Hymnal*. Originally published in 1931, it was revised in 1935 and 1958. (A new UCC hymnal was published in 1974 but was not widely accepted. Another has now been produced, and will soon go into distribution.) The prefaces to the revised *Pilgrim Hymnals* describe selection factors and the need for change as well as for maintenance of tradition:

> This book is a product of our Pilgrim heritage and of the conditions of life in the twentieth century. . . . It expresses our faith in Christ and in the God whom he reveals, and it seeks to bring this faith to bear upon the new problems and movements of our time. Here are more hymns of the social gospel . . . with no less provision for the gospel of personal evangelism and private devotion. (1935 ed., iii)

> This book was first conceived as a revision of the *Pilgrim Hymnal* of 1931, but the recent developments in hymnody, in church life, and in world history have made it necessary to plan our work in larger terms. . . . [T]he present volume draws more heavily on the best hymnody of the Church Universal, while at the same time making fuller use of our particular heritage. . . . Looking to the future, the hymnal has benefited from the broadening and enriching impetus of the ecumenical movement. (1958 edition, v)

In other words, the shared heritage is also a filtered heritage—hymnal compilers consider topics, specific historical frameworks, and language as well as music.

What is true about the "official" congregational hymn collection is even more the case for individual congregations' choices, especially when taken together with the less formally defined repertory of available choices. Consequently, the hymnbook in the pew provides only a hint of a particular congregation's practices; there is no one-to-one correspondence between the artifact and the process involved in hymnody.

The following, then, is an analysis of one UCC congregation's corporate singing over a five-year period. First Congregational United Church of Christ in downtown Washington, D.C. observed its 125th anniversary in 1990. General Oliver Otis Howard, head of the Freedmen's Bureau after the Civil War, was one of the founding members, and the establishment of Howard University grew from its Mission Committee. First Church became the first racially integrated church in the capital, though the congregation split over the issue, and some chose to go elsewhere. Other defining moments in the congregation's history were the decision in 1956 to remain a downtown congregation rather than to sell the property and move elsewhere, and the decision in 1973 to enter into covenant with the Metropolitan Community Church whereby MCC, a gay and lesbian congregation, was able to worship in the First Church sanctuary. The building is currently home to two feeding programs for the homeless. The congregation has donated office space for a Central American refugee assistance group. First Church voted to be a Just Peace church and has passed a Statement of Openness and Affirmation with respect to sexual orientation. As is apparent from such decisions, First Church is a very liberal congregation dedicated to social action.

Currently church membership stands at 221. Over the past few years, an average of 13 people have joined annually, four or five have died, and seven or eight have moved elsewhere. Only a small number of the members are originally from the D.C. area, and constant turnover is a fact of life in the Washington area as people relocate for new jobs and after retirement. And many travel frequently on business. Nonetheless, there are people who have been members since the 1940s and 1950s, and a core of perhaps 100 members who are present whenever they are in town. There is a genuine age mix among the adults (the oldest regularly-attending member is 85; the newly elected moderator is 26), and a bevy of babies, toddlers, and youngsters. Most of the congregation is white, but there are African American and Hispanic members. While the congregation consists predominantly of professionals (including at least 12 ordained clergy and several seminarians), some of the homeless women who attend the evening dinner program have also joined. There are gay and straight singles and couples. In other words, the congregation is diverse and perpetually changing, and yet experiences continuity and core stability. I have attended the church since 1983 and became a member in 1986, and thus have participant-observer status with regard to the information that follows.

During the period covered (1989 through 1993), the principal worship leadership came from one full-time and one part-time minister (a husband and wife) who came to the church in 1984 and from the part-time music director who had been there since 1977. The two ministers had gone to Union Seminary in New York; at about the same time, the music director had attended Chicago Theological Seminary. Some worship-related decisions were also made by a part-time Howard Divinity School student (who mainly worked with the Christian education program but also preached on occasion), guest preachers, and lay leaders (some of whom preach every year during August, when the clergy team has a month's vacation).

The primary source of text and music for the congregation's singing throughout the period of study was the 1958 edition of the *Pilgrim Hymnal*, but it was not the only source. In the 1980s, for example, the congregation began paying a fee to Hope Publishing Company in order to use its hymns. And there were other hymnals and songbooks in the church on which the worship planners drew. Part of the impetus for looking to other sources was certainly the issue of inclusive language. In 1980 a church committee looked at possible revisions of the church's covenant in order to arrive at gender-neutral or inclusive phrasings. The move in that direction was strengthened on the arrival of the present clergy team in 1984, since they were definitely committed to being inclusive. Worship planners, then, look for already inclusive texts or ones that require only a word or phrase substitution, as well as avoid texts filled with militaristic or feudal imagery. In addition, the minister spent part of one vacation month going through the *Pilgrim Hymnal* and creating a body of textual revisions as well as some totally new texts on which the church could draw.

During the last decade, there have been few total dissenters to this direction in the congregation's hymnody. (Only one person left the church indicating that this was a factor in her decision.) In 1994, when a newly created music committee surveyed the congregation regarding its preferences both in congregational, choral, and instrumental music, one of the questions was "how important is inclusive language in hymns?" Seventy responses were received. On a scale of one to five (from "not important" to "very important"), 45 persons ranked inclusivity as a four or five. Fifteen rated it as a one or two, and some made comments about finding the revisions of older hymns troubling as well as noting the chore it was to go back and forth from bulletin to hymnal to sing the designated words. Still, the support for this approach to church hymnody is clear, and that is reflected in the hymns chosen from week to week.

Most First Church services include three hymns, one in each of the sections of the service typically identified as "Awareness," "Proclamation," and "Response." On communion Sundays, an additional hymn is sung while people move out of the pews and circle the communion table. In addition, there were periodic hymn sings at the beginning of services, particularly in 1991 and 1992; these often included hymns known to be "old favorites." And special Sunday services, such as the one including the children's Christmas pageant, often included additional congregational songs.

In addition, the music director instituted the practice of using one or two hymn verses for congregational responses, particularly after the confession and for the doxology; responses tend to be used four to six Sundays in a row and then are changed, sometimes corresponding with a new liturgical season.

After an initial period following the clergy team's arrival at First Church, when decisions about the hymns were made collectively during weekly staff meetings, the system was modified; the music director would make initial choices which could be changed, if need be, at those meetings. The ministers did not usually follow a lectionary when choosing scriptures and sermon topics, so the music director could not necessarily anticipate a theme for the service. Singability and melodic characteristics entered into the selection process particularly with regard to opening and closing hymns. Judging both by experience and by many passing conversations with the music director, first hymns typically were chosen to express praise, the joy of creation and in coming together, while final hymns were of the "uplifting" sort (either in words or music or both) that—in the words of one of the most-used benedictions—take congregants back "out into the world, to love God and the people, to serve God and the people." In general, however, the middle hymn, preceding the sermon, would ultimately be chosen with sermon themes in mind, and thus might be more introspective in character. This position in the service was also the most opportune for introducing new hymns (that is, new text and new melody—new texts for familiar melodies occurred at any time).

With 52 Sundays in a year and rarely more than three hymns per service (apart from designated hymn-sings or the hymns used to move people up around the communion table once a month), our church would sing no more than 200 hymns per year even if every single one was different. But, in fact, there are repeats.

Tables 8.1 and 8.2 identify the hymns that were used during most of the Sunday services over the five-year period, 1989–1993. (There were several services in 1991 and one in 1993 at which I was not present and for which the church has no documentation.)

Over the five-year period, a total of 155 different *Pilgrim Hymnal* hymns were used, but the number of hymns chosen during a given year declined: 117 chosen in 1989, 89 in 1990, 84 in 1991, 88 in 1992, and only 71 in 1993. Meanwhile the number of hymns from other sources has basically increased: 25 in 1989, 40 in 1990, 43 in 1991, 54 in 1992, and back down to 35 in 1993. Many of these hymns are not only sung each year, but also multiple times each year: 62 *Pilgrim* hymns and 19 from other sources were sung during four or five of the years covered by the tally; of these, 21 and 8, respectively, were sung multiple times in three or more years.

The *Pilgrim Hymnal* contains more than 500 different hymns. While there are 594 numbered items, some are liturgical chants or simple responses (ten different Amen settings, for example) and some texts have multiple tunes. The hymnal is divided into 14 major categories (the largest of which are "Worship," "God the Father," "Our Lord Jesus Christ," "The Church of Christ," "Christian Life," and "Kingdom of God on Earth"). Most of the categories are broken down into subtopics for a total of 43 groups (containing anywhere from two to 31 hymns each). What becomes clear from a look at actual practice is that some sections have been more fully utilized while others have been avoided altogether.

Of the 31 "Adoration and Praise" hymns, for example, First Church used nine. Of the 26 "Passion and Cross" hymns, the church used only five, and only five of 28 "Pilgrimage and Conflict" hymns. Not surprisingly given that the services are on Sunday mornings, only one of sixteen "Evening" hymns was used. No hymns were chosen from the sub-categories "Jesus' Life and Ministry" (seven possible choices), "The Trinity" (six choices), and "Prayer" (five choices). The worship planners did, however, choose 22 of the 31 "Birth"

TABLE 8.1 Hymns from the *Pilgrim Hymnal,* with indications of hymn text changes, and the number of times a hymn was used for Sunday services in each of five years.

* = text changes

a = text changes all times the hymn was used

s = text changes some, but not all, of the times the hymn was used

For hymns with this designation, the number of times the text changes were utilized in a given year is indicated by the format: (number*)

Number and Title of *Pilgrim Hymnal* Hymns	*	1989	1990	1991	1992	1993
1. Our God, Our Help in Ages Past	a	3x	2x	2x	4x	x
7. Immortal, Invisible	a	2x	4x	2x	2x	2x
8. Joyful, Joyful	a	2x	2x	3x	2x	2x
12. From All that Dwell	s	2x	3x (1*)		2x	
15. Praise to the Lord (re-write called "Sing Praise to God")	a		x	x		
20. Sing Praise to God Who Reigns Above	a	3x	2x	5x	3x	3x
22. We Praise Thee, O God	a	x			x	
23. Ye Holy Angels Bright	a		x			
29. Now Thank We All Our God	a	x	x	x	x	
33. As the Sun Doth Daily Rise	s	x	3x (2*)	2x	2x	x
34. Awake, Awake to Love and Work	s	x	3x	x	2x (2*)	x (1*)
35. When Morning Gilds the Skies	s	x (1*)	2x (2*)	2x (1*)	2x (1*)	x (1*)
36. New Every Morning Is the Love		3x	2x	x	x	
37. Still, Still with Thee		x	x	x	2x	x
38. Morning Has Broken		2x	3x	4x	2x	2x
43. Christ Whose Glory		2x			2x	x
58. God that Madest Earth and . . .				x		
60. Savior, Again to Thy Dear Name		x	x	x	x	2x
62. God Be with You til We Meet	a			3x	x	x
63. Lord, Dismiss Us with Thy Blessing		x			x	
64. All Creatures of Our God . . .	a	x	x (*?)		x	
65. Glory Be to God on High	a					2x
66. For the Beauty of the Earth		x	x		x	x
67. God of the Earth, the Sky . . .	a	x	x	x	x	2x
68. I Sing the Mighty Power	a	2x	x	2x	2x	2x
72. The Spacious Firmament . . .		x	x	x		2x
74. O How Glorious, Full of Wonder	s	2x	x (1*)	2x (2*)	2x (2*)	2x (2*)
77. Be Still, My Soul	a	x				
82. High in the Heavens	a	2x	2x	x		2x
86. Our God, to Whom We Turn		x	2x	x	2x	x
90. Lord of All Being, Throned		x	x	x	x	
91. The Man Who Once Has Found Abode (changed to "The One Who Once . . .")	a	x				
92. I Look to Thee in Every Need		x	x		2x	2x
93. Guide Me, O Thou Great Jehovah		x			x	
97. God of Our Life, Through All			2x	2x	3x	2x

(continued)

TABLE 8.1 (*continued*)

Number and Title of *Pilgrim Hymnal* Hymns	*	1989	1990	1991	1992	1993
101. There's a Wideness . . .	a				2x	x
103. Come, Thou Long-Expected	s	x	x	x	x (1*)	x
104. Comfort, Comfort Ye My People	s	x	x (1*)	x (1*)	x (1*)	x (1*)
107. Let All Mortal Flesh		2x	2x	2x		
109. Watchman, Tell Us . . .	a		x	x		x
110. O Come, O Come, Emmanuel (segments on separate Sundays)	??	4x	x	x (1* ??)		x
114. Lift Up Your Heads, Ye Mighty Gates		x				
116. Angels We Have Heard on High		x	x	x	x	x
118. Break Forth, O Beauteous . . .					x	x
120. Hark the Herald Angels Sing	s	x	x (1*)		x (1*)	
121. From Heaven Above		x				
122. God Rest You Merry		x				
123. All My Heart This Night [Today] Rejoices	s		x	x (1*)		
124. Bring a Torch, Jeannette		x	x	x	x	
125. Good Christian Men [Folk/Friends], Rejoice	a	x	x	x	2x	
127. Christians, Awake, Salute the Happy Morn	a	x	x			
128. In the Bleak Midwinter		x	x	x		
129. It Came Upon a Midnight	s	x	x	x (1*)	x (1*)	x (1*)
130. Joy to the World	s			2x (1*)	3x (1*)	
131. Lo, How a Rose	a			x		
132. O Come, All Ye Faithful	s	x	x (1*)	x (1*)	2x (1*)	x (1*)
136. On This Day Earth Shall Ring	a		x	x	x	x
137. Away in a Manger		x		x		
138. Silent Night				x		
140. What Child Is This			x			
141. First Nowell		x	x	x	x	
143. We Three Kings				x		
145. O Morning Star, How Fair		x	x	x	x	x
146. While Shepherds Watched	a	x				
155. All Glory, Laud, and Honor				x		x
156. Draw Nigh to Thy Jerusalem		x			x	
161. Before the Cross of Jesus		x		x		
169. My Song Is Love Unknown	a	x	x	x		
175. Ride on, Ride on in Majesty			x	x	x	x
181. Alleluia! The strife Is O'er		x	x	x	x	
182. Christ the Lord Is Risen	s	x	x	x	x	x (1*)
184. Good Christian Men [Christians All] Rejoice	a	x	x	x	x	
185. Come, Ye Faithful, Raise the Strain	s	x	x (1*)		x (1*)	x
188. Joy Dawned Again on Easter		x	x	x	x	
190. Lift Up Your Hearts, Ye People					x	
192. The Day of Resurrection		x	x	x	x	x

Number and Title of *Pilgrim Hymnal* Hymns	*	1989	1990	1991	1992	1993
193. Thine Is the Glory		x	x	2x	x	
195. All Hail the Power of Jesus' Name		x				
197. At the Name of Jesus (At Your Name, O Jesus)	s	x	x	x (1*)		
202. Jesus Shall Reign Where'er . . .	a	x	x	x		
215–216. Lead, Kindly Light (2nd tune)		2x	x		x	x
217. Lord of All Hopefulness		x	x			
218. O Jesus, I Have Promised						x
221. How Sweet the Name of Jesus Sounds	a	x				
222. Jesus, Priceless Treasure	a					x
223. O for a Thousand Tongues to Sing	a	2x	x	2x	x	
227. Fairest Lord Jesus		x				
228. Love Divine, All Loves Excelling		2x	3x		3x	3x
232. Spirit of God, Descend Upon . . .	s	x		3x (2*)	3x	x
234. Breathe on Me, Breath of God		x				x
237. Send Down Thy Truth, O God		2x		x	x	x
238. Come, Gracious Spirit . . .	a	x	2x			
239. Come Down, O Love Divine	a	2x		x	x	
242. Holy Spirit, Truth Divine					x	
244. O Holy Spirit, Enter In		x	x	x		x
258. Lord, Thy Word Abideth		2x	x		2x	2x
259. We Limit Not the Truth of God	a	x	x			2x
260. The Church's One Foundation	a	x		x	x	
268. Lord, We Thank Thee for Our Neighbors			x			
272. Blest Be the Tie That Binds		x				
277. Jesus, Friend, So Kind and Gentle		x				
286. Come, Risen Lord		x		2x	x	4x
288. Let Us Break Bread Together		10x	8x	6x	8x	8x
293. Come, Labor On	a	x				
295. Christ for the World We Sing		2x	x	x		2x
305. The Morning Light Is Breaking						
306. For All the Saints	s	2x (1*)	x			
317. I Love to Tell the Story		x	2x	2x	x	x
318. Draw Thou My Soul, O Christ		2x		x	2x	x
322. Jesus Calls Us, O'er the Tumult						x
327. Savior, Like a Shepherd Lead Us			x		x	
341. Dear Lord, Creator		x			x	x
345. Rejoice, Ye Pure in Heart	a		x		x	
352. Lift Up Your Hearts		2x	2x	x	3x	x
353. Lord, I Want to Be a Christian						
362. Awake, My Soul, Stretch Every Nerve	s	x	x (1*)	x	2x (1*)	x (1*)
363. A Mighty Fortress	a	x	x			x
365. Faith of Our Fathers	a				x	
366. God of Grace and God of Glory	s	x	2x	2x (1*)	2x	

(continued)

TABLE 8.1 *(continued)*

Number and Title of *Pilgrim Hymnal* Hymns	*	1989	1990	1991	1992	1993
372. How Firm a Foundation	a		x	x	x	
390. As Pants the Hart	a	x			x	
391. Be Thou My Vision	a	x	x	x	x	2x
395. Behold Us, Lord, a Little Space		x	x	x		
397. Lord, Speak to Me That I May Speak		x	2x		2x	x
404. Take My Life and Let It Be		x	2x	x		
406. Forth in Thy Name, O Lord, I Go		x				
418. O Master, Let Me Walk With Thee		2x	x	2x		
419. Thou God of All, Whose Spirit Moves	a	2x	x	2x	2x	x
421. We Thank Thee, Lord, Thy Paths . . .	a				x	x
423. Where Cross the Crowded Ways of Life	a		x			
426. The Voice of God Is Calling	a	2x		x	x	
429. Eternal Father, Strong to Save	a					x
433. God of Our Fathers [The Ages]	a	x		x	x	x
435. Judge Eternal, Throned in Splendor	a				x	
438. O God, Beneath Thy Guiding Hand	a	x				
439. Not Alone for Mighty Empire		x				
440. O Beautiful for Spacious Skies		x				
444. O Day of God, Draw Nigh					x	x
447. O God of Love, O King of Peace (True Source of Peace/O Shepherd Mine)	a	x		x		3x
449. Let There Be Light, Lord God of Hosts	s	4x (3*)		2x	2x	2x
450. These Things Shall Be	a				x	
453. Ring Out, Wild Bells	a	2x	x			
454. Great God, We Sing That Mighty Hand	a	x	x	x	x	x
455. Tis Winter Now		x	x			
456. All Beautiful the March of Days	a	x				
458. Praise to God, Your Praises Bring		x				
460. We Plow the Fields and Scatter	a			x		
462. Come, Ye Thankful People, Come		x	x	x	x	x
464. Praise to God, Immortal Praise		x				
478. All Things Bright and Beautiful	a	x		x		
481. I Sing a Song of the Saints of God		x			2x	x
488. Go, Tell It on the Mountain		x	x		x	
514. Praise God from Whom All Blessings Flow	a		x			
576. Lord, Thou Hast Searched Me		x	x	2x	x	x
577. Great God Who Hast Delivered Us		x				

TABLE 8.2 Hymns from sources other than the *Pilgrim Hymnal*, and the number of times each was sung during the five-year study period.

Hymns from other sources	1989	1990	1991	1992	1993
A New Day Bids Us Wake	x	2x	x	2x	2x
All Who Tell the Gospel Story	x	x	x		x
Amazing Grace	x	x	x	3x	x
Be Not Afraid				x	
Behold a Broken World We Pray		x			
Behold That Star			x	x	x
Bread and Roses	x				
Bring Many Names		x		x	x
Christ Is Alive		x	x	x	
Christ Is the Sure Foundation	x				
Church of God/Christ in Every Age	x	2x	x	2x	x
Come Now, Holy Spirit			x	2x	
Come, Sing a Song of Harvest		x			
Come, Thou Fount of Every Blessing				x	
Creating God, Your Fingers Trace		x			
Deep River	x				
Down By the Riverside	x				
Earth Moves in a Mysterious Way					x
Every Morning Is Easter Morning				2x	
Every Time I Feel the Spirit	x	2x	x	2x	x
For the Fruit of All Creation		x	2x	3x	2x
For the Healing of the Nations		x	x		
Friendly Beasts				x	x
Go Down, Moses		x		x	
God Eternal, Touch Us				x	
God Moves in a Mysterious Way (different tune and partially different text from 87-88 in *Pilgrim Hymnal*)		x			
God of Abraham Praise	x				
God Whose Giving Knows No Ending		x	x	x	
Great God, Your Love Has Called Us			2x		
Great Is Thy Faithfulness				2x	3x
Help Us Accept Each Other		2x	2x	2x	x
Humbly in Your Sight			x	x	x
I Come with Joy	2x	3x	2x	x	
I Know the Lord			x		
I Want Jesus to Walk with Me			x	x	x
Jesus Walked This Lonesome Valley	x	x		x	x
Just a Closer Walk with Thee				x	x
Kum-ba-ya				x	
Leaning on the Everlasting Arms	x		2x	2x	2x
Lift Every Voice	x	x		x	x
Like a Mighty River Flowing		x	x	2x	2x
Live Gently	x				
Look Back and See the Apostles' Road		x			

(*continued*)

TABLE 8.2 *(continued)*

Hymns from other sources	1989	1990	1991	1992	1993
Lord God, Your Love Has Called Us		x			
Lord of the Dance		x			
Love Alone Unites Us		x			
Love's Goal (There Is a Love . . .)			2x	2x	x
Morning Light Is Breaking			x	x	4x
My God, My Shepherd, and My Guide		x	x	x	x
My Lord, What a Morning	x		3x	x	2x
Nobody Knows the Trouble				x	
Not for Tongues of Heaven's Angels			2x	x	x
Now in This Moment				x	
Now Let Us from This Table Rise	x	x	x	x	
O Christ the Healer			x		
O Come, All You Children		x	x	x	
O Freedom		x	2x	2x	x
O God of Every Nation		x			
One More River		x			
Palms, The	x	x		x	
Pass Me Not, O Gentle Savior				x	x
Prayer for Africa			x		
Precious Lord	x			x	x
Rise Up, Shepherd, and Follow		x	x	x	
Rock'a My Soul		x			
Shall We Gather at the River				x	
Sister Mary			x	x	x
Somebody's Knockin'	x				
Spirit of Gentleness	x	x	x		
Steal Away			x		
Swing Low			x		
Take Time				x	
Thank You				2x	
There's a Spirit in the Air			2x	x	x
This Is a Story Full of Love			x		
This Is My Song		x			
This Is My/Our Story, This Is My/Our Song				x	
This Little Light of Mine			x	2x	
Trees of the Field	x	x			
We Are a Gentle, Angry People			x		x
We Are Not Our Own			x	x	x
We Are Your People	x	2x	2x	3x	3x
We Shall Overcome		x		x	x
What Gift Can We Bring			x	2x	
When God Is a Child	x	2x		4x	4x
When in Our Music	x	3x	x	3x	3x

(Christmas) hymns, eight of the 15 "Resurrection" hymns, and seven of the 15 "Holy Spirit" hymns. In other words, the hymnal's selections for celebrative seasons were utilized more than those for "darker" liturgical seasons and doctrinal themes, and trinitarian formulas were largely filtered out (a very conscious choice on the part of the worship-planning team).

Further, certain hymns are "givens" for specific seasons or days, or have become traditions within the congregation: "Christ the Lord Is Risen Today" is sung each Easter; "When God Is a Child" is now sung in Advent, adding a verse each Sunday as a new candle is lit. A hymn such as "Take My Life and Let It Be" is typically sung on Pledge Sunday, while "We Are Your People" is often used on the annual Covenant Renewal Sunday. The logistics of the communion services are such that only three or four very familiar hymns have been used for the time when people are moving while singing. And it has also helped to have a familiar hymn at the end of communion, so people do not need hymnals but can simply follow the text printed in the bulletin.

To reiterate, then, hymn selection is ultimately a process specific to the congregation and its worship planners, a process in which the choices available from the hymnal in the pews are filtered, as well as augmented by other resources.

In the course of looking at hymns chosen (or avoided), I became aware of how many times hymn texts referred to the act of singing or, occasionally, to other forms of music-making. In Euro-American expressive culture, there are many instances in which one genre is used to depict another: there are paintings about music-making (Picasso's famous guitarist or Chagall's "Green Violinist"); there are dramas about painting ("Sunday in the Park with George"), and so on. But there are also occasions in which a genre comments on itself (a practice known in literary criticism as reflexivity): We sometimes see paintings whose topic is the act of painting (an early Rembrandt called "The Artist in His Studio" or the self-portrait of Judit Leyster, a contemporary of Franz Hals, depicting herself painting); we have plays about plays (everything from "Hamlet" to "Six Characters in Search of an Author" to "Chorus Line"); movies about movie-making (the documentary about the filming of Coppola's "Apocalypse Now"). We even talk about the process of talking—and not only in academic settings. A colleague whose dissertation was on aspects of Danish American Lutheranism commented on how much time these communities spend talking about talking, about the nature of appropriate speech, etc.[1]

And we sing about singing, both in secular (e.g., "Singing in the Rain" and "Sing, Sing a Song") and sacred contexts. What seems particularly interesting is that those whose religious expression includes singing about singing are not only the choir members—the designated song specialists—but rather all those in the pews. What is this about? Does this ultimately affect our religious experience? Is there a difference, perhaps, between singing "Praise God" and singing "Sing Praise to God?" These questions may not be answerable *per se*, but we can certainly see that singing about singing is no accident, but rather a common and effective aspect of congregational hymnody.

At least one-third of the *Pilgrim Hymnal* hymns, 177 to be exact, contain specific references to music-making. These hymns are not evenly dispersed through the hymnal categories; for example, only four of 26 "passion and cross" hymns contain references to song, while 14 out of 15 Resurrection hymns do. Two-thirds of the Christmas hymns as well as those in the "Adoration and Praise" category mention music-making (some of these hymns are based on Psalm texts which often use music-making imagery).

When we look at the hymns actually selected at First Church, we see a similar pattern: 49 of the 155 *Pilgrim Hymnal* hymns that were used include music-making references as do 22 of the 87 hymns selected from other sources. To this we must add the earlier-mentioned sung responses taken from hymns. In 1991, for example, First Church used seven doxologies on a total of 29 Sundays which typically command that songs be sung:

> "To God, creator, heavenly light . . . raise an endless song of thankful praise"
> "Rejoice, give thanks, and sing"
> "Praise God, from whom all blessings flow, sing praise, all creatures"
> "Honor God, give thanks, rejoice . . . sing through all eternity"
> "Glory be to God on high . . . let the whole creation cry . . . sing until the Day of Days"
> "We praise thee, O God . . . glad praises we sing"
> "Sing praise to God most joyfully"

While typically more introspective, one sung response to confession contains the line: "Why restless, why cast down, my soul?/Hope still and thou shalt sing the praise and honor of thy God."

In all, there were at least 54 occasions in 1989 when the congregation sang hymns with references to music-making, 61 occasions each in 1990 and 1991, 75 times in 1992, and 46 times in 1993—an average of more than once per service. Add in the sung responses, and a person who attends First Church is apt to sing about singing or music-making at least once a Sunday, and probably more often two or three times in a service.

Who or what does the singing or music-making in these hymns? There were ten first-person singular hymns ("I sing a song of the saints of God"; "This is my story, this is my song"), 11 if you count the one addressed to "my soul" [no. 23]. There were more than double that (24) in which "we" are the musicians ("we've no less days to sing God's praise" from "Amazing Grace"). There are some second-person examples; all of these are in the form of commands: "Come, ye faithful, raise the strain"; "rejoice, ye pure in heart," for example. Other categories of human singers who are identified include children, newborn souls, those on land and sea, toiling pilgrims, our ancestors, Christians, citizens of Jerusalem (as well as "the tribes"), shepherds, saints, the church, and simply-mortals. We also have "all" and "someone," both presumably human.

Then there are elements of nature, or nature itself—also birds, heavens or skies, flowing water, mountains, stars and planets, earth, and all creation. We even periodically revert to an earlier cosmology and sing about the music of the spheres: One of the great hymns of the Congregational tradition is "We limit not the truth of God to our poor reach of mind." Based on the parting words of Pastor John Robinson to the Pilgrims leaving England in 1620, it includes the line: "upward we press, the air is clear, and the sphere-music heard."

Heaven and citizens of heaven also are reported as singing: angelic music is a topic in twelve hymns. Two hymns address God (or facets of God?) directly, once as the "Spirit of gentleness" who "sang in a stable," the other referring to "thine eternal hymn" [no. 86]—so God may also be a participant.

Finally, there are some references that are hard to classify: "flaming tongues above," "every tongue or every voice," "all things seen and unseen," and references to singing where the source is unidentified or ambiguous: "praise for the singing" (in "Morning Has Broken"). There are also a few trumpet and organ blasts.

Whether descriptive or prescriptive, the music-making in the hymns is, for the most part, corporate. With our group singing, we primarily invoke collective entities (ourselves, all creation, angels, or every tongue). The uses of "I" and "my" are comparatively infrequent. Whether consciously chosen for that reason or not, this is a rather accurate representation of contemporary Congregational ideology—one in which personal salvation is not an emphasis, where membership is a function of the covenant to walk together rather than a statement about beliefs. (It would be interesting to see whether Christian churches that emphasize personal salvation sing more first-person hymns.)

What is the character of the music-making of all of these entities? The phrases that occur in the hymns include the following: triumph song of life, joyful music, grateful song, songs of true worship, glad or grateful praises, songs of love, canticle divine, eternal song, songs of heaven, mystic harmony, flowers of song, melody of peace. All affirm; they often celebrate. There are no dirges, no siren songs luring the unwary. And this is a Protestant tradition where, at one time, singing was looked upon with some suspicion. Probably the closest reference to aural discord linked to a musical symbol is the striking visual and sonic image in the hymn "Send Down Thy Truth, O God": "Earth's bitter voices drown in one deep ocean of accord."

There are, however, a few paradoxical instances of hymns that enjoin us to be quiet: Some of these are the lullaby-like songs for Christmas with "hush, hush" choruses, but also "God Himself is present, all within keep silence, prostrate lie in deepest reverence" (except for the angel choirs). The discrepancy between words and actions is striking—once it is noticed. But it seems likely that most of the references to music-making slip under our awareness. The persons in the congregation to whom I've spoken about this phenomenon find it intriguing but not something to be kept in mind Sunday after Sunday. And this is true even with the most "self-conscious" hymns: the ones specifically about music-making: "How Can I Keep from Singing" (Robert Lowry 1869), "When in Our Music God Is Glorified" (Green 1972), or "How Shall I Sing to God"[2] (Wren 1986). The latter, in particular, does not ask us to examine the process of singing about singing, only to own it.

Hymnody, after all, consists of text joined to music—ideas embedded in an affective medium. As Richard Viladesau has stated:

> Vocal music attempts to combine the intelligible revelation of word with that of sensible beauty. . . . Singing enables us to step back from the word's immediacy as communication, and to make it an aesthetic object; it allows us to contemplate and to celebrate the word rather than simply hear or speak it. (1992)

Hymns allow congregants to express thoughts or sentiments that they would not ordinarily express. As noted earlier, the music-making that goes on in hymn texts is very frequently in praise of God and God's actions. Judging from the results when several preachers have tried to evoke spoken responses, it is clear that First Church is one in which few people are comfortable saying something like "Praise God" except within the structured framework of unison readings or within hymns. The corporate activity and especially the music "lift" the weight of meaning from those words. Music takes those words, as Viladesau says, beyond the tasks of communication into the realm of sheer celebration; explicit, fully-thought-out meanings can wait.

So we combine Brian Wren's definition of hymns as sources of unification, expressions of faith, and empowerment (and the added confirmation from hymn texts themselves that singing of and in the faith is principally a corporate act) together with Viladesau's understanding of the effect of music, and add to this the selection and modifications of hymns used in a particular congregational setting. The result is an awareness of the complex processes at work "when[ever] in our music God is glorified."

NOTES

1. Private communication with Catherine Hiebert Kerst.
2. How shall I sing to God
   when life is filled with gladness,
      loving and birth,
      wonder and worth?
   I'll sing from the heart,
      thankfully receiving,
      joyful in believing.
   This is my song, I'll sing it with love.

   How shall I sing to God
   when life is filled with bleakness,
      empty and chill,
      breaking my will?
   I'll sing through my pain,
      angrily or aching,
      crying or complaining.
   This is my song, I'll sing it with love.

   How shall I sing to God
   and tell my Savior's story:
      Passover bread,
      life from the dead?
   I'll sing with my life,
      witnessing and giving,
      risking and forgiving.
   This is my song. I'll sing it with love.

WORKS CITED

Green, Fred Pratt. 1972. "When in Our Music God Is Glorified." Music by Charles Stanford.

Pilgrim Hymnal. 1931. *Pilgrim Hymnal*. Boston: The Pilgrim Press. 8th ed. 1962.

Viladesau, Richard. 1992. "Sacred Sound and Meaning: Theological Reflections on Music and Word in Christian Worship." In Vernon Wicker, ed., *Hymnology An-*

nual: An International Forum on the Hymn and Worship. Vol 2. Michigan: Vande Vere, 3–9.

Wren, Brian. 1986. "Hymnody as Theological Empowerment." *Chicago Theological Seminary Register* 76 (Spring): 12–13.

———. 1986. "How Shall I Sing to God?" Music by Joan Collier Fogg.

PART III

Individuals and the Agency of Faith

9

Fanny Crosby and Protestant Hymnody

Edith L. Blumhofer

I think of my blessed redeemer; I think of him all the day long. I sing, for I cannot be silent! His love is the theme of my song.

—Fanny J. Crosby, 1882

In the crowded auditorium of the Pacific Garden Mission on Chicago's near south side, where, for more than a century, hundreds of the city's homeless and dispossessed have congregated nightly, a capacity audience blend their voices in a rousing rendition of "Rescue the Perishing." A United Methodist congregation opens the denomination's new hymnal to sing "Blessed Assurance, Jesus Is Mine." A Baptist congregation prepares for its monthly communion service with the song, "Jesus, Keep Me Near the Cross." A mass choir at a Billy Graham crusade leads tens of thousands in the familiar words: "To God be the glory; great things He hath done." In each case, words provided by Fanny Crosby more than a century ago help mold how people today understand and express Christian faith.

Who was Fanny Crosby? Most churchgoing Protestants, especially those whose roots are in revivalistic denominations, know several Crosby songs, but few know anything about her—or about the hundreds of others whose contributions to the language of Christian faith are preserved and transmitted by Christian hymnody. In her day, Fanny Crosby was something of a legend. "Probably no person in the Christian world is better known than Fanny Crosby" was a typical claim in American publications in the 1890s (Fanny Crosby

Scrapbook [hereafter Scrapbook]).[1] A blind poet who wrote the lyrics for more than eight thousand gospel songs, Crosby was heralded by secular and religious media as the most prolific American hymnwriter of all time. Her lyrics both represented and shaped the ethos of evangelical Protestantism after the Civil War. The public adored her. Her blindness lent fascination to her accomplishments, and journalists of the Victorian era vied with one another in praising her. Some Crosby lyrics quickly became household words; others languished; many that were once sung have been long forgotten. But more than most of the hundreds of people who have contributed enduring words to North American hymnody over the years, Crosby helped mold the common memory of post–Civil War Protestants whose faith was nurtured in the Anglo-American revival tradition. They, in turn, took her lyrics around the world, translating and transmitting them as part of the Protestant missionary legacy.

The following pages offer a brief biographical sketch of Crosby, focusing on music but also suggesting other windows her life story offers on nearly a century of American Protestant experience.

Biography

Frances Jane Crosby was born to John and Mercy Crosby in the small village of Southeast, New York on March 24, 1820. Both of her parents were Crosbys. Their ancestors had arrived from England in the 1630s, settling on the outskirts of Boston. Over the years, the Crosby clan scattered, and one branch of the family made its way to Putnam County, north of New York City. Crosbys fought in the Revolutionary War and the War of 1812. It was commonly believed that James Fenimore Cooper's novel, *The Spy*, was based on the real exploits of one Enoch Crosby (see, e.g., Miller 1898, 307–19). By the time Fanny was born in 1820, then, her family had deep roots in the American experience. They were middle-class Protestants of Puritan stock fallen on hard economic times. Recent historiography often overlooks such people. Their story seems trite and uninteresting: they were white, Protestant, English, hard-working small farmers; moral, earnest people, proud to be descended from Puritan stock, and deeply devoted to God and country.

Before Crosby's first birthday, a quack doctor's mistreatment of an eye infection cost Fanny Crosby her eyesight, and a work-related accident claimed the life of her father. Mercy Crosby hired out to do whatever domestic work she could find and often left Fanny with her mother, Eunice. Eunice Crosby showered the child with attention and convinced Fanny that her blindness need not limit her. She taught Fanny to do almost everything sighted people did, and she spent hours cultivating the child's remarkable memory by helping her memorize scripture and poetry. Before Fanny was ten, she could differentiate among plants and birds and recite the four Gospels and long passages from the Pentateuch. "The books of the mind," she liked to say later, "are just as real and tangible as those of the desk and the library shelve—if only we would use them enough to keep their binding flexible and their pages free from dust!" (see Scrapbooks). Fanny's grandparents whiled away long winter evenings by reading aloud from Puritan classics and English poetry and fiction, and Fanny placed these on the bookshelves of her mind. Hard work and a hard life made Eunice Crosby seem to be an old woman long before her death in 1831 at the age of fifty-three. Fanny was eleven years old, but by then, despite her own lack of leisure and formal schooling, Eunice had opened her granddaughter's mind to the world around her and to literary resources that molded the child's future and stimulated her lifelong love of literature.

The Crosby family worshiped in a Presbyterian congregation that prided itself on its Puritan heritage. These non-instrumental churchgoers had preceptors who set the pitch with a tuning fork and lined out the psalms. By custom, the deacons provided an original hymn each week. The congregation sang these lyrics to standard tunes and used no hymnals.

As a child, then, Fanny Crosby had no knowledge of what she later called "the grand old hymns of the Christian faith." There were few hymnals in Southeast, New York, and the family held the few Isaac Watts hymns they knew in their memories, treasuring them as poetry as well as song (Crosby 1906, 26–27). Fanny's first exposure to a significant corpus of sacred songs came in 1832 when her mother's employment took both of them to nearby Ridgefield, Connecticut. There Fanny befriended a tailor who attended the local Methodist class meeting. At the humble Methodist meeting house in Ridgefield, she discovered a hymnic tradition that warmed her heart and summoned her to participate and respond. For a time, Fanny's mother worked among Quakers in Westchester County. From her playmates, Fanny learned plain speech and the faith story of another tradition.

Until she reached the age of fifteen, in 1835, Fanny had no formal schooling. She did, however, take advantage of classes offered locally by itinerant singing masters. Designed by a handful of people who hoped to influence American music with European song, these classes used materials written by Thomas Hastings and Lowell Mason.[2] Hastings (who wrote the common tune for "Rock of Ages" when Crosby was ten years old) and Mason (a Congregationalist known as an arranger and composer of hymn tunes, for example, "When I Survey the Wondrous Cross") helped introduce music into public school curricula and played leading roles in the emerging business of church music (see Rich 1946). Some may have regarded itinerant singing masters as part of a grand scheme to redirect popular music, but for people in villages like Southeast, the masters simply offered a welcome diversion from the monotony of the long, cold winters. Fanny Crosby did not have an exceptional voice, but she loved to sing.

In 1835, Mercy Crosby enrolled Fanny at the New York Institute for the Blind in New York City. The trip from Southeast to Manhattan was an adventure by horse-drawn carriage, train, and boat that brought Fanny into a vastly different cultural setting. Only the second school of its kind in the country, the Institute was an educational experiment rooted in the social reform movements energized by the Second Great Awakening. There Fanny first engaged in systematic studies in the liberal arts. She also began to study instrumental and vocal music, learning to play the piano, organ, harp, and guitar.[3]

One of the music instructors at the Institute was George F. Root, a New England colleague of Hasting's and Mason's, whose reputation as a composer of popular tunes was growing. Already as a small child, Fanny had shown poetic aptitude. Now she and Root pooled their talents to produce popular songs and several cantatas, some of which were performed in New York theaters (Root 1852; 1854; 1890, 81–82). With Root's encouragement, Fanny also published several small books of poetry (see, e.g., Crosby 1844, 1851).

Fanny's uncanny ability to express any idea poetically brought her to the attention of the steady stream of notables who visited the Institute to assess for themselves the feasibility of publicly supported education for the blind: Henry Clay, Martin van Buren, James Russell Lowell, James Knox Polk, William Seward, Horace Greeley. Grover Cleveland served for a time as a secretary on the Institute's staff, and Fanny came to know the future president. Fanny's way with words meant that she welcomed guests with an impromptu poem or traveled on behalf of the Institute to demonstrate what the visually challenged could accomplish with their minds. In 1843, Fanny addressed the New York State Senate, which came as a body to the Institute. During the 1840s, she visited Washington, D.C. several times to testify before congressional committees in support of education for the blind. During these visits, she dined several times at the White House and also heard a speech by former president John Quincy Adams, who had returned to Washington as a member of the House of Representatives (Crosby 1906, 76–110).

During her years at the Institute, Fanny attended churches of several denominations. The pastors of various local congregations offered regular chapel services at the Institute, and students were free to visit the churches of their choice. Fanny enjoyed participating in a nearby Methodist Church. She found parts of the Episcopal service appealing, so she often visited Episcopal churches for midweek prayers and vespers. She was seen frequently at Broadway Tabernacle, famous because the renowned evangelist Charles Finney had recently been its pastor, and was an occasional visitor at Baptist, Dutch Reformed, and Presbyterian congregations as well. All of these traditions molded her piety and her musical sensibilities.

Not until November 20, 1850, during revival services at New York's Thirtieth Street Methodist Church did Fanny Crosby reach the personal religious crisis that evangelicals called conversion. Fittingly for her future work, it occurred during the singing of Isaac Watts's hymn, "Alas, and Did My Saviour Bleed":

> When they reached the third line of the fourth stanza, "Here, Lord, I give myself away," my very soul was flooded with a celestial light. I sprang to my feet, shouting "hallelujah," and then for the first time I realized that I had been trying to hold the world in one hand and the Lord in the other. (ibid., 96)

Crosby's Calvinist upbringing had not emphasized certainty of salvation. In the Methodist revival she discovered the "blessed assurance" that her lyrics later wove into the vocabulary of popular Protestantism.

Meanwhile, changes had come to Fanny's family. Mercy Crosby had settled in Bridgeport, Connecticut where her brother, Joseph, was the proprietor of Crosby May and Co. Saddle Goods. In 1838, she married Thomas Morris, a widower who had migrated from Wales in 1836. In 1844, Morris became a Latter Day Saint and decided to join the growing Mormon community in Nauvoo, Illinois. Mercy refused to convert or to accompany him so he set off, taking with him a son and daughter from his first marriage. He arrived in Nauvoo shortly before Joseph Smith was assassinated and a few years later set out for Utah with an early part of Mormons. He eventually found work as a gardener to Brigham Young. The family he abandoned in Connecticut, including two daughters born to him and Mercy as well as his oldest son, never saw him again (Ruffin 1976, 42, 56).

In 1843, meanwhile, Fanny Crosby began teaching at the Institute for the Blind. She resigned early in 1858 to marry Alexander van Alstyne, a blind music teacher eleven years her junior. Van Alstyne had been first her pupil, then her colleague. The two left Manhattan to live near Maspeth, a small village in the sparsely settled county of Queens (Crosby 1906, 113–14). In 1859, they apparently lost a child. Motherhood was an experience to which Fanny seldom referred: Few of her cohorts knew about the child, and its name and gender have not survived. Fanny had left the security of the Institute to be a wife and mother; now she had neither job nor child (Alstyne, Crosby, and Jackson 1915, 55). For his part, van Alstyne held several posts as music teacher, organist, and composer. A restless Fanny needed something to occupy her, and the couple moved back to the familiar surroundings of Manhattan. There Fanny found her new sense of purpose in the soon-to-burgeon business of gospel hymnody.

In 1860, American Protestants were in the throes of change. Issues that would soon divide the nation had already split the denominations. A revival had recently poured new life into northern Protestantism. The country was moving westward, and new circumstances called for new resources, among them music. The rapid growth of Sunday schools, for example, seemed to warrant a new music idiom.[4] Some had already begun providing simple, easily sung songs that taught Christian values. The production of Sunday school hymnals quickly became a lucrative business. Prominent among the suppliers of new materials was William Bradbury, owner of a New York publishing firm. Bradbury was also a practicing church musician and a composer of tunes that are stamped indelibly on the Protestant cultural memory: "Just As I Am," "Saviour, Like a Shepherd Lead Us," "Jesus Loves Me." Early in 1864, a mutual friend introduced Crosby to Bradbury who was ever eager for talent to feed the growing demand. The two forged an alliance with far-reaching implications. Crosby agreed to provide poems for music Bradbury supplied. Sometimes he suggested topics; sometimes he asked what the music "said" to Crosby; sometimes she offered a poem, and he found a tune. Her first published hymns appeared in Bradbury's 1864 hymnal, *The Golden Censer* (see Bradbury, 1866). Before long, Bradbury began encouraging Crosby to use pseudonyms so that his heavy dependence on her work would not be evident (Crosby 1906, 115–25).

Crosby's association with Bradbury drew her into a growing network of hymnwriters and composers attempting to provide texts and tunes with simple harmony for congregational use. Their goal was a sacred repertory that both expressed and influenced the popular Protestant ethos. As her circle of acquaintances grew, Crosby began writing occasionally for other publishers as well. For most of her life, Crosby received $2 per poem. Composers commanded a few dollars more, but the profits went to the publishers. Fanny's Sunday school songs were selected by editors for use in hymnals designed for vastly different settings, ranging from the Reorganized Church of Jesus Christ of the Latter Day Saints to conservative evangelicals and the American Sunday School Union.

The sense that simpler words and tunes would help people "own" the songs was rooted as well in revivals. Just before the Civil War, the revival of 1857 and 1858 had swept the northeast. Immediately after the War, the National Camp Meeting Association for the Promotion of Holiness revived the venerable Methodist tradition of camp meetings where heightened emphasis on religious experiences, emotions, and testimonies assured music a prominent place. Then, perhaps even more influentially in time, came D. L. Moody and Ira Sankey, whose spectacular rise startled no one more than themselves. In Britain and the United States, Sankey introduced millions to simple, moving lyrics sung to easily learned melodies that often bore a striking resemblance to popular dances and marches (Sankey 1907). Moody and Sankey had many able colleagues in the United States, perhaps none more successful than the team of evangelist Daniel ("Major") Whittle and his songster, Philip Paul Bliss. Both Bliss and Sankey wrote text and music, gathered the work of others, and edited collections that became ubiquitous in revivals in the English-speaking world. Bliss's *Gospel Hymns* and Sankey's *Sacred Songs and Solos* were best sellers on both sides of the Atlantic (Bliss 1877). Combined, they became *Gospel Hymns 1–6*, one of the most successful religious books of all time. The royalties supported Moody's Northfield Schools (Mabie 1960). Sankey and Bliss are widely credited with being the models for the revivalistic "choristers" who have since become an accustomed part of the evangelistic circuit.

Crosby's association with Bradbury brought her into association with a growing group of gospel songwriters, who provided music for events and associations that were on the cutting-edge of evangelical Christianity after the Civil War; they were harbingers of a revolution in church music. Sunday schools, revivals, and related voluntary associations not only demanded change, they also facilitated adaptation. The new settings emphasizing Christian youth, Christian education, vibrant transdenominational movements focusing on religious experiences and testimony, and Christian mission naturally opted for stirring lyrics set to joyous music that at once elicited and expressed commitment and fervor. Renewed emphasis on evangelism gave songs of personal testimony a prominent place. At the same time, devotional piety focused increasingly on a sentimental, romanticized relationship between the believer and Christ. Crosby's experience encompassed these varied concerns of the evangelical soul. Her own piety, shaped by her exposure to a wide array of Protestant traditions, centered in devotion to Christ. She threw her energies into the causes of the day, and her songs testified as well to her confidence, experience, and perception of Christian mission. Crosby was equally at home at the immense annual Methodist camp meeting in Ocean Grove, New Jersey; socializing on the shores of Lake Chautauqua, and visiting the Chautauqua Institution; encouraging youth at Christian Endeavor conventions and YMCA rallies; or taking her place among evangelical notables on the platform at Moody's Northfield Conventions, where the Christ-centered piety of the British Keswick Conventions influenced a generation of prominent American Protestants. As the century waned, however, Crosby seemed increasingly drawn to another context, far removed from such centers of influence—the immigrant world of downtown Manhattan.

Crosby spent sixty-five years of her life in New York City. Lower Manhattan's teeming population of immigrants and the poor intrigued and attracted her. She lived the nomadic life of many propertyless New Yorkers, moving from apartment to apartment, choosing to settle in crowded districts rather than with her friends in affluent neighborhoods. From about 1878, she and her husband often lived apart. Little is known of their relationship beyond the fact that they remained on good terms and that she deeply mourned his loss in 1902. They had separate careers and interests, and Fanny opted for independence. In lower Manhattan she got to know the people for whom she wrote her songs. At about the same time that the Salvation Army discovered the appeal in the inner city of sacred texts set to popular tunes, Crosby found a new avenue of service in the rescue missions that proliferated to offer hope to the social outcasts in American cities. She became well known on the mission circuit as "Aunt Fanny" (Crosby 1906, 143–55). She preached, cajoled, sang, hugged, and cried with "her boys" as they huddled on backless benches or made their way to kneel at the front of the famous Jerry McAuley Mission (Hadley 1907). She started a new mission herself for trolley car operators. Each week, while cars were serviced at the end of the line, she preached to the trolley car operators on break. On other nights, she prayed with the prostitutes among whom Emma Whittemore worked at the Door of Hope (see Whittemore 1947). Her interests resonated with those of the Women's Christian Temperance Union, for which she also spoke. She frequented the Seamen's Mission at the Port of New York. These settings suggested to her some of her most enduring and widely sung lyrics, such as "Rescue the Perishing" and "Pass Me Not, O Gentle Saviour" (Crosby 1907, 145).

Such nondenominational associations claimed most of Fanny Crosby's energies. Denominational hymnals quickly incorporated some of her songs, too, but she wrote primarily from and to contexts shaped by the evangelical revival tradition and its language of piety.

By all accounts, Crosby was prolific and indefatigable. She liked to compose lyrics at night, sitting in the darkness of whatever flat she called "home" at the moment, holding a book. "After any particular hymn is done," she told the audiences who flocked to hear her wherever she traveled, "I let it lie for a few days in the writing desk of my mind . . . until I have the leisure to prune it, to read it through with the eyes of my memory. . . . I often cut it and trim it and change it" (quoted in Scrapbooks). She never dictated a song until she deemed it completely satisfactory. Crosby could barely write. She dictated to anyone who came by, sometimes keeping her poems in her mind for several days.

The popularity of Fanny Crosby's lyrics as well as her winsome personality catapulted her to fame. Her blindness made people curious, too. Only four feet, nine inches tall, she seemed fragile and frail—in fact, she had remarkable resilience and stamina. And she never forgot that much of her popularity depended on the composers who set her lyrics to music. One of her longest lasting and most successful collaborations was with a wealthy Cincinnati Baptist layman, William H. Doane, for whom she wrote her first widely acclaimed hymn in less than an hour in 1868—"Safe in the Arms of Jesus." Doane introduced it the same weekend at a Sunday school convention, and Crosby's publishers included it in a hymnal in 1871. Although it expresses Crosby's sense of the believer's intimate relationship with Christ in this life, its words also made it a popular funeral selection:

> Safe in the arms of Jesus, safe on his gentle breast;
> There by his love o'ershaded, sweetly my soul shall rest.[5]

Crosby wrote "Blessed Assurance," one of her best-known songs, to music composed by her eccentric wealthy friend, Phoebe Palmer Knapp. The wife of the founder of Metropolitan Life and the daughter of the prominent holiness evangelists Walter and Phoebe Palmer, Phoebe Knapp lived in a Brooklyn mansion with a large music salon where she entertained the political and social elite of her day. She and Crosby were an unlikely pair, but their collaboration yielded a song that has been translated into hundreds of languages and has been sung around the world for more than a century (Crosby 1906, 168; Sankey, McGranahan, and Stebbins n.d., no. 304).

Of all the New York churches Crosby attended, she sometimes said she liked Brooklyn's Plymouth Church best. A short ferry ride from lower Manhattan, Plymouth Church attracted thousands to Brooklyn Heights to hear its pastor, Henry Ward Beecher, who was not only acclaimed as a "prince of the pulpit" but was also an innovator with church music. A generation earlier, his father, Lyman Beecher, had encouraged and assisted Lowell Mason in his attempts to popularize German-style choral music. In the 1850s, Henry Ward Beecher decided to lead Plymouth Church in a new musical direction. To start, he oversaw the compilation of a hymnal for congregational use. "Beecher loved the old-fashioned hymns," one of his long-time associates reminisced, "though he had also a hearty welcome for new ones." Equally important to broadening the selection of music was Beecher's decision to entrust the music to volunteers among his own people rather than to paid musicians. Several hundred responded eagerly to his plea for a volunteer choir to lead the congregation in song.

Beecher cultivated spirited singing. "He was never satisfied," one of his ushers remembered, "unless he got everybody to singing":

> I have often seen him jump up from his chair right in the middle of a hymn and hold up his hand for silence. "You are not singing this hymn right," he would say. "Sing it with more spirit, and let everybody sing." The effect upon the congregation would be electric, and after that the church would fairly tremble with the volume of music the audience would pour forth. The result has been that it has always been the fashion for everybody in the congregation, strangers as well as members, to sing, and this undoubtedly has had a share in doing away with coldness and formality in the services. (Griswold 1907, 54–55)

Fanny Crosby resonated with Beecher's pro-Union politics, admired his sermons, and thrilled to the new style of congregational music that he ably implemented. Beecher adopted one of her songs as the theme for Plymouth Church's children's missions in Manhattan. Far-reaching changes in the music of American Protestantism happened simultaneously but in different ways in many places, influencing form and presentation and the function of music in congregational life. Both Crosby and Beecher were participants in a much larger movement of change.

Crosby frequented many churches, missions, camp meetings, conferences, and salons. Her friends were active in a wide range of thriving, expanding evangelical activities, always active and on the move. Not deeply rooted in a particular house, neighborhood, or congregation, she seemed a sort of generic white urban Protestant, standing squarely in the center of the piety, mission, and morality that defined the genteel, white, middle-class, revivalistic American Christianity of her day. Her piety was everybody's piety. She knew the rich and the poor, life's seamy side as well as its pleasures, the smells and close quarters of lower Manhattan tenements as well as the splendor of the drawing rooms of the wealthy. Touched by and sharing in a wide array of religious and social experiences, Crosby found herself embraced by different kinds of people. She wrote intentionally out of different experiences, sometimes especially for the impoverished and immigrant working-class people she knew as neighbors in lower Manhattan. She seemed unimpressed by money, moving easily from the drawing rooms of the city's rich, with whom she also spent parts of her summers at Chautauqua Lake and Ocean Grove, to the humble environs of lower Manhattan's East Side rescue missions. If she had more money than necessary for her frugal needs, she gave it away.

In 1900, eighty-year-old Fanny Crosby left New York to live with a younger stepsister in Bridgeport, Connecticut. Even then, she did not settle down. She returned frequently for weekends with friends in New York and traveled in the northeast to address conventions and conferences. Every year on her birthday (and especially when she reached yet another milestone—80, 85, 90), large numbers of the nation's Protestant churches paid her tribute by designating the Sunday nearest her birthday "Fanny Crosby Sunday" and singing her hymns in their services. A reporter's description of one summer season at the Methodist campground in Ocean Grove, New Jersey provides a snapshot of how she spent much of her last two decades. Her visit was "a continuous reception to oblige the hundreds of Christian visitors who clamor[ed] for a chance to meet and thank the venerable blind maker of verses that have echoed through every Sunday school in the land (*The New York Times* 1897)."

Crosby died at her home in Bridgeport on February 12, 1915 of a massive cerebral hemorrhage. The night before she had dictated her last poem:

In the morn of Zion's glory
When the clouds have rolled away,
And my hope has dropped its anchor
In the vale of perfect day,
When with all the pure and holy
I shall strike my harp anew,
With a power no arm can sever,
Love will hold me fast and true. (Ruffin 1976, 237)

Crosby's grave stands near the impressive monument that marks the grave of her childhood playmate, P. T. Barnum. Her grave, by contrast, is marked by a small stone with the simple engraving: "Aunt Fanny: She hath done what she could." "What she could" had enduring influence on the culture of post-Civil War Protestantism.

Legacy

Rooted in the flowering of evangelicalism in the decades following the Second Great Awakening, the lyrics of nineteenth-century gospel songs express the central message of the era's popular Protestantism and the mission it carried forward in Sunday schools, temperance rallies, urban revivals, and camp meetings. When one views the American Protestant landscape through the lens of gospel song, theological and denominational boundaries and doctrinal disputes blur and unitive assumptions and piety come into focus. Evangelical piety appears to have much more to do with devotion to Jesus, religious experience, testimony, and mission—and singing—than with carefully articulated theological points. Groupings defined by gospel song repertories cross denominational boundaries and also embrace the piety fostered in the vast nondenominational voluntary associations that have often channeled evangelical energies.

Gospel song lyrics tend to be dualistic, setting in sharp contrast this world and its problems with heaven and its bliss. Crosby's best-loved songs are about safety, assurance, the beauty of Jesus, and the anticipation of heaven. They are emphatically Christ-centered, expressing and cultivating a type of piety that flowered around the activities of Moody and Sankey as well as in the Methodist camp meeting tradition. Crosby wove strands of the piety nurtured at Keswick, Northfield, and Ocean Grove into the broader fabric of Protestant vocabulary. By appealing to religious affections, sacred songs could readily do such weaving. The language of the heart fostered and facilitated the expression of personal and communal piety in song. And Crosby reminded her generation that the act of singing was itself a core expression of evangelical faith:

> I sing for I cannot be silent;
> His love is the theme of my song.

Crosby's fame in Christian circles grew rapidly in the 1870s following the publication of "Safe in the Arms of Jesus." Like many of Crosby's other songs about the Christian being "hidden" in Christ for safety and shelter from life's inevitable storms, "Safe in the Arms of Jesus" juxtaposes the "corroding care" and "the world's temptations" with the safety and certainty of Christ's embrace. Crosby's hymn uses sentimental Victorian language to describe Christ: his gentle breast, his tender mercy, the light of his presence. For her, he was a loving, beautiful, precious Savior. On the one hand, this Christ has traditionally feminine attributes; on the other, he fulfills the traditionally masculine roles—the believer is held, protected, led; Christ makes life's decisions. The believer's ultimate lesson, the object of Christian growth, is the passivity of utter dependence and surrender.

In other lyrics, Crosby summoned her generation to duty and service:

> Rescue the perishing! Duty demands it;
> Strength for thy labor the Lord will provide.
> Plead with them earnestly, plead with them gently,
> Tell the poor wand'rer a Savior has died.

Above all, Crosby's lyrics remind one that Christians are happy people:

Redeemed, and so happy in Jesus!
No language my rapture can tell!
I know that the light of his presence
With me doth continually dwell!

Like many of her cohorts, Crosby forsook the strong descriptive language about sinners found in earlier hymns—depicting people as "worms" or "worthless" or "rebels"—for a gentler focus on redemption and reconciliation. For Crosby, the horrors of Christ's death were transformed by the meaning evangelicals assigned the crucifixion. Calvary was for her a place to linger and nurture the soul:

Jesus, keep me near the cross!
There a precious fountain
Free to all, a healing stream,
Flows from Calvary's mountain.

Near the cross a trembling soul
Love and mercy found me;
There the bright and morning star
Sheds its beams around me.

Crosby's lyrics conveyed notions of piety that extended the typical subject matter of gospel songs from testimony to include themes prominent in the higher life and holiness movements of her day: the uninterrupted and often conscious communion of the soul with Christ; the enthronement of Christ as king of the heart; passive waiting on God. For Crosby, the Christian life was not simply about repentance, forgiveness, assurance, and heaven; it also had to do with growing intimacy with Christ: "Take the world, but give me Jesus, sweetest comfort of my soul"; "Thou my everlasting portion, Saviour more than life to me, I am clinging, clinging close to thee"; "Thou, the spring of all my comfort, more than life to me; whom have I on earth beside thee, whom in heaven but thee?" Such language articulated and structured the exultation, testimony, and prayer of generations of evangelical believers.

Historians of American religion are only beginning to pay attention to popular piety in general and to music in particular. As scholars turn their attention to "lived religion," it becomes necessary to engage the forms in and through which ordinary people learn and express faith. Hymnody serves evangelical Protestantism as a primary didactic and expressive form. Exploring the role of music and the lives of people who shaped evangelicalism's musical repertoire brings into focus aspects of the religious culture that traditional studies of institutions and beliefs have often obscured. In other words, the point is that the story of gospel song in the late nineteenth century is also the story of immigration, education, social movements, and revivals.

Piety in general and songs in particular also illumine one of the areas of Christian practice in which women exercised extensive cultural authority. Though sometimes excluded from pulpits, they often provided words that shaped the vocabulary of generations of Protestants, popularized the evangelical message around the world, and helped mold North American evangelical identity. Crosby probably wielded far more enduring cultural influence through her songs than she could have in a pulpit.

Crosby's legacy is most obviously the language of testimony and worship that she offered American Protestants. Many of her hymns were immediately translated by missionaries, and some that fell into disuse in North America are still sung in other languages around the world. Her life, however, offers more than insights into the emergence of gospel hymnody.

Crosby's adoring public was always fascinated by her blindness. Her life provides a window on the emergence of education for the blind and the place of such enterprises in the Protestant subculture. Her blindness may have attracted some curious well-wishers, but her winsome personality, wit, and energy held them. Crosby not only helped advance opportunities for the visually handicapped, her life also demonstrated their potential contributions to the larger community.

Crosby was not a great poet, nor was her favorite collaborator, William Howard Doane, a great composer. She lived under pressure to produce and seldom had leisure to devote to writing. Demanding composers and publishers clamored for more, and she generally obliged. Her story offers a window on another fascinating aspect of her day: the emergence of the business of gospel music. Fueled by greed and skillful marketing as well as by the demands of new cultural situations and innovative religious movements, new musical forms generated deep animosity as well as strong support. Scholars have only begun to explore the financing of American evangelicalism. The business side of the evangelical enterprise is a fascinating and revealing story.

Crosby's story also offers a window on urban America: on the experience of both white Anglo-American middle-class Protestants and recent immigrants, the dispossessed and the working class. This daughter of Puritan stock had no scruples about mingling with the wealthy, attending social functions, and enjoying the cultural opportunities of her day. When she related to "the other half" of New York where they lived, she did so as both insider and outsider. She lived where they did, and she knew them well, but she was also carrying forward a white middle-class Protestant mission that defined what she meant by duty and "doing good."

Fanny Crosby interacted with some of the most prominent and powerful men in the popular Protestant arena of her day. She carried no torch for women's ordination or other feminist causes. She also found virtually no impediments placed in her path. Comfortable with who she was, she made others comfortable, too. Neither actively for nor against women's issues in the church, she offers a revealing glimpse at the many avenues open to women and at their contentment in filling those roles.

Crosby was strongly patriotic and wrote prolifically about the major battles of the Mexican and Civil wars. A proud member of the Daughters of the American Revolution, she was also devoted to the Grand Army of the Republic and to the King's Daughters. While the preceding pages have focused on Crosby's hymn writing, they could just as well have examined her secular popular and patriotic work that appeared in many publications. In her public persona, she was highly regarded as a competent professional who negotiated a difficult path with dignity and grace.

While the literature uniformly portrays Crosby as cheerful and successful, she clearly had a darker side. Her frequent separations from her husband suggest that her personal life was not uniformly happy. In public she refused to be drawn into bitter controversies over money that racked the emerging gospel music business, but she could not entirely avoid them.

Conclusion

Fanny Crosby was a village girl who became the cultural symbol of evangelical hymnody during one of its formative stages. She negotiated a path through the emerging music industry, found an outlet in urban evangelism, and advocated education for the visually impaired. Nothing delighted her more than to be known by one and all as "Aunt Fanny." Her lyrics expressed the yearnings and convictions of a generation of evangelicals in transition. The new trends in gospel music of which Crosby was part coincided with changes inspired by others, but also stood somewhat apart. Generated amid the vast new evangelical cooperative endeavors of the nineteenth century, evangelicalism's new music mirrored piety and mission far broader than that defined by any denomination. Crosby stood squarely in the center of this emerging tradition in Protestant evangelical song. She became, at least for a generation, its cultural symbol.

NOTES

1. The Scrapbook is filled with clippings and articles by Crosby's contemporaries echoing such sentiments. This quote comes from a publication issued by the Albany (NY) Railroad YMCA.

2. A sample of materials used by these itinerants and of the anticipated results is preserved in George F. Root's *The Diapason* (1860).

3. Yearbooks of the New York Institute for the Blind are at the New York Historical Society. They include lists of pupils, their courses, and instructors.

4. On Sunday schools, see Boylan (1988) and Lynn and Wright (1980).

5. For the full text, see Sankey, McGranahan, and Stebbins n.d.: no.6.

WORKS CITED

Alstyne, Van, Frances Jane Crosby, and Samuel Trevena Jackson. 1915. *Fanny Crosby's Story of Ninety-four Years.* New York: F. H. Revell.

Banbury, William B. 1866. *The New Golden Trios: On Bradbury's Golden Series of Sabbath School Melodies, Comprising the New Golden Chain, New Golden Shower, and Golden Censer.* New York: William B. Bradbury.

Bliss, P. P. 1877. *Memoirs of P. P. Bliss.* New York: A. S. Barnes.

Boylan, Anne. 1998. *Sunday School: The Formation of an American Institution, 1790–1880.* New Haven: Yale University Press.

Crosby, Frances J. 1844. *The Blind Girl and Other Poems.* New York: Wiley & Putnam.

———. 1906. *Memories of Eighty Years.* Boston: James H. Earle.

———. 1851. *Monterey, and Other Poems.* New York: R. Craighead.

Fanny Crosby Scrapbook. Fanny Crosby Scrapbook. Music Reference Divison, New York Public Library. Scrapbook of clippings, portraits, letters and other memorabilia of Fanny Crosby, presented to the New York Public Library by Mr. H. Adelbert White on July 17, 1950.

Griswold, Stephen M. 1907. *Sixty Years with Plymouth Church.* New York: Fleming H. Revell.

Hadley, Samuel. 1907. *Down on Water Street: A Story of Sixteen Years Life and Work in Water Street Mission.* New York: Fleming H. Revell.

Lynn, Robert, and Elliott Wright. 1980. *The Big Little School: Two Hundred Years of the Sunday School.* Birmingham, Ala.: Religious Education Press.

Mabie, Janet. 1960. *The Years Beyond: The Story of Northfield, D. L. Moody, and the Schools.* East Northfield, Mass: Northfield Bookstore.

Miller, H. E. 1898. "Spy of the Neutral Ground: Enoch Crosby." *New England Magazine* 18 (May): 307–319.

Rich, Arthur Lowndes. 1946. *Lowell Mason, the Father of Singing among Children.* Chapel Hill: University of North Carolina Press.

Root, George F. 1852. *Libretto of the Flower Queen, or, the Coronation of the Rose.* Words by Fanny J. Crosby. New York: Mason Brothers.

———. 1854. *The Pilgrim Fathers: A Cantata in Two Parts.* Composed by George F.

Root. Assisted in the preparation of the words by Miss Frances J. Crosby. New York: Mason Brothers.

———. 1860. *The Diapason: A Collection of Church Music, to Which Are Prefixed a New and Comprehensive View of "Music and Its Notation" [by Lowell Mason], Exercises for Reading Music, and Vocal Training.* New York: Mason Brothers.

———. 1890. *The Story of a Musical Life.* Cincinnati: John Church.

Ruffin, Bernard. 1976. *Fanny Crosby.* Cleveland: Pilgrim.

Sankey, Ira. 1907. *My Life and the Story of the Gospel Hymns and of the Sacred Songs and Solos.* New York and London: Harper.

Sankey, Ira, James McGranahan, and George C. Stebbins, eds. n.d. *Gospel Hymns Nos. 1 to 6 Complete.* Chicago: Biglow & Main.

Unique Hymn Writer, A. 1987. "A Unique Hymn Writer." *The New York Times,* 22 August 1897, p. 12.

Whittemore, Emma Mott. 1947. *Mother Whittemore's Records of Modern Miracles.* Edited by F. A. Robinson. Toronto: Missions of Biblical Education.

10

Prayer on the Panorama: Music and Individualism in American Religious Experience

Philip V. Bohlman

The Panorama of American Religious Experience

This chapter attempts to tease out and unpack the multiple meanings that the title of this volume embodies: Music in American Religious Experience. In particular, I concern myself with the cluster, "American religious experience," which, multivalent and even nebulous as it might seem at first glance, was essential to the inclusiveness that the volume's contents represent. The authors in this volume have viewed religious experience as changing and responsive to shifting practices. Indeed, religious experience is by no means limited to the sanctuaries of organized religious institutions, nor is it bounded by the strictures of liturgies or professionally sanctioned repertories. Perhaps most important, the experience of religion in the United States and Canada is at base highly personal, starting with individual responses to religion. Music provides one of the most powerful voices for the expression of the individual's religious experience, not least because music in American religious life more often than not provides an active form of performing one's faith. As a means of experiencing religion, music in North America engages the individual through performance.

It will not be my task in this chapter to define American religious experience, or even to lay out a series of definitions of the individual terms. I want, instead, to concern myself with the ways representation enters into the processes of experiencing religion. At a very fundamental level, the "experience" to which the title of this book refers is a personal and individual experience, indeed *the experience* that conjoins music and religion. Music is, in a very real sense, inseparable from the experiencing of religion and from experiencing through religion.

American church historians traditionally turn to a stock of metaphors that evoke the vastness of religion in North America: The continent comprises sweeping landscapes, onto which denominational and ethnic churches are mapped, their overwhelming presence enveloping entire areas of the United States and Canada (see Marty 1976 and Noll 1992). Whereas such cartographic metaphors consider religious experience from the top-down, in this essay I prefer to introduce a metaphor with which I want to represent the experience from bottom-up, still without discarding the vast stretches of space and history into which certain religious experiences evolve. My concern has been, moreover, to find a persistent metaphor that locates diverse forms of music on the larger canvas of American culture. The metaphor I shall be employing is the "panorama," the American panorama, the depiction of scenes and events from American history and life through murals or vast paintings, in churches, municipal buildings, schools, and public spaces of all kinds throughout North America. The panorama has been a trope to which Americans and Canadians have often turned, and in both tangible and symbolic senses it has provided one of the most persistent forms of depicting the long history of North America.

First achieving popularity in the United States in the early decades of the nineteenth century, the panorama quickly assumed massive proportions. Entrepreneurs developed ways to set vast walls of history or geography in motion, creating the "moving panorama," which accordingly enabled the individual viewer to witness each event as it occurred (Hyde 1988; von Plessen 1993). John Banvard's panorama of the Mississippi River, displayed first in 1846, consisted of some 400 meters that depicted the landscape stretching from New Orleans to St. Louis (Avery 1993, 67; Banvard 1847). By the mid-nineteenth century American panorama artists were specializing in the moving panorama, capitalizing on its narrative potential to describe the westward expansion (Avery 1993). As American history changed, panoramas were adapted so that they might better narrate the new and popular images. With advancements in photography, the panorama quickly followed suit (D'Ooge 1994). In the twentieth century, public murals, ranging from those created for public spaces by the artists of the Works Progress Administration (often abbreviated as WPA) during the Great Depression to the billboards proliferating apace with the American highway system, became one of the most popular and populist forms of narrating the American experience in general.

There are two other reasons that this representational metaphor will become an aesthetic and religious metonym in this chapter. First, music has frequently appeared in the scenes of the panorama. That music has been fundamental to the location of experience on the panorama is evident in Daniel Kingman's choice of the panorama as the metaphor for American music history itself (1979). Music's presence on the panorama is both universal and local. In panorama scenes from great fairs or national celebrations, musicians appear to represent difference, for example, the foreign musical troupes on the Midway at the 1893 World's Columbian Exposition in Chicago. Musical performance even accompanied the moving panorama, indeed participating in the power of this particularly American form to narrate history. Nineteenth-century music publishers recognized the close relation between music and panorama, choosing at times to conflate the two as if they were a single performative experience. Collections of popular song, for example *Christy's Panorama Songster* (ca. 1840), were named in such ways as to signify their narrative connection to the American experience. Publishers also used lithographs in the forms of panoramas on the covers of sheet music, in a sense situating each song on the experience of American culture evoked by the cover; numerous prints by Currier and Ives, who embraced the panorama for their prints, were used for sheet-music covers in this way (see, e.g., Peters 1942, plates 91–94).

Religion, too, has always appeared in the scenes of the panorama, either as a unifying feature of North American histories or as a fragmenting feature, deliberately depicting the differences and variation that are evident at different times and places narrated on the canvas. The Jesuit missionary, Joseph-François Lafitau, represented the rituals of Native North and South Americans using panorama techniques (fig. 10.1), intentionally connecting different musical and religious practices in the etchings prepared for his 1724 ethnography of indigenous religious customs (Lafitau 1724; see Bohlman 1988). The diversity of American religious experiences, civil and secular, individual and collective, also attracted the attention of American painters who frequently used panorama techniques in their paintings, for example Thomas Hart Benton.

The scenes on the panorama function at once as individual experiences and as components of an entire experience, and to capture this narrative quality, this chapter, like the American panorama, will consist of individual experiences, experiences in which music and religion are coextensive and coterminous. When we turn toward the scenes on the American panorama, it is the individual experiences that come into focus and attract our attention, and therefore these will be the scenes that I situate in the foreground of the chapter.

FIGURE 10.1. Native American Ritual Panorama from Lafitau (1724)

To some degree I look closely at music as a means of redressing the frequent historiographic tendency to consider religion as a primarily collective experience. The individual often disappears in the historiography of American religious experience, replaced by congregational song and denominational experiences. Thus to say that the individual sings alone and that religious experience undermines the community is counterintuitive to what many hold to be fundamental to sacred music in North America. The scenes I sketch in this chapter, nonetheless, are counterintuitive, for I use them to argue for the importance of the individual musician in American religious experience. Moreover, I wish to argue for the larger thesis—my theoretical panorama—that it is in the dialectical tension between individual and community that American religious experience resides. Music intensifies both that tension and the complex practices of faith that it makes possible.

Community in the Imagination of American Religious Experience

Exodus, diaspora, ingathering. The sacred journey of the American religious experience passes through these three stages in the historical accounts chronicling it. For most religious historians, the American religious experience begins with emigration as a response to unacceptable socioeconomic and religious conditions. The experience continues as a journey through a vast North American liminal space, represented, for example, as the "wilderness" or "frontier." In this space, as in a rite of passage, the sojourner has been freed from one world, but has not yet established the *communitas* of another. The trajectory of the historical journey is toward the community that forms at its conclusion, therefore symbolizing its successful completion. A new American religious experience begins with the community, called variously assimilation, acculturation, or Americanization. At the moment the sacred journey is complete, the American experience begins (see Turner 1993).

Historians of American religion stress the importance of "social religion" as the centripetalizing force in the history of the American religious experience. Whether written by theologians surveying their own denomination, or by social historians concerned with the processes that hold the entire narrative of history together, one comes closer to understanding the American religious experience, in Marty's words, by "mapping group identity and social location" (1976, 1–17). Martin Marty's cartographic notion of history depends on the formation of groups and the dynamic among them as they extend their identity, shaping the place they choose to make their own. These groups, formed differently at different historical moments, compete for the same spaces, and then resolve the competition by laying claim to certain regions or urban areas as their own.

In the long history of the American religious experience, colonial narratives were dominated by the tropes of exodus, which in turn gave way to diasporic descriptions in the nineteenth century. During the twentieth century, the concept of "community" has come to dominate the ways in which we describe and understand American religious experience. Its importance has become even greater as the possibility to respond to acute emergency with exodus is greater and the sacred journey itself can take place in a matter of days, as immigration officials settle Hmong Buddhists, Cuban Catholics, or Russian Jews in predetermined communities, ready-made points of ingathering. The twentieth century has witnessed a flattening of the diversity that communities may once have represented, coming into existence after very different sacred journeys.

The "congregation," *Gemeinde* (German) and *kehillah* (Hebrew), has undergone transformations as if it were entirely synonymous with a community of believers, whose religious and musical practices were the same. Indeed, the terminology of multiculturalism recognizes changing forms of community on new American religious panoramas where communities are also urban neighborhoods, as well as ethnic and racial polities. It is through sharing religious and musical practices that a community forms and solidifies itself. In the United States the importance of ethnicity as a form of identity often derives from its inseparability from community, that is from an "ethnic group." Yet religious communities, if nothing else, change. What they are imagined to be also changes through the course of history, revealing them to be adaptive strategies and constructed senses self-determined by distinguishing differences vis-à-vis various others. The differences result from the distinctive motivations for exodus and the contrastive experiences of diaspora. They powerfully influence the need to form as a group capable of finding ways to share the experiences of past and future.

To some extent, then, American religious communities are imagined in the sense of Benedict Anderson's notion of nationalism (1991). I should argue even that the imagination of religious communities might be one of the most powerful forms of American nationalism, in which the group or community establishes its self-interests by imagining them in such ways that they are parallel both to the self-interests of other communities and to those of the nation. If imagined, American religious communities are no less real than any other kind of community. They are, nonetheless, attempts to imagine and instantiate American religious experience in specific ways. They depend on a model of music-making in which religious song and worship are primarily shared experiences. Accordingly, we witness a historiographic tendency to imagine religious music as if it were entirely shared, transforming the repertory, enacted ritual, or the denominational hymnal into metaphors for community. The community defines both the texts and contexts of music, and reproduces these by publishing music or prayer books, or by establishing the boundaries of ritual performance. Music becomes religious because of the extent to which a community can imagine itself through the performative acts of music-making.

Similarly, we witness the importance of actively grappling with the religious, experiencing it performatively in public spaces. The religious community, it follows, moves music into the public space, where its power depends on collective experience. In this way, I want to suggest yet another way in which we might understand the concept "experience" found in the title of this volume, namely as engendered by the music itself. I shall be concentrating on the power of this experience and music as a fundamental voice and vessel for it. Because of the diverse settings for music on the panorama of American experience, music and musical practices provide means of imagining communities and constructing the dialectics of selfness and otherness, private and public worship, individual belief and community cohesion.

The Unsung Presence of Pietism and Prayer

In contradistinction to the communal performance of music in the public sphere, many musical practices exist only in the private sphere, in pietism and prayer, in the performance of the individual. The experience of music in the private sphere often remains unrecorded, just as that of the individual outside the community fails to be heard as representative of the collective, of an entity we might call *the* American religious experience. In many religions, the private practices of music, notably Judaism and Islam, may not even be considered to be music, but rather simply prayer or reading. Recognizing their power to evoke religious experience in the context of the individual is therefore even more complex, for it requires a rethinking of the ontology of music and its metaphysical presence as a component of religion. I should also argue that rethinking the individual and private experience of religious musical practice forces us concomitantly to rethink the nature of religious practice itself in American or Canadian society (see Qureshi in this volume). In this essay I concern myself with recovering the unrecorded and personal sacred music experience, and I make a case for resituating it on the panorama of North American history and historiography as a means of more completely understanding American religious experience.

Even though the individual musical voice is largely absent from the historiography of American religious experience, theories of the individual have been essential to the construction of American history. Among the earliest observers to stress the individual and space necessary for individual acts as essential for democracy in America was Tocqueville ([1835] 1945). In a somewhat similar way the historian, Frederick Jackson Turner, defined the frontier in American experience as the space in which the individual could exercise her or his independence (e.g., Turner 1935). Because of its expansion westward, the frontier provided the individual with the opportunity to move elsewhere when threatened by the encroachment of the group. The processes of dispersion and individualism provided the privileged metaphor for the American experience itself.

Religious historians have been less wont to concern themselves with individual actors. Martin Marty, concerned primarily with the ascription of identity from the group, has charted the American religious landscape with categories that broadly include all individuals, in one way or another. He writes of this landscape that, "if there are spaces between these clusters, these spheres of belonging that are not species of these genera, voids or unmapped areas, they have escaped me entirely" (1976, 17). Recently, nonetheless, we might observe a new interest in the individual and the personal practices of music in the work of American church historians, and it is interesting to note that at least Mark Noll has taken the hymn as emblematic of how "the common people" worship (Noll 1992, 1–2). The hymn is, of course, a vehicle for the voice of the individual. So, too, are the prayers and liturgy in American Jewish prayer books. So, too, are spirituals, those of African Americans and those received in silence as gifts by Shakers. There is indeed a multitude of individual voices and personal religious experiences that lend constant variation to the American panorama. I now turn to some of the places we can hear those voices and some ways in which more careful listening might provide the basis for rethinking the music's essential presence in the American religious experience.

Scene 1 on the Panorama: Music and the Production of an American Musical-Religious Literacy

Expansion of literacy and musical literacy accompanied the great religious movements of westward expansion. To fulfill the needs of the faithful on the frontier, new genres of music books for the individual came into existence and then proliferated. With the onset of the Federalist period, new settlements spread across the Allegheny and Appalachian mountains into the South, as the soil on the prairies was broken and urbanization and trade spread along the waterways of the Midwest. The vastness of the frontier and the highly signifying significance of the individual provided one of the most common of all nineteenth-century panorama themes (Avery 1993).

Religious revival, of course, accompanied westward expansion. One might even observe that rapid expansion necessitated revival as a means of drawing the individual back into the context of the community. Descriptions of revival generally situate it in camp meetings, mass gatherings of various kinds in which the word of God was shared with all. In order to sustain the revival movements, the several "Awakenings" before and during the first half-century of American independence, new forms of literacy were necessary.

The first scenes on the panorama of American religious experience, then, evoke the power of musical literacy as a means of representing westward expansion. A new musical notation visually encoded this scene, namely shaped-note hymnody, which persists today in *Sacred Harp* (see, e.g., Denson et al. 1936) and other offshoots of early nineteenth-century hymnody. Shaped-note hymnody belongs to the panorama of American religious experience, I suggest, precisely because it is about becoming an American, namely, it is about experiencing what it is like to live in America. One initially encounters the American experience of religious music, moreover, visually, and its virtually immediate legibility transforms it into a means of quick access to a wide range of different musical repertories and styles. The different shapes provide an easy-to-learn notational system, devised specifically for American repertories. Some of these repertories comprise fuguing tunes or other hymns composed in North America (see Bohlman 1993). Others mix together different American and ethnic styles, creating a panoramic logic only because the hymns occupy the same canvas. Shaped-note hymnals, then, offered something for everyone, a musical democracy constituted of different tastes and needs.

The potential to Americanize was not lost upon early hymnal publishers, who even adapted shaped notations to immigrant and ethnic repertories, such as those in the *Pennsylvanische Sammlung von Kirchen-Musik* (1840; see fig. 10.2). Although such hymnals still use hymns from the Old World, they are no longer about an Old-World musical experience, but rather about shaping new musical experiences, if indeed the familiarity of the old experiences serve as a means of mollifying the shock of musical contact. The new and the familiar, moreover, are mixed in different ways; sometimes, it is the text that remains familiar, whereas at other times it is the melody. Performance style

FIGURE 10.2. "America" from *Pennsylvanische Sammlung*

also mixes old and new, for example in the juxtaposition of bar-form German hymns with American fuguing tunes in the *Pennsylvanische Sammlung*. The panorama of an American hymnal was complete, albeit punctuated through performance by the individual, even idiosyncratic presence of the individual hymn, which existed outside of any liturgy or ritual. Experiencing America was possible, so the panorama of shaped-note hymnals suggest, the moment one could properly read its songs.

Narrative Metaphor 1: American Religious Music as Discourse Network

Sacred music in the history of North America juxtaposes reading and experiencing. Its forms and uses depend on the interaction between written and oral traditions. Music becomes individualized because of the various forms of literacy that it accompanies and in which it participates. Hymnbooks, the technical designation for books lacking musical notation, require individual literacy for the performance of the text, but are still inseparable from the oral knowledge transmitted through congregational performance. The hymn is a musical genre, then, that allows the individual to negotiate between private and public spheres. If we examine different genres and sites of music-making, we quickly witness the ways in which religious music was conceived for individual and home use, while at the same time being necessary for public performance. Hymnbooks and prayer books are pocket-sized, with clear indications that they are portable, often the claims of publishers on the title page, assuring the owner (and purchaser) that the hymnbook can be used virtually anywhere.

Religious publishers both created and adapted musical publications for home consumption and performance in the private sphere. Literacy made music a link between private and public religious experience. In his study of the

German American Lutheran publication, *Die Abendschule,* Brent Peterson has examined the ways in which these links were produced among German-speaking Midwesterners from roughly the mid-nineteenth to the mid-twentieth century (1991). Dependent on the reading practices of the family as a unit, and on a literary patriarchy dominated by the father, the magazine *Die Abendschule* situated ethnic culture in the home. Covering a broad range of social, aesthetic, and moral issues, *Die Abendschule* mediated the public sphere by creating a forum in which the individual could encounter it in the home.

The Missouri Synod, the denomination that published *Die Abendschule,* also produced vast numbers of home songbooks in multiple editions for the home. These songbooks consciously gathered a diverse repertory and represented it as American. Just as the bulk of the songs were German, many familiar folk songs and hymns, the "Star Spangled Banner" was rarely absent from the contents. With their mixture of traditional German chorales, American hymn tunes, and patriotic songs, home songbooks such as the Missouri Synod *Liederperlen* (see, e.g., 1905) made the American panorama legible and singable (see fig. 10.3). The books themselves, moreover, reproduced the musical tradition on the local level, for most passed from one generation to the next, in some areas of the Midwest at least, until the late twentieth century.

The individual religious experience was joined to the American through

Lieder-Perlen.

Eine Sammlung

von

Liedern geistlichen und gemischten Inhalts, theils in deutscher, theils in englischer Sprache, nebst einer Anzahl Spiellieder, ein-, zwei- und dreistimmig gesetzt

für

unsere Schulen.

St. Louis, Mo.
CONCORDIA PUBLISHING HOUSE.
1905.

FIGURE 10.3. Title page, *Liederperlen,* Concordia Publishing House (1905)

the complex network of a musical print culture (see, e.g., Armstrong and Tennenhouse 1992). Without claiming this to exemplify all the conditions of what Friedrich Kittler (1987) has called "discourse networks" (*Aufschreibesysteme*), I should nonetheless like to suggest that music as reading and performance practice contributed substantially to the networks that formed American religious experience. Religious song, published in formats that bore no visible relation to formal liturgy, provided a means of articulating personal experiences and yet contextualizing them within a larger tradition shared by coreligionists. Interpreted in this way, religious songbooks in the home belong at once to the everyday person and to the institutions of American religious culture. In the different domains, music comes to function in different ways and to have complex meanings, because the contexts of performance—of reading—are different. Published in mass numbers, song-, hymn-, and prayer books nonetheless individualize musical practice and instantiate the differences of the everyday religious experience on the American panorama.

Scene 2: The Body as Site of Individual Musical Experience

Sacred music in North America is frequently distinguished by its intense physicality, its reliance on the body as a site of musical experience. Through such experiences, song not only acquires power but also conveys power. It is a means whereby music sacralizes the individual. Among the Native Americans of the American and Canadian Plains, for example the Blackfoot people (see Nettl 1989), individuals receive songs directly through dreams, in direct physical exchange with mythological animals. The individual, it follows, owns the song he or she has received. The ability to acquire such songs accrues only to those with sufficient sacred knowledge to undergo the forms of stress, such as sensory deprivation, that heighten the body's musical receptivity. Songs thus composed, of course, are immensely personal, located in the single experience of a single individual.

It is important here, I believe, to address Native Americans in order not to separate them from the American religious experience—the nineteenth-century panoramas always include them, if only to portray them as vanishing from the expanding frontier—but to locate their practices on the soundscape of North America. Native American hymnody, for example, fits the discourse network, though alters it because of the ways in which it resists or because of the ways it must seek to accommodate traditional musical practice and, say, Methodism or Catholicism. Certain Native American peoples, for example, may retain, or even revive, their languages in their hymnals, even in mainline

Protestant denominations, long after that language has ceased to function as a vernacular, thereby performing and preserving the sense of selfness in the sanctuary (O'Grady 1991; Levine 1993). That accommodation, I want to suggest, is only possible because of the intensively physical act of reception traditional in Native American spirituality.

Shaker spiritual, too, provides a moment in which the body receives and experiences song, and therefore establishes new patterns of connection in the panorama of American religious experience. Shakers, like Native Americans of the Plains, received songs in a direct, physical way, dependent on the individual's ability to transform her body into a site of musical experience. We witness this in the texts of Shaker spirituals, with their stress on sacred gift and direct physicality, even on the physicality of dance. Drawings of reception and performance make this direct physicality of the body extraordinarily evident (see, e.g., Patterson 1979).

By focusing on the body as a site of musical experience, we also recognize the power of music to alter the body, thereby physically altering its agency in spirituality. The ecstasy of a Sufi *dhikr* (lit. "remembrance") ceremony connects recitation and prayer directly to the body, indeed measuring their efficacy by their ability to bring the worshiper physically closer to Allah. The chanting of Buddhist mantras, too, heightens spiritual receptivity in ways dependent on physical alteration. It may seem that, by turning to Sufism and Buddhism, I am also departing from the American religious experience, but in fact I deliberately choose these examples because they have become increasingly evident in the sacred musical landscape of many American cities, unquestionably so in Chicago. The ecstasy of Sufi *dhikr*, for example, is increasingly attractive among Muslims on the predominantly African American South Side of Chicago. The musical instigation of ecstasy, however, has long been an element of the larger sacred landscape, where it was also a measure of efficacy in many African American evangelical Christian traditions. If we recognize the body's presence as a site of sacred musical performance, we concurrently admit many new kinds of musical and religious experiences to the panorama of the late twentieth century.

Scene 3: Personal Charisma and the Pioneer's Journey

Alfred Grimm of Antigo, Wisconsin epitomized the pioneer church musician; he did it all. He wrote hymns and popular songs; he arranged Lutheran chorales for "the church band," and then specialized in publishing the scores and parts for these. Indeed, he published all of the music,, prose, and dramatic works he and a small stable of composers wrote. He was so prolific that he sometimes published under pseudonyms, for example Alfred Ira. Alfred Grimm *was* the Antigo Publishing Company, whose mission was to open a more expansive space for German Protestant immigrants in the Midwest. Throughout his life he actively employed music to broaden the American religious experience.

Grimm was also a voice in the wilderness. As a Lutheran church musician, he represents that model of the pioneer on the frontier, first sighted by Tocqueville and then argued forcefully by the historian, Frederick Jackson Turner. He adapted music—specifically, the German chorale tradition—to the frontier conditions of the Upper Midwest, producing a musical commodity for the German-speaking parishes spreading westward across the Great Plains. He published his creative works explicitly for the institutions of the American immigrant context, for example, town bands and church youth groups. The texts of his popular songs, though in German, chronicled the events of American history and the everyday world of American society (see fig. 10.4). His novels and short stories described local subjects, even when he needed to contribute new words to the German vocabulary to do so.

There is another reason we must understand him as a voice in the wilderness, namely the fact that his voice fell silent almost immediately after his death in 1922. This was due in part to the declining use of German, particularly after World War I. But it was also due to the challenge that Grimm offered to the musical traditions of the German Lutheran Synods. Grimm's music specifically addressed the conditions of the American settler and the American frontier. He prescribed a way of faith rather than promulgating that of the denominational institution. His musical compositions, even when they had unequivocally Protestant texts, were to be performed outside the liturgy, in the public sphere of small-town America. Alfred Grimm represents, then, a religious charisma that illuminated new musical possibilities, which nevertheless did not catch on. His musical voice offered an alternative to tradition, but in so doing failed to form itself into tradition. The intriguing quality of his individual voice notwithstanding, his charisma did not resonate for the American religious experience to which he wished so passionately to contribute.

Narrative Metaphor 2: Professionalization of Religious Song

The case of another charismatic religious musical voice, David Einhorn, intersected with tradition in quite different ways. Einhorn, the editor of one of the first Reform prayer books in North America, used the power of his own per-

FIGURE 10.4. Alfred Grimm, "Und es waren Hirten auf dem Felde"

sonality to create one of the most influential traditions of Jewish song in the nineteenth and early twentieth centuries. Einhorn was rabbi of Congregation Har-Sinai in Baltimore, and in 1858 he published a new prayer book for German-speaking Reform synagogues in North America (Einhorn 1858). Einhorn's prayer book enjoyed immediate success, accounts in rabbinical and cantorial writings suggesting that it was more or less a cult object. Einhorn and his prayer book appear in descriptions as if they were the same, the book, though a German and Hebrew version of the *siddur,* an embodiment of Einhorn himself. Einhorn's presence in a direct, physical way was palpable during prayer and ritual, as we read in the following passages from Emil Hirsch's "Preface" to the first English translation:

> [The prayer book] mirrors the great mind and man whose very soul—it is not too much to say—found incarnation in the pages of the book. Jewish to the core, deeply convinced of the glorious responsibility incumbent upon Israel for the rearing of the temple of humanity, Einhorn in his ritual has given us in truth, an epitome of the aspirations and beliefs of modern Judaism. (Hirsch, iii)

David Einhorn, thus, was himself present, making prayer and song a personal dialogue, almost as much in the presence of Einhorn as in the presence of God:

> We know that there will always be a few congregations that will continue to love *their* Einhorn; for many decades they have by this book been led to the fount of true edification. They know no reason why they should now exchange their old and well-tried friend for a newcomer that, at its best, can only give what the old possesses so abundantly. (ibid., v)

David Einhorn is only one of many charismatic American religious figures whose personality forms the path along which a musical and religious tradition develops. Charles Wesley, William Billings, Thomas A. Dorsey, and Fanny Crosby, these are among the figures, who, like David Einhorn, left an indelible, yet highly personalized, impression on sacred music in North America. These are the figures, also, who professionalized the diverse strands that make up that history. Like David Einhorn, these composers and writers of hymns became cult figures, whose works stand out vividly in the sacred music history of North America.

The professionalization of Einhorn, a rabbi and prayer book editor, draws our attention to another specifically American phenomenon of the panorama, namely that of the professionalized Jewish cantorate. Mark Slobin has argued that the cantorate as an institutionalized body of religious musicians is unique to the American experience (1989). He plots the ways in which certain specifically American experiences play themselves out in the cantorate through activities of its constituent members. The liberal politics of the civil rights and anti-war movements of the 1960s, for example, entered the synagogue together with guitars, symbols of political engagement of many Jewish singer-songwriters in the folk-music revival. During the following two decades, women began to enter the cantorate, first the Reform and then the Conservative, signaling the impact of feminist thinking on the sacred communities of

American Jews (ibid., 112–32). Musically, too, style changes enter traditional Jewish music through the sanctioned professionalism of the cantorate (see Summit in this volume). The professionalization of musical life had become one of many pathways between the sacred space of the synagogue and the public sphere in which American Jews participated.

Scene 4: Moments of Otherness, Resistance, and Assertion of Individuality

During fieldwork in German American Lutheran areas of the Midwest from the late 1970s to the mid-1980s, I conducted almost all my recording sessions in the kitchens or living rooms of rural houses, that is in the social domain created and maintained by women. The religious traditions I recorded belonged to the home, having been transformed to reside there within the family. The home was the locus of piety, distinct from the church, which had become the center for community and celebration. When I first began to collect sacred songs in this way, I was unprepared for the ways in which music represented the personal sacred space of the home. The pious women of the German American Lutheran tradition of the Upper Midwest, however, focused their religious practices on the home, which was for them the most fitting place for religious devotion and ritual. In sparsely settled northern Wisconsin, these German American Lutheran women, even at the end of the twentieth century, hardly represented an isolated phenomenon. In the rural Midwest, at least in those areas with which I am familiar, many women use the home as the center of religious practice. Although they acquire musical materials for these domestic practices through a discourse network connected to the public sphere, many women shape specific religious practices of their own with these materials. In the German American Lutheran tradition, as well as others I have not researched, musical materials are published for the home. This instance of song and prayer on the prairie, then, is by no means isolated as a scene of American religious experience, if indeed it seems isolated from community and nation.

Although I have spent considerable time during the past two decades interviewing and recording women in their homes, it has taken recent feminist scholarship in music (including the chapters by Regula Qureshi and Janet Walton in this volume) to force me to reflect on the position of women's musical practices within the panorama of American religious experience. Surely, these are voices that are not heard, voices absent from the texture of sacred music polyphony in North America. And yet, American religious experience is unimaginable without them. Women's musical practices perform other sacred spaces into existence, and they transform the nature of the sacred in the public sphere in which community ritual occurs. Historically, it has been women's voices that have reconfigured the sacred spaces of the synagogue, first when women joined in public prayer in the nineteenth-century Reform synagogue, and then when women entered the cantorate in the late twentieth century. In the case of ethnic religious practice, it is usually women whose musical practices retain language the most extensively. Women also most frequently play the central role in the musical transmission of sacred texts. This is surely another of the reasons that women have begun to have such a profound impact on the American Jewish cantorate, which still relies on knowledge of Hebrew.

When feminist analysis of women's sacred musical practices potentially yields complex forms for the articulation of otherness within American religious experience, religious and musical scholars might well undertake a broad rethinking of the nature of difference, even otherness, in American religious experience. How, for example, do voices of gays and lesbians integrate themselves into the fabric of American religious life? And they do, which we witness in the task forces within denominations such as the United Methodists, where song might even become the site for interlocutions about sexuality in the church. Where are the sites of resistance for individuals engaged in actively opening the American religious experience to the expression of difference? The hymn texts of primitivist and pietist movements have historically voiced resistance, weaving it already into the fabric of American religion (see Hughes 1988; Schelbert 1985). Native American Protestant hymnals and Catholic ritual unquestionably serve as vehicles for resistance from within. The African American spiritual has powerfully inscribed resistance onto American religious experience. And the polka mass has not just brought popular music into the sanctuary, but the voice of the people as well (Walser 1992). Pilgrimages and rituals enacted on American city streets or Canadian prairies (Taft 1983) alike become sacred paths for the inscription of religious otherness on modern panoramas. Music, individual and local, inflects the panorama of American religious experience in ways far more varied than ever before, fully witnessing the diversity and difference in American society.

Conclusion: The Everyday Religious Experiences to which Music Gives Voice

Sacred music practices suggest, in fact, that difference emerges from within American religious experience at least as extensively as it accrues from the arrival of new immigrant and ethnic groups or from the new directions resulting from denominational splintering. Indeed, I want to suggest in this chapter that it could be one prevalent characteristic of American religious experience that music provides text and context for the articulation of change beginning with individuals at the local level, even when this undermines the collective nature of some religious practices. To some extent, we might think of individuality and community actually existing in a sort of dialectic, synthesized by music. Music and song make this dialectic dynamic, allowing the individual her voice, while at the same time gathering the community in song.

Music gives an added dimension to the panorama of American religious experience, individualizing its scenes and giving voice to those whose faith is different, yet still part of American religious experience. It is because of music's inseparability from sacred practices that it would be quite impossible to change the name of this book to "the American religious experience," or likewise to a pluralized form, "American religious experiences." Like the panorama throughout American popular history, American religious experience confronts us with a view of the past and present that is replete with contradictions. Its vastness, on one hand, evokes a sense of wholeness, but, on the other, makes it impossible to see the whole while focusing on the individual scene. Music does nothing to eliminate such contradictions. Quite the contrary, it brings them into sharper relief and enriches the whole with its presence. Music, because it articulates contradiction and difference so fundamentally, transforms religion in North America, offering us the possibility of experiencing as many individual voices as possible.

WORKS CITED

Anderson, Benedict. 1991. *Imagined Communities: Reflections on the Origin and Spread of Nationalism.* Rev. and expanded ed. London: Verso.

Armstrong, Nancy, and Leonard Tennenhouse. 1992. *The Imaginary Puritan: Literature, Intellectual Labor, and the Origins of Personal Life.* Berkeley: University of California Press.

Avery, Kevin J. 1993. "Go West! Das Moving Panorama als Kunstform der nordamerikanischen Frontier-Bewegung." In von Plessen 1993, 64–73.

Banvard, John. 1847. *Description of Banvard's Panorama of the Mississippi River, Painted on Three Miles of Canvas: Exhibiting a View of Country 1200 Miles in Length, Extending from the Mouth of the Missouri River to the City of New Orleans; Being by Far the Largest Picture Ever Executed by Man.* Boston: J. Putnam. (Copy in Special Collections of Regenstein Library, University of Chicago)

Bohlman, Philip V. 1988. "Missionaries, Magical Muses, and Magnificent Menageries:

Image and Imagination in the Early History of Ethnomusicology." *The World of Music* 33 (3): 5–27.

———. 1993. "Die 'Pennsylvanische Sammlung von Kirchen-Musik': Ein Lehrbuch zur Deutsch-Amerikanisierung." *Jahrbuch für Volksliedforschung* 38: 90–109.

Christy's Panorama Songster. ca. 1840. *Christy's Panorama Songster; Containing the Songs as Sung by the Christy, Campbell, Pierce's Minstrels and Sable Brothers*. New York: H. Murphy. Available in Special Collections. Regenstein Library, University of Chicago.

Denson, T. J., et al. 1936. *Original Sacred Harp: The Best Collection of Songs, Hymns, Odes, and Anthems Ever Offered the Singing Public for General Use*. Haleyville, Ala.: Sacred Harp Publishing Co.

D'Ooge, Craig. 1994. "Taking a Wider View: Photos Show the Panorama of History." *Library of Congress Information Bulletin* 53, 8 (April 18): 160–64.

Einhorn, David, ed. 1858. *Gebetbuch für Israelitische Reform-Gemeinden*. Baltimore: C. W. Schneidereith.

———. 1896. *Book of Prayers for Jewish Congregations*. Trans. from the German original by Emil Hirsch. Chicago: S. Ettlinger.

Hirsch, Emil. Preface to Einhorn 1896.

Hughes, Richard T., ed. 1988. *The American Quest for the Primitive Church*. Urbana: University of Illinois Press.

Hyde, Ralph. 1988. *Panoramania! The Art and Entertainment of the 'All-Embracing' View*. London: Trefoil.

Kingman, Daniel. 1979. *American Music: A Panorama*. New York: Schirmer.

Kittler, Friedrich A. 1987. *Aufschreibesysteme 1800/1900*. 2nd expanded ed. Munich: Wilhelm Fink.

Lafitau, Joseph-François. 1724. *Moeurs des sauvages amériquains, comparées aux moeurs des premiers temps*. 2 vols. Paris: Saugrain et Hochereau.

Levine, Victoria Lindsay. 1993. "Musical Revitalization among the Choctaw." *American Music* 11 (4): 391–411.

Liederperlen. 1905. *Liederperlen. Eine Sammlung von Liedern geistlichens und gemischten Inhalts*. St. Louis: Concordia.

Marty, Martin E. 1976. *A Nation of Behavers*. Chicago: University of Chicago Press.

Nettl, Bruno. 1989. *Blackfoot Musical Thought: Comparative Perspectives*. Kent, Ohio: Kent State University Press.

Noll, Mark A. 1992. *A History of Christianity in the United States and Canada*. Grand Rapids, Mich.: William B. Eerdmans.

O'Grady, Terence J. 1991. "The Singing Societies of Oneida." *American Music* 9 (1): 67–91.

Patterson, Daniel W. 1979. *The Shaker Spiritual*. Princeton: Princeton University Press.

Peters, Harry T. 1942. *Currier & Ives: Printmakers to the American People*. Garden City, N.Y.: Doubleday, Doran.

Peterson, Brent O. 1991. *Popular Narratives and Ethnic Identity: Literature and Community in* Die Abendschule. Ithaca, N.Y.: Cornell University Press.

Pennsylvanische Sammlung. 1840. *Pennsylvanische Sammlung von Kirchen-Musik/The Pennsylvania Collection of Church Musick.* Harrisburg, Penn.: Wyeth.

von Plessen, Marie-Louise, ed. 1993. *Sehsucht: Das Panorama als Massenunterhaltung im 19. Jahrhundert.* Frankfurt am Main and Basel: Stroemfeld/Roter Stern.

Schelbert, Leo. 1985. "Pietism Rejected: A Reinterpretation of Amish Origins." In Frank Trommler and Joseph McVeigh, eds., *American and the Germans: An Assessment of a Three-Hundred-Year History.* Vol. 1: *Immigration, Language, Ethnicity,* pp. 118–27. Philadelphia: University of Pennsylvania Press.

Slobin, Mark. 1989. *Chosen Voices: The Story of the American Cantorate.* Urbana: University of Illinois Press.

Taft, Michael. 1983. *Discovering Saskatchewan Folklore: Three Case Studies.* Edmonton, Alberta, Canada: NeWest.

Tocqueville, Alexis de. 1945. *Democracy in America.* Trans. by Henry Reeve. New York: Alfred A. Knopf. Orig. 1835.

Turner, Frederick Jackson. 1935. *The United States, 1830–1850.* New York: Holt, Rinehart, and Winston.

———. 1993. *History, Frontier, and Section: Three Essays.* Albuquerque: University of New Mexico Press.

Walser, Rob. 1992. "The Polka Mass: Music of Postmodern Ethnicity." *American Music* 10 (2): 183–202.

11

Women's Ritual Music

Janet Walton

> Songs are a way to get to singing. The singing is what you are aiming for and the singing is running the sound through your body. You cannot sing a song and not change your condition. (Reagon 1991)
>
> —Bernice Johnson Reagon, Founder, "Sweet Honey in the Rock"

For centuries an androcentric and, sometimes, misogynist fixed tradition has dictated the way people pray. Gender, culture, race, class, sexual orientation, physical abilities played no role in decisions about the language, symbols, sounds, leadership, or actions of public prayer. Women, among others, have identified the limitations and inherent injustice of this situation. As one of a number of correctives, women are designing their own rituals to express what has been missing and to eliminate what is not true.

Women's rituals are about "changing our condition," a dynamic process that includes letting go, leaving behind, risking, experimenting, claiming, and acting. Music is one of the components of this ongoing work. What we listen to, sing, or play is chosen with utmost care. We scrutinize the choice of music by the same criteria we apply to every aspect of what we do when we gather. What Bernice Johnson Reagon says of singing is true for us: Women's ritualizing changes our condition. That is our hope, and that is our experience.

"Sound" in women's rituals cannot be easily categorized. It extends to all expressions: classical music, new-age, feminist, rock, rap, country, jazz, ethnic music as well as other styles. It may be well known or newly composed, sung or instrumental, recorded or live. Women's ritual music is differentiated from the music of other ritual gatherings not so much by a particular "sound" but by what it communicates through its words or through the emotion it arouses. Music of many composers is commonly used, though in some groups there is a preference for music by women. As with everything else (word, gesture, action, readings, etc.), what is chosen reflects the agreements made by the particular group of women about what it is they hope for when they gather.

Women's rituals are usually concerned with freedom, power, survival, relationships, and justice. Feminist liturgical scholar Mary Collins explains: "This involves both symbolically negating the patriarchal culture that has denied and actively suppressed women's power or demonized it, and actualizing redeemed and redeeming relationships that allow women to claim their full power as human persons" (1993, 11). We rely on symbols, ancient and emerging, to make these connections. In order to know what is true and to claim it in our lives, we depend on power within and among ourselves and surely that power beyond ourselves, called God, Goddess, the Holy One.

Such rituals are taking place more and more often. Some occur within institutional religious settings where there is space and opportunity to explore uncharted territory. Others intentionally avoid denominational affiliations. Women feel restricted in them and, in the worst scenarios, abused. Ritualizing may take place in homes or other spaces, such as out of doors in some beautiful natural setting. Most women's rituals are conducted with some or all of the following guidelines in mind:[1]

1. The power, indeed the responsibility, to express divine and human relationships is assumed to be within *all* who gather for the ritual. That is, the power/responsibility is not mediated by one or several persons, though a ritual may be led by a few.
2. What is "authoritative" for a group (whether it is a choice of symbol, text, sound, etc.) is *discovered* and critiqued. Its authority derives from repeated use where layers of meaning continue to emerge. Nothing from the past, or even from the present, for that matter, is taken for granted.
3. We understand our bodies as well as our minds to be reflections of the holy. Bodily functions, such as giving birth, menstruating—for so long considered to be unclean experiences that regularly required purifications—are particular expressions of the holy.

4. It is imperative to name what hurts women. By identifying what is destructive we recognize its power and we work to let it go.
5. Our struggle connects with all people whose rights have been denied because of class, race, physical abilities, sexual orientation, age, culture. What we do in our rituals explicitly reflects this solidarity and understanding.
6. Our search for what is meaningful (and for mythology and frameworks that express it) reaches to the entire cosmic reality. All nature, animate and inanimate, is included.
7. There are no set models for our ritualizing. We constantly experiment, drawing freely from the traditional legacy of symbols and actions to rediscover what is good, to note what has been excluded, and to add what is appropriate. We enjoy the spontaneity of the moment and expect from one another rigorous evaluation of our work together.

When we get together something happens. Not only do we imagine a different future in which justice reigns for all people but we also feel the power to make it happen. Side by side we sense our possibilities, both personal and collective. Music is an important vehicle of that knowledge.

Specific research on the music of women's ritual groups is quite minimal. Only in the last decade have there been significant data gathered on women's rituals in general.[2] A comparative or detailed analysis of the music is yet to come. Therefore, for the purposes of this chapter, I will offer a descriptive glimpse: some examples of music that are heard in such gatherings. The list is not exhaustive, but rather, illustrative.

Music Composed for the Occasion

Songs written for particular women's ritual gatherings, but general enough that they may be used again and again are very common. They may be new words set to familiar melodies, new compositions (both tune and text) or words for the first time set to music. Some examples follow:

1. *New tune*

A simple chant set for an Advent service, example 11.1 was used initially as a congregational response interspersed throughout a spoken reflection on the meaning of Advent in our time. The text reflects the experience of the move-

"Walker" Chant

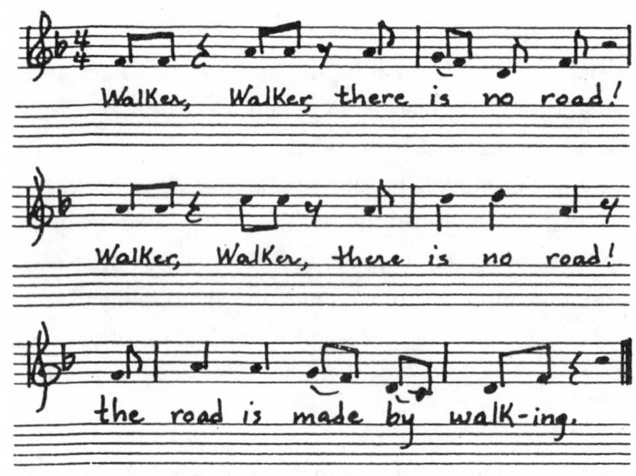

Excerpt from a Spanish poem
by Antonio Machado
Music by Annette Covatta

MUSIC EXAMPLE 11.1. "Walker" Chant

ment toward freedom, for women, but also for all people on a similar journey. The community sang and moved in a circle, dancing to it. It has been used many times since then in the same group of women. Repeated use offers more interpretations, and memories provide layers of meanings.

2. *New text*

A new and profoundly disturbing epidemic requires our attention. How can we verbalize our concern and our solidarity? This fresh text sung to a well-known tune (*Sine Nomine* "For all the Saints" often sung at memorial services) expresses our pain, our compassion and our faith.

For Those Who Died With AIDS (an excerpt)

For all the young whose prospects now are gone,
Whose tender life was cut off in its dawn:

You met your death with faces gaunt and drawn—
Now live in our mem'ry, Alleluia!

For outcast all, the lesbian and gay,
Fighting for rights each hard step of the way:
What fearful price your love has had to pay—
Now live in our mem'ry, Alleluia! (Ware 1993, 13)

3. Songs for Lent and Christmas revised

Major seasonal celebrations present difficult challenges in women's ritual groups because our memories and expectations are rooted so deeply in a common patriarchal tradition. We gather at such times expecting something different, but what seems to work best does not completely overlook the past. In the following two examples the tunes and the texts express continuity and at the same time our search for what author Ann Patrick Ware points to as a "look behind romantic and somewhat sentimental expressions" to discover "a meaning which dear and familiar melodies can convey to contemporary adult Christians." We seek texts that "call us to honor God's grace but to know at the same time that the doing of justice is our primary task" (Ware 1993, ii).

Lenten Song

In bleakness of the winter
The world is mute and grey.
We long for summer sunshine
To take our gloom away,
But radiance of the sunshine
Will not hide wounds still there:
The homeless crouch in doorways,
The poor are everywhere.

This time of Lent reminds us
Where one in need is found
There all are, poor and wanting,
Yes, all in need are bound.
Come, let us rouse our courage,
Make justice our demand,
And keep our eyes on this world,
Not some far Promised Land. (Ware 1993, 10)[3]

Joy to the World (excerpt)

Joy to the World, for Christmas comes
With songs of hope and mirth.
  While fields and floods,
  Rocks, hills, and plains
  And all the sites of earth
  Recall to us Christ's birth,
And teach us and preach to us
Our wondrous worth.

Joy to us all who strive to be
A sister and a friend;
  We want to act
  With honesty,
  Good humor and integrity.
  Our energies we'll spend (Trying never to offend)
In aiding, persuading
All hate to end. (Ware 1993, 3)[4]

For some women, the relationship between the "sacrifice of Jesus on the cross" and the abuse of women is intimately interconnected. Womanist theologian Delores Williams argues that the action of Jesus of submitting voluntarily to the will of God for the sake of sinful humanity conveys the message that surrogacy is a sacred act. For black women especially, whose history is marked significantly with surrogacy roles (as mammies, or as "masculine" women whose bodies were so strong they could sustain more pain than white women), a surrogate Jesus can continue to reinforce their own exploitation. Thus Williams asks, "If black women accept the image of redemption, can they not also passively accept the exploitation surrogacy brings?" (Williams 1991, 9–14). This excerpt addresses this concern:

If God Is Love

If God is love, how can we say
he gave his only son?
Are torture, shame, and senseless death
the way our grace is won?

In Jesus Christ we meet a God
whose love embraces all,
who weeps when children are abused

who sees each sparrow fall. . . .
When grace is ancient as the earth,
how can we worship death?
So let us live in tender care
for all whom Love gives breath. (excerpts from Duck 1993)[5]

The next hymn is a rewriting of a traditional canticle using a female pronoun (she) for God and rephrasing some sections to express a more contemporary understanding of justice. It is critical for women to make repeated use of female pronouns and words to express the divinity, not so much because women believe that gender can be attributed to God but rather to overcome the long, unexamined tradition of the maleness of God that is part of the conscious and unconscious experience of every person. To claim female images is to claim oneself as an image of God, a significant development for women.

Magnificat

My soul gives glory to my God.
My heart pours out its praise.
God lifted up my lowliness
in many marvelous ways.

My God has done great things for me:
Holy is Her Name.
All people will declare me blessed,
And blessings they shall claim.

Praise God, whose loving Covenant
supports those in distress,
remembering past promises
with present faithfulness. (excerpted from Winter 1987, 219)[6]

4. *Newly composed tunes and texts*

Music example 11.2 is a chant that elicits solidarity with all female energy, human and divine, especially from women who have died. One of the most poignant experiences in traditional religions is to hear again and again the names of only men cited as models of sanctity. Women's ritual groups make consistent efforts to offer the names of women. Such a chant is used in many different ways to call forth those memories.

Created as a refrain for a blessing over milk and honey, music example 11.3 calls to mind that the physical experiences of women are good, are in fact,

For our mothers, grandmothers, aunts, and sisters. . .

All: She who has gone before us, rise up and call her name.

MUSIC EXAMPLE 11.2. "She Who Has Gone before Us"

symbols of what is Holy. It also names God, Sophia, an ancient female symbol of wisdom.

Music from a Variety of Traditions

Not only texts recount women's stories but the tunes as well. Music of a variety of cultural traditions is drawn upon to express the diversity of human experience. For example, in the "Reimagining" conference (November 4–7, 1993, in Minneapolis, Minnesota) where 2200 women and a few hundred men gathered, there was music from Hawaiian, Asian, Lakota, African American, Hispanic, Appalachian, Zulu, and European American traditions. Women understand that sexism is intimately related to other forms of oppression and we want to address them as well, but always with respect for the particularities of these traditions.

1. *Recorded music*

In this category the list is endless, reaching from the most ancient chants to the most recent rap. Recorded music focuses our attention, sets a particular ambiance, evokes specific emotions, engages our bodies, and conveys a memory, just as music does in any ritual. One example, heard often in women's ritual settings, is the music of "Sweet Honey in the Rock," a female *a cappella* ensemble that creates its sounds by listening to their own voices, using only percussion instruments as accompaniment.

> With mature Black singing, you can't sound like a feeling, you can't act like you're feeling, you have to feel, be in the feeling, and have the feeling establish the quality of your sound. . . . If it is right, those sitting in the sound of your voice will not only hear you singing,

Blessing over Milk and Honey

by Hilda Kuester

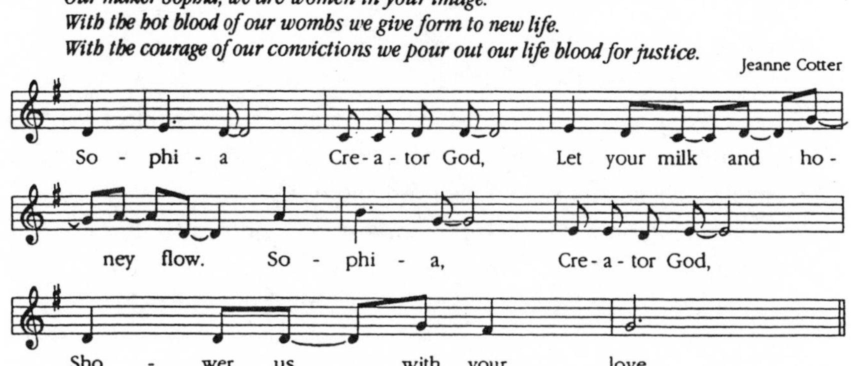

MUSIC EXAMPLE 11.3. "Blessing over Milk and Honey"

they will feel you singing in a deeper part of themselves. (Reagon and Sweet Honey in the Rock 1993, 141)

Sweet Honey's texts are about freedom, justice, the horrors of oppression, and a celebration of power. As African American women they are particularly committed to express the legacy of blacks. They remind all of us of our history, and they point to what is yet possible. In women's ritualizing we listen to such groups. We sing their songs. We, too, want to find our music from deep within. We, too, want to remember the past and bring about a different future.

2. *Instrumental music*

Again no one sound prevails, but more commonly than not (often because women meet in places where there are no large instruments) small percussion instruments are used. As happens universally for all people, these instruments evoke a physical reaction and therefore involve us in movement. As women we want to claim the revelation of our bodies, and their various shapes, weights, and colors. We want to remind ourselves of the beauty of flesh and the power of touch. Percussion instruments are a lively vehicle of that connection.

However, when possible, women "pull out all the stops." One wonderful example is the music for the "Reimagining" conference (cited above). The accompaniment for the rituals included twenty women on each of four stages in the room using woodwind and percussion instruments and a keyboard player at each place. The music was vibrant. It filled the room. It offered threads of energy that engaged the entire assembly.

Music Adapted for the Occasion

While making any exhaustive list in this category is impossible, I want to offer and comment on an illustration, only one of many ways in which a wide spectrum of published music can be heard and used.

Luciano Berio wrote the vocal composition *Sequenza III* in 1966. As Berio describes it: "There are forty emotive successions (tense, serene, frantic, coy, desperate, joyful etc.) which pivot about various forms of laughter" (1985, 96). The hearing of it, Berio proposes, will connect with "a huge range of associations: cultural, musical, emotive, physiological, or drawn from everyday life" (ibid., 94). There is no recognizable or memorable melody in *Sequenza III*, rather it is a quick succession of sounds and actions expressing a broad range of emotion from frantic to serene. Singer Isabelle Ganz depicts it this way: "Sequenza III is a dramatic essay based on the relationship between the soloist and her voice alone. Many aspects of that voice are exhibited, expressing the chameleon-like emotional states and the many layers of her personality." She continues: "Cathy Berberian, Berio's former wife for whom and with whom most of Berio's vocal music was written, has said that this work 'is like an x-ray of a woman's inner life' " (Ganz 1990).

I heard the piece performed in two different contexts, first during a series of services for a women's history week, the theme of which was "Weaving Our Lives," with this particular service subtitled "Refusing to be Comforted." The performance of *Sequenza III* set the tone for the entire experience. It was followed by only lamentation, both biblical and spontaneous. Women (and men with them) expressed their pain and their resistance to any "cheap grace." Hope was difficult to feel. The second performance was a ritual about suffering and healing (as known in the life of one particular woman) where the piece was sung to express the quixotic changes a woman often experiences in her painful journey to health.

In both situations (certainly influenced by the context) the music was performed to suggest the turmoil inherent in the lives of many women. There are few words to describe it. The sound and actions of the performer felt like the journey of women to claim their own voices and experiences, a struggle, at times frantic, sad, confusing, frightening, ecstatic, unbalanced, dreamy, urgent, uncontrollable, determined, needy, monotonous, calm.

Political Music

Aware that the struggle against sexism is connected to every other fight for justice and freedom, women sing in understanding and solidarity. We know and sing songs such as James Oppenheim's "Bread and Roses" (inspired by the 1912 strike of textile workers in Lawrence, Massachusetts where young girls carried a banner that read, "We want bread and roses too"), "We Shall Overcome," "Lift Every Voice and Sing," or "We Are a Gentle Angry People" expressing in turn the battles against sexism, classism, racism, and homophobia.

General Comments

One of the primary goals of women's ritual gatherings is maximum participation. This objective affects the choice of music to be sung. Though in some situations where the same women gather regularly and therefore can build a repertory to draw from, more commonly, we cannot count on it. So there is a varied use of music. Less complicated music or short repeated responses are used; hymns or any music that requires a keyboard accompaniment are rare. Often heard are songs with easy refrains, hymns that have a relatively uncomplicated melodic range or are well known, and chants that are familiar or that people can learn on-the-spot.

In contrast to situations where women have to reinterpret words and symbols to include their particular experiences or to tolerate those that do not, in women's ritual groups we can let go of such strain. We are at home with ourselves, stretching ourselves from our strengths without fear of criticism that would destroy or undermine our attempts to experiment. We try new words and images and listen to new sounds, then scrutinize them to see whether we should continue to use them.

Words that have proved dangerous for women are flagged immediately. Hymnist and theologian Ruth Duck points to hymns such as "Awake, Awake to Love and Work" which "glorifies self-giving without counting the cost" or "where we are called to the risk of unprotected living" as "dangerous" (Duck 1993, 61, in Proctor-Smith and Walton). They can lead to unconscious acceptance of behaviors that destroy women, like doing so much for everyone else that one's own life, one's own self-care and self-esteem are undermined seriously. Such words can suggest that putting oneself in situations where abuse is taken for granted is redemptive.

Women's gifts of composition are celebrated. We search for music written by women not only for our own benefit but also to support their work. Texts and tunes written by men are not excluded. We use and appreciate the efforts of those who are willing to change along with us.

The talents and good will of women seem to be ever flowing in women's ritual groups. The attitude toward new compositions is not first to resist them (as it is in many congregational settings) but rather to welcome them. Much leeway is given to bold attempts: revisions of seasonal music (the most difficult to rewrite because of deeply rooted memories), new sounds and irregular or complex rhythms. An innovator can expect to have the benefit of every doubt until the new musical form absolutely, unquestionably fails.

Still difficult for us is the freeing of our voices to make spontaneous sounds like wailing or groaning, sounds of ecstasy or anger. Although these sometimes occur there is a lingering self-consciousness and culture-consciousness that inhibits our utterance of these sounds more often.

We have learned in our ritual groups that the source of our music is deep within us and the response to that search will take us to a place we have not been to before (Reagon 1993).

We are most successful when we respect this wisdom and follow where it leads. When we sing, dance, laugh, and pray, thus giving form to rituals that affirm our worth, challenge our commitments, and support our dreams, we claim the power and relationships to participate fully with the Holy One in the healing and transformation of this world. Like "Sweet Honey in the Rock," we "sing for our lives" (ibid.).

NOTES

1. These guidelines are drawn from a variety of sources: personal experience (fourteen years gathering semimonthly with women, and occasionally some men, to discover and experience what connects with women's lives; and my work with the daily worshiping community of Union Theological Seminary); the collected wisdom of scholars in a seminar group of the North American Academy of Liturgy which studied "The Teaching of Feminist Liturgy" as summarized in its 1990 *Proceedings* by Marjorie Procter-Smith; the work of Mary Collins entitled "Principles of Feminist Liturgy" in Walton and Procter-Smith, *Women at Worship* (Collins 1993).

2. Some of the most recent resources include Charlotte Caron (1993).

3. Text by Ann Patrick Ware; tune: Passion Chorale.

4. Text by Ann Patrick Ware; tune: Antioch.

5. Text by Ruth Duck; tune: Kingsfold.

6. Text by Miriam Therese Winter, adapted from Luke 1:47–55; tune: Nettleton. Text by Hilda Kuester; tune, Jeanne Cotter; from Kuester and Cotter (1993, 32).

WORKS CITED

Berio, Luciano. 1985. Two interviews. An interview by Rossana Dalmonte in David Osmond-Smith, trans. and ed., *Luciano Berio Two Interviews*. London: Marion Bayors.

Caron, Charlotte. 1993. *To Make and Make Again: Feminist Ritual Theology*. New York: Crossroad.

Collins, Mary. 1993. "Feminist Liturgical Principles." In Marjorie Procter-Smith and Janet Walton, eds., *Women at Worship: Interpretations of North American Diversity*, 9–26. Louisville: Westminster/John Knox Press.

Duck, Ruth. 1993. Unpublished hymn text.

———. 1993. "Sin, Grace, and Gender in Free-Church Protestant Worship." In Marjorie Procter-Smith and Janet Walton, eds., *Women at Worship*, 55–69. Louisville: Westminster/John Knox Press.

Ganz, Isabelle. 1990. Notes from a lecture-recital given at Eastman School of Music.

Kuester, Hilda, and Jeanne Cotter. 1993. "Blessing over Milk and Honey." In the Reimagining Conference booklet, Minneapolis November 4–7, 1993.

McDade, Carolyn. n.d. *This Tough Web*. Plainville, Mass.: Plainville Womancenter.

Proctor-Smith, Marjorie. 1990. "The Teachings of Feminist Liturgy." In *Proceedings of the North American Academy of Liturgy Annual Meeting*. Valparaiso, Ind.: The Academy

Proctor-Smith, Marjorie, and Janet R. Walton, eds. 1993. *Women at Worship: Interpretations of North American Diversity*. Louisville: Westminister-John Knox.

Reagon, Bernice Johnson. 1991. With Bill Moyers. *The Songs Are Free*. VHS. New York: Mystic Fire Video.

———. 1993. "Singing For My Life." In Bernice Johnson Reagon and Sweet Honey In the Rock, *We Who Believe in Freedom*, 133–68. New York: Anchor, Doubleday.

Ware, Ann Patrick. 1993. *New Words for Old Songs*. Privately printed. St. Louis: Loretto Community, 590 E. Lockwood, St. Louis, Mo. 63119. Reprint: Ibid. 2000. *New Words for Old Hymns and Songs*. New York: Women's Liturgy Group.

Williams, Delores. 1991. "Black Women's Surrogacy Experience and the Christian Notion of Redemption." In Paula M. Cooey, William R. Eakin, and Jay B. McDaniel, eds., *After Patriarchy*. Maryknoll: Orbis.

Winter, Miriam Therese. 1987. *WomanPrayer WomanSong*. Oak Park, Ill.: Meyer-Stone.

PART IV

Congregation and Community

12

Nusach and Identity: The Contemporary Meaning of Traditional Jewish Prayer Modes

Jeffrey A. Summit

This chapter examines the construction of identity among a cross section of American Jews in the greater Boston area, focusing on worshipers' ideas about the meaning and function of traditional prayer modes in contemporary Jewish worship.[1] In the broader study from which this research is taken, I concentrate on the Friday evening, *Kabbalat Shabbat* service across five different traditions, as a means to understand how these Jews define, maintain, and present their identity (Summit 2000).[2] Three of these worship communities represent "mainstream" Jewish movements: Reform, Conservative, and Orthodox. In addition, there are two "edges" of the Jewish community: the Bostoner *Rebbe*'s (title of a Hasidic leader, Yiddish) community and a "new age" *havurah*—a fellowship where it was not unusual to find interpretive dance or Hebrew text set to Buddhist chant included in a *Shabbat* (Sabbath) service. My research is based upon analysis and transcriptions of the services of these five communities as well as upon interviews with the communities' members and leaders.

The music of the synagogue can be divided into *nusach*, traditional Jewish prayer modes, and metrical songs. This chapter is concerned with the study of *nusach* from an emic, that is, insider's, perspective.[3] The word *nusach* comes from the Hebrew root meaning, "uprooted" or "torn away." The term originally referred to a specific section of Jewish liturgy that a scribe had copied out of a particular prayer book or text (Nulman 1975, 189). The term was later applied in a broader way to indicate a particular community's tradition of prayer or, more generally, the way that the prayers were publicly presented. In her work on the study of "flowing rhythm" in *nusach*, Judit Frigyesi explains: "*Nusach* means something like 'the traditional way (of singing) according to the given liturgical function and local custom.' . . . And whereas metric tunes can be replaced or omitted, *nusach* is indispensable—without it there is no ritual" (1993, 69; also see Elbogen 1993, 381–86).[4]

In traditional Jewish worship the leader intones the ending and occasionally the beginning lines of individual prayers, marking the place and setting the pace of the service. These short sections of the liturgy are chanted in *nusach*. Joseph Levine provides a description of *nusach*, concentrating on the leader's role as an improviser working within a traditionally accepted framework to construct a musical representation of the liturgy. As the leader chants the service, he "concentrates on the melodic line, selecting from a stock of prescribed motifs, bridging them through reciting-tones and melismatic flourishes. Each cantor varies the selection of motifs, their rhythm, intervallic spacing, and how the notes sound. Flexibility comes foremost. Prayer modes may be varied endlessly, limited only by the cantor's imagination, yet they are always recognizable. Hence a prayer mode is a sacred vocal pattern of traditional motifs that retains its identity even though melody, rhythm, and note-intervals and note-sequences change. . . ." (1989, 79–80). Because of its relatively free nature, *nusach* allows the leader considerable opportunity for improvisation. The following example of *Kabbalat Shabbat nusach* was transcribed from the modern Orthodox community considered in my research.

FIGURE 12.1. *Arba'im shanah* ("Forty years"—Conclusion of Psalm 95)

It is also important to add that *nusach* is specific for the time of day or the time of year in the holiday cycle. Thus, there is a particular *nusach* for the High Holidays, for *Shabbat* morning or for a weekday afternoon service. The fact that *nusach* is occasion specific has caused Avenary and others to compare it to the oriental *māqām* and the Indian *raga* (Avenary 1972, 1284; Idelsohn 1929, 24–34).

Many attempts, both historical and contemporary, to name, describe and categorize *nusach* tend to separate and analyze the song quite apart from the singer. Also, they have almost entirely ignored the congregation's reception of *nusach*, paying little attention to the worshipers' conception of the meaning and function of liturgical chant. My approach here is different: My research is built upon interviews with community members in which I examine their understanding of the role of *nusach* in the synagogue service. I see this approach as a continuation of Mark Slobin's research in his final chapter of *Chosen Voices*, where he presents the first emic consideration of *nusach* (1989, 256–79).[5] In both my interviews and participant observation, I found *nusach* to be an unexpectedly loaded subject, eliciting strong, contrasting responses across denominational lines. As one Conservative cantor stated, "*Nusach* is a real 'hot potato' in the Jewish community right now." Some members of the Jewish community, for example, see *nusach* as the last holdout of traditional Jewish liturgy. Others view it as a magic door to Jewish authenticity. One Reform worshiper said *nusach* was unintelligible, calling it a "mumble-fest." A Bostoner Hasid insisted that *nusach* was "the first rap music." My questions concerning *nusach* were purposely general and open-ended, addressing a number of related themes. Following are examples of different contemporary understandings of *nusach* drawn from my research with the communities selected for this study.

Nusach and Authenticity: A (Tenuous) Connection with Tradition

Across denominational lines, worshipers spoke about the importance of *nusach* as "authentic" or "traditional" Jewish liturgical music. B'nai Or (Children of Light), the most eclectic congregation studied, was no exception. This *havurah* is a fellowship of about 175 unit members that meets weekly for Friday evening and holiday services in a local Masonic Temple.[6] B'nai Or is open to many musical styles in constructing its *Shabbat* worship. Hasidic *nigunim* (tunes with vocables in place of words), Israeli folk songs, *nusach*, Hindu chant with Hebrew lyrics, modern musical compositions, movement, and dance all find their way into the service. Participants strongly affirmed the importance of *nusach* as a historical connection to Jewish tradition. One member stated, "[Without *nusach*], there would be no continuity with our tradition." His wife continued, "I think there's got to be some connection with tradition—as creative as we get—because part of the thing about Judaism is how this chain has gone on."

Both the leader and the ritual committee at B'nai Or exercise control over the atmosphere and decorum of the service. Still, worship is creative and participants spoke of their services as having an atmosphere where "anything goes." Here, *nusach* is seen as an anchor to authenticity, an example of normative religious practice that serves as a connection to mainstream Jewish worship. Another member expressed this clearly when she said, "I love (*nusach*). It makes me feel like I'm really doing Jewish and that I'm not just being a new age hippie."

For this congregation, *nusach* becomes a touchstone, a tether to the past. Many members of this congregation are not ritually observant. They do not keep kosher, observe the Sabbath, or visibly mark themselves as being Jewish. Yet once these identity markers have vanished, *nusach* becomes invested with more importance and meaning as a connection to authentic Jewish practice. At the same time, this congregation's creative and nontraditional approach to Jewish liturgy has considerable influence on their approach to *nusach*. For example, it is not unusual for members to chant the English translations of the Hebrew prayers in *nusach*, a practice pioneered by Rabbi Zalman Schachter-Shalomi in the late 1960s. They sometimes even announce the number "in *nusach*." Also, a leader may switch from Hebrew to English, chanting alternatively in both languages. At other times there are two leaders, one chanting the Hebrew, one the English. While this practice is sometimes referred to by members as "stereo" English/Hebrew davening (from the Yiddish word *davenen*, meaning praying), it would be considered unacceptable to the Orthodox where no English is used in the service, and silly to Conservative and Reform Jews who simply do not pray that way. Yet at B'nai Or it is a common practice as a way both to connect to traditional practice and make the English translations of the prayers more "Jewish." With such musical choices, the community defines itself simultaneously as traditional and innovative.

In a community where most participants have not had a traditional Jewish education, however, there are few gatekeepers to judge whether a tradition or melody really does have a connection to Jewish tradition. In fact, it was clear to me that the leader's *nusach* did not sound like Ashkenazi chanting of the *Shabbat Ma'ariv* (evening) service, a fact that bothered his congregation very little. When I questioned the leader on the source of his *Ma'ariv nusach*, he stated, "I think that just came out of me. I'm into this major kind of mode." This leader understood that *nusach* was connected to time of day and time of the week, stating "they're like ragas to me. They each evoke something." In fact, the *Ma'ariv nusach* for *Shabbat* in the Ashkenazic tradition is commonly in the minor mode. Then what constitutes "authentic" *nusach* for this congregation? In this case, it was not the traditional modal structure of the chant that established its authenticity. Among members of this community, melodic distinctions between specific *nushaot* (pl.) were lost; the canvas was painted in broader strokes. Certain characteristics of Jewish chant—such as free rhythm, reciting tones, a cadential formula—bolstered by a respected community leader were enough to establish this *nusach* as authentic as well as to link it comfortably to the chain of Jewish tradition.

Participation versus Correct Performance

In Temple Israel, the Reform congregation I studied, both professional and lay people were committed to "proper *nusach*." Historically, traditional Jews criticized the Reform Movement for introducing instrumental music, first the organ and more recently the guitar, into *Shabbat* worship. This "Protestant" influence, together with the formation of large synagogue choirs, the diminution of the cantor's traditional role, and the shortening of the liturgy were seen as musical and liturgical evidence of the Reform Movement's increasing assimilation to the dominant culture, a move away from traditional Jewish practice. Since the 1960s, however, Reform Judaism has found it increasingly difficult to involve members in worship and communal life without embracing particular rituals and more traditional practice. The Reform Movement even published its first code of Jewish law in the late 1970s, fearing that Jewish life without significant connections to tradition would simply not hold an appeal to Jews searching for community and rootedness.

When I spoke to the cantor of this large Reform temple, he spoke passionately of his commitment to teach the congregation to use and appreciate the special *nushaot* for the High Holidays and the festivals, Passover, *Shavuot* and *Sukkot*. He was frustrated with the fact that while his congregants were familiar with the Sabbath *nusach*, they lacked knowledge about the unique musical traditions for the holidays. In trying to teach the congregation the occasion specific music, however, he was faced with a dilemma: using the "right" music at the expense of congregational participation, or sacrificing the "right" music for the sake of engendering more congregational participation:

> I think it's good for people to be singing the right thing at the proper moment, the correct melody, [but] I have fudged my philosophy on this with the High Holidays because everyone knows the [prayers] with *Shabbat nusach*, and the first year I sang High Holiday *nusach*, and it was "Death Valley Days." I looked out: it was quiet. I may have done it for two years and then I decided I'm going to compromise my belief here because I think it's more important for them to be singing rather than hearing me sing the proper melody, and just watching me.

He went on to say that, with his wife's encouragement, he decided to continue with his educational program for the congregation. Eventually, he believed, they would come to learn, appreciate and participate in the special, occasion specific melodies. The fact that a Reform cantor at a large urban temple is so committed to educating and introducing his congregants to traditional *nusach* contradicts the stereotypical view that Reform Jews do not value "traditional" practice.

It is also important to note the cantor's sensitivity to congregational participation. One might think that the cantor would primarily wish to perform for his congregation. In fact, we know that the early virtuoso cantors and cantorial composers purposely varied their tunes so that they were more difficult for the congregation to learn. The famous nineteenth-century cantor and composer, Salomon Sulzer, is credited with writing a rotating series of Sabbath liturgical pieces to make it more difficult for the masses to sing along with his music. He supposedly said, "Better one person singing beautifully than the entire congregation howling like wolves." This dynamic has clearly changed. This cantor is disturbed when his congregation seems like "Death Valley Days." He is caught between his desire to facilitate greater congregational participation and his feeling that the liturgy should be sung in the correct, traditional manner. This question would only be an issue of debate in a Reform congregation, where the use of *nusach*, like the performance of commandments, is seen as a choice. More traditional Conservative and certainly Orthodox congregations perform proper *nusach* at the expense of congregational participation.

At this temple the cantor is not alone in his dedication to traditional chanting. Several of his congregants spoke hyperbolically of *nusach* as ancient tradition, powerfully connecting them to thousands of years of Jewish history and experience. Much classical Reform liturgy is read, in unison or responsively, as opposed to chanted. But one woman, a former president of the congregation, stated, "I don't feel good just sitting there reading." She explained that the very experience of chanting the Hebrew opened up greater possibilities for spiritual experience and participation:

> [Chanting] comes from here . . . in your soul . . . the more senses you use, the more connection you feel. . . . [*Nusach* puts these] mediums together—to read it and sing it and then to move with it—it just raises your level of participation and your sense of belonging. . . . I love using more senses.

The "multi-sensory" nature of *nusach* (singing, chanting, breathing, moving, swaying) is seen to enhance prayer. To this worshiper, *nusach* facilitates a more integrated involvement in worship as well as a deeper understanding of the Jewish tradition. *Nusach*, more than any other musical choice, brings the worshiper into direct contact with traditional Hebrew texts. This congregational leader said that the introduction of more *nusach* in the service encouraged her to renew her study of Hebrew. While the older members of this "Boston Brahmin" synagogue do not approve of this move toward traditional practice, it represents a cultural and spiritual awakening for a new generation of Reform leadership.

Nusach as Normative Practice

Among the liberal congregations considered in this study, *nusach* was just one of the many possible musical choices for the performance of sacred text. In contrast, the modern Orthodox have chosen to limit their musical and liturgical choices. When asked why *nusach* was so important to Shaarei Tefillah (Gates of Prayer), a modern Orthodox congregation, one member answered:

> Identification with tradition. . . . If you asked [Orthodox Jews], "What's traditional about you? Do you study Talmud?" Some do, a lot don't. "Do you know the *Shulhan Arukh* (major code of Jewish law)?" "Never look in it." "So what's traditional about you?" "Well, I do things right. I go to a synagogue where it's done right. . . . We do the tunes in the correct way."

When the members of this Orthodox congregation insist that they "do things right," they leave little room open for other musical choices in the service. *Nusach* becomes normative liturgical practice and they have chosen to have no choice in this matter. In many aspects of their lives—their social circles, the food they eat, their leisure activities, how they spend their Friday evenings and Saturdays—they establish careful boundaries, limiting and narrowing their choices. Below, I consider the comments of another member in this congregation, a physician who grew up in the Conservative Movement and has become more observant since having children. He feels this constriction and expresses how he sees it reflected in the congregation's music:

> What's interesting, at least for me is that the *nusach* that I learned at Camp Ramah and U. S. Y. (United Synagogue Youth—the Conservative Movement's summer camp and youth movement) was pretty fixed [but] is different than what my children are learning. There are similarities, but I think it's [different]. . . . It's not quite as melodic as we learned.

He proceeded to sing his *nusach* and his rendition of the *nusach* his son has learned. He commented on his son's *nusach*: "It's kind of more straightforward, . . . limited" and continued, punctuating his comments with laughter, "I think that that's probably where we're going religiously too. . . ." He spoke about how his *nusach* had greater intervallic range and was more expansive, with more "flourishes." He perceived his son's *nusach* as simpler and more austere. While there is not a dramatic difference between the two versions, these observations are born out in transcription (Summit 2000, 118, 119).

He drew a general comparison from this musical observation and went on to describe the ways that becoming more Orthodox has restricted and limited his life, affecting his job and determining the neighborhood in which they live. He viewed all these developments as positive. He sends his children to Orthodox day school and in many ways they live a life much more regulated and segregated than his experience growing up as a committed Conservative Jew. He explained that his family used to eat out in restaurants but as their standards of keeping kosher became stricter, they stopped this too. He went on to talk about their decision to separate themselves from many aspects of American society and concluded, "by choice I think we've ghettoized ourselves, and I don't think that we're any worse for it." He spoke of the legal restrictions on the Sabbath as "totally freeing," allowing him to spend time with his family. He went on to explain how these choices enriched both his personal and professional life:

> I think that . . . if you're strong in who you are, I think you can go out and face other people and appreciate them for who they are, and respect them for who they are better. . . . It doesn't get in the way of being a doctor. The only way to be a doctor these days, more than ever, is to have some kind of faith in something bigger than medicine.

In the Orthodox community, musical traditions are often passed from father to son, yet this doctor was not bothered that his son's *nusach* was different, and their social sphere in general ranged less freely. He saw this tighter focus toward family and community as a way to enrich their lives, strengthen his marriage, and allow him to spend more time with his children, marking them—and their values—as different from the larger culture.

Still, with this stress on the importance of *nusach*, I repeatedly heard members of Shaarei Tefillah insist that they "did not know *nusach*." Another member went on to speculate what percentage of the congregation is committed to and actually knows these musical and liturgical traditions: "I would say [only] . . . about ten per cent really know. I may be exaggerating, but not by much. A lot of people pay lip service—oh, *nusach* is very important, but if you sang them the *nusach* . . . they wouldn't know."

It was notable that even knowledgeable members of this congregation played down and derided their own liturgical skills and knowledge of "correct" *nusach*. Listening to members of this Orthodox congregation discuss this as they stood around outside their synagogue was rather like sitting in a locker room hearing semiprofessional players insist that they "didn't really know basketball."

What does it mean when these members assert that "no one really knows *nusach*"? Their manner was not like that of the self-effacing gamelan master who says he "knows a little gamelan." Objectively, the level of Jewish knowledge at Shaarei Tefillah is as high as or even higher than any Orthodox congregation in town. The vast majority of the members are liturgically skilled enough to lead services. Members of this *shul* (synagogue) know *nusach* as well as any "nonprofessional" cantor can be expected to know these musical traditions. I think that when they insist that they do not know *nusach*, they are asserting that their musical and liturgical traditions are precise, detailed, historically specific, and not easily known. They are saying that the tradition they have chosen is subtle, varied, and complicated. It is difficult to know. In doing so, they affirm that there is a correct musical and liturgical tradition, rich in nuance and complexity. These modern Orthodox Jews are conscious that they live in a unique historical time: Anti-Semitism is minimal in greater Boston and their access to American society is broad. However, they specifically choose not to fully enter the "Goldena Medina," the golden country that lies spread out before them. They find many ways to assert that the tradition they have chosen in its place is venerable and valuable. This is in line with general trends in the modern Orthodox community. They search out more ways to make distinctions between Jews and non-Jews, to affirm their unique separateness in the face of the challenge and appeal of the seductive non-Jewish culture.

"Down-Home Elitists": An Aversion to Performance

Even while asserting that members "did not know *nusach*," I found that there were some styles of davening that simply were seen as unacceptable to the members of Shaarei Tefillah. The physician quoted above stated that in order to bring down community censure, "for people to exchange looks or something," a leader would have to chant the wrong melodies or pronounce the Hebrew improperly. Yet a leader could also stretch things to the point of censure if he did a "*dreylich, hazanishe shtick*" (overly ornamented cantorial performance, Yiddish) while davening. The physician continued: "I think we have no tolerance for that stuff. Who does he think he is? . . . Look who thinks he's a *hazzan* (cantor)! . . . We don't do *hazzanut* (cantorial performance) here (laughs). We do davening with *nusach*!" He went on to explain:

> A lot of people have made a conscious decision against that kind of *shul*. If you wanted a *hazzan*, you would have stayed in a *shul* with a *hazzan*, or hired one, even though we don't have the money to do that. . . . There's a very interesting dichotomy here because, on the one hand, I think—not totally wrongly—there's a perception of a certain elitism that we pride ourselves in being more *frum* (observant, Yiddish) than the *shul* we came from. . . . But at the same time, if someone wants to come in and start with a big time *hazanus* (*hazzanut*, Yiddish) . . . we won't allow that! (laughs). So, it's kind of—"don't be too grandiose" . . . we're down-home elitist.

"Doing it right" is not only knowing the correct tunes for traditional prayer modes. In some communities, it is also connected to the nature of performance practice and musical style of the leader. This member went deeper in explaining this antipathy toward "fancy," cantorial davening:

> One of the reasons our *shul* was founded was because people didn't like to have a *hazzan*, and so, to the extent . . . if you're talking about . . . formal cantorial singing, I think my reaction and the reaction of my contemporaries has been a strongly negative one. . . . Our generation has been reacting against formal institutionalization, and cantorial singing with its distant and performative aspects . . . is almost a symbol of the kind of large, empty edifice in which we are to varying degrees rejecting.

These "down-home elitists" have fairly simple goals when leading davening: pronounce the Hebrew properly; know what prayers are required at a specific service; know the tune for the appropriate *nusach;* do not stand out or call attention to the leader; do not get too fancy. One very knowledgeable member described his goals when he led the congregation in prayer:

> I think what I try to do is not embarrass myself. . . . So my own personal goal, and I think this holds true for many, although obviously not all, is just to get it in a way that's perceived as right—not to jar people, so that they don't wake up from their mental torpor, which is the usual state of mental alertness in a synagogue. In other words, if they don't say "What the hell was that?!" then I've succeeded.

So here, the emotional davening of the cantor that once was considered pious and spiritually heartfelt is seen as performance centered, showy and removed from true religious expression. In breaking away from the professionalism of the old-style Orthodox *shul* with a full time *hazzan,* this modern Orthodox congregation has chosen to be more involved and observant in all aspects of their Jewish lives, including their service leading skill, which is shared by many in the congregation. They approach *nusach* with an understated simplicity, technical precision, and attention to detail that is in keeping with their general approach to modern Orthodox life.

Nusach and the Interpretation of the Text

In previous research with part-time cantors, many leaders told me how they used *nusach* to interpret the meaning of the liturgical text (Summit 1988, 101–103). These semi-professional leaders often saw their role as teachers. *Nusach* was a tool to explain the prayers. In this study, it was only among the Hasidim of Beth Pinchas, the Bostoner Rebbe's *shul,* that *nusach* was discussed as a means of explaining and understanding the meaning of the liturgical text.

When I spoke to the Bostoner Rebbe's son, Rav (Rabbi) Naftali Horowitz, about the purpose of *nusach,* he differentiated *nusach* from other kinds of music. He was quick to contemporize his explanation by comparing *nusach* to rap music:

> *Nusach* is also a type of melody but it's not a melody where it's song. If you want to get more to the secular world, it's more like rap music. Rap music's not like song. [It's closer to speech,] like Jesse Jackson speaks, . . . we basically created the first rap music and that's called *nusach* . . . and basically we have . . . different parts of *nusach.*

> The way we bring it out is the type of moment that we're looking for.

It was notable that the only one who used contemporary metaphors in his explanations of Jewish liturgical music was a Bostoner Hasid, who, ironically enough looked as if he had stepped out of nineteenth-century Poland. Though working hard to isolate himself from secular American culture, Rav Naftali showed that he was hip to it. His proprietary claim of historical authenticity ("We created the first rap music") was his way to underscore the historical validity of the Torah, its teachings, and traditions.

Rav Naftali explained that *nusach* might deal with feelings of joy or awe, mourning or longing for the *mashiah* (Messiah) as it is applied to specific texts. In every case, he stressed:

> The music gets the words across and your *kavanah* in *tefillah* (your intentions in prayer), [is] much stronger. . . . Through the music and the melody, you can reach much more the feeling of the moment, that's what music does, brings over and clearer across to the soul, the *neshamah*, the feeling of the moment.

Here music is more than a way to interpret the meaning of the text: It is seen as a "shortcut," a direct path to the moment, the feeling, the truth and experience of the liturgy. Music intensifies the meaning of the prayers, allowing the worshiper to forge a connection between the soul and the text.

This function of music is in line with a Hasidic view of music in general, as a way to lift and elevate the soul. A Hasidic aphorism states "Great is a melody with words but greater still is a melody without words" (see Idelsohn 1929, 416). There is a sense that the music itself contains and can convey pure emotion, short-circuiting the text in order to convey a deeper truth. In this way, *nusach* functions to bring out the spiritual meaning in the text. Rav Naftali's father, Rabbi Levi Yitzchak Horowitz, the Bostoner Rebbe, spoke at length about the function of *nusach*. He described the transformative role of music, explaining that music facilitates the transition from the weekday to the Sabbath, from the ordinary to the holy, from the everyday to the nearly-messianic state of *Shabbat*. This heightened musical and spiritual intensity does more than convey the meaning of the words, it embodies the experience of the events. He continued:

> It is the *nusach* that tends to guide you to what's happening, it's via the tune of the *nusach* that you get the meaning of the words and you get the meaning maybe even more than the words, you get the meaning of the events, which is the ultimate of what we would like

> to have. . . . There is the six chapters before *Lekhah dodi* ("Come, My Beloved," Sabbath hymn) which represent the six days of the week and getting closer every day, every *kapitel* (each *Kabbalat Shabbat* psalm, Yiddish), to the ultimate of your goal, the *Shabbas* (Sabbath).

The Rebbe states that the actual tune of the Friday night *nusach,* itself, might be arbitrary. Still, history and tradition have imbued it with power and meaning and this *nusach* has become the tune that "gets us off":

> I don't know whether we can say that we know . . . exactly what the meaning of the tune [of *Kabbalat Shabbat nusach*] is as applied to the words. . . . Now, it's basically the *nusach* of the world, but of course, everyone has their little *kvetch* (emphasis), their little *drey* (ornamental turn). . . . You hear the *Arba'im shanah* . . . you know we're taking off. So . . . there is no explanation why we are taking off with *this* tune. Maybe we could have taken off with another tune but we've taken off with this tune for millennia, forever, . . . so that's the tune that gets us into the new position. . . .

Even if this particular tune, the melody for *Kabbalat Shabbat nusach,* might be arbitrary, history has imbued it with meaning. It has become an effective way for the leader to convey the *experience* of the text, the *feeling* of the liturgy. The text of the liturgy is the script for this weekly rehearsal for the coming of the Messiah, the precursor of the World to Come. The Rebbe stresses that the *shaliah tsibur* (prayer leader) must feel and understand the meaning of the prayers, or else the melody, the *nusach,* does not work. In other words, the leader's sincerity is paramount. As the Rebbe emphasizes, "you just can't convey the message if you're not the messenger." On *Kabbalat Shabbat, nusach* is the means to tell the story and translate the experience of the Jewish people moving towards redemption. It conveys that story with an emotional intensity deeper than intellect, strengthened and bolstered by generations of musical meaning and associations.

Conclusions

The *Mahzor Vitry,* a twelfth-century religious manual, quotes a tradition by stating that the melodies of the synagogue were taught to Moses by God on Mount Sinai: Jews have strong feelings about music (1893, 91). The quote helps highlight the contemporary conceptions of *nusach* in the above discussion: These Jews' conceptions of *nusach* are bound up in their struggles with modernity as well as their efforts to clarify their religious and cultural identity. For some of them, *nusach* serves as a powerful connection to Jewish community and tradition as external markers of identity fall away. Others see *nusach* as the key to a more participatory prayer experience, reconnecting them with traditional texts, with the rhythm of the body and their breathing. For some, a commitment to performing "correct" *nusach* is a way to show their dedication to traditional religious practice; they reject other possible musical—and communal—choices as they separate themselves both from other Jews and from American culture. Still for others, *nusach* conveys the experience of Jewish history—past, present, and moving towards a messianic future. *Nusach* is performed and interpreted strategically, one part in a continuing process as these American Jews define and present their identity.

NOTES

1. I wish to thank Mark Slobin, Philip Bohlman, Mark DeVoto, Marc Perlman, and Richard Israel for their valuable advice, criticism, and direction in this work.

2. In the context of this study, the term "identity" indicates a sense of belonging, of membership, of place, and of connection to a particular community. One belongs to a community by participating in the social, communal, and religious activities of that group. In this way, identity is functionally determined by a series of individual and collective choices, made by technical means. This study considers the concepts of "ethnic group" and "ethnic identity" from several different perspectives. My understanding of the two concepts is in line with that offered by the anthropologist and dance ethnographer, Anya Peterson Royce, who states, "An 'ethnic group' is a reference group invoked by people who share a common historical style (which may be only assumed), based on overt features and values, and who, through the process of interaction with others, identify themselves as sharing that style. 'Ethnic identity' is the sum total of feelings on the part of group members about those values, symbols, and common histories that identify them as a distinct group" (1982, 18). See Royce's first chapter, "Neither Christian nor Jewish . . ." on the problems inherent in defining ethnic identity and ethnicity.

3. Most explorations of *nusach* analyze the musical aspects of Jewish chant and examine such concepts as mode, scale, and the art of cantorial improvisation. Other studies have considered the historical development of Jewish prayer modes or their relation to the religious music of other cultures. For an overview of chant in Ashkenazi liturgical music, see Schleifer (1992, 13–58). Also see the sections on liturgical chant and prayer modes in Avenary (1972), Kligman (2000), Werner (1976, 46–61), Idelsohn ([1929] 1967, 72–91). For a detailed discussion of prayer modes, see Wohlberg ([1954] 1972), Glantz ([1952] 1972), and Cohon (1950). For cantorial art music, see Avenary (1968).

4. Frigyesi discusses both the history of the term *nusach* and the approach to its study. She notes: "the study of *nusach* goes back to the treatises of the eighteenth- and

nineteenth-century cantors who first described the melodies and scales of Jewish music, either as part of the introduction to a collection of melodies or as a separate theoretical study. . . . In these studies, usually the word *Steiger* appears, literally meaning 'scale' but referring actually to the mode of the prayer. In cultural areas influenced by the Austrian-German cantorate, the word *nusach* often has been replaced by or used alongside with *Steiger* among cantors. Scholarly study in the ethnomusicological sense started with Idelsohn, who did not, however, use the word *nusach* but introduced the ethnomusicological term, 'mode' (Idelsohn 1914–32, 1929, 1933)" (1993, 82, 83 n. 19). While Frigyesi states that Idelson's classification and terminology of the modes are still used today, I would stress that these are familiar to professionals (cantors, musicologists, choir directors), rather than to lay people.

5. Slobin describes the difficulty of establishing any single understanding and approach to *nusach* and observes that the "dividing up of a core insider term is bound to be artificial, as is any one gloss for a cultural concept." He continues, "Experiences such as mine in trying to map nusach are commonplace these days in ethnomusicology, with its recent stress on emic data; but despite all the lip service paid to the interior view, no one has turned up a good methodology for doing so honestly or comprehensively" (1989, 276 n. 4). In *Chosen Voices*, Slobin constructs a comprehensive picture of *nusach*, presenting quotes from his informants to draw a broader picture of this fluid cultural term.

6. Several important works have been written on the *Havurah* movement. One of the best and earliest anthologies is edited by Neusner (1972); also, see Prell (1988) and Hecht (1993).

WORKS CITED

Avenary, Hanoch. 1972. "Nusach." *Encyclopedia Judaica*. vol. 12. cols. 1283–84. Jerusalem: Keter.

———. 1968. "The Cantorial Fantasia of the Eighteenth and Nineteenth Centuries—A Late Manifestation of Musical Trope." In *Yuval: Studies of the Jewish Music Research Center*. Ed. Israel Adler. Jerusalem: Magnes Press, Hebrew University, 68–85.

Ben Samuel, Simha. *Mahzor Vitry*. 1893. S. Hurwitz, ed. Berlin: H. Itzkowski.

Cohon, Baruch. 1950. "Structure of the Synagogue Prayer Chant." *Journal of the American Musicological Society* 3 (1): 17–32.

Elbogen, Ismar. 1993. *Jewish Liturgy: A Comprehensive History*. Translated by Raymond P. Scheindlin. Based on the author's *Der jüdische Gottesdienst in seiner geschichtlichen Entwicklung* (1913) and the Hebrew version, *Hatefila beyisra'el behitpathutah hahistorit* (1972). New York and Philadelphia: Jewish Theological Seminary; Jewish Publication Society.

Frigyesi, Judit. 1993. "Preliminary Thoughts Toward the Study of Music without Clear Beat: The Example of "Flowing Rhythm" in Jewish *Nusach*." *Asian Music* 24 (2): 59–87.

Glantz, Leib. [1952] 1972. "The Musical Basis of Nusach Hatefillah." In *Journal of Synagogue Music*, vol. 4 (1, 2). New York: Cantors Assembly of America, 23–37.

Hecht, Shirah Weinberg. 1993. "When Tradition Leads: Prayer and Participation in the Contemporary Jewish Equalitarian Minyan." Ph.D. diss., University of Chicago.

Idelsohn, A. Z. [1929] 1967. *Jewish Music in its Historical Development.* Boston: Holt, Rinehart and Winston. Repr., New York: Schocken, 1967.

Kligman, Mark. 2000. "Music in Judaism." In *The Encyclopaedia of Judaism*, edited by Jacob Neusner, Alan J. Avery-Peck, and William Scott Green, vol. 2. Leiden: Museum of Jewish Heritage; Brill, 905–24.

Levine, Joseph. 1989. *Synagogue Song in America.* Crown Point, Ind.: White Cliffs Media.

Neusner, Jacob, ed. 1972. *Contemporary Judaic Fellowship in Theory and Practice.* New York: Ktav.

Nulman, Macy. 1975. *Concise Encyclopedia of Jewish Music.* New York: McGraw-Hill.

Prell, Riv-Ellen. 1988. *Prayer and Community: The Havurah Movement and the Recreation of American Judaism.* Detroit: Wayne State University Press.

Royce, Anya Peterson. 1982. *Ethnic Identity: Strategies of Diversity.* Bloomington, Ind.: Indiana University Press.

Schleifer, Eliyahu. 1992. "Jewish Liturgical Music from the Bible to Hasidism." In *Sacred Sound and Social Change: Liturgical Music in Jewish and Christian Experience*, eds. Lawrence A. Hoffman and Janet R. Walton. Notre Dame, Ind.: University of Notre Dame Press, 59–83.

Slobin, Mark. 1989. *Chosen Voices: The Story of the American Cantorate.* Urbana: University of Illinois Press.

Summit, Jeffrey A. 1988. "The Role and Function of the Part-time Cantor: A Regional Study based on Oral Histories of Part-time Cantors in the Boston Area." M.A. thesis, Tufts University.

———. 2000. *The Lord's Song in a Strange Land: Music and Identity in Contemporary Jewish Worship.* New York: Oxford University Press.

Werner, Eric. 1976. *A Voice Still Heard . . . : The Sacred Songs of the Ashkenazic Jews.* London: Pennsylvania State University Press.

Wohlberg, Max. [1954] 1972. "History of the Musical Modes of the Ashkenazic Synagogue and Their Usage." In *Journal of Synagogue Music*, vol. 4 (1, 2). New York: Cantors Assembly of America, 41–61.

13

Reflections on the Musical Diversity of Chinese Churches in the United States

Maria M. Chow

The Chinese population in the United States is diverse. Besides American-born Chinese (often abbreviated as ABC), there are Chinese immigrants from mainland China, Taiwan, Hong Kong, Indonesia, Vietnam, and Singapore, in addition to other nations in Asia and throughout the world. In spite of the fact that they are reckoned as Chinese in the United States for various reasons, Chinese Americans constitute individuals from different social and cultural backgrounds and often do not share the same language or dialect. When the Christian believers among these Chinese Americans congregate to worship with hymns and prayers, how do their music and worship reflect such diversity?

This chapter explores the use of music in Chinese American worship services by presenting the results of a fifteen-month study, which was conducted between October 1992 and February 1994, with conclusions gathered through a survey.[1] While the study prior to the survey shaped the way in which I designed the survey, the results of the survey, in turn, caused me to develop new perspectives for handling the information gathered earlier in the study. Since the survey represents a greater diversity of congregations than those covered in the earlier study, I focus the following chapter mainly on the survey. But first I show how the earlier study served as the survey's foundation and as the point of departure for future studies of Chinese churches in the United States.

Precepts and Assumptions of the Survey

Members of Chinese churches in the United States know from first-hand experience that Chinese congregations in the country differ remarkably from one another in their languages, dialects, cultural backgrounds, and worship practices. Intercongregational diversity is often reflected at the intracongregational level; each Chinese congregation may well have different services in different languages (or dialects) and worship styles. The Chicago congregation in which I did fieldwork at the beginning of my study clearly reflects such diversity.

The Chinese Christian Union Church (often abbreviated as CCUC) is located in Chicago's Chinatown, itself lying southwest of the city's downtown, the Loop. As an independent and interdenominational congregation, it had a membership of around one thousand, I was told, but the number of members regularly attending the Sunday services was around four hundred. The CCUC is one of the largest Chinese congregations that I have visited in the United States. During the period I visited the congregation, three services were held every Sunday: one in Cantonese, one in Mandarin, and one in English. Like most independent congregations, this one does not adopt any specific liturgy for worship; the style and order of the services change from time to time. In addition to differences in the structure and style of worship, each of the services also has its own distinctive musical features. The services differ from one another in their repertoires of congregational hymns, music sung by the choir, the choice of musical instruments, and the style of accompaniment for congregational singing.

The musical practices of this Chicago congregation served as my starting point in formulating the issues and questions for the subsequent study. First, all three services share a core of hymns from the same service hymnal, *Hymns of Life* (1986), which seems to be widely used among Chinese churches both within and outside of the United States.[2] The hymnal, like many other hymnals of Chinese churches, contains a large number of European American hymns from the Baptist, Methodist, and American revivalist traditions.

Second, the music and musical practices of the two Chinese-language services are very similar to what one would find in many Chinese congregations in Hong Kong or Taiwan. Hymns are accompanied primarily by the piano and sometimes by the organ, with chordal harmony. The English service, however, differs to some degree. Besides singing hymns from the service hymnal, participants in the English service also sing many contemporary American Christian songs to the accompaniment of guitar, percussion instruments, and synthesizers. In short, the English service differs from the Chinese-language services not only in language but also in musical practice. Finally, numerous Christian songs of various styles are sung in activities outside the Sunday services, such as Bible studies, fellowship meetings, Sunday school, and other special occasions.

Based on these preliminary observations, I raise three questions: (1) To what extent do other Chinese congregations in the United States display a similar diversity of musical expressions? (2) How is musical diversity related to the linguistic diversity reflected by the presence of services in different dialects and languages? (3) How is the greater variety of musical styles at the other church activities related to the more homogeneous musical expressions at each of the services? To take this last question further, how are the musical expressions of the individual members or groups of members being negotiated in the process of deciding the music and musical practices of the services?

These are the three main questions upon which I reflected throughout the entire period of this study (i.e., from October 1992 to February 1994). At the beginning of the study, I talked to ministers, musicians, and lay people whom I knew personally, and I asked various organizations for statistical data concerning the overall situation of Chinese congregations in the United States.[3] Through these organizations, I was able to contact more people and organizations for further information and advice. During the summer of 1993, I also visited nine Chinese congregations outside of Chicago, including three in California, to acquire more direct knowledge of certain congregations that I may not have known otherwise. Towards the end of the study, when I designed the survey, I had already formulated some preliminary opinions regarding the three questions I was trying to answer. These opinions became the assumptions that I intended to verify through the survey.

My assumptions, which I formulated into hypotheses, are the following: (1) The linguistic diversity of a congregation is proportional to the size of that congregation. (2) At the Chinese services, most of the congregations sing more or less the same repertory of Baptist and Methodist hymns and American revivalist gospel songs (all with translated Chinese texts), which is related to the fact that several Chinese-English bilingual hymnals are widely used among the congregations. (3) The singing of contemporary Christian songs in English, together with the use of musical instruments other than the piano and the organ, are characteristic of the English services. (4) The repertory of hymns sung at the Chinese services is considerably different from that used for other activities.

The Survey—Objectives

The survey consists of twenty-two questions in both Chinese and English.[4] Twenty are multiple-choice questions; the others were simple yes/no questions. Copies of the survey were sent to 110 congregations chosen from China Horizon's mailing list. The decision about the initial screening was based on various factors, one of which was the unsatisfactory response to past surveys conducted among Chinese congregations.[5] Given limited resources, priority was assigned to the more responsive congregations, even though such an initial screening would inevitably increase the survey's potential bias. While processing the data from the questionnaires, I phoned more than twenty-five of the congregations in order to clarify my questions or to obtain information about certain details.

In addition to inquiring about general census information—denominational affiliation, size of membership, and the number of Sunday services—the questionnaire aimed at soliciting information concerning two musical aspects of the Sunday services: (1) the repertory of congregational hymns, and (2) the relationship of musical style to the use of musical instruments.[6] In addition, in order to understand how the musical expressions of the services are related to congregational members personally, the survey contains a question about how often ("rarely, seldom, sometimes, regularly, or always") the congregations used the service hymnal for other activities.

Churches Represented by the Survey

Sixty-six of the 110 congregations surveyed, that is, 60 percent,[7] returned their questionnaires; this is an unusually high percentage in comparison with those of past surveys conducted among Chinese churches.[8] In spite of the initial screening, the denominational affiliation of the 66 churches is in line with earlier statistics and what is generally known among ministers and church leaders: The percentage of independent churches among Chinese churches in the United States is the highest, and the next on the list is the Baptist Church (cf. tables. 13.1 and 13.2).[9]

When we take the size of membership into consideration, the distribution of the churches represented in the present survey differs slightly from what is commonly known. The percentage of congregations of the "100-or-below" category, however, is somewhat lower than usual. According to a survey conducted in 1990 by the Chinese Coordination Center of World Evangelism (CCCOWE),

TABLE 13.1 Denominational Affiliation of Chinese American Churches in the Survey

Number of congregations (percent)	Denominational affiliation
34 (52)	nondenominational, interdenominational, independent
14 (21)	Baptists (Southern Baptist and American Baptist)
8 (12)	Christian and Missionary Alliance
10	• Christian Reformed Church • Evangelical Formosan Church • Evangelical Free Church • Evangelical Lutheran Church of America • Mennonite Church • United Presbyterian Church of America

TABLE 13.2 Size of Chinese American Churches in the Survey

Number of congregations (percent)	Size of membership
12 (18)	500 or more
20 (30)	300–400
13 (20)	200
21 (31)	100 or below

and taking into consideration what is generally known among ministers and church leaders, more than 40 percent of the Chinese congregations in the United States have a membership of 100 or below; the percentage is significantly higher than the 31 percent in the present survey. Furthermore, the percentage of congregations in the 300- to 400-member category in the present survey is higher than what one might generally expect; however, no past statistics are available for comparison.

This survey's slightly different distribution of congregational membership size could be due to the initial screening that eliminated less responsive congregations. Judging from the unusually high percentage of congregations responding to the survey, it seems that larger congregations were among the more responsive.[10] Although larger congregations generally display greater intracongregational diversity, it will become clear below that the high percentage of larger congregations represented in this survey has little bearing on this discussion of the diversity of Chinese Americ an churches.

Number of Sunday Services

The phenomenon of having more than one Sunday service is quite widespread among the 66 churches. Twenty of the 66 congregations have only one Sunday service, while the rest have at least two services, each in a different dialect or language—Chinese or English.[11] All but one (91 percent) of the congregations in the "500-or-more" category have three or four services. Among the 20 congregations that have only one Sunday service, 17 indicate that their service is either bidialectal or bilingual; one of the services is conducted in Cantonese and Mandarin as well as English. In total, 127 services are held each Sunday at the 66 congregations. Since, however, there is no information about what language is used in three of the services, there are in fact 124 services for this discussion; of these, 39 are in English, 63 in one or two Chinese dialects, and 22 are bilingual services (i.e., English plus any one Chinese dialect). Hence, English is used in 61 out of the 124 services (49 percent).

Hymnals and Songbooks

The titles of no fewer than 30 hymnals and songbooks were collected from the survey. These included around 20 hymnals that are used as service hymnals at all the different services. With only two exceptions, each of the 63 Chinese services uses one hymnal as the service hymnal. Among these service hymnals, *Hymns of Life* (1986) is used by 26 congregations (ca. 39 percent) at 46 services every Sunday (ca. 36 percent); *Hymnody* (1972) by 19 congregations (ca. 29 percent) at 27 services (ca. 21 percent); and *Hymns for God's People* by nine congregations (ca. 14 percent). The hymnals used by the remaining congregations at the Chinese services include *Church Hymnal, New Hymnal,*[12] *New Songs of Praise,*[13] and others.[14] In the two congregations that do not use a specific service hymnal, the person responsible for leading the congregational singing during the service chooses the hymns and Christian songs for each week's service.[15] However, it seems that this practice of singing hymns and songs from various sources is also found at some of the Chinese services that do use service hymnals.

Among the song collections often used for this kind of free selection, *New Songs Ringing* deserves special attention. This is a collection of 400 translated contemporary American Christian songs in four volumes with English texts of the songs provided at the end of the songbooks. Most of the time, when such songs are selected for congregational use, the text is projected onto a screen by an overhead projector, a practice common among many American evangelical churches.

Among the 34 congregations that have at least one English-only service, 19 indicate that their English services share to some extent the same hymnal with their Chinese services; this includes ten English services using *Hymns of Life* and eight using *Hymnody*. Many of the 19 congregations, however, also list a number of other English song collections that are used specifically at the English service. In my conversations with the staff of some of these congregations, I was often told that the English congregation would sing at least one hymn from the service hymnal, but sing primarily contemporary songs from songbooks such as *Praise* and *Worship Songs of the Vineyard*. As a matter of fact, it seems that most of the English services sing similar contemporary Christian songs to varying degrees; only two of the 25 congregations that I contacted do not have such a practice. The congregations that do select hymns and songs to be sung at the English services from different sources generally use the services of Church Copyright License, Inc., which allows them to reprint songs published by over 120 publishers.

Instruments and Music Outside Worship Services

The primary musical instrument used to accompany congregational singing at the Chinese-language services is the piano. When I asked the congregations to represent the importance of the piano in each of the services on a scale of one to four in order of increasing importance, 117 services (92 percent) rated a "three" or a "four." The next most widely used instrument is the organ, similarly represented by a "three" or "four" in 47 services (37 percent). The guitar is widely used to accompany hymn singing in services that, to some extent, involve English. Of the 29 services in which the use of the guitar scores a "three" or a "four," 24 are conducted either in English alone or in both English and Chinese. Of the 39 English services, 33 (85 percent) use the guitar to varying degrees from time to time, whereas the instrument is used in only 24 of the 63 Chinese services (38 percent).

Finally, when asked whether hymns are sung at other weekly church activities (e.g., Bible studies, prayer meetings, and fellowship meetings), six congregations (nine percent) answered "always"; 20 congregations (30 percent) answered "regularly"; 20, "sometimes"; 11 (16 percent), "seldom"; 12 (18 percent), "rarely"; and one answered "never."[16]

Linguistic Diversity

The results of the survey both confirm my initial assumptions and suggest some revisions to them. First of all, judging from the fact that more than 91 percent of the congregations in the "500-or-more" members category provide at least three services every Sunday, each in a different language (or dialect), while only three of the congregations in the "100-to-200" category have three separate services in different languages (or dialects), it seems that, indeed, greater linguistic diversity is characteristic of the larger congregations. Yet, because the growth of any community usually lends itself to increasing diversity, it is perhaps more important to notice that a significant degree of linguistic diversity is present in nearly all 66 congregations. Such diversity, in fact, is experienced more directly in the smaller congregations than the larger ones.

In the larger congregations, separate services are usually held in at least some of the languages or dialects spoken by the members, but in the smaller congregations, members speaking different languages or dialects often attend the same service.[17] In the case of the latter, the service is usually conducted in one language or dialect with simultaneous interpretation of the sermon and certain other parts of the worship. Under such circumstances, the members of the congregation will sing the hymns in different languages or dialects simultaneously. We are, therefore, able preliminarily to conclude that the linguistic diversity in the larger congregations' services is only one instance of the cultural diversity that characterizes most Chinese congregations in the country.

A Common Repertory

The survey shows that *Hymns of Life* is by far the most widely used bilingual hymnal among these Chinese American congregations. This hymnal is the official hymnal of the Chinese and Missionary Alliance Church. Figure 13.1 is hymn number 459 from the hymnal, George C. Stebbins's "Fully Surrendered." The hymnal contains no fewer than 510 hymn texts by Western authors, as well as 517 hymn tunes either by Western composers or from Western sources. According to the survey's results, this hymnal is used not only by the Christian and Missionary Alliance congregations but also by many independent Churches and congregations of other denominations.[18] The 26 congregations that use *Hymns of Life* as their service hymnal include four Baptist, one Evangelical Free, and one Presbyterian. The case of the Presbyterian congre-

信徒生活—事奉獻身

完全的奉獻

Fully Surrendered

459

將身體獻上，當作活祭，是聖潔的，是神所喜悅的。 羅12:1

Offer your bodies as living sacrifices, holy and pleasing to God. Rom.12:1

FIGURE 13.1. "Fully Surrendered" in *Hymns of Life*

gation (more than 500 members) is particularly revealing. This church conducts three services every Sunday, one in Mandarin and two in Taiwanese. However, while the Mandarin service uses *Hymns of Life*, the Taiwanese service uses two separate hymnals: the Taiwanese hymnal *Sèng-si* (1965; contains Chinese hymn texts and romanized Taiwanese pronunciation of the texts; see fig. 13.2)[19] and *The Hymnbook* (1955). Occasionally, hymns will be selected from a third hymnal, *Grace Hymnal* (1981),[20] which has the Chinese and English hymn texts plus the romanized Taiwanese pronunciation.

When asked why the Mandarin congregation uses a different hymnal from the Taiwanese congregation, the church's minister replied that the cultural background of the two congregations is very different; many members of the Taiwanese congregations are first-generation immigrants who are used to the Taiwanese hymnal. Also, the translations of the hymn texts in the hymnal are meant to be sung in Taiwanese,[21] and are awkward to sing in Mandarin. According to the minister, the reason for the use of two hymnals in the Taiwanese services, one in Chinese and one in English, is that some members of the Taiwanese congregation speak Taiwanese but cannot read Chinese characters. These include Chinese from the Philippines, from Indonesia, and second-generation Taiwanese. The church, therefore, provides this group of Taiwanese-speaking members with *The Hymnbook*. In this case, when a hymn is sung from the Taiwanese hymnal, the same hymn has to be present in the English hymnal so that the two groups of members can sing together.[22] Since there are more and more members among the Taiwanese congregation who cannot read Chinese characters, the church is in the process of starting a separate English service. The minister expressed his hope that in the future the three services—Mandarin, Taiwanese, and English—would all use the same hymnal.

The other widely used bilingual hymnal is *Hymnody*, which consists primarily of American revivalist gospel songs. It used to be the service hymnal of many congregations now using *Hymns of Life*. Among its 591 hymns, *Hymnody* shares with *Hymns of Life* around 268 hymns (both tunes and texts).[23] For some of the congregations that have been using the former for years, replacement by the latter means a significant loss of familiar hymns coupled with a sharp increase in unfamiliar ones. A staff member from a Baptist congregation that had replaced its service hymnal, *Hymnody*, with *Hymns of Life* a few years ago, commented that the latter contains many hymns that they "do not know" and therefore they "have fewer hymns to sing now." However, the minister of another Baptist congregation that made the same replacement in 1987 states that the new hymns in the latter hymnal have not caused much difficulty because the parishioners sing "mostly the familiar hymns," just as they did with the former service hymnal.

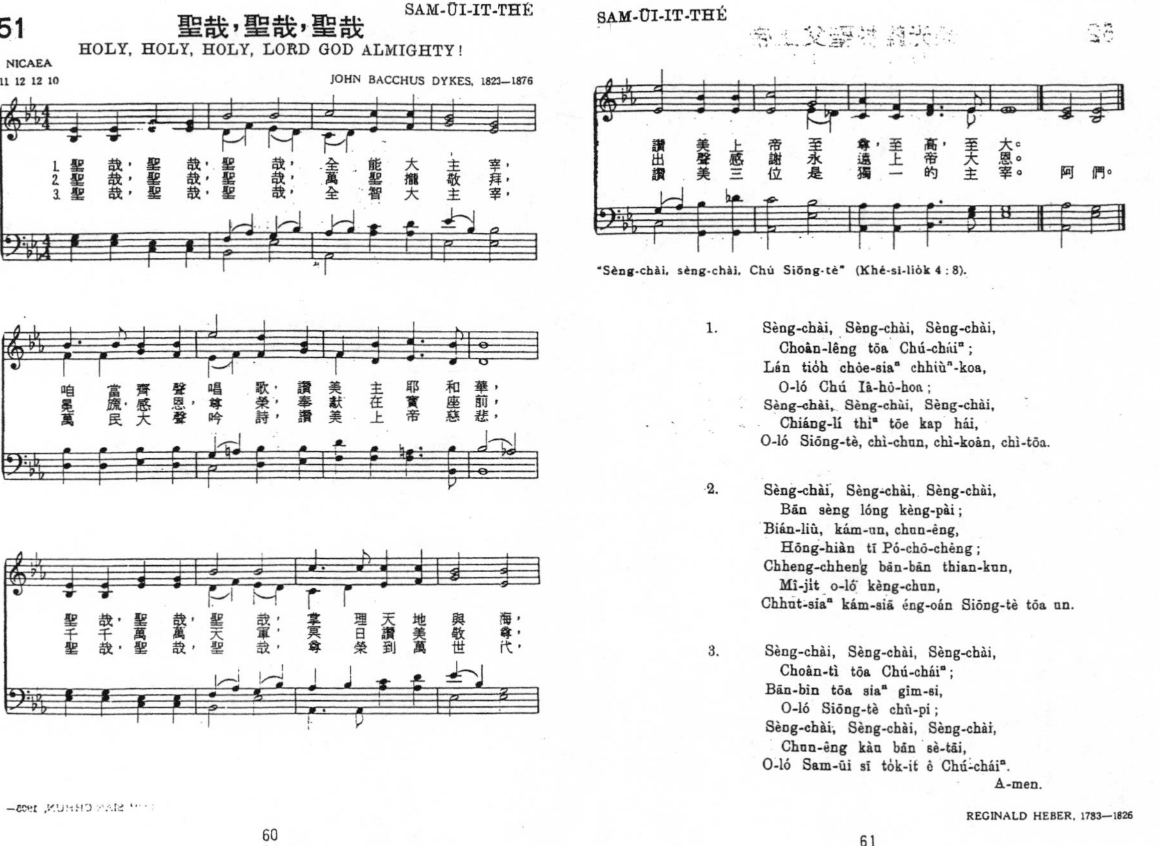

FIGURE 13.2. The Taiwanese hymnal *Sèng-si*

While it is hard to judge to what extent the Chinese services share a certain repertory of hymns or gospel songs, this picture of congregation hymnal use, suggests that perhaps it is more important to examine some of the factors that shape the congregations' hymn and song repertory sung by the congregations. First, while there are many English- or Chinese-only hymnals, there are still very few Chinese-English bilingual hymnals, in spite of the pressing need for them among Chinese American churches. One reason for this is the significantly increased time and effort required to produce a bilingual hymnal. The production of a Chinese-English bilingual hymnal, especially a service hymnal, requires not only specialized knowledge in music, theology, hymnology, and English poetry, but also a perfect command of the Chinese dialect involved. The selection of a bilingual hymnal for service use is usually further limited by other factors such as a particular congregation's cultural and denominational background.

The minister of a Christian Reformed congregation (not involved in the survey) explained to me that in choosing a hymnal for his congregation, he had to strike a balance between denominational theology and a good Chinese translation of the hymns. He had to choose between a hymnal that suited their denominational theology but not their linguistic practice and one that deviated from their denominational theology but better suited them linguistically. At the present time, having chosen the hymnal that has the better Chinese translations, he avoids using the hymns that do not suit their theological stance.

Second, in some congregations the repertory of service hymns can be seriously limited by the availability of musical resources, including proper musical leadership. Traditionally, musicians in Chinese American churches are volunteers from the congregation. Only two of the 66 congregations have full-time musicians, and five have part-time; the musicians in the remaining congregations are all volunteers. The larger congregations generally do not have problems finding volunteer musicians among their members: the larger the congregation, the more the volunteers. The smaller the congregation, the more difficult it is to find among its members a musician with the necessary skill to play in the service or to provide musical leadership for the congregation. Hence, some smaller congregations, particularly the newly established ones, often have to sing the service hymns without accompaniment.[24]

Third, perhaps the most fundamental factor influencing the service hymn repertory of Chinese American congregations is that, as a group, such churches typically do not emphasize denominational differences and affiliations. There are probably many reasons behind this phenomenon, which itself deserves a separate study. The large number of nondenominational or interdenominational churches certainly constitutes one of the reasons. It is estimated that as many as 50 percent of the roughly 800 Chinese congregations in the United States fall into this category.[25] The two largest denominations among Chinese churches in the United States are the Baptist and the Christian and Missionary Alliance Church.[26] In the nondenominational or interdenominational churches, denominational ties are very often either completely absent or subject to the training and leadership of the ministers. Under most circumstances, without a strong sense of denominational affiliation, the congregations tend to be more flexible regarding the style of worship and the choice of hymns.

Musical Styles of the English Services

The survey's results clearly indicate some general differences between the musical practices of the English-language and Chinese-language services. Stated simply, the singing of contemporary Christian songs with the accompaniment of guitars, drums, and other less traditional instruments is found more often in the English services than in the Chinese services. In a sense, this is perfectly understandable, for the members of the English congregations are mainly second-generation Chinese or younger foreign-born Chinese, who are used to contemporary popular music, from which contemporary Christian songs draw many of their musical characteristics. Accordingly, the members of English congregations are more familiar with the musical idiom of contemporary Christian songs than that of traditional hymns. Judging from the descriptions given by the staff members and ministers of some English congregations that have adopted such musical practices, it seems that their services are very much like what I observed in the English service at Chicago's Chinese Christian Union Church mentioned at the beginning of this chapter.

Although this impact is more noticeable in the English services, it is by no means absent from the Chinese services. In some congregations, the singing of contemporary Christian songs in Chinese, such as those in *New Songs Ringing*, is accompanied not only by various less traditional musical instruments, but also by clapping and other bodily movements—both of which are still rather uncommon among the Chinese congregations. Like the English congregations, these Chinese congregations sometimes also sing traditional hymns in the same way they sing contemporary Christian songs; the accompaniment patterns, instrumental combinations, and vocal technique completely transform the musical styles of the traditional hymns.

Singing contemporary Christian songs and using various media related to popular music in the worship service is certainly not unique to Chinese congregations; rather, as pointed out by Milburn Price (1993), it represents the strong impact of popular culture on Christian churches in general. The Chinese churches in the United States are subject to the same influences as other American churches. Also similar to the situation of American congregations, perhaps, is the fact that not all Chinese congregations are receptive to this trend. Some Chinese congregations are still reluctant to change their accustomed style of worship.[27]

In short, the musical styles and practices of contemporary Christian songs characterize some Chinese services to the same degree they characterize many of the English services. In both types of services, the average age of the membership seems directly related to the adoption of more contemporary musical styles. The younger the members, the more likely one is to find such musical styles and practices in the service. Furthermore, the musical styles of the hymns and songs sung in these services are not restricted to the music notated on the printed page; traditional hymns are often played and sung in the same style as contemporary Christian songs.

Personal Expression

Thus far, I have focused on the music of Sunday church services. Apart from attending the Sunday services, however, many members of the Chinese congregations are also active in a number of other church activities, such as Bible studies, prayer meetings, and fellowship meetings, in which hymns and songs are regularly sung. The survey shows that in more than half of the 66 congregations, the hymns sung at these activities are not from the service hymnals. This phenomenon suggests that the musical styles or expressions favored by some individual members could be quite different from those adopted by their congregation's corporate worship.

Understandably, the larger the congregation, the more difficult it is to incorporate the diverse musical preferences of all the individual members into the corporate worship. In comparison, at the meetings that involve fewer members, individual musical expression is usually better represented and personal musical expression is more prominent. Some of the hymns and songs sung at the church activities outside the service unmistakably reflect the cultural background of the individual members, especially the foreign-born. For example, some Cantonese-speaking members from Hong Kong will sing contemporary Cantonese Christian songs. The musical style of these songs is akin to that city's "Cantopop" style.

Conclusion

Upon surveying the contexts of music-making in the Chinese churches described above, three aspects deserve special attention. First, the linguistic diversity in each of the Chinese congregations is only part of the much greater sociocultural diversity among the members. The existence of services conducted in different dialects and languages is itself a means of negotiating this diversity. This kind of negotiation not only varies over time, but also often varies within the same congregation. For example, in some churches, Chinese from Mainland China, Chinese from Taiwan, and Chinese from Indonesia all have to attend the Mandarin service, while their church provides another service for the large number of Cantonese-speaking members. At other churches, the cultural differences among these three groups of Chinese are mediated by having a Mandarin service, a Taiwanese service, and an English service. Under such circumstances, while the Indonesian members can choose between the Taiwanese and the English services, the Cantonese-speaking members, who, supposedly, would be the minorities in this case, usually choose between the Mandarin and the English services.

The individual experiences underlying such negotiations can sometimes be rather intense. Yet a number of the people whom I interviewed indicated that adjusting to the language or other elements of a worship service was less problematic than adjusting to a worship service's particular musical expression. For them, the type of hymns and musical styles in a service often play a primary role in deciding which service to attend or even which church to join. Very often, one person's reason for choosing to attend a service may be another's reason for choosing not to attend. Either way, there are many reasons other than linguistic ties or shared geographical origin behind each decision. For example, Chinese who speak different dialects or even languages but share a common educational background or profession sometimes have the same interests or aesthetic preferences; as a result, they may be attracted to the musical styles of the same worship service. In other words, it is important to realize that besides linguistic ties and shared geographical origins, there are other factors that cut across these categorical distinctions within a Chinese congregation.

Second, in order to understand and appreciate the subtleties of the musical practices of Chinese congregations in the United States, it is necessary to have some knowledge about the musical traditions of the members' birthplaces. Most members of Chinese congregations in the United States are foreign-born

Chinese, who carry with them, to varying degrees, the aesthetics and musical practices of their countries of origin. Westernization in these countries, such as China, Hong Kong, Indonesia, the Philippines, and Taiwan, defies an essentialist view of what it means to be "Chinese." The Chinese in these countries do not listen only to their own, already westernized, traditional musics, they also listen to Western classical music and multiethnic popular music; all of these are part of their culture. At the same time, in many Asian countries, the Chinese churches have a long tradition of singing translated Western hymns. Hence most Chinese Christians, even the new members, do not consciously identify the hymns they sing as "Western."

There is, nonetheless, a marked distinction between the hymns of the Western churches and the translated hymns of the Chinese churches. Every translation involves interpreting or even transforming the "original meaning." Every translated Chinese hymn text is a union of some tradition of Christian expression and the cultural experiences embedded in the Chinese language. Within the realm of so-called orthodox interpretations, understanding of the Chinese hymn texts is constantly shaped by the ways in which these hymns are used and sung as well as by the multifarious discourses carried on in the life of the Chinese churches. As a result, in order to appreciate the values and meanings of the hymns for a particular Chinese congregation, one needs not only to know the necessary Chinese language and the dialects, but also to understand their congregational life.

Third, the musical aesthetics of the translated Chinese hymns are inseparable from the aural experience of the Chinese dialects. Many who regularly sing translated Chinese hymns or Christian songs, such as those in *New Songs Ringing*, speak English fluently and are able to appreciate the original English texts without any problem. They still choose, nonetheless, to sing the translated texts in the dialects they speak because, for them, the experience of singing in their own dialect is different from singing in English. The point can best be illustrated by the Cantonese dialect. As a tonal language, Cantonese has more tones than most other Chinese dialects; different characters bearing totally different meanings are often pronounced with the same sound but with different tones. To sing in Cantonese a Chinese song not intended to be sung in that dialect often results in serious tonal errors and, therefore, makes the lyrics aurally incomprehensible. To avoid the musical restrictions imposed by the dialect's tones, composition of Cantonese songs usually begins with the melody; when the melody is completed the lyrics are written in such a way that the Cantonese pronunciation of each word matches each musical pitch. Under these circumstances, the choice of words can be very limited; this makes the composition of lyrics difficult and creation of good lyrics even more demanding.

In the past, most hymns sung by the Cantonese-speaking congregations were translated into Chinese without considering their dialect's tones; hence, the hymns were generally very awkward for such congregations to sing. This issue has apparently received more attention in recent years. In *Hymns of Life*, for example, although tonal errors still exist when the hymns are sung in Cantonese, the errors are much less serious than in earlier hymnals.[28] For some Cantonese-speaking members among the Chinese congregations, nonetheless, especially the younger generations, a perfect match between the music and their dialect's tones is an essential part of their singing experience. In recent years, Christian songs have been composed particularly for the Cantonese dialect. The musical styles of the songs resemble those of Western popular songs and American contemporary Christian songs; hence, their aesthetic quality for the Cantonese speakers may easily be overlooked if one focuses only on the music instead of the union of music and dialect. That which constitutes a "good sing" for native Cantonese speakers is precisely the perfect union of music and the dialect in these songs. In short, the issue of the tones in the Cantonese dialect demonstrates that translated Chinese hymns—or, for that matter, original Chinese hymns in Western musical styles—should not be judged on the basis of the music alone. Each Chinese hymn should be viewed in its own right, that is, as the union of music and the Chinese language, or a particular dialect of that language.

Epilogue

I began this study with many assumptions about Chinese churches in the United States, even more than those mentioned in this chapter. Those assumptions, in light of Geertz's concepts of "experience-near" and "experience-far," reflected my relation as both "near" and "far" from the churches. Simply put, I was "near" because I was brought up within one of the Chinese Christian traditions.[29] I was also "far" for a number of reasons, one of which is the sheer diversity of the Chinese churches demonstrated in this chapter. Such diversity makes generalizations about the congregations extremely difficult.

One of my initial assumptions was that the question of what musical styles are appropriate for worship is much debated among Chinese congregations in the United States. One realizes this immediately upon reading discussions on the subject in some journals and magazines widely circulated among the congregations.[30] I soon suspended my own attempt to test this assumption, however, because the opinions I collected during the survey were too diverse to yield any fruitful discussion without further research. In fact, some of these opinions reflect the interplay of many underlying issues, such as the recognition of a musical canon, a Western concept, and the emphasis on keeping the tradition of the Church, which is also generally understood as Western. These factors also deserve in-depth study.

Another assumption that I only partially discuss here is the sharing of hymnals by the Chinese-language services. To test fully the assumption that these services use more or less the same repertory of Baptist and Methodist hymns as well as American evangelical songs, it is at least necessary first to obtain a list of the hymn texts and tunes common to the service hymnals mentioned in the survey and then subject it to further examination. While this task cannot be carried out here, comparisons between several Chinese-English bilingual hymnals and English hymnals would perhaps shed some light on why I held the assumption in the first place.

The significant role of Methodist hymns for the Chinese congregations can be illustrated by the fact that *Hymns of Life* shares 210 hymn texts with *The United Methodist Hymnal* (1989), whereas it has only 112 hymn texts in common with *The Hymnal 1982*, the hymnal of the Episcopal Church. These two statistics, however, are notably smaller in comparison with the 268 hymns shared between *Hymns of Life* (1986) and the other widely used Chinese-English bilingual *Hymnody*. Furthermore, the collections of hymns in both *Hymnody* and *Hymns of Life* are apparently quite different from those in the Taiwanese hymnal *Sèng-si* (1965), which is published in Taiwan and is the official hymnal of the Taiwanese Presbyterian Church in the United States. *Hymnody* shares with *Sèng-si* only 91 hymn texts; *Hymns of Life*, 116. In this respect, it is interesting to notice the difference between *Sèng-si* of the Taiwanese Presbyterian Church in the United States and the *Sin Sèng-si* of the Evangelical Formosan Church in the United States. The latter was first published in 1982 by the Evangelical Formosan Church in the United States and also has romanization of Taiwanese pronunciation of some hymn texts to meet the needs of the Taiwanese congregation members in this country.[31] Markedly different from *Sèng-si*, this new Taiwanese hymnal shares 216 hymn texts with *Hymnody* and 217 with *Hymns of Life*. Such data do seem to suggest that the Chinese-English bilingual hymnals used by certain Chinese congregations in the United States share a relatively large number of hymns.

In retrospect, some of my assumptions at the beginning of this study were rooted in the various ties I perceived between some Chinese congregations in the United States and those in Taiwan or Hong Kong, the two places I happen to know rather well. One of these ties comes unmistakably from the considerable number of immigrant Taiwanese and Hongkongese ministers whom I found serving congregations composed mainly of Taiwanese or Hongkongese immigrants. In visiting these congregations, I was often struck by how similar their worship services and community life were to what I was accustomed. Before long, however, the differences underlying the similarities came to the foreground.

As pointed out by some ministers I interviewed, unlike Chinese congregations in Hong Kong or Taiwan, those in the United States are ethnic minority groups; the Chinese churches often attract new Chinese immigrants as a kind of refuge, a place to pursue the community life they may otherwise lose. In light of this, regardless of the similarities between Chinese congregations in this country and those in Taiwan and Hong Kong, the different situations confronted by the former are easily conceivable. For example, the participation of second-generation members in the former will almost necessarily cause significant cultural diversity.[32] While the first-generation immigrants in a congregation often emphasize their differences from the rest of the community at large and hold on to certain Chinese traditions, the second generation readily identifies themselves as Americans and shares the dominant values of United States society.

There is, however, the saying that "what the son tries to forget, the grandson wants to remember." I have also encountered some second-, third-, and even fourth-generation members among the Chinese congregations who do not hesitate to call themselves "Chinese" and are also greatly interested in incorporating indigenous Chinese hymns into their worship. Under such circumstances, it seems that in trying to understand a "Chinese" congregation, one must also consider to what extent that congregation views itself as "Chinese."

While much more could be said about the music of Chinese congregations in the United States, and for that matter, about the congregations themselves, I hope that the picture of diversity presented here can provide some directions for further studies of their cultural complexity. Pluralism itself, moreover, is part of American society: Many of the issues raised above, as the contributors to the present volume witness, are not unique to Chinese congregations, but also characterize other ethnic communities in the United States. Viewed this way, the cultural diversity within Chinese churches presented by this chapter constitutes only one prominent aspect of the complex American religious experience.

NOTES

1. The space here does not allow me to thank individually all those who have helped me in this study—some of them will be duly mentioned in the course of the chapter. However, I am particularly indebted to Philip Bohlman, my thesis advisor, for his unyielding support at every stage of this study. I am also deeply thankful to Rev. Samuel Ling, Director of the China Horizon, for his full support in conducting the survey; without his help the survey would not have materialized. China Horizon provided all the necessary funding and logistics for the survey.

2. I got this impression early on in the study from the Chinese ministers I interviewed. They spoke unequivocally about *Hymns of Life* as a major hymnal among Chinese American congregations. The result of the questionnaire I conducted for this study supports what they said; see under the subheadings "Hymnals and Songbooks" and "A Common Repertory."

3. I thank Dr. Stephen Ng, former Director of the Information Department of the Chinese Coordination Center of World Evangelism in Hong Kong (CCCOWE-HK), for his advice in the early stage of this study. I also owe my special thanks to Leonard Man, former staff member of CCCOWE-HK and former Executive Editor of *Chinese Churches Today*, for providing me promptly with the materials I needed throughout this study.

4. The questionnaire was sent to 110 congregations in the United States. Conducted without a professional statistician, the survey was subject to various limitations. Be that as it may, the information and advice I received from experienced ministers and church leaders have greatly compensated for these limitations.

5. In a survey conducted by CCCOWE-US in 1990, for example, questionnaires were sent to 708 congregations in both the United States and Canada. Less than 20 percent of 139 congregations (89 in the United States, 34 in Canada) responded by returning their questionnaires (see CCCOWE 1991, 136). According to the opinions I gathered, various factors account for the low response rate. For example, some congregations received as many as three copies of the same questionnaire, each addressing a different church. At the same time, many questionnaires were incorrectly addressed and returned to the post office.

6. The survey is also partly intended to help understand the role of music among the Chinese congregations. Hence, the questionnaire also includes questions trying to understand what factors would inevitably shape a congregation's musical life. The factors comprise whether there is a person responsible for supervising the musical programs of the congregation, the status of that person (whether he or she is full-time, part-time, or volunteer), how far in advance the service hymns would be chosen, and so forth.

7. All percentages in this article are rounded to the nearest whole number.

8. See note 5.

9. Thus far, I have not succeeded in obtaining any official data about the number of independent Chinese churches. But the ministers and church leaders that I contacted stated unanimously that approximately 50 percent of Chinese American

churches are independent. Part of the difficulty in finding out or estimating the number of independent churches is that they are not registered by denominational offices and that most of them are not connected to organizations such as CCCOWE or the Ambassadors for Christ, Inc.

10. According to the opinions I gathered, the congregations that do not respond to surveys are generally the smaller ones with a membership of fewer than 100, or even fewer than 50. While these congregations are usually understaffed, leaving the ministers too busy to fill out the questionnaires, it is also possible that the ministers may want to avoid revealing the "unsatisfactory" situation (poor attendance or lack of staff) at their congregations.

11. There are two congregations, however, that have services in other languages: Vietnamese and Spanish. In both cases, the non-Chinese congregations are said to be independent from the Chinese congregations; the Chinese congregation and the non-Chinese congregations are connected only by denominational affiliation—the non-Chinese service is part of the denominational mission program. In addition, there are three Taiwanese congregations that use the Fokien dialect in their services.

12. This is the hymnal of the Evangelical Formosan Church. The title exists only in Chinese although it is a bilingual hymnal (i.e., English and Chinese); the English translation of the title is mine.

13. This is a bilingual hymnal published by the Baptist Press in Hong Kong and is the hymnal of the Baptist Church of Hong Kong.

14. Among the other hymnals and song collections, there is one that was first published in 1937 in China, and some others were published in the 1950s and 1960s in other Asian countries.

15. The practice of designating a person to lead the singing of the congregational hymns in the service is common in Chinese churches.

16. One congregation did not answer the question.

17. Parenthetically, the three congregations that have only one Sunday service conducted in one language or dialect all have memberships of fewer than 100. One of them is a congregation of mostly American-born Chinese; however, while their service is in English, they provide a Sunday service in Chinese for the foreign-born Chinese members.

18. According to the opinions of some church leaders, the popularity of the hymnal, in the United States at least, is due to both proper timing and design. On the one hand, when the hymnal first appeared in 1986, not only was there an increasing demand for bilingual hymnals among the Chinese congregations, but also the several bilingual hymnals then existing were already deemed dated. On the other hand, the hymnal consists of hymns related to a variety of Christian themes and occasions, making it more suitable for corporate worship. Also, it seems that the "Worship Resources" (doxology, responsories, etc.) and scriptural excerpts at the end of the hymnal are useful for many congregations, especially the independent churches that, without specific liturgies, have to design the services themselves. *Hymns of Life* is also used by the Chinese congregations in Canada, Latin America, England, Taiwan, Australia, Austria, and Africa. I thank Dr. Daniel Law, Senior Lecturer at the Music De-

partment of the Chinese University of Hong Kong, for providing me with this information.

19. *Sèng-si* is the hymnal of the Presbyterian Church in Taiwan, the largest denomination there.

20. The hymnal was prepared in the Philippines and contains more than 1,000 hymns. In addition to the Chinese and English hymn texts, the romanization of the Taiwanese pronunciation of the Chinese texts is also provided.

21. The Taiwanese dialect, also known as Minnan dialect, is originally the dialect from the southern part of Fujian province, which is on the coast of China right across the Taiwan Strait.

22. *Sèng-si* and *The Presbyterian Hymnal* share 149 hymn texts.

23. In addition to the different musical settings of the Amen and doxology, some hymn texts are sung to more than one hymn tune.

24. There are also congregations that sing along with hymns recorded on cassette tapes.

25. See note 10.

26. This includes Southern Baptist and American Baptist congregations.

27. Asked if contemporary Christian songs and related musical practices are used in his congregation, one Chinese minister commented that his congregation was relatively "conservative" and that they did not use the guitar for accompanying hymns either.

28. While the translations in some major Chinese-English bilingual hymnals published in recent years obviously take the pronunciations of both Mandarin and Cantonese into consideration, priority is usually given to the former since it is the official language of mainland China, and is considered the lingua franca samong Chinese.

29. I am a native Hongkongese and was brought up in a Christian family.

30. For example, there was an exchange of views on contemporary Christian music between Rev. Joshua Law (1991) and Rev. Samuel Ling (1991). The whole issue of *Chinese Churches Today* 171 (1993) was devoted to the discussion of "sacred music," in which there were discussions about "gospel rock" as well as the "sacredness" and "profanity" of music.

31. *Sèng-si* means "hymns"; *Sin Sèng-si* means "new hymns." (I am grateful to David Yang of the Board of Directors of the Evangelical Formosan Church in the United States for helping me obtain information about the publishers of the two Taiwanese hymnals.)

32. Cultural differences between first generation immigrants and their children, however, are by no means absent in Chinese churches in Taiwan, Hong Kong, or other Asian countries. In our Lutheran congregation in Hong Kong, for example, my parents are immigrants who arrived in the city from the northern provinces in 1949. As first-generation immigrants from northern China, they speak Mandarin and always differentiate themselves from the Cantonese speaking Hongkongese. I am one of the second-generation members, having attended the same congregation with my parents since I was born. The cultural difference between the first- and second-

generations in our congregation is also expressed in the simultaneous use of at least two dialects, Mandarin and Cantonese, in our worship service.

WORKS CITED

Chinese Coordination Center of World Evangelism. 1993.

Chinese Churches Today 171. Hong Kong.

———. *Diaspora Chinese Church–North America.* vol. 5. Hong Kong: CCCOWE. Prepared and edited by Research Department, Chinese Coordination Centre of World Evangelism.

———. 1993. *Diaspora Chinese Church–North America.* Hong Kong: CCCOWE. Prepared and edited by Research Department Chinese Coordination Centre of World Evangelism.

Grace Hymnal. 1981. *Grace Hymnal* (*Ling hui sheng shi*). Chinese and English, with Amoy romanization. Quezon City, Philippines; Rockville, Md.; Ling hui jidu jiao hui.

The Hymnal 1982. 1982. *The Hymnal 1982: According to the Use of the Episcopal Church.* New York: Church Publications.

The Hymnbook. 1955. *The Hymnbook.* New York: Presbyterian Church in the United States.

Hymns of God's People. 1985. *Hymns of God's People.* Alhambra, Calif.: First Evangelical Church Association.

Hymns of Life. 1986. *Hymns of Life.* Hong Kong: China Alliance Press.

New Hymnal (Sin Sèng-si). 1991. New Hymnal (*Sin Sèng-si*). Revised edition. El Monte, Calif.: EFC Communication Center.

New Songs of Praise. 1988. *New Songs of Praise.* Bilingual version. Hong Kong: Baptist Press.

Law, Joshua. 1991. "A Closer Look at Christian Music." *Challenger* 30 (July 1991): 1–4.

Ling, Samuel. 1991. "The Discussion Continues . . ." *Challenger* 30 (7): 1–5.

———. 1991. "Reaching the Total Person with Contemporary Music." *Challenger* 30 (April 1991): 1–3.

Praise. n.d. *Praise.* (Purple Books). Costa Mesa, Calif.: Nashville, Tenn.: Maranatha! Music.

Price, Milburn. 1993. "The Impact of Popular Culture on Congregational Song." *The Hymn* 44: 11–18.

Sèng-si. 1965. *Sèng-si.* Ed. by Sid Hormell. Hymns in Taiwanese dialect. Taipei: Taiwan Presbyterian Church.

The United Methodist Hymnal. 1989. *The United Methodist Hymnal.* Nashville, Tenn.: The United Methodist Publishing House.

Worship Songs of the Vineyard. 1991. *Worship Songs of the Vineyard* Anaheim, Calif.: Vineyard Ministries International.

14

"Tuned Up with the Grace of God": Music and Experience among Old Regular Baptists

Jeff Todd Titon

About ten years ago, I played a field tape recording of Old Regular Baptist singing for a classical music composer friend of mine. Seventy voices arose more or less together as the eastern Kentucky group gave out a highly elaborated, folk hymn melody with no discernible pulse beat in an unaccompanied, heterophonic singing style at least four centuries old. "Of course they have a conductor," he said. "No," I said, "actually they don't." "Then how do they stay together?" he asked. How, indeed? This is the problem of rhythm in their music. How they solve it is the subject of this chapter. My thesis is that while their familiarity with the melodies helps, it is not a sufficient cause. Rather, a commonly experienced spirituality accounts for their musical integration.

A visit to an Old Regular Baptist church would not help my friend to sing along very much better. First, he would not be able to follow the tune in a hymnal, because the congregation is not provided with songbooks. (Old Regular Baptists speak of a "song," not a "hymn.") A few songbooks are kept in the churches for the songleaders (always male), but these contain words only; the tunes are remembered and live in oral tradition. He might catch the words from the songleader, who would, as the Old Regulars say, "give them out." In Old Regular Baptist practice, giving out a song (or "lining out," as scholars call it), is a type of antiphony (call and response) in which songleaders sing each line of verse fairly rapidly (about three to four seconds) to let the congregation know the words. Then the congregation joins the leader to repeat the words just sung, very slowly (about 16 to 21 seconds) but to a tune different from the lining tune. Secondly, because the melodies are melismatic—that is, most syllables of text occupy two or more melody notes (see fig. 14.1)—he would not be able understand the placement of the syllables. And because the melodies are so elaborate, he would have difficulty recalling them as they repeat from one stanza to the next. But third and most important, the rhythm would continue to befuddle him, for there is no instrumental accompaniment, no regular pulse beat is apparent, and no signal indicates when to move to the next tone. No doubt my composer friend tried to sing along in his mind with the tape recording, found himself flummoxed, and determined that they must have a conductor.

This seemingly technical musical problem—how do they stay together?—raises a difficult issue concerning knowledge of religious behavior: When competing explanations exist, how can one decide which is best? It might seem as if the best explanation for the group's musical integration would be familiarity over a long period of time. Indeed, Old Regular Baptists sing these songs (without conductor or accompanist) in church and at home, often over a period of many years.

This kind of explanation (they sing well together because they sing together often) typifies the research approach of a social scientist, who, using Occam's razor, would dispense with any religious explanation which the singers might give, on the grounds that if it were not needed, we should give it no credence. In college that point was driven home to me by a physics professor who enjoyed playing devil's advocate with the students: We were to ask him what caused friction, and he explained and elaborated what he called the "demon theory of friction." For the sake of argument he claimed that tiny demons on the peripheries of objects caused friction. Why, then, do objects slide more easily when oiled? Oil drowns demons, he replied. When sandpapered? Sandpapering squishes them. Why do objects slide more easily on ice? Demons slip on ice. And so on. He could find an after-the-fact explanation for any question we might have, and we could not show him wrong except by applying Occam's razor: A demon theory was simply not necessary in order to explain friction. The obvious, but never stated, analogy was to explanations of events on the basis of myth or religion: Science did not traffic in that kind of nonsense.

Yet just that kind of explanation enables one fully to understand how and why Old Regular Baptists sing in so integrated a way. It is not just that they "practice" but also their inner religious experience that enables this musical integration. (Lack of "practice" fails to explain those times when they do not, in fact, sing well together. The same group may sing well one Sunday but not a month later.) What they think ought to happen during a singing—the Christian belief they should be of one mind and accord in worshiping God—acts to empower them toward that end and bring it about. And when one does not feel right, he or she sometimes refrains from singing.

Furthermore, like others who take a phenomenological approach to human behavior, I claim that we can find our most satisfying knowledge if our goal is not just explaining behavior but also understanding experience. To understand people's experience we must pursue their ideas about it, even though scholars involved in the "scientific study of religion" would allege that this pursuit is peripheral. Of course, understanding Old Regular Baptist musical experience requires background on their history and music, and I offer that in the first two of the following sections. In the last section I take up this specific case of musical integration in detail.

The Old Regular Baptists

Approximately fifteen thousand members comprise about three hundred Old Regular Baptist churches, the vast majority located in the mountain areas of southeastern Kentucky and southwestern Virginia, the heart of the coal mining country of Appalachia. Another fifteen thousand or so attend those churches but are not currently members. Although confined to a small geographical region, these churches are prominent within it. Each Old Regular Baptist church is a part of a larger Association, of which there are fifteen: Union, New Salem, Thornton Union, Indian Bottom, Old Indian Bottom, Sardis, Old Friendship, Philadelphia, Northern New Salem, Mud River, Bethel, Kyova, two Mountain Associations, and Mountain Liberty (Dorgan 1989, 8–12). Most of my fieldwork with Old Regular Baptists has been among people in the Indian Bottom Association. In typical Baptist fashion, many of these associations do not agree entirely in points of doctrine and practice, and therefore they are not "in correspondence" or fellowship with other associations.

Nonetheless, the Old Regular Baptist associations are in agreement over key matters of doctrine, matters that will emerge from the following brief historical sketch.[2] Old Regular Baptists began calling themselves that late in the nineteenth century; before that they were United Baptists; before that, "Particular" (Calvinist) Baptists. In their orientation and doctrine they maintain much of the Reformation's Calvinist wing, while giving the human will a greater role than Calvin allowed. Additionally, many aspects of American frontier revivalism have been grafted into Old Regular Baptist belief and practice. Finally, Old Regular Baptists share with other conservative Baptist denominations an opposition to benevolent organizations and other worldly church involvements.

Early Baptist theology was Calvinistic, emphasizing God's sovereignty and humankind's depravity. "Calvin's Institutes of the Christian Religion (1536)," writes theologian John Wallhausser,

> became the work that organized the Protestant Reformation. God is revealed—so said the Institutes—in both nature and reason. But since the Fall from grace into sin, humans are unable to 'read' the testimony to God present in this general revelation. Scripture is given as a particular revelation in which God's will is made clear. Since the Fall of Adam all humankind has become impotent to do the will of God and stands outside the community of God. . . . God has ordained a plan of redemption through the divine decree of election and reprobation, a 'double predestination,' singling out both the elect and the damned. The elect, without merit on their part, find it possible to do God's will by grace. The church consists of those called to redemption (membership known only to God). Members involve themselves in civic and political life as citizens of their community. (unpublished manuscript portion of the notes accompanying Cornett, Titon, and Wallhausser 1997)

Debates among seventeenth-century Baptists divided them into "Particular" (Calvinist) and "General" (Arminian) camps. The Particular embraced Calvin's doctrine of predestination while the Arminan reacted strongly against it. The latter adopted the teachings of the Dutch theologian Jacob Arminius, arguing that God had not predetermined an elect ("limited atonement") but that any individual's will was free to work with God's will and accept or reject redemption ("general atonement"). Most Particular Baptists migrated to the northern English Colonies in seventeenth-century America, General to the southern Colonies.

The First Great Awakening further split these Baptists into "Separates" (who approved of the experiential emphasis and took part in the revivals) and "Regulars" who did not. Late in the eighteenth century in Virginia and North Carolina they combined into "United" Baptists, a union effected in Kentucky in 1801 on the eve of the Cane Ridge Revival and the Second Great Awakening. Nineteenth-century Baptist developments in the United States, which included a split over slavery into northern and southern wings, and the eventual emergence of the two large groups that would become the Southern Baptists and the American Baptists, moved in a liberal and progressive direction.

This provoked a conservative reaction among some Baptists, who, as a result, formed their own alliances. In the southern Appalachian Mountains, or "Appalachia" as the region is popularly known today, "Old School" ("Primitive") Baptists split from the Uniteds in the 1830s, while other churches and associations returned to the name "Regular." To complicate this further, in 1845 Kentucky's New Salem Association, originally formed in 1825 from the Burning Spring Association, changed its name from United to Regular, and in 1870 to Old Regular Baptist (Perrigan 1961, 127). Meanwhile Burning Spring became Primitive. These conservative denominations opposed the Sunday school and mission movements, and retained the Calvinism of the 1707 Confession of Faith of the Philadelphia Association (the first Baptist cooperative body in the Colonies). But continued debate over predestination led to further division and realignment, and while the Primitive Baptists maintained Calvin's doctrine of double predestination, Old Regulars moved in the direction of general atonement.

The Indian Bottom Association of Old Regular Baptists is a group of twenty-six churches in Letcher, Knott, and Perry Counties in southeastern Kentucky. The original Indian Bottom church, located in Letcher County not far from the town of Blackey, was founded in 1810 as a member of the Burning Spring Association, later becoming a member of New Salem. In 1876 New Salem declared itself in "non-fellowship with all modern institutions called benevolent; such as missionary, Bible and tract societies, Sunday-school Union and Masonry and all societies set on foot by men, whether secret or open, religious or political, outside the word of God" (ibid., 48).

Thereupon nine dissenting churches, including the Indian Bottom church, organized the Sandlick Association. It is not clear whether they established any "modern benevolent institutions"; if so, none has lasted. In 1896 the Sandlick Association, riven over the doctrine of predestination, split into a predestinarian group, which retained the name Sandlick Association, and a group that believed in general atonement and, meeting at the same Indian Bottom church, formed the Indian Bottom Association (ibid., 332). In 1960 the Indian Bottom Association split into the more conservative Old Indian Bottom Association and another, larger group that retained the name Indian Bottom Association.

The latter (the group I have most closely followed) consists of thirty churches and approximately 2,000 members, with another 1,500 or so attendees who likely will become members some day. Church membership usually is entered into as an adult, often (particularly for men) in middle age. Although Old Regulars believe that those who know the Lord should belong to a church, and certainly they encourage it in their communities, they also believe that it is not necessary to be a church member in order to be a child of God; and it is not unusual for people to attend church for several years before taking on the responsibilities of membership.

Old Regular Baptist doctrine today retains the Calvinist emphasis on God's sovereignty, unmerited grace, and the divine plan of redemption; but it rejects predestination and declares a general atonement. Article 16 of the Indian Bottom Association's Articles of Faith reads: "None of the above articles shall be construed as to hold with particular election or reprobation as to make God partial directly or indirectly so as to injure children of man."[3] Salvation is open to all, and a person's will is free to accept or reject it. Thus the Old Regular Baptists insist upon this limited role of the human will in salvation, and maintain, "God does the saving."

Furthermore, Old Regular Baptists, unlike Freewills and other Baptist denominations of a more Arminian persuasion, retain the Calvinist doctrine of the perseverance of the saints: that a person truly redeemed will not, cannot, "backslide" or lose his or her salvation (Article 6: "We believe in the perseverance of the saints."). A person cannot, therefore, be assured that he or she is saved; the most that one can have is a "hope" of redemption. At times, however, that hope becomes stronger, as when singing in church awakens the indwelling Spirit and provides them with a glimpse of what heaven will be like (Wallhausser 1983).

A cluster of other conservative traits for which they claim a basis in Scripture characterizes Old Regular Baptist practice (Dorgan 1989, 6–8). Some of these are shared by other Baptist denominations in Appalachia (see Titon 1988; Dorgan 1988). For example, each church observes communion but once a year, in the summertime; and besides taking the bread (unleavened, baked by the sisters) and wine, foot washing is practiced as an ordinance (John 13:14). Taking off their shoes and socks, and using water, basins, and towels, men kneel at the feet of other men, and women at the feet of other women, washing one another's feet in an act of humility and reconciliation which, among other things, becomes in effect a sacrament and powerfully bonds families and friends within this community.

As in many conservative Baptist denominations that follow Pauline teachings, women are denied certain leadership roles: They are not permitted to preach, to lead songs, or to speak out in church business meetings. (Of course, they make their opinions known to one another and to the male members of their families, and thereby they are represented at these meetings even though they maintain silence in them.) Men are to rule their households; disputes between church members should be settled by the church, not in civil court; divorce, except on grounds of adultery, is considered wrong; men should keep their hair short and women should let theirs grow long and avoid dressing in men's clothing (pants). In daily life, of course, women do take on leadership roles, and they deal with the patriarchal heritage by gently making fun of the men when they fail.[4]

Many of the practices of Old Regular Baptists are the result of eighteenth- and nineteenth-century developments on the American frontier. For example, their preaching delivery is a legacy of the intoned, spontaneous preaching of the First Great Awakening and the styles of preachers such as Whitefield and Davenport. To an outsider it appears that Old Regular Baptist preaching is chanted in a singing voice. Old Regulars are careful not to make this chant a necessary and sufficient condition of good or effective preaching, or to say that this delivery is an infallible sign of inspiration. Nevertheless, it often appears to be so, and young preachers hope to acquire it. Another Old Regular Baptist legacy of the Great Awakenings is the pietist emphasis upon personal experience and the theme of regeneration, or being "born again."

Yet other traits of the Old Regulars today arose a century ago in an effort to resist innovations such as mission societies and Sunday schools. Like the Primitive Baptists, Old Regular Baptists have neither. They believe in bringing the gospel to others, and indeed their sermons urge the unsaved to answer God's call and repent; but they do not wish to divert their energies from congregational responsibility to outside professional agencies. And their distrust of radio and television evangelism springs from the same impulse. Without Sunday schools, youngsters sit near their parents, and are free to move quietly about the sanctuary, sometimes making trips to the altar as the service progresses to get a drink from the water cooler or a piece of hard candy wrapped in cellophane.

Churches hold worship services once a month: a business meeting and short service on Saturday, and a fuller service on Sunday morning. This does not mean, however, that an Old Regular attends church only once every month: He or she attends the home church on its regular weekend services, and then visits any of several nearby Old Regular Baptist churches on the other three. This constant visiting strengthens the community beyond the confines of any single congregation. A typical Sunday morning service begins as people arrive between 9 and 9:30 A.M., walk into the sanctuary, and shake hands with everyone—and I do mean everyone—who is already there. Frequent handshaking and embracing are striking features of Old Regular Baptist fellowship. At 9:30 one of the elders will line out a song and the rest will join in. Other elders will follow, lining songs of their choice, or as requested informally by members of the congregation.

There is no program indicating an order of service and who will lead the songs, what their titles are, who will preach, and on what topic and Scripture passages; the elders informally arrange these elements as the service progresses. Yet because there is no program and things appear to run spontaneously, it would be incorrect to deduce that there is no liturgy (see Wallhausser 1983). The order of worship is clearly understood by the congregation, and it follows the same pattern every Sunday. After a half hour of singing, the moderator (elected head) of the church appoints one of the elders to "open" the service by preaching a short sermon. The moderator arranges the preachers in order of preaching experience (least experienced to most), but no one knows prior to the service exactly which preaching brothers will attend, and visiting preachers are almost always given preference when, at 10 A.M., the moderator asks who is willing to try to preach. All sermons are spontaneous and led by the Spirit. No preacher relies on a printed manuscript or brings one to the pulpit. If a preacher does not feel the Spirit after a couple of moments, he sits down. After five or ten minutes the first preaching brother closes, a leader gives out a song, the congregation stands, and everyone shakes hands with their neighbors. At the close of the second or third stanza, an appointed elder sinks to his knees and improvises and intones a prayer, often for two or three minutes, in which he not only thanks God but also asks God's help for the nation's political leaders as well as the church community, and mentions by name several of those within that community who are in need of special help (typically because they are seriously ill). Next, anywhere from three to five elders preach, seriatim, each sermon preceded by a song. At the close of the last sermon, an elder lines out a song, the congregation joins in, stands, and shakes hands, and a collection is taken up. At this point, the church is formally open for nonmembers to become members on the basis of their testimony or by letter if transferring from another church. Afterwards an elder gives a closing prayer, announcements of upcoming meetings at other churches are given out, the moderator makes whatever closing remarks are needed, and the service is over, usually between noon and 12:15 P.M. Altogether, singing has taken up about 60 of the service's 150 minutes.

Music among Old Regular Baptists

Like almost all Christian hymns, Old Regular Baptist congregational songs consist of rhymed, metrical verse in a series of stanzas to which a repeating tune is set. The metrical verse patterns include common meter (alternating lines of 8 and 6 syllables; i.e., 8,6,8,6, and represented in their songbooks by C. M.); long meter (represented by L. M.—8,8,8,8); short meter (or S. M.—6,6,8,6) and various others. The leader sings the very first line and the congregation joins in when they recognize the song. After that the song proceeds line by line: The leader briefly chants a line alone, and then the group repeats the words but to a tune that is much longer and more elaborate than the leader's chant or lining tune. Congregational singing is not the only kind of singing to be heard in Old Regular Baptist worship services. In the Indian Bottom Association, it is now customary for a preaching brother (preacher) to sing, or lead a song, before preaching. He may line one out, or he may just lead one without lining. Sometimes he sings a solo gospel song instead, or a duet with his wife, prior to his sermon.

Old Regular Baptist songbooks are kept only at the altar, for song leaders' use. The songs are printed with their words but no music. The oldest lyrics are the eighteenth-century hymns, written chiefly by familiar English or American devotional poets and hymnwriters such as Isaac Watts. These fill their two favorite songbooks, the collections *Sweet Songster* (Billups 1854) and the *Thomas Hymnal* (E. Thomas 1877). The newer songbooks, including *Some of Our Favorite Songs* (Smith 1988), *The New Baptist Song Book* (Conley 1989), and the *Old Regular Baptist Song Book* (Osborne 1989) (now the *Baptist Hymn Book* [Osborne 1991]) are contemporary collections published nearby. These newer songbooks contain a mix of the older hymns, nineteenth-century camp meeting songs and spirituals, gospel hymns from the later nineteenth century onwards, and finally a number of contemporary gospel songs—some written by Old Regulars known to have this gift, others popular on the radio and recordings. The singers catch the words from the song leader as he lines out the song. They know their favorites by heart.

In general, Old Regulars choose songs that emphasize God's sovereignty (e.g., "Guide Me O Thou Great Jehovah") and humankind's depravity ("O Ye Young, Ye Gay, Ye Proud"). They also sing those that speak of the Christian's personal relationship with Jesus. Although they chose some that offer a glimpse of heaven ("On Jordan's Stormy Banks I Stand") they neither dwell on a heavenly homecoming reunion, nor do they choose gospel songs centered on "Mother." Not all the songs in these books fit well with Old Regular Baptist theology, and therefore the sung repertory is not coextensive with the songbook repertory. As a result, no accurate conclusions about Old Regular Baptist beliefs could be drawn from a content analysis of the entire body of lyrics in their hymnals. This should be a caution to those students of American religious history who would perform gospel song content analysis on hymnals in order to attempt to understand nineteenth-century popular religion (for examples see Bruce 1974; Sizer 1978).

The tunes that go with the Old Regular Baptist songs are passed along from one singer, one generation to the next. Singers learn by following and imitating others, not by reading notes. The elaborate melodies are melismatic: Some syllables carry three or more tones. About one-third fall in major keys; the rest are pentatonic, gapped, natural minor, dorian, or mixolydian. The pentatonic lacking scale degrees 2 and 6 is the most frequent for the older hymns; the fourth degree is prominent. Melodic elaborations that emphasize a shift from tonic to subtonic are striking and characteristic, and they reveal these melodies' kinship with, and descent from, the traditional music of Ireland, lowlands Scotland, and the northern English borderlands.

Some of these tunes are quite old. The tune used for both "Guide Me O Thou Great Jehovah" and "Every Moment Brings Me Nearer," for example, can be traced to "Adew Dundee" in the Skene manuscript (ca. 1620; Dauney 1973 contains a reprint of the manuscript). Others are more recent compositions in the same folksong style. Some tunes, such as those for "Salvation O the Name I Love" and "The Day Is Past and Gone," are clearly related to tunes that were printed in nineteenth-century shape-note hymnals: the former to a tune usually called "Bourbon" and the latter to "Idumea." But this does not mean that the Old Regulars' songs came at some point in the past from those printed versions, for in many instances the book tunes were written down from melodies in oral tradition. More likely, the Old Baptists were already singing the tunes before the editors of nineteenth-century shape-note hymnals wrote them down.

Newer tunes are either adaptations of gospel hymn tunes ("Precious Memories," for example, done in a lined-out format) or compositions by local and regional song writers that draw on the resources of all available melodic traditions. Each singer is free to "curve" the tune a little differently, and those who are able to make it more elaborate are admired. Outsiders are mistaken if they think the intent is singing with unified precision and that the result falls short; on the contrary, the singing is in step and deliberately just a bit out of phase—and this, I think, is one of its most powerful musical aspects.

Music historian Nicholas Temperley writes that the Old Regular Baptist practice of lining-out derives from the music of the sixteenth-century English parish church (1981, 511–44). In 1644 the Westminster Assembly of Divines, appointed by Cromwell's Parliament, recommended the practice of lining out, and it was adopted in Massachusetts a few years later. By the end of the seventeenth century it had become the "common way of singing" among Anglicans and in other Protestant denominations (Lutherans excepted) throughout Britain and her colonies (see Chase 1987, 19–30). African Americans learned it and carry a parallel tradition today, particularly among Baptists in the rural South.

As the great wave of settlers moved during the eighteenth and early nineteenth centuries into the frontier South, to the Shenandoah Valley and later across the Cumberland Gap, they carried the "common way" (now called "the old way") of singing with them. The majority of Appalachian settlers from the English/Scottish borderlands were familiar with this form of music, for it had persisted there well into the eighteenth century after it had begun to decline in the southern parts of England and the more urban parts of the new American nation.

Undoubtedly the new texts called for new tunes, and the Old Baptists did what many had done before: They used well-known secular tunes and composed other, similar-sounding tunes to carry the sacred texts. Nineteenth-century camp meetings gave rise to spiritual songs—usually easily sung, rapid choruses with refrains; but the more conservative Old Baptist ancestors of the Old Regulars clung to the old ways in singing as well as other aspects of church life, resisting missions, Sunday schools, and other progressive developments while they held fast against Arminianism. Another musical novelty that the Old Regulars resisted was musical notation in shaped notes, a reform designed to teach people to sing by reading notes and to drive out the "old way of singing." Shaped notes spread via singing schools from New England to Appalachia and the South in the nineteenth century and were featured in such prominent hymn collections as the *Southern Harmony* (Walker 1835) and *The Sacred Harp* (1844), and in various gospel hymn collections from the late nineteenth century onward.

While the shape-note collections, which printed music in parts (harmony) and discouraged lining out, influenced some of the Old Regulars' Appalachian neighbors, such as the Primitive Baptists, who have now lost lining out probably beyond recovery, the greatest challenge to "the old way of singing" among the Old Regulars today comes from the gospel songs on radio and recordings. Some of the churches have succumbed to part-singing and many include a far higher percentage of gospel hymnody, but in the Indian Bottom Association most remain steadfast in keeping the older hymns lined out.

Because folksong collectors in Appalachia have overwhelmingly pursued secular ballads, scholarship in religious music has suffered from neglect. The standard, if overly simple, definition of a folk hymn, as a tune that lives in oral tradition to which a written religious text is set, had not been formulated early in the twentieth century, when Appalachian religious folk song came to the attention of researchers. In the first third of the twentieth century, folklorists sought Negro spirituals, old British carols, and religious ballads, not hymns.

Among the first writers to bring lined-out hymnody to the attention of outsiders was the author, Kentucky native, and folk festival promoter Jean Thomas. In *Devil's Ditties* (a book devoted chiefly to secular music, as the title suggests) she described lined-out hymnody and printed a bit of it in musical notation; but her description was incorrect in a few important particulars—for example, she described a woman song leader (women are forbidden to lead songs)—and the point of view of her narrative was limited by the conventions of local color writing that she embraced in her work (Thomas 1931, 20–22). George Pullen Jackson, the pioneer scholar of folk hymnody in the United States, seems not to have paid attention to Thomas's earlier work. Jackson's research concentrated on the nineteenth-century shape-note songbooks and their continuing uses in the twentieth century. He mistakenly thought that lining out had disappeared long ago. But that did not deter Thomas. An unpublished 1930s Kentucky WPA collection, which she supervised, contains melodies (although without the lining written in) for several folk hymns in the Old Baptist (i.e., Old Regular Baptists, Primitive Baptists, and United Baptists) repertory in the mountains (Thomas et al. n.d.). Partly through Thomas's festival and her promotion of Appalachian folk culture, a small number of other folk-song collectors active in the 1930s and 1940s, most notably Alan Lomax, became aware of the mountain religious folksong tradition, and recorded a small amount of it—again, in the singers' homes, as part of their individual repertories, and without the lining. No doubt the bulky recording equipment would have been impossible to operate in a church without disturbing the service, but also, in folklorists' conventional wisdom of the time (a convention which Thomas opposed), it was the song that was important, not the singer or context.

The folksinger Jean Ritchie wrote about lined hymn-singing in her marvelous autobiography, *Singing Family of the Cumberlands* (1955); and lined hymn from her family's home church in Jeff (Perry County), Kentucky was issued on a record album, *The Ritchie Family of Kentucky*, not long afterward (Ritchie 1959). John Cohen also collected some lined hymnody at the church in Jeff, and a selection was issued on *Mountain Music of Kentucky* (1960). His film, *The High Lonesome Sound*, features some of this Old Regular Baptist singing on its sound track (1963). In a 1959 music-collecting survey throughout the South, Alan Lomax stopped off and recorded a service at one of their churches, in Blackey—his visit is still recalled among the church members; and a few selections (lined hymns and an excerpt from a sung sermon) were published on albums for folk music enthusiasts (see Lomax n.d., 1977).

Activity picked up in the 1960s when it became plain to music scholars that the old way of singing from the American colonies had survived in central Appalachia. After hearing one of the Lomax recordings, William Tallmadge spent two summers recording music in eastern Kentucky, eventually moving from his professorial position at the State College of New York at Buffalo to the music department at Berea College, in Kentucky. From 1968 until about

1973, he collected a major portion of the Old Baptist repertory of lined-out hymnody, later publishing the first scholarly articles on their music. One was a general introductory article, and another argued that in some of the churches a harmony could be heard in fourths and fifths that suggested, to Tallmadge, how medieval organum might have arisen (Tallmadge 1975, 1984).

The Old Regulars were featured in an Appalshop documentary film, *In the Good Old-Fashioned Way* (Smith 1973). In the 1970s, in the course of research on lined hymnody in general, ethnomusicologist Terry Miller recorded some Old Regular Baptist singing in Ohio. He continues this research on the Old Regular Baptists and hopes some day to publish it.

During the spring of 1981 Philip Rhodes, a professor of music at Carleton College, visited churches in the Indian Bottom Association and recorded their services. His recordings and field notes are on deposit at Berea College, and he has pursued the connection between their lined hymnody and Gaelic lined hymnody from the Scottish Isle of Lewis. About 1982, John Wallhausser, professor of religion and philosophy at Berea College, began visiting with the Indian Bottom Association and continues to do so. His article, "I Can Almost See Heaven from Here," is an outstanding introduction to their way of worship and one of which the Old Regulars approve (Wallhausser 1983). Loyal Jones has also contributed significantly toward understanding Old Baptists in their own terms (e.g., 1977).

Sammie Ann Wicks wrote her dissertation on a neighboring association of Old Regulars (1983). It features a carefully detailed description of a single service, with elaborate musical transcriptions of the hymnody and some of the sung preaching. She later published an article demonstrating that contemporary country music singers utilize the same kinds of melodic elaborations as Old Regular Baptists, although not to the same degree (Wicks 1989, 59–96). Of course, this type of melodic elaboration (what would be termed ornamentation in other contexts) belongs to the British and Irish folk-song tradition and its descendants abroad—it can be found in ballads and in traditional instrumental music for the dance, for example. While the elaborations are not exclusive to Old Regular Baptists, it appears that they have carried them as far as any group in this tradition save perhaps Irish *sean-nós* singers.

Howard Dorgan, professor of communications at Appalachian State University, surveyed six Baptist denominations in the mountains (1988) and wrote an overview of the Old Regulars that, while sensitive and accurate in matters of history, doctrine, and polity, had little to say about their music (1989). He called it "a slow, wailful hymnody that seems to ignore customary melodies" (ibid., 6). Dorgan's reaction is no doubt shared by many outsiders, who are unfamiliar with these intricate folk melodies and whose basic frame of melodic reference is popular music. Brett Sutton and Beverly Patterson have made significant contributions toward our understanding of Primitive Baptist hymnody, a related tradition, but one that does not present the problem of integration that the Old Regular Baptist songs do. For Primitive Baptist singing has a regular pulse beat. Many of their songbooks contain musical notation, and although lined-out hymnody has been collected from them, most of their churches no longer practice it (see Sutton and Hartman 1982; Patterson 1994).

That only a small number of scholars have written about Old Baptist hymnody in Appalachia may be partly the result of an academically unglamorous subject, religious music, which, when coupled with obscure denominations from a border region, simply does not interest very many. But it is also partly because Old Baptists are guarded toward outsiders and uncooperative with visiting documentarians when it means disturbing their worship. Like many natives of Appalachia, they feel that outsiders misunderstand them and exploit them and their region. They resent the stereotypes of poverty and ignorance that have harmed the mountain people, not only in media portrayals but also in scholarly writings by historians and sociologists (see Titon 1988, 157–62 for an indictment of this literature). Today, most Old Regular Baptist churches do not allow cameras; nor will they allow outsiders to make recordings except under special circumstances and then only after they have gotten to know and to trust the outsider. Some groups are willing, however, to demonstrate their singing in an appropriate setting. For example, singers from one of the churches in the Indian Bottom Association have sung at conferences on religious music at Berea College, for the College Music Society's annual meeting, and at the 1997 Smithsonian Institution's Folklife Festival

My research with the Old Regular Baptists began in Kentucky in 1979, when I observed a Sunday service at the Left Beaver church, a member of the Thornton Union Association. Their singing captivated me, and I resolved that after completing current research with a Baptist group in Virginia's northern Blue Ridge I would try to return to the Old Regulars (see Titon 1982 and 1988; Titon, Dornfeld, and Rankin 1989). At the start of the spring semester of 1990, when I was Goode Visiting Professor of Appalachian Studies at Berea College, John Wallhausser introduced me to Elwood Cornett (the moderator, or elected leader) and to others in the Indian Bottom Association, and he assured them that my intentions were honorable and long-term. I spent most Sundays with them, and got permission to tape-record services from my seat with a small tape recorder. I got to know some of them, particularly over delicious Sunday dinners at their homes after church, and I arranged interviews in which I learned about their lives and more about their religious beliefs and practices. Near the end of my stay I was permitted to videotape an outdoor memorial service and a baptism. In their homes I also recorded songs from some of the outstanding singers. Since then I have returned many times, collaborating with Cornett and Wallhausser on two CD recordings of their lined hymnody published by Smithsonian Folkways (Cornett, Titon, and Wallhausser 1997, 2002).[5]

Singing Together

I return now to the issue that generated this essay: How do the Old Regular Baptists achieve rhythmic integration in their singing without the aid of a conductor, accompanist, and a regular pulse beat? By now it should be clear that because each person curves the tune a little differently, they do not sing in perfect unison. Their texture is better described as heterophonic. Singers have the chance to exercise their individuality and at the same time feel the bonding power of the group, a liberal ideal throughout American religious history here realized in the traditional musical practice of a conservative denomination. I find the integration all the more remarkable because they are not striving to do the same thing at the exact same time.

Although I eventually learned to do it, I must confess my initial frustration in trying to sing along with the Old Regulars. I have always had confidence in my ear, and I thought I could pick up the tunes and sing them without difficulty, as I have done with all the other orally transmitted music I have tried to sing or play. But although I was able soon enough to catch the basic pitch structures, the rhythms eluded me. Trying to puzzle it out, I thought I should be able to hear a pulse but was somehow missing it. Try as I might, I could not honestly hear it, construct it, or convince myself it was "there."

Was there something wrong with my ear, then? Tallmadge had transcribed a few Old Regular songs in Western notation and he stated that it did have a pulse beat (1975). Wicks's transcriptions buried any pulse beat in so much detail that the music was virtually unsingable, yet she asserted that she, too, heard a regular pulse (1983). I did not. Perhaps I just did not have enough experience. I decided to ask my friends among the Old Regulars whether they felt a beat when they sang their songs. Every one of them said no. This wasn't "beat music," one said. They couldn't tap their foot to it.

I never directly asked them how they could stay together so well without a beat, accompanist, or conductor. I thought the question would be presumptuous, and worse: They would infer that this music department professor thought something was lacking in their music that an accompanist or conductor would supply, which of course was quite the opposite of how I felt. When

I did ask them to tell me more generally about affect or meaning in their music they almost always gave their explanations in the language of religious experience, which was what I expected. I could not see at that time how such language might serve as an explanation of what I considered a technical problem: the integration in their music.

When I left Kentucky in June of 1990 after spending four months with the Old Regulars, I felt at an impasse concerning the problem of rhythm. I loved the music, and I had been listening to, and singing with, the tape recordings I had made. As the time passed I found myself becoming more easily able to sing with the tapes on songs I particularly liked. Was I just memorizing the songs, or was I also learning some principle of singing? I did not consciously practice singing with the tape; rather, at moments when I felt in a meditative mood, I listened to a tape, felt the music envelop me, and I sang along, softly and happily, and increasingly together with them.

Returning to Kentucky in 1992 and 1993 to record music for the forthcoming compact disc, I found that not only could I sing together with them on familiar songs, but that at certain moments when I was able to put everything else out of my mind and, to speak in an idiom familiar to me, "get in a groove." I could now sing together with them even on songs that I had heard only once or twice before. It felt very good, and I remarked on this to a professor and his wife. "How can you sing with them," his wife wanted to know, "when you're not an Old Regular Baptist and you don't believe as they do?" "But I think I believe in music the way they do," I replied.

And that is where the matter lay for a little while longer. Then as I was writing up my part of the notes for the forthcoming CD of their music, I once more faced the vexing problem of rendering the rhythm of this music in musical notation. It would be nice to have a transcription of their music in the brochure notes accompanying the album, I thought. But how to transcribe it? Earlier I had tried a few transcriptions in Western notation, in free rhythm; and I gave one to Elwood Cornett, their Association leader (fig. 14.1). Like the other Old Regulars he does not read music, but I showed it to him after he asked me whether their music could be rendered in notation. He had one question for me: "Could someone sing it back from that?" "Not without a lot of musical training," I said, "and even then I'm not sure anyone would think it was a good way to learn the songs. I like your way of catching the tunes better." "Well," he said, pointing to my transcription, "could you sing it from that?" I began singing. "That's pretty much it. Of course, you already know the tune," he responded.

Frustrated with my attempts to render their rhythms in Western notation, in 1992, I decided to see if I could make more accurate transcriptions using

FIGURE 14.1. "On Jordan's Stormy Banks I Stand" (transcribed in standard musical notation by Jeff Todd Titon)

the computer. I used a relatively simple Macintosh computer program called SoundEdit to measure the durations of each melody note, and I found no basic time unit that could be understood as a pulse beat. Figure 14.2 shows why. It is a printout of a sound spectrogram of one of the eight-syllable lines from "On Jordan's Stormy Banks" as they sing it together: "There rock and hill and brook and vale." For a rough guide in musical notation consult the eight-syllable lines in figure 14.1; of course this is for a different verse, but the melody repeats. Horizontally atop the figure is the running time in seconds; at the bottom are the words. Measuring the duration of each word results in the following series (in seconds): 2.5, 2.0, 3.8, 2.8, 2.6, 1.6, 2.2, and 3.3. This series cannot be translated into the kind of easily divisible small integers that would reveal a pulse beat. (Of course, one might argue that there is an extremely rapid pulse

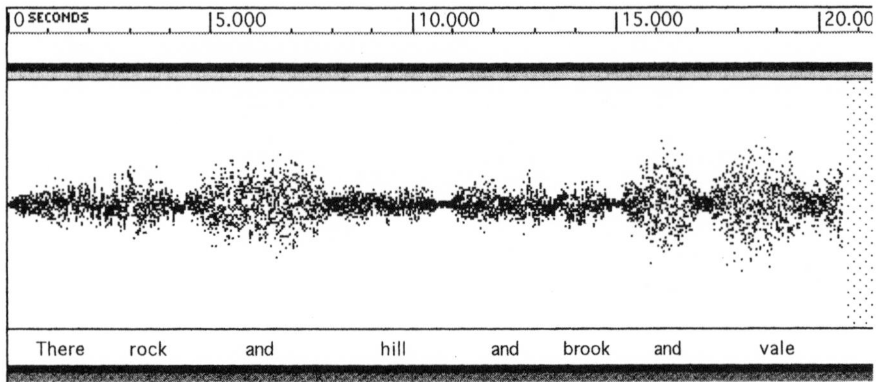

FIGURE 14.2. "On Jordan's Stormy Banks I Stand" (spectrogram)

beat, recurring every tenth of a second, but there is no other evidence to suggest it.) And after measurements at the syllable level, it was even clearer that there is no regular pulse beat unit. I could not use the computer to construct a pulse beat that was hidden from my unaided ear.

But early in 1994 while mastering the first compact disc (Cornett, Titon, and Wallhausser 1997), I decided to include some of the Old Regular Baptist statements about music. Cornett knew that I was interested in what people had to say about the significance of the singing (he was interested in it, too), and after the recording sessions he had asked people to volunteer and step in front of the microphone and say what the singing meant to them. I recorded the statements as well as the singing. As these statements played back again and again while I edited them for the master, what I had previously interpreted as religious metaphor began to take on, by virtue of their replay, the force of fact. Was it really metaphor when they spoke of being tuned up with the grace of God? When they spoke of how the Holy Spirit made a melody? Or was it not metaphor at all but their habitual way of thinking, their quite literal belief? I went back over my interview transcripts for possible clues to their experience as a way of understanding how they were able to integrate their singing.

I had, of course, realized that they experienced an unusual state of consciousness when singing, one which had the potential to unify them. I knew that their descriptions of it were similar to others I had obtained (Titon 1982, 1987, 1988). When I asked them what went through their minds when they sang, they replied that if they were in a proper state of mind, they meditated on the words. Squire Watts said, "It's best not to even sing if you're not going to, I think, not going to put your heart into it. I like to dwell on what a song means, and it's helpful to get in step with it, you know" (Watts and Watts 1990).

I asked Kenzie Ison, "When you sing 'On Jordan's Stormy Banks I Stand,' does a picture run through your mind?" "Of course," he replied. "When Elwood got up there and started [leading] 'I am a poor wayfaring stranger,' we were sitting there being honest with ourselves. We weren't out here pretending. . . . We are poor, wayfaring strangers, really. And we're going to be on Jordan's stormy banks, sooner or later" (Ison 1990).

One telling phrase that several Old Regular Baptists used when discussing their ideas about music was "singing from the heart." They contrasted one kind of music, which satisfied the body, with the kind that satisfied the soul. Kenzie Ison likened the sense of satisfaction to being at peace: "When you sing from the heart, you know, your vocal cords are, this is a theory of mine [laughs]: If you sing from the heart, if you sing at peace, your vocal cords are at ease to do what they do instead of being jittery or lackadaisical" (ibid.) Singing from the heart allows a person to sing well. Ison continued: "But we start singing, I think, for more reasons than one. We want to start thinking about the message that is in the song. There's a message of compassion, there's a message of the love of God, and Christ's purpose. There's a message for a sweet and old time way of religion, I guess you could say. And then we begin to become less aggressive and more humble and we start thinking like this and we become more at peace, inside of us. And the Spirit of God starts to well up in us" (ibid.)

When they feel the Spirit of God inside, it serves to link them to one another and to God in this state of consciousness that (ideally) occurs during the singing (and at other times, such as communion): thus the sacramental integration they are able to achieve. Squire Watts said, "Well, sometimes the singing, of course, it's going there to worship God in the Spirit. He teaches us the Spirit and truth. That's all we worship him. Sometimes, I think, what it is when we say we worship him in Spirit and in truth, his Spirit connects up with our Spirit, and we're overjoyed sometimes. And you feel that in the singing sometimes. We've had some wonderful meetings just in the singing" (Watts and Watts 1990). Singing this way, the ego disappears in order to make way for the kind of group bonding that Victor Turner called "communitas" (Turner 1969). Kenzie Ison describes it as a loss of self-centeredness and a desire to join the rest in their "peaceful war" against evil: "The idea of Elwood getting up and singing, 'I Am a Poor, Wayfaring Pilgrim' or 'Stranger' is something that is not self-centered at all. See, I had this big desire that I wanted to help, assist, with this peaceful war, fight. . . . I wanted to be on the side of good. . . . We sing because it's necessary" (Ison 1990). Elwood Cornett emphasized the outward-radiating power of the Spirit to unify the singing group: "You see, the love of God, I think, is manifested in more directions than one. In one way it's from God to us individually. But then there's that love that God, if God is in me, and God's in him, and God's in her, then there's that love that is manifest among us as well. And certainly singing is a good opportunity. Sometimes I may just want to sing real loud. And if so, that's my individual relationship with God. But then being a part of the whole group singing does something for me also" (Cornett and Back 1990). And I. D. Back suggested the link between singing together, singing from the heart, and being "tuned up" in the Spirit of God: "Of course, you know, we don't have any music [musical instruments] or anything, but we believe in being tuned up with the grace of God and his Holy Spirit, and when that begins to, it makes a melody, makes a joyful noise, and I'm sure the Lord's pleased with it because we feel good in doing it" (Back 1992).

It was not difficult for me to infer from this that, in their way of thinking, being "tuned up" in the Spirit of God literally enables them to sing together. My thoughts then began to turn toward the similarity between Spirit and breath[6]. Could they be breathing together? Perhaps instead of measuring the length of each note, I should measure large units, breath units. Thinking of Charles Olson's essay "Projective Verse" and its impact on my earlier ethnopoetic transcriptions (see, e.g., Titon 1976), I decided to measure line lengths first. Here was a most remarkable result: I found that in many, though not all, of their songs, corresponding lines lasted almost the same amount of time, in some cases with differences of only a few tenths of a second over a twenty-second line period. Table 14.1 shows the durations of lines in "On Jordan's Stormy Banks" and in "Guide Me O Thou Great Jehovah." The corresponding lines last almost the same period, even though the lines are "cut up" in irregular durations that defeat the notion of a pulse beat at the word or syllable level, but here was a regular period every 16 or 20 seconds.

Could they possibly be taking twenty seconds of singing on one breath, I wondered? Not likely; but they had an unerring sense for a long period. I listened for breathing in my recordings and discovered that they did breathe together, but not in equal increments. For example, in songs in an iambic meter, like "On Jordan's Stormy Banks," they seem to take a breath after the even syllables, or in other words, after every other syllable. Of course, the durations varied for each syllable and two-syllable group, and there was no way to render this in simple Western notation.

I have no doubt that "practice" is an explanation for the remarkable ability of this group of singers to stay together. But this explanation is misleading without an understanding of their experience while singing. "In one mind and one accord" they are able to integrate their singing as a group without external aid. Once "tuned up" and singing in that spiritual consciousness, characteristic

TABLE 14.1 Corresponding line lengths, "On Jordan's Stormy Banks" and "Guide Me O Thou Great Jehovah"

"On Jordan's Stormy Banks" (Aug. 20, 1992, Defeated Creek Church, Defeated Creek, Ky., led by Elwood Cornett).

First and third lines:	*Duration (sec.)*
On Jordan's Stormy Banks I Stand	22.558 (beginning)
To Canaan's Fair and Happy Land	20.413
There Gen'rous Fruits that Never Fail	20.614
There Rock and Hill and Brook and Vale	20.614
All Oe'r those Wide Extended Plains	20.522
There God, the Son, Forever Reigns	19.690
Second and fourth lines:	*Duration (sec.)*
And Cast a Wishful Eye	17.048
Where My Possessions Lie	16.358
On Trees Immortal Grow	16.335
With Milk and Honey Flow	16.519
Shines One Eternal Day	16.480
And Scatters Night Away	18.014 (ending)

"Guide Me O Thou Great Jehovah" (Aug. 20, 1992, Defeated Creek Church, Defeated Creek, Ky., led by I. D. Back).

First and third lines:	*Duration (sec.)*
Guide Me O Thou Great Jehovah	20.867
I Am Weak and Thou Art Mighty	21.281
Bread of Heaven, Bread of Heaven	20.637
Open Thou the Crystal Fountain	20.614
Let the Fiery Cloudy Pillar	19.947
Strong Deliverer, Strong Deliverer	19.947
Second and fourth lines:	*Duration (sec.)*
Pilgrim Through this Barren Land	20.660
Hold Me with Thy Powerful Hand	20.108
Feed Me Till I Want No More	20.102
Where the Healing Streams Do Flow	19.348
Lead Me on My Journey Through	19.855
Be Thou Still My Strength and Shield	20.499

of worship generally and transcending the boundaries of any individual religion; once breathing together as one, they are enabled through music to express themselves quite individually and yet simultaneously to bond to the others in the group—a powerful and transcendent experience indeed.

NOTES

1. This essay, written in 1994 and updated for this volume, was based on two earlier presentations (Titon 1991, 1993). I am grateful to Berea College for the Goode Visiting Professorship in Appalachian Studies in 1990 which permitted me to undertake fieldwork with the Old Regular Baptists; to the Appalachian Center of Berea College for a Mellon Foundation-funded Appalachian Fellowship which allowed me to return in 1992; to the Weatherford-Hammond Collection of the Hutchins Library at Berea; and to the Indian Bottom Association of Old Regular Baptists in southeastern Kentucky. I am grateful also to several individuals who have aided me in this work: Loyal Jones, John Wallhausser, William Tallmadge, Howard Dorgan, Philip Rhodes, Gerald Roberts, Elwood and Kathy Cornett, Ivan and Mae Amburgey, Squire and Claudette Watts, Don and Shirley Pratt, John Preece, I. D. Back, MacKenzie Ison, Ruth Frazier, Mary Ison, Manus Ison, Jr., and Valeria Ison.

2. Much of this history is drawn from John Wallhausser's essay in Cornett, Titon, and Wallhausser (1997).

3. The Articles of Faith are published in the Association's minutes of their annual meetings.

4. That is, when they fail in ordinary things, like forgetting directions. See Titon (1999).

5. A small grant was provided by the Folk Arts Division of the National Endowment for the Arts to enable me to teach them how to make professional tape recordings and document their song repertory. Most of my field recordings are on deposit at Berea in Special Collections at the Hutchins Library where the public can hear them; I gave copies to Cornett for Association use as well. Nearly two thousand of the two Folkways CDs have been sold at cost in the Old Regular Baptist communities.

6. In both Old Testament Hebrew and New Testament Greek, "spirit" and "breath" are the same word: *ruakh* in Hebrew and *pneuma* in Greek.

WORKS CITED

Back, I. D. 1992. Statement after music recording session, Defeated Creek, Ky., Aug. 20.

Billups, Edward W. 1854. *The Sweet Songster: A Collection*. Reprint. Wayne, W.Va.: Arrowood Bros.

Bruce, Dickson D. Jr. 1974. *And They All Sang Hallelujah: Plain-Folk Camp-Meeting Religion, 1800–1845*. Knoxville: University of Tennessee Press.

Chase, Gilbert. 1987. *America's Music: From the Pilgrims to the Present*. 3rd ed. Urbana: University of Illinois Press.

Cohen, John, comp. 1960. *Mountain Music of Kentucky*. Folkways FA 2317.
———, director. 1962. *The High Lonesome Sound*. The Cinema Guild.
Conley, Roland H. 1989. *The New Baptist Song Book*. Salyersville, Ky.: By the author.
Cornett, Elwood, Jeff Todd Titon, and John Wallhausser. 1997. *Songs of the Old Regular Baptists: Lined-Out Hymnody from Southeastern Kentucky*. One compact disc and cassette recording. Smithsonian Folkways Recordings SF 40106.Washington, DC: Smithsonian Folkways Recordings.
———. 2002. *Songs of the Old Regular Baptists: Lined-Out Hymnody from Southeastern Kentucky*, Vol. 2. One compact disc and cassette recording. Smithsonian Folkways Recordings SFW 50001.Washington, DC: Smithsonian Folkways Recordings.
Cornett, Elwood and I. D. Back. 1990. Interview by Jeff Titon and John Wallhausser, Blackey, Ky., Apr. 1.
Dauney, William. 1973. *Ancient Scottish Melodies* [1838]. Reprint. New York: AMS Press.
Dorgan, Howard. 1988. *Giving Glory to God in Appalachia: Worship Practices of Six Baptist Subdenominations*. Knoxville: University of Tennessee Press.
———. 1989. *The Old Regular Baptists of Central Appalachia: Brothers and Sisters in Hope*. Knoxville: University of Tennessee Press.
Ison, MacKenzie. 1990. Interview by Jeff Titon, Slemp, Ky., Apr. 14.
Jones, Loyal. 1977. "Old-time Baptists and Mainline Christianity." In *An Appalachian Symposium*, ed. by J. W. Williamson, 120–130. Boone, N.C.: Appalachian State University Press.
Lomax, Alan. 1977. *The Gospel Ship: Baptist Hymns and White Spirituals from the Southern Mountains*. LP Recording, 33 1/3 rpm. New World Records NW 294.
———. n.d. [ca.1961]. *White Spirituals*. LP Recording, 33 1/3 rpm. Southern Folk Heritage Series. Atlantic SD-1349.
Osborne, Baxter, and Roy B. Akers. 1989. *Old Regular Baptist Song Book*. Ashland, Ky.: By the authors.
Osborne, Dorothy. 1991. *The Baptist Hymn Book*. Ashland, Ky.: By the author.
Patterson, Beverly B. 1994. *Sound of the Dove: An Ethnography of Singing in Primitive Baptist Churches*. Urbana: University of Illinois Press.
Perrigan, Rufus. 1961. *History of Regular Baptist, and Their Ancestors and Accessors*. Haysi, Va.: By the author.
Ritchie, Jean. 1955. *Singing Family of the Cumberlands*. Repr., Lexington, Ky.: University Press of Kentucky, 1988.
———. 1959. *The Ritchie Family of Kentucky*. LP recording, 33 1/3 rpm with notes. Folkways Records FA 2316.
Sacred Harp, The. 1844. *The Sacred Harp*. Rev. ed., 1991. Edited. by Hugh McGraw et al. Bremen, Ga.: Sacred Harp. Sizer, Sandra S. 1978. *Gospel Hymns and Social Religion: The Rhetoric of Nineteenth-Century Revivalism*. Philadelphia: Temple University Press.
Smith, C. B. 1988. *Some of Our Favorite Songs*. Pippa Passes, Ky.: By the author.
Smith, Herbie, director. 1973. *In the Good Old-Fashioned Way*. 16mm, color documentary film. Distributed by Appalashop, Whitesburg, Ky.

Sutton, Brett, and Pete Hartman. 1982. *Primitive Baptist Hymns of the Blue Ridge.* Chapel Hill: University of North Carolina Press.

Tallmadge, William. 1975. "Baptist Monophonic and Heterophonic Hymnody in Southern Appalachia." *Yearbook for Inter-American Musical Research* 11: 106–36.

———. 1984. "Folk Organum: A Study of Origins." *American Music* 2: 47–65.

Temperley, Nicholas. 1981. "The Old Way of Singing." *Journal of the American Musicological Society* 34: 511–44.

Thomas, E. D. 1877. *Thomas Hymnal: A Choice Collection.* Repr. Wayne, W.Va.: Arrowood Bros., n.d.

Thomas, Jean. 1931. *Devil's Ditties.* Chicago: W. Wilbur Hatfield.

Thomas, Jean, et al. n.d. [1939?]. "Kentucky Folk Songs." Collected through the Federal Music Project (Works Progress Administration). Unpublished manuscript in the Library of Congress, Folklife Reading Room.

Titon, Jeff Todd. 1976. "Son House: Two Narratives." *Alcheringa: Ethnopoetics,* NS 2 (1): 2–9.

———. 1982. *Powerhouse for God: Sacred Speech, Chant, and Song in an Appalachian Baptist Church.* Two LP recordings, 33 1/3 rpm with booklet. Chapel Hill: University of North Carolina Press.

———. 1987. "God'll Just Bless You All Over the Place: Hymnody in the Fellowship Independent Baptist Church, Stanley, Virginia." *Appalachian Journal* 14: 348–58.

———. 1988. *Powerhouse for God: Speech, Chant, and Song in an Appalachian Baptist Church.* Austin: University of Texas Press.

———. 1991. "Singing from the Heart." Unpublished paper delivered at the Annual Meeting of the Society for Ethnomusicology, Chicago.

———. 1993. "The Problem of Rhythm in Old Regular Baptist Singing." Unpublished paper delivered at the Chicago Humanities Institute Conference on Music in American Religious Experience.

———. 1999. "'The Real Thing': Tourism, Authenticity, and Pilgrimage among the Old Regular Baptists at the 1997 Smithsonian Folklife Festival." *The World of Music* 41 (3): 115–39.

Titon, Jeff Todd, Barry Dornfeld, and Tom Rankin. 1989. *Powerhouse for God.* 16mm, color, documentary film. Distributed in 16mm and VHS by Documentary Educational Resources, Watertown, Mass.

Turner, Victor. 1969. *The Ritual Process: Structure and Anti-Structure.* Chicago: University of Chicago Press.

Walker, William. 1835. *The Southern Harmony and Musical Companion.* Repr., Lexington: University Press of Kentucky, 1987.

Wallhausser, John. 1983. "I Can Almost See Heaven from Here." *Katallagete* (Spring): 2–10.

Watts, Squire, and Claudette Watts. 1990. Interview by Jeff Titon, Red Fox, Ky., Apr. 29.

Wicks, Sammie Ann. 1983. "Life and Meaning: Singing, Praying, and the Word among the Old Regular Baptists of Eastern Kentucky." Ph.D. diss., University of Texas, 1983.

———. 1989. "A Belated Salute to the 'Old Way' of 'Snaking' the Voice on its (ca.) 345th Birthday." *Popular Music* 8: 59–96.

15

Aesthetics and Theology in Congregational Song: A Hymnal Intervenes

Don E. Saliers

Every generation or so in the life of American Protestant denominations, a new hymnal is published. The appearance of a new hymn collection always generates both resistance and enthusiasm in local congregations. This is in part because hymn singing forms and expresses communities of faith in belief and experience. What we learn to sing in public worship and devotion is at once experiential and theological. The poetry of the text and the musical setting of the tune, once brought together, carry the meaning and import of theological belief at a deeper level than does homiletical discourse, much less doctrinal teaching, by themselves. Therefore change in what is sung is both threat and promise.

In this sense St. Augustine was certainly right: Those who sing, pray twice. The act of breathing, sounding the air, and reproducing the musical form embodies the words in a more than cognitive way. Sung texts, especially those repeated with some frequency over time, become part of the *body memory* of faith—a point to which we shall return. Of course, what and how congregations sing also encodes and reveals social and class identity, musical tastes, and deeper patterns of religious sensibility. A hymnal, analogously to the Bible itself, is also an identity symbol. Debates over new hymns versus familiar hymns are therefore symbolic of political, moral, and ecclesiastical divergences as well.

In what follows, I wish to explore issues bearing upon relations between aesthetic and theological dimensions of congregational singing, drawing upon a particular research project in one American denomination. During 1993 and the first few months of 1994, I studied, with a research team, thirteen United Methodist churches. We began with a basic question: How has the *United Methodist Hymnal* (1989) been received and begun to shape the worship and faith life of these local churches? Through survey instruments, group and individual interviews, field observations, and participation in the worship life of these congregations, a distinctive picture of how a new hymnal takes hold has begun to emerge. While not yet fully elaborated and interpreted, this research sheds interesting light on the singing practices in American Protestant worship today.

An Initial Proposal

In his posthumously published *The Divine Formula*, Erik Routley observed:

> Transfer, change, and the removal of domestic landmarks . . . bring discomfort, and that must be acknowledged. When a group makes changes in its liturgical customs it is dislodging much that its members held in affection and through which they genuinely worshipped and the effect is as if those people had been moved to an unfamiliar place as well as being faced with unfamiliar demands. Therefore two things are needed in any program of reconstruction if that discomfort is to be reasonably short-lived. The new words and actions must be such as will as soon as possible "come naturally," and they must be assisted in their purpose by being . . . works of art. (Routley 1986, 137)

Routley has clearly identified two major points with which we are concerned: the disorientation brought about by liturgical-musical change, and the role of aesthetic form in the process of new materials entering the congregation's "body memory."

Building upon these points, let us formulate a proposal concerning the reception process of a new Protestant hymnal: The authorized appearance of a denominational hymnal represents a simultaneous semantic and acoustical shift in the primary theology of the worshiping community. *How* the new hymn repertory is assimilated will reveal social and cultural features (especially the aesthetic sensibility) of that community's theology.

Some Anecdotal Points of Departure

One of my most memorable interviewing experiences occurred in a group interview of some twenty women whose average age was mid-to-late seventies. They were members of an established morning devotional group in a historical Methodist congregation in Charleston, South Carolina. We began the interview by asking them to name some of their favorite hymns. The expected replies were forthcoming: "Amazing Grace," "Blessed Assurance, Jesus Is Mine," "How Great Thou Art," "I Love to Tell the Story," and others of the same era and style. That these would be in the top group of favorite mainline Protestant hymns is not surprising. It was in their responses to the question about how they learned these hymns that insights began to unfold.

One by one the women spoke of these hymns as old friends. While eventually they recited texts and hummed phrases, they invariably began by remembering the sound of their grandmother's or grandfather's voice, the squeak of the parlor pump-organ, the comforting feeling of leaning on their mother's shoulder while the family sang. Memories were evoked of Sunday night services and Wednesday evening prayer meetings, of singing these hymns and songs in Sunday school assemblies, and of family and friends gathered for social singing through the year. They were sharing with me, and with one another, what we might call the deep "body memory" of the hymns. Here in miniature, I heard first-person accounts of the profound associative power of words and music fused together. Their generation had experienced the liturgical and devotional uses of these hymns that had, at the same time, encoded a broader set of familial and social meanings in their lives.

Thus, one of the hallmarks of church members whose formation in singing their faith came in times and places where church and social life were more coterminous, is a homogeneous field of associative memory. At the same time, the physical act of singing together was part of their expected churchly and social behavior. Very different factors come into play when the music is heard in electronically reproduced forms, as we shall note later. Rote learning by repeated singing has a deeper bodily location.

Toward the end of that interview several women began revealing how much they liked some of the "new songs" in the *United Methodist Hymnal* (1989). One remarked on how Natalie Sleeth's "Hymn of Promise" had actually changed her attitude toward singing at funerals. Upon further questioning she observed, "The tune is so pretty, and I love the words. It reminds me of some of the songs we used to sing." I then began to listen for these criteria as others spoke of having learned to like new things in the hymnal. Another then said how much she enjoyed "Jesus' Hands Were Kind Hands," especially when the children sang it in worship. The tune to which those words are set is a familiar French folk melody.

Once we moved beyond texts and tunes which made some immediately accessible connection with their familiar base repertory, I found some of the women commenting on enjoying hearing the choir sing things which had not been familiar to them. For example, "When in Our Music God Is Glorified," and "Lift High the Cross." Neither of these had been in any previous hymnal they had used. In these cases, most of those who spoke had either sung in the choir at one time or tended to read poetry. That is, the more sophisticated texts and musical forms were mentioned by those whose background included more than rote learning. Yet it is also true that those two hymn tunes echoed their own more formal Sunday morning experiences.

While I did not have an exact equivalent group in other congregations to interview, the same phenomena surfaced in different ways. So, in a United Methodist church of twelve hundred members in Atlanta, we found one of the Sunday school classes (having had the same teacher for forty years!) singing the same repertory of hymns the women in Charleston had first named. In the Atlanta congregation, the Sunday school class holds what amounts to its own "church" prior to the main Sunday service in the sanctuary, and we found relatively little overlap in what was sung in the two gatherings. But it was at a Wednesday night weekly supper with an intergenerational program that the two repertories, to a certain extent, interfaced.

Studying these two contexts helped me understand some of the larger patterns of data from a national sampling of one hundred thirty-five churches geographically distributed across the United States. People across the entire age spectrum are learning new hymns, as did an older generation. When asked which new hymns—not in previous United Methodist hymn collections—had actually established themselves in the congregation's singing, six new hymns were consistently named: "Hymn of Promise," "Lift High the Cross," "Here I Am, Lord," "Spirit Song," "Lord, You Have Come to the Lakeshore," and "God of the Sparrow." Of these, the texts show a number of affinities to earlier popular songs and hymns, except for "Lift High the Cross," and for "God of the Sparrow," which shows a remarkably new poetic form. The musical shape of "Lift High the Cross," the tune *Crucifer*, harkens back to more classical nineteenth-century hymn tunes. All the rest are lyrical and quite accessible, tending toward popular and folk harmonic and melodic features.

Here we note a strong strand of continuity of sound—how a hymn tune "feels" in relation to what has been in the central repertory. At work is a kind of acoustical iconography, if you will. The vast majority of worshipers learn the new by way of assimilation to the familiar. But there are notable exceptions, especially where the congregation has a high percentage of members who read music, who have sung in choirs, or whose liturgical concerns include prophetic and/or global, multicultural experience. In such contexts, openness to learning new texts and new musical form becomes more explicit and intentional. But precisely these differences create tensions within local congregations and often produce the clash of separate musical/liturgical subcultures within the same congregation.

There is much about worship in these churches that appears to look backward. Hymns and songs learned in early formative experiences and stages of faith constitute a "feeling of familiarity." A great deal of effort is expended on evoking a simpler time, when the experience of God and neighbor was less ambiguous, and life less complex. At the same time in these churches, the chief concern is one of relevance. As one interviewee remarked: "I don't understand why we have to be so concerned with history and with the Bible. Some of us want a more psychologically healthy and relevant upbeat accent in worship and our music."

Such a mix of sensibility and assessment of music in worship cannot be easily reconciled. The current "church growth" movement emphasizes meeting people's needs, whatever they are. This surfaces in clashes between pastors, musicians, and church members in the pew. What happens, in effect, is that in most cases different generations or groups sing only their "canon" of hymns and songs within the hymnal. The new hymnal is judged according to how well it represents the "canon" at issue. Thus, in one congregation the hymnal had a surprisingly high approval rating among those 65 and older because "it brought back some of the old time favorites." Another congregation approved because of the eighteen hymns in Spanish and English and the 33 from African American sources. This very pluralism has been at work in the formation of hymnals of much broader textual and musical range than almost any hymnal published before the last two decades of the twentieth century.

The Broadening of Style and Performance Practice

So far we have focused on the significance of body memory and the associative power of text and music in certain samplings of congregational repertory and learning. From my study it is clear that the vast majority of church members over 60 exhibit a proclivity for continuity of "sound" and "feel" in receiving a new hymnal. Musical training and broader cultural exposure can either exist alongside such continuity, or produce the need for discontinuity. This is seen especially in the attitude and practices of many of the youth groups included in the study.

In a large metropolitan congregation in Minnesota, I found that the youth were singing almost an entirely different set of songs when they worshiped and had "social singing" time. They consistently referred to the new hymnal in the pews as belonging to the "older folks in church," even though there were songs from the hymnal they knew well such as "Pass It On" and "Morning Has Broken." Most of their words and tunes were also on recordings, particularly from contemporary Christian singers. But it was really their style of singing and the performance practice of solo voices that seemed more central. This phenomenon is but one aspect, although exaggerated in urban congregations, of the larger question a new hymnal raises: Is there an emerging appreciation for a wide diversity of texts and tunes as well as musical practices represented in the latest generation of Protestant hymnals?

While there are marked differences in general between urban and rural settings, and considerable regional differentiation within United Methodist congregations, depending upon the configuration of neighboring denominations, it is quite clear that the new hymnal itself is a product of a new, increasingly strong diversity of theological and aesthetic sensibility. Generally speaking, the congregations we studied are fairly evenly divided between those who favor more "evangelical" (of the late nineteenth and early twentieth centuries) and those who prefer more "classical" hymnody such as "Holy, Holy, Holy," or the chorale tradition. But nearly every congregation has a significant population who said they loved the new diversity, including a range of Hispanic, African American, and other global sources, alongside the more recent "folk" style.

This represents a new set of factors in how mainline Protestants approach and use recent hymnal collections. The challenge of many of these, such as the *United Methodist Hymnal*, is found in the diversity of texts and musical forms, and, more significantly, in the new musical demands in performance style. It is one thing to learn gradually to assimilate words and music that display a great deal of continuity; it is another to learn a new style of singing. Here the tension emerges between identity in body memory and relevance to a new world.

No previous official collection of hymns for United Methodists has moved so broadly in both form and style. The same thing can be said of the recent Presbyterian (*The Presbyterian Hymnal* 1990) and the United Church of Christ (*United Church of Christ Hymnal* 1996) hymnals. Here the learning and the assimilation of hymns, psalm settings, and related congregational song require serious examination of the creative tension between identity and relevance. Musical exposure to singing in diverse styles requires an ability to cross over into a sociocultural context not our own. At the same time this process alters what counts as being "our" acoustic or musical form and "theirs."

We return, then, to Routley's observation about the "removal of domestic landmarks" in what churches sing. What makes a widely diverse set of words/music and performance styles "come naturally" is quite different from the more homogenous patterns of learning and singing featured in most official hymnals before the 1970s. We are now asking congregations to develop a new aesthetic; perhaps, more accurately, new aesthetics. For as we move away from either the dominant evangelical and popular styles, or from the received "classical" shapes of hymns, we also shift theologically and liturgically. This is particularly so where Protestant worship is still carried by congregational hymns.

Hymnal as Theological/Aesthetic Interventions

Let us draw some working inferences from our inquiry, particularly in its bearing upon the American Protestant congregation in the midst of so much change in both liturgy and music. This much is clear, we are in the midst of long-term shifts in sensibility which have both aesthetic and theological import. What constitutes the "sound" of prayer and praise is shifting, particularly with the addition of instruments and percussion beyond piano and organ. This is especially so with the advent of synthesized accompaniments. Often the same tune and text, rendered on a midi keyboard, will appeal to younger singers, and become difficult for those who prefer unsynthesized and less inflected singing.

How and what we sing shapes and expresses our religious existence. How we think about what we sing raises a critical self-consciousness. But this is simply to remark that the process of liturgical reform and renewal among Protestants in America is still underway. Since music is intrinsically the praise of God, the proclamation of faith, and the body memory of images of human life before God, such worship reform and renewal entails congregational awareness of singing practices. What a congregation sings "by heart" is often the deepest part of its identity. What a congregation is prepared to learn, or at least to consider for its religious growth, may tell us much about its spirituality.

A division is emerging between and among congregations who are open to the new ecumenical and cultural diversity, and those who are not. Such openness to hymns and musical styles from widely different sources is itself a significant theological viewpoint. While recent hymnals may be simply regarded as eclectic by those with more unified musical aesthetics, the issue is not simply eclecticism versus purity. Rather, real theological differences are behind the open and closed stances. At the same time, tensions between cultural and subcultural aesthetic judgments make it increasingly difficult to assess hymns and hymnals on strictly doctrinal or dogmatic grounds.

Two points follow from this. We are reminded, in the first place, that hymn texts and tunes have never been assessed by congregations on poetic and musical grounds alone. The longer-run faith experience of singing assemblies is a significant factor in what is retained and what is discarded in the next generation. In the second place, late twentieth-century ecumenism and cultural broadening of acceptability in Christian worship have begun to shape a new liturgical aesthetics. The result of all this is that common judgment on what constitutes "good" or "bad" hymnody is much more difficult than was the case in midcentury. Contemporary hymnals, such as the United Methodist or Presbyterian collections, are themselves ongoing "conversations" and "debates" within those denominational families.

I believe it was Iris Murdoch who quipped that we are like persons who, having admired the landscape through the front window of their house for years, suddenly noticed the glass. Such self-consciousness is one of the burdens of modernity (and post-modernity for that matter!). What is crucial to the Protestant spirit is maintaining the tension of both seeing the view and noting the potential distortions the glass may involve. Whole-heartedness in singing the Christian faith is a hallmark of Protestant hymnody, but so is self-reflective faith.

The publication of a new hymnal is indeed an intervention into the lifestream of worshiping assemblies. When new poetry and new musical forms begin to make their way into people's expression and self-understanding of the Christian faith, tensions are to be expected: identity and relevance, the familiar and the novel, the "classical" and the "popular" or "contemporary." The currents in American cultural taste and the impact of commercial interests have always played a role in the style and the mode of Protestant worship. This is part of the ever-shifting aesthetic dimension of lived theology.

As a practitioner in the field of church music I confess to my concern for the loss of a deeper historical continuity and an appreciation for the larger tradition in much local church practice, both Protestant and Roman Catholic. In a culture that finds it increasingly difficult to distinguish immediacy of feeling from depth of emotion, it seems crucial to foster the sense of awe, of delight, of honesty, and of beauty as part of the sense of authentic worship. At the same time, if my research and my experience has taught me anything, it is that the *interplay* of the "learned" traditions in church music with what I have described here as the *body memory* of the faithful, is crucial to the theological well-being of future Protestant hymnody and liturgy.

A new century will doubtless produce new hymn collections. I do not foresee the lessening of ferment. Some of those future collections will not be in bound book form. This may accelerate the current tendencies toward more immediate, disposable music. But if part of the distinctiveness of Protestant Christianity is found in the singing assembly, then the test of the new will be the integrity of wholehearted praise of God, mediated and formed by art that is adequate to awe, delight, honesty, and beauty.

WORKS CITED

Routley, Erik. 1986. *The Divine Formula: A Book for Worshipers, Preachers, and Musicians, and All Who Celebrate the Mysteries.* Princeton, N.J.: Prestige Publications.

United Church of Christ Hymnal. 1996. *United Church of Christ Hymnal.* Cleveland: United Church Press, Pilgrim Press.

The Presbyterian Hymnal. 1990. *The Presbyterian Hymnal.* Louisville: Presbyterian Publishing Corporation.

The United Methodist Hymnal. 1989. *The United Methodist Hymnal: Book of United Methodist Worship.* Nashville: United Methodist Publishing House.

Index

Abenaki, 57, 59, 61–62, 65, 71–72, 75, 77 n.8, 79 n.31
Abendschule, 243
Acadia, 57, 60, 68–69, 71, 78 n.23
acculturation, 62, 185, 237
Adams, John Quincy, 218
adhān, 24, 28
Advent, 207, 257
aesthetics, 52, 335–43
Africa, 76 n.4
African Americans, 198, 240, 245, 250, 262–63, 320, 339–40
AIDS, 258
Alexander I, Czar, 86, 113 n.8
Algonquian languages, 57, 59, 64
Alstyne, Alexander van, 219–20
"Amazing Grace," 16–18, 78 n.19, 109, 123, 139, 209, 337
America
  antebellum, 124, 127, 134, 142–43, 145, 147
  Colonial, 15, 68, 179, 182, 315
  See also United States
"America"
  hymn by William Billings, 3, 5, 8
  shaped-note hymn, 242
American Indians. *See* Native Americans
Americanization, 185, 237
Amish, 178, 181, 190
Anglicans, 166, 169
Antigo Publishing Company, 245–47
apnā, 24, 41 n.8
Appalachia, 313, 315–16. 321, 324
Arabic, 25, 27–28, 30–33, 38–39
Arminius, Jacob, 314
Asbury, Francis, 130
Asia, 287
assimilation, 62, 182, 237, 339–40
Atlanta, 338
Ausbund, 180–81
Australia, 86
authenticity, 6, 9, 273–75, 282, 342

Back, I. D., 330–31
Baker, Houston A., Jr., 52
ballad, 52, 147
Baltimore, 180, 247
Banvard, John, 234
Baptists, 105, 109, 123, 127, 130, 150, 188, 215, 219, 288–90, 294, 304, 313–15
Barnum, P. T., 225
Bay Psalm Book, 4
Beecher, Lyman, 223–24
Benson, Louis F., 132
Benton, Thomas Hart, 235
Berea College, 322–24, 332
Berio, Luciano, 264
Berlin, 187
beseda, 92–93, 105–6, 114 n.19
besednik, 90–92
Biard, Pierre, Fr., 60–61, 65, 67
Bible, 49–50, 88, 92, 110, 114 n.19, 137, 339
Billings, William, 3–6, 8, 146, 248
Bliss, Philip Paul, 167, 221
blues, 12, 50–55
blues, gospel, 12
Blumhofer, Edith L., 15, 215–31
body memory, 336–37, 339, 343
Bohlman, Philip V., 3–19, 185, 233–53
Boston, 4, 59, 62, 79 n.34, 146, 216, 271, 277, 279, 281–82
Bradbury, William, 220–21
Brazil, 78 n.20
Buddhism, 245, 271
Buddhists, 238
Burrison, John, 53
Burma, 144
bush meeting. *See* camp meeting

California, 85, 104, 116 n.32, 289
call to prayer. *See adhān*
Calvinism, 16, 313–15
Calvinists, 8, 126–27, 129, 219, 314, 316

camp meeting, 123, 147, 167–68, 221, 224–26, 319, 321
Canada, 28, 36, 40, 57, 76, 77 n.13, 178, 233–34
canon
 of literature, 132
 as standard repertory, 14, 138, 339
cantillation, 24
Cantonese, 292, 300–3, 309 n.32
Cantopop, 300
cantor, 16, 273, 276, 279–81, 285 n.4
cantorate, 248–50
Carey, William, 144
Catholicism, 9, 57–58, 60–65, 68, 74–76, 78 n.22, 244
Catholics, 58, 65, 67, 190, 238
Cennick, John, 134, 137
chant, 65–66, 69, 74, 76, 169, 200, 258, 275, 277
Charleston, 337–38
Chautauqua, 221, 224
Chicago, 16–19, 177, 186, 215, 235, 245, 288–89, 299
China, 287, 302
China Horizon, 290, 306 n.1
Chinese Americans, vii, 15, 188, 287–309
choir, 17–19, 164, 208, 215, 288, 339
chorale, 28, 157–58, 160–63, 166–68, 170–71, 246
Chow, Maria M. W., 16, 287–309
Christ, 64, 75, 87, 115 n.26, 125, 127–29, 131, 136, 138–40, 150, 152, 223, 226–27, 260, 319, 329
Christian, 88, 125–26, 136, 145, 150, 259
Christianity, 87, 110, 136–37, 139, 184, 224, 343
Christmas, 72, 199, 207–8, 210, 259–60
Christology, 139, 151
Civil War, 125, 137, 146, 181, 197, 216, 220–21, 225, 229
Cleveland, Grover, 218
Clinton, Bill, 182
Cohen, John, 322
"Collection," the, 6–8
Collins, Mary, 256
colonization, 36
communitarianism, 14–16, 25
communitas, 54, 237, 329
community
 immigrant, 23, 28–29, 36, 39–40, 83–84, 94, 109, 112 n.2, 155, 207, 305
 Native American, 62–64, 68–69, 72–75
 religious, 4, 9–11, 13, 19, 24–25, 38, 51, 83–85, 88, 90–91, 95–96, 99, 105, 110–11, 143, 170, 177, 179, 237–39, 241, 248–50, 258, 269, 272, 275, 279–80, 284, 294, 305, 315–18, 335–36
composer, 4, 6, 10, 14, 19, 220, 228, 256, 294, 311
Cone, James, 47–52
confessionalism, 183
congregation, 3, 6, 10–11, 16–17, 19, 43–45, 53, 65, 72, 76, 92, 170, 182, 186, 188–89, 197–99, 207, 210, 215, 217–19, 224, 238, 269, 273–74, 276–79, 281, 288–95, 298–301, 303–4, 311–12, 318–19, 338–42
congregational song, 335–43
Congregationalism, 14, 188, 195–212. *See also* United Church of Christ
Congregationalists, 123, 127, 129, 143, 146, 217
Conkling, Robert, 61
Conservative Judaism, 271, 273–74, 278
conversion, 58, 76 n.4
Cooper-Lewter, Nicholas, 50–52
Cornett, Elwood, 326, 328–29, 331
Cowper, William, 132, 139–40, 161–62
Crimea, 86
Crosby, Fanny, 15, 215–31, 248
Crosby, Eunice, 216–17
Crosby, Mercer, 216, 218–19

Danish Americans, 207
Davie, Donald, 132
deistvie, 96–97
denomination, 87, 113 n.11, 126, 130–33, 137, 166, 175–77, 181, 183–84, 196, 215, 222, 226, 229, 234, 239, 243, 245, 251, 256, 294, 298–99, 314, 316, 320, 324–25, 335–36
Devji, Faisal, 36
dhikr, 245
diaspora, 8, 25, 39, 109, 237–38
Disciples of Christ, 123
discourse network, 242, 244, 249
diversity
 in sacred music, 287–309
Doane, William H., 223, 228
Doddridge, Philip, 134, 137, 161–62, 166
Dorgan, Howard, 323
Dorsey, Thomas A., Jr., 12–13, 248
Douglass, Frederick, 48
du'ā, 32–34
Dublin, 67
Duck, Ruth, 265
Dukhobors, 85–86, 109
durūd, 27–28, 30–31
Dwight, Timothy, 127, 129–31, 133, 143

East Africa, 41 n.4
Easter, 17, 207
Easter, John, 130–31
Edmonton, 23, 29, 35, 38
Edwards, Jonathan, 126, 129, 141, 145–46
Einhorn, David, 246–48
Eliade, Mircea, 140, 147
England, 184, 209, 216, 221, 320–21
English
 as language of sacred music, 62, 155, 161, 168–69, 178–83, 185, 187, 189, 274, 288–89, 292–93, 295, 298–300, 302, 304, 339
Enlightenment, 137
Episcopal church, 190, 218, 304
Erickson, Vincent, 69
eschatology, 49, 140
ethnicity, 188, 238
Europe, 60, 167, 175–76
"Europe"
 hymn by William Billings, 8
evangelicalism, 124–25, 131, 134–35, 137–38, 145, 151, 189–90, 216, 227–29, 293
evangelicals, vii, 8, 123, 133–34, 137, 139, 143–46, 149, 152, 226
ethnicity, 13–14, 19, 251
exile, 8
exodus, 8
experience
 American religious, 3–4, 6, 8–9, 12, 14, 16, 18–19, 131, 176, 233–53, 305
  human, 262
 individual, 234, 243–44, 332
 musical, 83, 241, 245, 311
 Protestant, 216
 religious, 60, 83, 208, 221, 226, 243, 277, 312, 326

Fellerer, Karl, 179
feminism, 15, 248–50
First Nations, 60–63, 74
folk hymn, 311, 321–22
folklore, 45
folk song, 103, 113 n.5, 321–22
Franklin and Marshall College, 164, 183
Freitag, Sandria, 36
French, 58, 60, 68, 70, 73, 77 n. 8
Fresno, 94
fuguing tune, 147, 242
fundamentalism, 40

Gabriel, Lillian, 73
Gabriel, Mary, 73
Gates, Henry Louis, Jr., 53
Geertz, Clifford, 134–35, 145, 148–49
genealogy, 10
Gentiles, 6
German Americans, 155–73, 175–94, 243, 249
Germantown, 155, 180
Germany, 86, 155, 169, 176, 182, 186
glossa, 44–45
Gordon, Robert, 47–48, 50
Gospels, the, 125, 128, 217
gospel music, 51, 170, 216, 220, 225–28, 289, 295, 298, 319–20
gospel song. *See* gospel music
Graham, Billy, 215
Grand Army of the Republic, 229
Gray, Judith, 14, 195–212
Great Awakening, 11, 123, 126–27, 129, 133, 137, 141, 145–46, 177, 184, 241, 314, 317
  See also Second Great Awakening
Great Lakes, 176
Greeley, Andrew M., 180
Grimm, Alfred, vii, 245–47

Habsburg Monarchy, 17
Halle, 179, 181
hamd, 30–31
Harbaugh, Henry, 155, 163–68, 170, 171 n.5
Hart, Joseph, 140
Hastings, Thomas, 217–18
Hatch, Nathan, 124, 137
hazzan. *See* cantor
Hebrew, 103, 247, 250, 271, 273–74, 277, 280
Heidelberg, 175
Helmuth, J. H. C., 156
Hendel, John William, 156–58
hermeneutics, 48–50, 114 n.19
hieroglyphs, 74–75, 79 n.38
High Holidays, 273, 275–76
Hirsch, Emil, 248
Hispanic Americans, 198, 262, 340
historicism, 10
historiography
  of American music, 4, 237, 240
history
  African American, 14
  American, 8, 10, 123, 234, 240, 251
  cultural, vi
  intellectual, vi
  Jewish, 15
  of American music, 3, 10
  of sacred music, 6
  political, 11
  religious, 9, 11, 14, 319, 325
  social, vi
Holzapfel, Otto, 14, 175–94
Hong Kong, 287–88, 300, 302, 305
Hongkongese, 305, 308 n.29
Hutterites, 9, 178
hybridity, 9
hymn, 3, 8, 10, 12, 14–15, 23, 26–28, 30–31, 34, 37, 47, 51, 63, 65, 72–73, 75, 77 n.15, 123–54, 156–63, 165–67, 169–70, 179, 181, 187–90, 195, 197, 199–207, 208, 210–11, 220, 224, 226–28, 241–42, 261, 265, 283, 287–90, 293–95, 298–300, 302–5, 318–21, 335, 337–43
hymnal, 4, 14–15, 17–18, 64, 124–28, 130–33, 137, 148, 155–57, 159, 162, 165–66, 168–69, 175–94, 197, 207–8, 215, 217, 220, 222, 239, 241–42, 244, 250, 288–89, 292–95, 297–300, 304, 307 n.12, 311, 320, 335–43
hymnbook, 6, 9, 14, 165, 179, 197, 242, 244
hymnody, 8–9, 12, 14–16, 18, 121, 123–54, 155–73, 195–96, 199, 208, 210, 215–31, 244, 321–25, 340, 342–43

icon, 110
identity
  American, 184, 188
  cultural, 284
  ethnic, 175–94, 271–86
  evangelical, 228
  Islamic, 23, 25
  religious, 36, 38, 64, 191, 271–86, 341
  self, 88
Illinois, 180
immigrant, 4, 18, 23–26, 28–29, 34, 39, 176–78, 180–84, 186, 222, 224, 246, 251, 287, 305
immigration, 29, 177, 183, 188, 228
India, 36, 144
individualism, 233–53
individuals
  as sacred musicians, 213
Innsbruck, 176
Institute for the Study of American Evangelicals, x
Ira, Alfred. *See* Grimm, Alfred
Ireland, 320
Islam, 13, 23–42, 239
Islamism, 34, 36, 38–40
Islamization, 36, 41 n.7
Ison, Kenzie, 329
Ives, Charles, 6–7

Jackson, George Pullen, 322
jazz, 18, 256
Jerusalem, 209
Jesuits, 71, 77 n.5, 235
Jesus. *See* Christ
Jews, 6, 238, 249, 271, 276, 279, 283–84
Johnson, Robert, 53
journey, sacred, 8
Judaism, 6, 9, 239, 248, 274
Judson, Adoniram, 144
Jumpers
  as Molokan community, 96, 115 n.23
Jung, C. J., 46–47, 53

Kabbalat Shabbat, 271–72, 283
Kauder, Charles Christian, 74–75
Kentucky, 311, 313–15, 321–22, 324, 326
khushihani, 30
Knapp, Phoebe Palmer, 223
kratophany, 44

Lacy, Rubin, 53–54
Lafitau, Joseph-François, 235–36

lament, 97–98, 115–16 n.29
Lancaster, 164
landscape
  musical, 9–10
  sacred, 3–4, 6, 10, 16, 18–19
language transformation, 175–94
Latin, 66, 69, 75, 104, 145
Layriz, Friedrich, 189
Leadbelly, 53
LeClerq, Chrestien, 74
Lent, 17, 259
Léry, Jean de, 78 n.20
Lescarbot, Marc, 66
Lewisburg, 164
liberation theology, 49–50
Linyova, Evgeniya, 99, 116 n.34
litany, 31
literacy, 240–42
liturgy, 4, 9, 63–65, 72, 76, 95, 104, 121, 169, 182, 200, 272–74, 276, 279, 282, 318, 341, 343
Lobwasser, Ambrosius, 156
Lomax, Alan, 322
Los Angeles, 83, 86, 103, 111, 112 n.2, 114 n.18, 116 n.35
Louisville, 180
Luther, Martin, 152, 169, 181, 185
Lutheran Church—Missouri Synod, 168–69, 180, 183, 185–87, 189, 243
Lutherans, 8, 28, 156, 162–63, 165, 169–71, 181–83, 185, 189, 207, 246, 249

Mack, Alexander, 175
Maine, 57, 62–63, 65, 68, 70–72, 78 n.26
mainstream, religious, vii, 16, 18
Maliseet, 57, 59, 61–62, 69–71, 75, 77 n.9, 79 n.29
Māqām, 273
Mandarin, 292, 295, 301, 308 n.32, 309 n.32
Marburg, 155
Marini, Stephen A., 123–54
Marty, Martin E., 237, 240
Mason, Lowell, 170, 217–18, 223
Massachusetts, 68, 126, 167
Maximisty, 86
Mazo, Margarita, 14, 83–119
McCarty, Paul, 63–64
McKendree, William, 130–31
medeolinuwok, 57, 61, 76
Memphis Minnie, 53
Mencken, H. L., 180
Mennonites, 165, 178–79, 190
Mercer, Jesse, 129–31
Mercersburg, 160, 164, 166, 168, 171 n.7, 186
Metcalf, Barbara, 36
meter
  in American hymnody, 161–62, 166–67, 318
Methodism, 126, 131, 244
Methodists, 123, 127, 185, 215, 217–19, 221, 225, 288–89, 304, 336–37, 342
Michigan, 180
Midwest, 18, 170, 176–77, 196, 241, 243, 246, 249
Mi'kmaq, 57, 59, 61–62, 66–68, 72, 74–76, 77 n.6, 79 n.38
milad, 13, 26–30, 32–37, 39–40
Miller, Terry, 323
Minnesota, 340
mission, 57, 69–71, 130, 144, 221–22, 224–26, 228, 317, 321
missionary, 14, 57, 60–62, 66–68, 71–74, 76, 78 n.19, 79 n.37, 216, 235
missionization, 57–58
Mississippi River, 176, 234
Mitchell, Henry, 50–52
modernism, 6
modes
  in Jewish prayer, 271–86
molokane, 85, 113 n.8
Molokanism, 83–85, 87, 89, 98, 106, 110
Molokans, 14, 83–119
Montgomery, James, 134
Montréal, 59
Moody, D. L. 221
Mormons, 219–20
Morrison, Kenneth, 76 n.4, 77 n.8
Moscow, 112 n.1
mosque, 23–24, 26, 38–40, 41 n.12
Muhammed. *See* Prophet Muhammad, the
Mühlenberg, Heinrich Melchior, 179–80, 182, 184, 191
multiculturalism, 238
multicultural music, 4
music
  African American, 12, 14, 43–56
  AngloAmerican, 123, 146, 171
  of the Bible, 43
  ethnic, 170, 256
  feminist, 256
  folk, 50–51, 273
  German American, 14
  practice of, 39
  sacred, 8–9, 11, 14–16, 46, 50, 55, 123, 237, 239, 242, 244, 250, 284 n.3, 324
music, black. *See* music, African American
music, religious. *See* music, sacred
Muslims, 13, 23–42, 34, 36–40, 41 n.3, 245
mysticism, 44, 87
myth, 46
mythology, 51, 53, 257

narrative, 53
na't, 27, 30–32
National Anthem, vi
nationalism, 186, 191, 238
Native Americans, 4, 53, 60, 62, 64, 67, 77 n.8, 244–45
  See also First Nations
Native peoples. *See* Native Americans
ne nashi, 85, 88, 106, 111
New Brunswick, 62, 69, 71, 78 n.26
New England, 57, 143, 149, 167, 196, 218, 321
New-England Psalm-Singer, 8, 146
New Testament, 48, 50, 87, 125
Newton, John, 134, 139, 161–62
New World. *See* United States
New York State, 178
New York Institute for the Blind, 218–19, 230 n.3
New York City, 179, 182–84, 187, 198, 216, 218–19, 221, 223, 225, 228
Nicholas I, Czar, 86
nigun, 273
Noll, Mark, 240
North
  of the United States, 48
North America, 4, 9, 14, 24, 36, 39, 57, 70, 74, 190, 233, 237, 241–42, 244, 246–48, 251
North Carolina, 314
Northrup, Solomon, 48
Nova Scotia, 62, 71

nusach, 15, 271–86
nutonan, 69

Oberlin College, 132
Ohio, 163–64, 183, 323
Old Believers, 109, 113 n.6
Old Regular Baptists, 15, 311–34
Old Testament, 48, 50, 87, 125
Old World. *See* Europe
"On Jordan's Stormy Banks I Stand," 327–31
ontology, 10, 13, 239
oppugnancy, 44–45, 48
Oregon, 85, 105
Orthodox Church
  Russian, 85–87, 113 n.6, 114 n.16
Orthodox Judaism, 271–72, 274, 277–79, 281

Pacific Garden Mission, 215
Pakistan, 26, 37, 41 n.7
Palatinate, 175
panorama, 15, 233–53
Passamaquoddy, 57, 59, 61–65, 68–75, 77 n.15, 78 n.19, 79 n.29
Passover, 211, 275
Patterson, Beverly, 324
Patton, Charlie, 53
Pennsylvania, 155–56, 163, 170, 175, 180–84
Pennsylvania Dutch. *See* Pennsylvania German culture
Pennsylvania German culture, 163, 165, 168, 178
Penobscot, 57, 59, 62, 68, 70, 72, 75
Pentateuch, 217
Pentecostalism, 16–18
Pentecostals, 105
Persia, 86
Persian, 28
Peterson, Brent, 243
pevets, 90, 91–93, 95–96, 99, 101, 103–4, 106, 114 n.15
Philadelphia, 156, 181–82
Philadelphia Church of God, 16–18
pietism, 239
Pilgrim Hymnal, 188, 196–98, 200–6, 208
pilgrimage, 8, 85, 110, 113 n.9, 150, 250
pilgrims
  as religious community in colonial New England, 184, 196, 209
  as travelers on sacred journey, 209
plainchant, 65
plurality
  of American religious experience, 12
Poland, 282
Postoyannye, 86
prayer book, 6, 9, 18, 74, 179, 239–40, 242, 244, 246, 248, 272
preaching
  in the African American church, 43–45
Presbyterians, 123, 127, 129, 217, 219, 294, 304, 340, 342
prestol, 90, 92–93, 114 n.14, 115 n.22
presviter, 90–93, 97, 106
priest, 61–62, 66–67, 69–70, 72, 151
Proctor, Henry Hugh, 47, 50
promised land, 8–9
Prophet Muhammad, the, 25–33, 37–38, 41 n.2
Protestantism, 16, 68, 137, 151, 177, 210, 215–31, 275, 343
Protestants, vii, 8, 12, 18, 28, 57–58, 62, 65, 87, 113 n.11, 123, 155, 183–84, 186–89, 215–16, 220, 224, 228, 320, 340–41
protyazhnaya, 101–2
Pryguny, 86
psalm, 84, 91–93, 95, 97–101, 103–7, 113 n.4, 115 n.24, 116 n.33, 125–26, 145, 152 n.8, 156–61, 166, 208, 340
public sphere, 239, 250
Puritans, 149, 216–17, 228

Qawwali, 27
Québec, 59, 70–71, 75
Qur'an, 24–30, 37, 41 n.9
Qureshi, Regula Burckhardt, 13, 23–42, 249

raga, 273, 275
Reagon, Bernice Johnson, 255
recitation, 23–30, 32, 34, 36–40
Reform Judaism, 246–48, 250, 271, 274–76
Reform Molokans, 86, 105–6, 108–9
Reformation, 136–37, 141, 314
Reformed Church
  Evangelical and Reformed Church, 169, 196
  in America, 155–57, 159–65, 170–71, 181, 183, 189, 298
  of Germany, 155
religion, public, 39
Requiem mass, 74
resistance, 249–50, 335
revival, 10, 123, 140, 152, 160, 177, 216, 220–21, 225, 228, 241, 248, 288, 313–14
revivalism, 124, 129, 152, 224
Revolution of 1848, 176
Rhodes, Philip, 323
rhythm and blues, 52
Ritchie, Jean, 322
ritual, 9–10, 34, 40, 58, 77 n.9, 97–98, 115 n.27, 145, 147, 151–52, 248, 250, 256, 266, 272, 274
  of women, 255–67
  with women's music, 255–67
riwāyāt, 30–31
Roman Catholic Church, 180. *See also* Catholicism
Romania, 18
Romanian Americans, 16–18
Root, George F., 218, 230 n.2
Routley, Erik, 336, 341
Russia, 83, 85–87, 98, 103–4, 108–10, 112 n.1, 113 n.5, 114 n.15, 115 n.29, 116 n.30, 117 n.41
Russian
  in Molokan worship, 90, 104–6, 108
Russian Americans, 83–119

Sacred Harp, 241
Saliers, Don E., 16, 335–43
Salvation Army, 222
San Francisco, 114 n.20, 117 n.41
Sankey, Ira, 167, 221
Saur, Christopher, 155, 180, 191
Schaff, Philip, 160–61, 166–68, 170, 171 n.6, 186–87, 191
Schlatter, Michael, 175
Schmucker, Samuel S., 183, 190
schools, singing, 4
Scotland, 320
Scrapbook
  with Fanny Crosby memoirs, 216–17, 222, 230 n.1
Second Great Awakening, 165, 168, 185, 218, 225, 241, 314, 317
  See also Great Awakening

sermon, 46
Shabbat Ma'ariv, 274
Shakers, 240, 245
shaman, 61, 67, 77 n.5
shaped-note music, 241–42, 320–21
Siberia, 86
siddur, 247
Signifying Monkey, 52
singularity
  of American religious experience, 12
Sipayik, 63–65, 68, 72, 77 n.13, 79 n.35
skazatel', 90–93, 101, 104, 106
slaves, African American, 44, 46–47, 49
Slobin, Mark, 248, 273, 285 n.5
sobranie, 90–98, 103, 105–6, 111, 114 n.13, 115 n.23, 116 n.32
songbook, 9, 18, 175–94, 243–44, 292, 311, 319, 324
South
  of the United States, 46, 52, 241, 320–21
South Asia
  immigrants from, 24–26, 28–29, 34, 39–40, 41 n.4
  region of Muslim practice, 36–39
Soviet Union. *See* Russia
Spand, Charlie, 54
speech, liturgical, 66
Spencer, Jon Michael, 14, 43–56
Spinney, Ann Morrison, 14, 57–82
spirituality, 149, 151, 245
spirituals, 43–44, 46–51, 240, 250, 319, 321
St. Louis, 189, 234
Stavropol', 98, 111, 113 n.10, 116 n.37, 117 n.41
Steadfasts
  as Molokan community, 96–97, 117 n.41
Steele, Anne, 134, 138, 140, 161–62, 166
Stennett, Samuel, 134, 142, 162
Sufis, 27, 245
Sufism, 245
Sulzer, Salomon, 276
Summit, Jeffrey A., 6, 15, 271–86
Sunday school, 167, 185, 220, 225, 230 n.4, 289, 317, 321, 337–38
Sutton, Brett, 324
Sweet Honey in the Rock, 255, 262–63, 266
syncretism, 9, 12, 75

Taiwan, 287–88, 301–2, 304–5
Taiwanese, 295, 297, 301, 304–5
"Take My Hand, Precious Lord," 12–13
Tallmadge, William, 322–23, 325
Temperley, Nicholas, 320
Tennent, Gilbert, 141, 145
theomusicology, 14, 43, 51–52
theology, 43, 46–47, 50–53, 129–31, 140, 168, 298, 314, 335–43
Thomas, Etienne, 69
Thomas, Jean, 321–22
Thomas Kyrie Manuscript, 69–71
Thorpe, Earl E., 46–47
Tillich, Paul, 47, 50
time, sacred, 10
Titon, Jeff Todd, 15, 311–34
Tocqueville, Alexis de, 240, 246
Torah, 282. *See also* Pentateuch
tradition, oral, 4, 9, 44. 72, 76, 98, 103
transmission, oral. *See* tradition, oral
trickster, 52–54
Turkey, 86
Turner, Frederick Jackson, 240, 246
Turner, William C., Jr., 44–46, 48
Transylvania, 18

Uklein, Semen, 98
Underground Railroad, 49
Union Theological Seminary, 266 n.1
United Church of Christ, 196–97, 340. *See also* Congregationalism
United Methodist Hymnal, 16, 336–37, 340
United States, vi, 4, 11, 28, 40, 46, 85–86, 98, 105, 108, 111, 112 n.1, 116 n.30, 117 n.40, 144–45, 155, 167, 171, 175–76, 179–83, 186–88, 191, 221, 233–34, 238, 287–91, 299–301, 303–5, 314, 322, 338
Urdu, 27, 32–33, 41 n.8
utopia, 9, 40

Vatican II, 75, 190
Vetromile, Eugene, 65, 72, 74
Victorian era, 216, 226
Vienna, 74–75
Viladesau, Richard, 210–11
Virginia, 130, 313–14, 324

Wabanakik, 57, 59–60
Wabanakis, 14, 57–82
Walther, C. F. W., 186, 189
Walton, Janet, 15, 249, 255–67
War of Independence, 11, 68, 70, 184
Ware, Ann Patrick, 259
Washington D.C., 197–98
Watts, Isaac, 125–27, 132–33, 137, 139–41, 144–48, 150, 161–62, 166, 219, 319
Wesley, Charles, 126, 132–34, 138–39, 141, 161–62, 166, 248
Wesley, John, 126–27, 130–31, 133, 136–37, 145–46
Westermeyer, Paul, 14, 155–73
Westernization, 302
Wheatstraw, Peetie, 53
Whitehead, Ruth Holmes, 66
Whittier, 111
Wicks, Sammie Ann, 323, 325
Williams College, 144
Williams, Delores, 260
Wimbush, Vincent, 50
Wisconsin, 176, 178, 180
Woodbury, I. B., 167
World War I, 171, 176, 178, 180, 186, 188, 190, 246
World War II, 109, 171
Wren, Brian, 195, 211
Württemberg, 180, 182

Yale University, 127
Yoder, Don, 165

zakon, 88–89, 94, 103, 105, 110, 114 n.17